Gender &
Difference

in a Globalizing World

Gender & Difference

in a Globalizing World

Twenty-First-Century Anthropology

Frances E. Mascia-Lees

Rutgers University

WAVELAND

PRESS, INC.

Long Grove, Illinois

For information about this book, contact:
Waveland Press, Inc.
4180 IL Route 83, Suite 101
Long Grove, IL 60047-9580
(847) 634-0081
info@waveland.com
www.waveland.com

To Nancy Black for thirty years of friendship,
and to the wonderful men in my life:
Anthony C. Mascia, Frank Lees, Matthew Lees, and Alexander Lees
for holding me close
and for keeping me laughing.

Brief Contents

Detailed Contents

Preface

Audience for the Book

Gender and Difference in a Globalizing World is designed primarily for courses in Anthropology of Gender, Anthropology of Difference, and Feminist Anthropology. However, it is also well suited to an Introduction to Anthropology course. It offers perspectives and insights that all anthropology students increasingly need as anthropology's traditional objects of study are transformed, and as more and more people are subsumed within complex networks of global power and inequality. It illustrates how anthropologists today reframe traditional areas of anthropological concern to understand the twenty-first century's globalizing world, making *Gender and Difference in a Globalizing World* appropriate for broadly conceived anthropology courses.

Themes

The book introduces students to the core concepts and central topics of the cultural anthropological study of gender, difference, power, and inequality in today's world. It focuses on the following:

- Introducing students to the idea of the **politics of difference,** on how the intersection of gender, race, class, ethnicity, and sexual preference produces different degrees of privilege and experiences of oppression for different groups of people both within and across nations

- Analyzing the **impact of global processes** on women's and men's lives around the world today, paying particular attention to how gender and other forms of difference are shaped and transformed by global forces and how global processes are themselves gendered and raced

- Providing a **historical contextualization** of ideas about gender, difference, power, and inequality, with particular emphasis on the impact of colonialism on late-nineteenth- to mid-twentieth-century ideas and the postcolonial and global context of current conceptualizations

- Tracing the history, and analyzing the assumptions and conclusions, of the following **theoretical orientations** used in anthropology to study gender, difference, power, and inequality:
  — Feminist anthropology
  — Black feminist anthropology
  — Lesbian/Gay/Bisexual/Transgendered (LGBT) and Queer Theory
  — Marxist anthropology
  — Social evolutionism
  — Sociobiology and evolutionary psychology
  — Structural anthropology
  — Symbolic anthropology
  — Postcolonial anthropology
  — Postmodern anthropology (the "Writing Culture Critique")
  — Practice anthropology
  — Psychological anthropology

Organization of the Book

Part I. Situating Gender and Difference within Anthropology

The chapters in this section place ideas about gender and other forms of difference, as well as approaches to the study of power and inequality, in historical and contemporary contexts.

1. Gender, Difference, and Globalization

This chapter introduces students to the concepts of gender and difference, placing them within the context of global interconnections. It highlights major ideas and debates about the nature of contemporary globalization and focuses on how women's and men's lives are differentially constructed, constrained, and experienced due to global processes.

2. A History of Gender and Difference

Chapter 2 places feminist anthropology within the political context of the 1970s out of which it arose as well as within the discipline of anthropology itself. It highlights the rise of feminist anthropology and traces how its early emphasis on gender has shifted over time to a focus that considers gender as only one "axis of domination."

3. The Politics of Anthropology

This chapter explores how anthropology's commitment to cultural relativism may conflict with feminist anthropology's commitment to political engagement and on how cultural rights are often in conflict with gender or human rights. It helps students think critically about how to work through these tensions. It situates anthropology within the postcolonial critique, which has raised questions about the politics of anthropological fieldwork and ethnographic representation.

Part II. Naturalizing Gender and Difference

In this section, students are introduced to processes that maintain power differentials among groups of people by making differences appear natural, normal, and inevitable, rather than political and ideological. It offers a critique of the belief that science produces unquestionable truths and analyzes scientific ideas as cultural products.

4. Sex Differences: Nature and Nurture

Chapter 4 introduces students to the debate over whether gender and other differences are the result of innate biological differences (nature) or social and cultural factors (nurture). It analyzes the assumptions and conclusions of scientific studies of difference, understanding science as a social activity that helps to naturalize inequalities.

5. The Evolution of Gender and Difference

This chapter focuses on theories that explain gender difference as the natural outcome of evolutionary processes. It assesses the assumptions and approaches of nineteenth-century social evolutionism, twentieth-century sociobiology, and contemporary evolutionary psychology.

Part III. Political Economy and the Production of Culture

Part III compares and contrasts materialist and ideational approaches to the study of gender and difference, highlighting feminist anthropological revisions of Marxist explanations of inequality, on the one hand, and structural and symbolic explanations, on the other.

6. Production, Capitalism, Ideology, and the State

This chapter explores Marx and Engels' materialist explanation of class and gender inequality and its impact on twentieth-century feminist anthropology. The relationship between women's subordination and differing modes of production is assessed, with particular emphasis on the development of capitalism and the rise of the state.

7. The Global Economy, Neoliberalism, and Labor

Chapter 7 focuses on the nature of the contemporary global economy and the impact that the neoliberal ideologies underlying it have had on worldwide inequalities, gendered labor relations, and the nature of work.

8. Producing Culture: From Structure to Agency

This chapter is centrally concerned with theories that focus on how cultural symbols construct and maintain inequalities. It poses the question of whether oppressed people are completely determined by a society's ideas and structures or whether they are able to resist their subordination through the production of new meanings and daily practices.

Part IV. The Personal as Political

Part IV focuses on areas of life that in Western thinking have tended to be relegated to the personal sphere but yet in reality are deeply embedded in political processes and help to maintain inequality relations. It exposes the body, identity, subjectivity, sex, sexuality, reproduction, marriage, and the family as sites of power.

9. Embodying Politics

This chapter treats the body as a symbolic construct, focusing on the relationship of particular conceptualizations of the body to power, control, and domination. It analyzes how discourses differentially construct and discipline bodies marked by gender and race and it assesses the implications of a consumer society for the body in a global economy.

10. Minding Gender and Difference

This chapter focuses on how power, inequalities, and language shape who people think they are and how they situate themselves in the world. It assesses theories of personality and gender, focuses on not only how identity underlies a person's sense of self but also on how identity is embedded nationally and culturally, and looks at how gendered subjectivities are formed and performed.

11. Reproducing Gender and Difference

This chapter focuses on sex, sexuality, reproduction, marriage, and the family as sites of power. It stresses the historical and cross-cultural variation in these areas of life to complicate the idea that they are natural and to disrupt simple ideas about the connection among sex, gender, and sexuality.

Learning Aids

- An **In this chapter you will . . .** feature appears at the beginning of each chapter to alert students to the major topics that will be covered.

- **Global News** items draw attention to timely issues of special interest to help students link concepts with "real-life" happenings.

- Each chapter contains an **Ethnography in Focus**, an excerpt from an ethnography that illustrates how anthropologists approach the ideas and issues raised in the chapter within a particular cultural context.

- **Close-Ups** offer engaging information that expands on a concept or topic presented in the chapter.

- Key terms appear in bold print in the text and their definitions appear alongside them. Placing definitions within the chapters allows students to contextualize individual terms within larger discussions. Students can also turn to the end of each chapter for a complete alphabetized glossary, called **Word Portfolio.**

- **Recommended Reading** provides suggestions for more in-depth coverage of some of the topics discussed in the chapter.

Note on Terminology

The language for describing differences in today's world is inadequate, reflecting a moment of transition in which realities, concepts, and ideas have changed more rapidly than the vocabulary available to us. At one time it seemed acceptable and adequate to describe a major cultural, geopolitical, and economic divide with the terms "West" and "non-West," "Occident" and "Orient," "developed" and "developing," "First World" and "Third World." But these are problematic terms today, not only because of their insufficiency, but also because of their ideological content. It is, therefore, preferable to describe the configuration of world power today using the terms "Global North and "Global South." In this usage, "North" refers to the industrialized countries of Europe, North America, Japan, and northern Asia and "South" refers primarily to Africa, the Asian subcontinent, and Latin America. But these terms are already somewhat out of date: as nations develop economically they are designated "North," regardless of geographical location, while nations that do not qualify as "developed" are considered as "South." However, the designations "West" and "non-West" are used when speaking about U.S. and European ideas that have dominated relations between peoples of the Global North and South. "Developed" and "First World" or "developing" and "Third World" appear throughout the text when these terms are used by the theorist or theoretical orientation being discussed or when they are needed for clarity.

We encounter similar difficulty when describing differences within societies. The terms "gender" and "race" for example, have been made problematic by the discourses described throughout this book. Yet, these terms remain useful when describing social differences because they continue to be used that way in people's everyday lives and, consequently, have real social effects. When these terms are introduced in the text, I try to point out their ideological content and limitations. Neither "sexuality," "sexual orientation," nor "sexual preference" are adequate terms for capturing the multiple factors that affect how individuals understand and experience themselves as "desiring beings." Even though it is also inadequate, I use the term "sexual diversity" instead to signal the complexity and multiplicity of factors that combine to produce "sexuality."

There is no one definition of "globalization," as the discussion in chapter 1 indicates, not only because of different conceptualizations among theorists but also because it is the result of processes that are constantly in flux. I do, however offer the following *working* definition in that chapter: "globalization" refers to "a set of processes that have given rise to a widening, deepening, and acceleration of worldwide interconnections in all aspects of contemporary life." I use the phrase today's "global world" in reference to the entity that is increasingly produced through these processes and employ "globality" to refer to the condition or state that globalization has thus far produced. I use "globalizing world" whenever possible to indicate the ongoing nature of globalization processes and to underscore that a fully interconnected global world is not completely formed.

Acknowledgments

This book would not have been possible without Nancy Black, to whom I give my deepest thanks. She introduced me to Waveland Press and her generosity has enabled me to weave text from our small book, *Gender and Anthropology,* throughout this one. I am indebted to all my research assistants: Alex Lees, Emily McDonald, Noelle Molé, and Nell Quest for their careful reading, editing, feedback, and work on "Close-Up," "Ethnography in Focus," and "Recommended Reading" features. Without the generous support of Rutgers University, their help would not have been possible. Noelle Molé also made significant contributions to the body of the text of several chapters, most notably chapters 6 and 7. Her expertise was invaluable. I would also like to thank Rebecca Etz for reading the manuscript and making helpful suggestions. I deeply appreciate Tom Curtin at Waveland for his encouragement and patience, and Jeni Ogilvie for her enthusiasm and careful editing. I am indebted to Frank Lees.

Situating Gender and Difference within Anthropology

What we need to search for and find, what we need to hone and perfect into a magnificent, shining thing, is a new kind of politics. Not the politics of governance, but the politics of resistance. The politics of opposition. The politics of forcing accountability. The politics of slowing things down. The politics of joining hands across the world and preventing certain destruction. In the present circumstances, I'd say that the only thing worth globalizing is dissent.

—*Arundhati Roy*

Gender, Difference, and Globalization

In this chapter you will . . .

examine the relationship of personal experiences to global events • be introduced to the idea of gender and race as social constructs that form the basis of systems of social inequality • learn about what anthropology contributes to an understanding of gender, difference, and globalization • examine various conceptualizations of globalization • gain exposure to major debates concerning globalization • look at examples of the impact of globalization on women and men around the world • explore the challenges to anthropology posed by global changes

Our exploration of gender and other forms of difference in today's globalizing world begins with a scenario. It is a composite based on actual recent events and situations. Its aim is to suggest how, in the contemporary moment, an individual's seemingly personal and private opportunities, experiences, ideas, and choices are connected to events occurring thousands of miles away.

Kate, a young Canadian woman student, has decided to travel to Costa Rica for spring break for an ecotour of the country. She has become increasingly concerned with environmental issues. She hopes one day to become an attorney who specializes in cases brought against big-business interests like those of the transnational corporations destroying the rain forest for profit. She hopes this visit will give her a better sense of the problems involved. However, she ends up spending much of her free time in Central America commiserating with her U.S. friend, Wilson. He is currently stationed in Egypt and the two of them instant message each other via an e-mail connection she accesses at local Internet cafes along the way. She and Wilson met two years ago when they worked together to form a biracial student organization dedicated to finding ways to bring together students of color with white students to overcome racial biases on campus. They have been close friends ever since.

Wilson is experiencing a crisis, and Kate feels she must help in whatever way she can. Wilson thinks he's in love, but he is

questioning the attraction between himself and a local woman, Fatima. He and Fatima met a few months ago at a showing of The Legend of Sigh, *a film directed by the Iranian filmmaker, Tahmineh Milani, whose trial—for waging a "war against God"—they have both been following anxiously. Although at first their conversation seemed awkward, they quickly found that they shared other interests, not only in current independent films but also in old silent Hollywood movies and the music of Thornton and Ramzy, a British multi-instrumentalist and an Egyptian percussionist, who together made some of their favorite CDs.*

But despite these remarkable commonalities, Wilson is uneasy. Fatima is talking marriage, and he worries that Fatima might be attracted to him for what he fears are the wrong reasons. Does she see him as desirable because she equates the power and wealth of the United States with his own? He hopes not, because he knows back home he has little chance for his preferred career as a writer due to an economic recession, and he's not sure how he'll make a living. That's one of the reasons he joined the army in the first place; he needs to postpone entering the U.S. job market for a few years, without accruing additional debt or having to repay his student loans on his own. His parents were disappointed with his decision. They had hopes that, as the first member of his family to go to college, he would go to medical school and ultimately make enough money to pay off his loans easily. They wanted to see him free of the economic burdens that had always plagued their lives.

4

For the moment, Wilson is less concerned about that than his doubts about Fatima's feelings for him. He is also worried that her attraction to him is based on the pressure she feels to marry soon, even as she resists other pressures to find a "suitable" partner from within her own community. Fatima is certain about her choice of Wilson despite Wilson's doubts and her parents' objections. She knows that she loves him because he is a devout man. Even though her Islamic and his Southern Baptist beliefs seem quite different on the surface, she is more concerned with the fact that God is central to his life and that Wilson respects her piety and modesty than with whether he is Muslim. She has even begun to think about taking up the veil, covering her hair to demonstrate her devotion to Allah. Her family has always told her that being a wife is the essential element in being a good Muslim woman, and she feels eager to get married now so she can further fulfill her commitment to God.

And what about Wilson's attraction to Fatima? Kate warns that his emerging feelings for Fatima may not be genuine. Kate tells him that instead, the very things he seems to find appealing about Fatima—her mystery and exotic beauty— might grow out of something else. She reminds Wilson about what they learned in their anthropology classes last year about "Orientalizing." He feels guilty when he realizes that he might be experiencing the very feelings he found so awful when he read about them in a book on the colonial harem. As a black man, he was appalled to find out about the racist ideas that fueled a long history of the colonization of Eastern peoples by Western nations. He was shocked to read about how this colonial domination gave rise to sexual fantasies about Muslim women. As a devote Christian he is disgusted by the idea that his attraction to Fatima today may arise out of this history of sexualization in which Western men viewed non-Western women primarily as objects for sexual use.

Indeed, he feels he is attracted to Fatima because she is a good religious woman, not a sexual object; but how can he be sure?

He pours his heart out to Kate in his e-mail messages, but she is becoming distracted now that she is having her own crisis. She has just learned that her father will soon be laid off from his job as a welder in Montreal due to the crash in the global financial markets and that he won't be able to help her pay for her last year of college. Instead, he has made the difficult but, he thinks, sound decision to use his savings to pay for his son's education. He feels that, even if Kate has a career and works after she is married, she will not be the main income earner in the family like her brother will be. He is sure she will be able to depend on her husband's income to support her. Kate does not tell him just how unlikely his plans for her are: she has "come out" at school but not at

home, fearing her parents' reactions. Kate cuts her vacation short so that she can look for a job. But the economic downturn in her country will make it hard for her to find a job, let alone one she likes. Luckily, after only two weeks she is hired to work in a local flower shop that specializes in selling fresh flowers grown in Guatemala only one day earlier. The store is owned by a Korean family that has only recently arrived in Canada. She hopes that by taking this job she will at least have something at the end of the day in addition to her minimal wage. Perhaps learning about Korean ways of life will give her another perspective on global issues, one she can use if she is ever able to complete her degree and move on to law school. But at the rate she is being paid, she sees her dreams of a satisfying career as an environmental attorney becoming more and more elusive.

In this chapter we investigate the relationship of global occurrences such as those mentioned in this story to gender and other forms of social differentiation. We also learn the role anthropology can play in helping us understand women's and men's lives all over a world, increasingly characterized by the movement of people, information, ideas, products, and images.

What Is Gender?

There is a good deal of controversy over the meaning of gender, and to a large extent, this entire book is an answer to this question. However, let's begin with a good working definition of **gender:** the socially and culturally produced ideas about the differences between females and males in a particular society.

These differences are based on a society's *interpretation* of physical **sex differences:** those features, usually of anatomy, that a society or group assumes distinguish females and males. Although physical sex differences form the basis of a society's ideas about gender, gender is not a biological reality. This is made evident by societies that have more than the two gender categories of female and male, as we will see in chapter 11. Thus, gender is a socially constructed characteristic; it is not an innate property of individuals. It is a social attribution that individuals embody, and from which they derive identity. **Gender identity** is the very idea of what it means to be a man or a woman in a particular society. In the story above, Fatima's gender identity, what it means for her to be a Muslim *woman*, influences her desire to marry and perhaps even her attraction to Wilson. Because gender is social, not biological, individuals can contest, negotiate, shift, and change gender ideals and identity, although this is often a difficult and painful process.

In almost all societies, the traits thought to distinguish a girl from a boy, and a woman from a man, are valued differently. This differential evaluation produces gender inequality because it differentially expands and constrains women's and men's choices, opportunities, rights, privileges, access to resources, degree of autonomy, and the extent of their **power**—the ability to act effectively and the capacity to exercise control over oneself and others. Gender inequality is not a monolithic, homogeneous phenomenon but a set of different, interlinked problems (Sen 2001:35). Therefore, uncovering, analyzing, and understanding it requires multiple approaches, methodologies, and strategies.

Because gender is used as a basis for socially differentiating people in terms of access to social rewards, it is a form of social stratification called **gender stratification.** We can see gender stratification operating in the story above; Kate and her brother have different opportunities in terms of their higher education

Global News

1.1: Iraq: Continued Violence Causing Gender Role Swap

BAGHDAD—Until 2003, Salwa Khatab Omar had been driven around by two drivers and accompanied by at least three guards who lived in a caravan next to her house in Baghdad. She lived in some style and without many responsibilities.

Since the 2003 US-led invasion, however, Salwa, the wife of a former senior army officer, has found herself responsible for virtually everything.

"My husband can't leave the house at all for fear of being targeted like other former regime officials," said Khatab, a 51-year-old mother of four.

"Unlike before, I have to accompany my sons and daughters to their schools and colleges in addition to dealing with other household stuff," said Khatab. She said they had to leave their home and rent a house where nobody knows her husband and his background.

Iraqi men are traditionally the breadwinners, while most women take care of other duties inside the house.

Iraq's continuing violence, however, especially with threats against men, has forced some women to take on more family responsibilities—a phenomenon called "gender role swap" by some specialists.

"Our society does not respect a man who sits at home while his wife works and feeds the family," said Kholoud Nasser Muhssin, a researcher on family and children's affairs at the University of Baghdad.

"This phenomenon will definitely weaken the role of the father and reduce respect among children for their fathers in some families. It will adversely affect an already devastated society," Muhssin added.

IRIN News, August 18, 2007. Reprinted by permission of IRIN News. Copyright © 2007 IRIN (www.irinnews.org)

because of the different expectations their father has for them. These **gender role expectations** arise from society's ideas about the social skills, abilities, and behaviors thought appropriate to individuals depending on whether they are male or female.

What Is Difference?

In a number of instances in this chapter's opening story, it is not just gender but also other forms of social **difference,** such as race, class, and sexuality that affect the characters' ideas, opportunities, and experiences. These social factors position women and men differently in relationship to power, opportunities, and access to privilege and rewards. What is important to remember about each of these forms of difference is that they are *social* differences. There are no simple objective measures for placing individuals in one group as opposed to another. For example, as described in Close-Up 1.1: *Race and Racialization,* **race** is not a natural biological division among people; instead, it is an arbitrary social category created through racialization. **Racialization** is the term used to describe the race-making process in which individuals are grouped together based on a certain set of physical features that have social significance. This constellation of traits is, in turn, attached to a set of assumptions and stereotypes about a certain group. So, for example, in the recent immigration debate in the United States people perceived as "Hispanic" are often assumed to be in the United States illegally, regardless of their actual status, and are demonized as having crossed the border to take jobs away from "real and deserving" citizens, that is from white Americans.

Similarly, identifying one's **class** position can be difficult, since class is not merely a matter of income level. It may also include a consideration of one's level

Close-Up

1.1: Race and Racialization

As you may have noticed, authors sometimes place quotation marks around the word race each time they use it. They do so to indicate that what we think of as race is not real. That is, they wish to indicate that race does not exist as a natural, biological trait that clearly differentiates one group of people from another but is, instead, a culturally constructed category of difference.

Historically, in Western thinking, race has been understood as a natural feature of individuals and groups. Traits associated with race were, and continue to be, used to categorize people into distinct groups, forming a racial classification system or typology. Some racial typologies classify the people of the world into as few as three groups, others into many, many more, suggesting the inherent imprecision and difficulty with such categorizations. Sometimes religion has been used to underscore the God-given nature of racial categories. At other times, science has played the role of supporting the idea that race and racial classifications are natural. In the nineteenth century, for example, scientists wrote voluminous tracts about the biological basis of racial difference. Not surprisingly, the physical characteristics that supposedly differentiated people were then linked to supposed differences in abilities, behaviors, moral attributes, and the like. These assumptions about the natural difference in behavior and ability were then used to explain and justify the unequal access to, and allocation of, social rewards, creating a system of racial stratification.

(continued)

However, during the early twentieth century, anthropologists, using new ideas from the science of genetics and new statistical techniques, interrogated the assumption that race is a scientifically valid concept. They discovered that race has no such biological validity and concluded that race as a biological category does not exist. In other words, they showed that there is no way to take a trait such as skin color or nose shape or hair type and definitively categorize individuals based on it into discrete groups called "races." This is because the variation in such human traits is continuous. Take skin color as an example: if all the individuals of the world were lined up from the person with the darkest skin color to the person with the lightest, you would observe a very gradual and continuous movement from dark to light skin. Any attempt to break this continuum of variation into distinct categories would result in very arbitrary groupings.

As an illustration, take the following grey-scale spectrum.

Divide it into three groups indicating three distinct categories of color, calling the group on the left "light grey," the one in the middle, "medium grey," and the one on the right, "dark grey." How did you decide where to divide the spectrum? You may have made equal-sized groupings just because that seems to make sense. But whether you did or not, ask yourself how the color immediately to the left of each of your dividing lines differs from the one immediately to the right of it? You should see that your choice of where to put the line in terms of actual differences in color is arbitrary. Someone else could very well put the lines in different places, but each of you would have trouble justifying the definitiveness of your choice.

Just as it is impossible to tell where one color of grey definitively ends, and the other begins, so it is impossible to tell where one group identified as a race ends and another begins. Skin color is a continuous variable that has historically been divided into discrete groups called races, without much concern for the arbitrary nature of the distinctions, just as the grey scale divisions you made were arbitrary. This is one reason there has been such disagreement over the exact number of races that exist.

Although race has no biological or scientific validity, it certainly has a *social* meaning. Indeed, race is perhaps best understood as a social classification system designed to deal with cultural and political issues. During the colonial period in Middle and South America, for example, the Spaniards introduced a rigidly hierarchical social system consisting of hundreds of different categories or *castas* (castes) based on skin color and ethnic ancestry. A person's racial designation determined his or her legal status and rights. Spaniards, not surprisingly, placed themselves at the top of the hierarchy and were granted prestige, access to power, and resources, while African slaves were relegated to the lowest level and denied any legal rights. In many places in the world today, racial designations continue to have great significance for how individuals are judged and treated every day of their lives and what opportunities are opened or closed to them.

Because of the lack of natural racial divisions among humans, and because race has been, and continues to be, the basis of a system of social stratification, race is best defined in the following way: race is a social category that uses arbitrary external physical characteristics to categorize humans into what are mistakenly thought to be biologically distinct human groups.

Great social significance continues to be attached to certain human features; individuals with these features have a "racial character" imposed on them based on a set of assumptions and stereotypes about a certain group of people. This imposition *creates* race. The social and political process of race-making is called racialization. Racialization assigns rights, resources, power, prestige, privileges, and other social rewards based on the categorization of individuals into groups based on assumed differences, usually, but not always, physical traits. Just as "blackness" is one such social category, so too is "whiteness."

Thus, even though the assumption throughout this book is that race has no biological reality, it continues to have great social validity and real-world consequences because of processes of racialization. To indicate this social reality, I have chosen not to put the word race in quotations marks.

For more information, see: Marable Manning, 2004. Globalization and Racialization: Building New Sites of Resistance to the New Racial Domain, http://www.manningmarable.netowrks/pdf/globalization.pdf+racialization&hl= en&ct=clnk&cd=6&gl=us (accessed 7/8/08).

of education, occupation, and cultural factors such as taste and style.

People's sexuality is also a complex social construction, which puts individuals into different positions in relationship to power and access to privilege. In North America, people's sexuality is most often defined in terms of their "sexual orientation"—with whom they have sex—and/or their "sexual preference"—with whom they prefer to have sex. If individuals have and prefer sexual relations with someone of the same sex, they are usually considered to be homosexual, gay, or lesbian. If they have and prefer sexual relations with someone of the opposite sex, they are generally considered to be heterosexual or straight.

Neither "sexual orientation" nor "sexual preference," however, reflects the range of differences among people who are usually grouped together based on these simple criteria. Multiple factors affect how individuals understand and experience themselves as "sexual beings," as is discussed more fully in chapter 11. These understandings and experiences intersect not only with other aspects of identity, such as gender, race, and class, but also, for example, with national identity, producing a large range of variation, or **sexual diversity.**

Many people around the world experience multiple forms of oppression simultaneously based on an intersecting set of social variables. Kate, for example, is not only a woman; she is also a white, North American working-class lesbian. These distinctions position her in a particular way, giving her more and less access to societal rewards in comparison to other men and women living in her own and in other societies. She may, for example, be privileged by race in relationship to some men and women within her own society but disadvantaged in relationship to men and women from the middle and upper classes; she has less access to resources and opportunities than wealthier women and men in her own society.

Gender, race, class, and sexual diversity come into play in understanding someone's relationship to power, but so may, for example, age, ethnicity, nationality, religion, and able-bodiedness. Each of these factors affects individuals and groups of people in dissimilar ways; that is, they affect people *differentially.* Difference is used as a broad category to highlight what some people share with one another in relationship to other people, as well as what distinguishes certain categories of people from others in terms of access to opportunities, privileges, and power. Difference, then, is socially constructed, not based on inherent biological dissimilarities from a more powerful and privileged reference group, usually understood to be white, wealthy heterosexual men. One way in which ideologies of difference work to sustain inequality, however, is to assert that the traits and characteristics that distinguish one group from another are natural ones, as we will see in chapter 4.

Intersecting forms of difference not only construct and constrain individuals' opportunities differentially, they also affect the very ideas individuals from different social locations have about how to act, what to believe, how to make sense of their experiences, and how to think about themselves and others. Each individual, thus, has a range of identities that inform her or him about who she or he is. These differences constitute an individual's social identity.

How Are Personal Lives and Global Forces Connected?

The chapter-opening scenario shows how distant events affect our personal lives and gender identities. This occurs because no society is an isolated entity composed of individuals merely holding on to traditional cultural beliefs about masculinity and femininity passed on through the generations. Every society, whether in the past or in the present, has permeable boundaries. People, ideas, assumptions, values, and images have always crossed societal borders. As the story also indicates, what might appear as very personal and intimate ideas and choices are influenced by such crossings, and the historical and contemporary relations among societies and nations within which they arise. These relations have had, and continue to have, profound consequences for women's and men's lives and how they interact with each other. A history of unequal power relations between colonizers and colonized peoples may be impinging on Wilson's romantic and sexual attraction to Fatima, and perhaps hers to him. As we will see in the following chapters, such economic and political power relations were, and continue to be, perpetuated and rationalized through ideas about ideal gender relations, as well as ideas about race, class, sexual diversity, and other forms of difference.

With recent changes in communication technologies, ideas about difference circulate throughout the world more widely than ever before and with increasing speed. As more and more people move to new places, whether through leisured travel, voluntary immigration, or forced movement, varied constructions of gender come increasingly into contact with one another. In addition, images of gender, especially in Western advertising and film, are now exported to almost every corner of the globe. As a result of these movements, many individuals now routinely confront complex and contradictory identity constructs and expectations.

The impact of the circulation of such constructs is not a simple one. Individuals and groups of people do not merely accept wholesale "new" cultural conceptualizations of difference. Instead, they react in complex ways to them, sometimes integrating bits and pieces of new conceptualizations into preexisting models of femininity and masculinity. At other times they contest and resist them. The end result is often the creation of new values, social identities, and tensions. In the realm of gender, exposure to others' constructs has also resulted in the emergence of new and diverse conceptualizations of masculinity and femininity, what it means to be a male or a female. These new conceptualizations, in turn, circulate beyond particular places, inextricably connecting local and globalizing worlds.

Why Study Anthropology to Learn about Today's Globalizing World?

Traditional Anthropology

Since its beginning in the late nineteenth century, anthropology has been committed to describing and explaining human diversity. Anthropologists have also traditionally been concerned with exploring how societies change and with understanding the forces propelling contact among societies. Given these long-standing emphases, anthropologists are in a prime position to understand the contemporary world of interconnections, in which people with diverse traditions come into ever-increasing contact with one another to produce new forms of culture.

Feminist Anthropology

Anthropology's traditional commitment to describing and explaining cultural diversity did not, for the most part, take other aspects of diversity into account. For example, it largely ignored and rendered invisible gender, race, class, and sexual differences as important influences on people's lives. It is in response to this invisibility that **feminist anthropology** emerged in the United States in the 1970s, as we discuss in more detail in chapter 2. At its inception, feminist anthropology was particularly concerned with how gender affected individuals and groups of people differently cross-culturally.

Black Feminist and Lesbian/Gay/Bisexual/Transgendered (LGBT) Anthropology

In the last decades of the twentieth century, feminist anthropologists studied other forms of difference along with gender. They, together with black feminist anthropologists and LGBT anthropologists, came to understand that no culture can be adequately described or explained without attention to differences within societies. Yet, these approaches are seen by many as a special kind of anthropology, as mere off-shoots of a more general or fundamental type of anthropology.

What feminist, black feminist, and LGBT anthropologists do, however, *is* fundamental anthropology. They recognize that cultural and other forms of difference are socially created and typically involve differential power relations between and among groups of people. Indeed, it is these approaches and other politically engaged approaches that have been able to fulfill the unrealized promises of traditional anthropology. We use the phrase **twenty-first-century anthropology** to make this clear whenever possible throughout the text. However, "feminist anthropology," "black feminist anthropology," and "LGBT anthropology" are used when necessary for clarity, for historic accuracy, and to specify the differences among these three approaches.

Twenty-First-Century Anthropology

Twenty-first-century anthropologists understand that what has been called "culture" cannot be understood without placing difference at the center of their studies. They also know that understanding the characteristics of our globalizing world is a prerequisite for comprehending how differences shape local lives and cultures. The connection between local and personal meanings and global events like those described in the opening story makes this evident. Twenty-first-century anthropology, thus, explores the impact of global changes on how people live their lives, how they conceptualize the world and their place within it, what they find meaningful, what they imagine, and what values they hold. It also explains how people interpret global forces, adapting them within their own systems of meaning and to their own beliefs and practices.

Close-Up

1.2: Minority or Majority? by Peter Rigby

One obvious characteristic women share with both the working class and racial "minorities" is that they are in actual fact a majority. Of course in certain communities and places around the world, men outnumber women, but the world population statistics tell another story. The same is true of the "non-white" or non-European races of the world: the populations of Asia and Africa together account for over 70% of the world's total (Brantlinger 1990:147). So, too, the "working class," or those "who perform physical labor for wages or . . . produce food from land they do not legally own," are in the global majority.

[How] does it come about that [the terms race, class, and gender] are perceived in the dominant culture [of the West] as relevant to "minorities" instead of majorities? How has the map of the world become so distorted . . . that questions of class, gender, and race seem marginal, "special" topics for seminars and graduate courses, perhaps, but not for the main agenda? These categories signify the *major* forms of division and difference between people. [From: Peter Rigby, 1996. *African Images: Racism and the End of Anthropology.* Oxford: Berg. Cited: Brantlinger, *Rule of Darkness: British Literature and Imperialism, 1830–1914.* Ithaca, NY: Cornell University Press.]

It is also important to understand that the globalizing world is made up of complex intersections of people, technology, media, capital, commodities, and ideas. A globalizing world, in other words, does not exist outside of the groups of people who inhabit it and interact within it. Global economic flows, or the global economy, for example, are not propelled by forces unattached from the people who are a part of it.

Twenty-first-century anthropologists have developed concepts and methods capable of helping us better understand a globalizing world. Before we describe some of these changing concepts, it is necessary to get a clearer sense of the world those concepts are meant to map. To do so, we turn to a discussion of how today's worldwide interconnections have been, and are being, conceptualized.

What Is Globalization?

No Single Definition of Globalization

Over the last century, goods, services, information, people, and money and other forms of finance have surged across borders in unprecedented numbers and at unparalleled rates. This flow has led to a complex set of interconnections among the world's nations and people. Today, developments in transportation and especially in communication and information technologies have made even the remotest parts of the world accessible, connecting people and places in new ways. It is not uncommon for people from the Global North to have experiences similar to the ones described in the opening scenario: to travel to Central America for an ecotour, to electronically communicate in real time with friends all over the world, and to experience job layoffs due to fluctuations in distant financial markets. Neither is it unheard of in today's world to find a native (aboriginal) Australian watching the latest episode of *Sex and the City* on a television produced in Japan or to find a Mayan woman in highland Guatemala growing Asian snow peas that will be served to customers of the newest fusion restaurant in New York City's trendy Chelsea district.

The term "globalization" is frequently used to describe the complex interconnections occurring throughout the world. There is, however, no one single or simple definition of globalization. Theorists from different fields and with differing political orientations define globalization in various ways and equate different processes with it. The essential feature included in almost all definitions of globalization, however, focuses on the vast network of interconnections among peoples and places that exists today and even more specifically on the speed with which these interconnections are made. Most theorists also agree that these interconnections are more extensive and intense than ever before. Given these basic commonalities, the following working definition of **globalization** is offered: a set of processes that has given rise to a widening, deepening, and acceleration of worldwide interconnections in all aspects of contemporary life (see Held et al. 1999:2).

How and Why Definitions of Globalization Differ

If we look beyond the basic definition of globalization that is shared by most people, we find that conceptualizations of globalization vary considerably. For example, there is significant difference among various writers on the issue of whether globalization is something new or merely a variation on processes that have affected cultural interconnections for centuries. Where one stands on this debate influences whether today's globality is seen as a phenomenon that can be adequately understood using traditional concepts and methods or whether new concepts and approaches are required.

How globalization is defined also affects whether someone evaluates globalization as a positive or negative force in people's lives. For example, some policy makers equate globalization with free trade and praise its virtues, seeing in it the possibility for the creation of one harmonious, "global world." Others question just how "free" free trade actually is and whom it benefits. People also disagree about what globalization produces: a homogenized world or one that is increasingly diverse? We will look at each of these viewpoints when we consider debates over globalization later in the chapter.

Is There a Better Term?

Researchers differ over which term best captures today's interconnectedness. Since these interconnections occur across preexisting national boundaries, some scholars prefer to refer to them as **transnational** in nature. Anthropologists tend to be among the group of thinkers who prefer to use the words "transnational" and "transnationalization," rather than "global" and "globalization." There are several reasons for this, including the following:

- As we have discussed, globalization is a difficult term to pin down and means different things to different researchers. Using it may reinforce definitions that are counter to what anthropologists have in mind when they explore worldwide interconnections.

- Globalization is now used so frequently that it has become a virtual "buzzword." Some people worry that this popular use of the term has emptied it of its analytical power.

- Unlike "globalization," transnationalism does not assume a universal and even flow of capital, commodities, people, images, ideas, and technologies across the globe. Instead, transnationalism focuses attention on cross-border interactions.

The word "transnational" has limitations as well. It assumes that national boundaries are the most significant borders across which people and things move. But this is certainly not always the case. In today's shifting world, regional, ethnic, and cultural boundaries are routinely crossed and the movement across them is often more significant to people's daily lives than those taking place across national borders. Although you will see the terms transnationalism and globalization throughout this book, the preferred term is "globalizing world" because it better signals the understanding that a number of processes—not only economic but also political and cultural—continue to establish new, and to transform existing, interconnections among people and places. The world is not truly global. Even though people, places, ideas, and social systems have become less separate from each other, different people and different societies continue to be integrated into a world system in different ways, granting advantages to some people in comparison to others who are more disadvantaged by changes occurring around the world.

How Has Globalization Been Conceptualized?

Globalization as Multidimensional

Since globalization unfolds in multiple spheres of life simultaneously some people conceptualize it as a having a number of dimensions. The emphasis on globalization as multidimensional is helpful in broadly categorizing and distinguishing the main kinds of processes characterizing major changes occurring in the world today. Figure 1.1 (on the following page) provides one such conceptualization of globalization. It describes four spheres in which global processes take place: economic, political, demographic, and cultural. It also outlines the major forms of global transformations occurring within each of these spheres.

This figure lists global processes and transformations in separate spheres to help make globalization more understandable. But in doing so, it oversimplifies and obscures the interconnection between and among the processes and changes occurring in each sphere. The relationship among different spheres of globalization is complex. For example, demographic globalization, the movement of people throughout the world, has contributed to extensive cultural globalization, the spread of images, symbols, meaning systems, modes of thought, and modes of communication worldwide. But demographic globalization is not solely responsible for cultural globalization. Ideas and values may be brought to new places by the people who hold them and they also may be widely transported through the media and other forms of telecommunication.

Knowledge of globalization's multiple dimensions can allow us to better conceptualize the impact of globalization on women and men and how it has restructured many aspects of women's and men's lives worldwide. Some of this restructuring is based on standard social divisions along lines of gender, race, class, social diversity, and other differences and, therefore, reinforces them. For example, in the political sphere, large-scale transnational political-economic structures, such as the World Bank and the International Monetary Fund, have tended to lend money to men more readily than to women, based on assumptions about gender difference (discussed further in chapter 7). In many places in Africa, for example, men who wish to borrow money to set up agribusinesses are often given preference over women, thereby displacing women's traditional economic activities.

Globalization can also bring mixed blessings to women and men around the world. For example, whether in Tunisia, Honduras, or Thailand, economic globalization has allowed an increasing number of women to move out of the domestic realm and into factories. But this comes with costs. Factory work may grant women a degree of independence but with a high price: as corporations cut costs in the face of increasing worldwide competition, women must often work under appalling conditions for meager wages, sometimes making a third less than their male coun-

Definition	Characteristics
Economic globalization: the internationalization and spread of capitalist market relations throughout the world.	• higher-than-ever levels of trade; • unprecedented high levels of finance and capital flow across national boundaries facilitated by electronic technology allowing vast amounts of money to be transferred across the globe in seconds; • high rates of investment in, and lending to, poorer countries by wealthier ones.
Political globalization: the extension of political power and activity across the boundaries of nations, resulting in a decrease in the autonomy of sovereign states.	• proliferation of international regulatory regimes such as the World Bank; • developing infrastructure for political decision making at international, transnational, and global levels; • increasing number of transnational pressure groups; • increasing scope of international law.
Demographic globalization: high levels of movement of people across national boundaries.	• increase in the number of countries affected by migration in comparison to earlier historical moments; • growing diversity in migrants' areas of origin and final destinations; • increase in number of multiethnic and multicultural societies.
Cultural globalization: the worldwide proliferation of images, symbols, meaning systems, modes of thought, and modes of communication.	• dominance of multinational industries in creation and ownership of infrastructure and organizations for the production and distribution of cultural goods; • increase in intensity, speed, and volume of cultural exchange and communication of all kinds, enabled by telecommunication technologies and international media corporations; • rising complexity of cultural interactions across societies; • erosion of cultural self-sufficiency and autonomy on the local, regional, and national levels; • production simultaneously of cultural homogeneity (McWorld) in some areas of life and cultural heterogeneity in others.

Information compiled from Pieterse 1995 and Held et al., 1999.

Figure 1.1   Spheres of Globalization

terparts, then go home to work a "second-shift," doing housework and caring for children.

Transnational corporations often rationalize underpaying women by drawing on widespread cultural assumptions about femininity and marriage. For example, as anthropologist Faye Harrison (1997) describes, transnational garment corporations have used the assumption that activities such as sewing are "natural" women's tasks, to take advantage of women. Since this work is seen as natural, it is thought to re-

quire no special skill or training, which justifies paying women little for their work. Men's work, in contrast, is more often seen as involving special knowledge and training—as skilled work in need of appropriate compensation. Underpaying women in comparison to men is also justified by the assumption that women's wages merely supplement the wages of their husband or father, who is assumed to be the actual breadwinner in the family, as discussed more fully in chapter 7 (Harrison 1997:457).

Globalization as Flows, Scapes, and Disjunctures

Categorizing global processes in terms of the primary spheres in which they take place can help us conceptualize "globalization." But it is not the only useful way of doing so. Anthropologist, Arjun Appadurai (1997) suggests that globalization is best understood when conceptualized in terms of a number of types of cultural global flows. This emphasis on flows highlights the importance of the movement of people and things to today's world. Appadurai refers to these dimensions as **scapes.** He identifies five scapes with the following flows:

- capital flows throughout the world in financescapes;

- people move as tourists, immigrants, refugees, exiles, or guest workers in ethnoscapes;

- technology circulates in technoscapes;

- media images travel in mediascapes; and

- political ideologies and images flow in ideoscapes.

Appadurai chooses the term "scape" to get at the idea that the processes taking place in these dimensions look different to people situated in various land*scapes* (places) across the globe.

Appadurai is interested in these different views of global flows because he is concerned with how people use them as raw material for imagining themselves and their worlds. People, images, ideas, capital, and products intersect in different ways in different places producing new ways of seeing the world and understanding one's self and place within it (Appadurai 1997:8). Flows can also result in unpredictable combinations and effects, what Appadurai calls "disjunctures." The idea of disjunctures implies that global flows are not a set of circulating ideas, people, images, and capital that will increasingly expand outward until the world is "one." Instead, it suggests that global flows can create clashes, misfires, confusions (Tsing 2000), and even chaos (Appadurai 1997).

Disjunctures among flows can create significantly different circumstances for men and women and affect their lives in very gender-specific ways as global flows both reformulate and reinforce old patterns. For example, as capital flows to produce multinational corporations (MNCs) with offices and clients throughout the world, it can produce different requirements for men and women moving in ethnoscapes. Aiwha Ong provides an illustration of this in her book, *Flexible Citizenship: The Cultural Logics of Transnationality* (1999). She describes how an elite Hong Kong male executive may be able to jet all over the world today, expanding business networks and opportunities. His wife however might be ensconced in a house in the United States, where she has moved with her children in order to establish residency rights for her family. She is left to care for their children in this new unfamiliar setting, perhaps even knowing that her husband might start a second family "back home" (Ong 1999:20).

Globalization as Deterritorialization

For many anthropologists, what is most significant about globalization is that it deterritorializes the world. **Deterritorialization** is the process by which the cultural, social, and political contexts that affect and define people's lives cease to be confined by territorial borders, boundaries, and distances. Because social interactions, exchanges, and encounters now occur so quickly, so frequently, and so easily over large distances, people's social spaces are no longer confined to, or arise out of, a single geographic area. Personal lives have been significantly refigured for many people due to this process: now, for example, a person's most important family members and friends might routinely live hundreds or thousands of miles away (see Rouse 1991).

Personal interactions have been reformulated as people talk to others on different continents in real time, order products from a distant country by using the Internet, watch films made in another hemisphere, and even travel to meet and marry someone on the opposite side of the planet. Belief systems, political ideologies, food preferences, and artistic styles and genres, which may once have been more easily defined by specific geographic areas, now defy territorial categorization.

Deterritorialization weakens ties between culture and place as people move from their traditional homelands to one, two, and even three new locales over the course of their lifetime. But it has also led to the reinsertion of culture into new contexts (Inda and Rosaldo 2002:11). One important consequence of deterritorialization is that cultural identity has become increasingly significant to numerous people as they move to new places and seek to imagine and carve out new lives. In other words, globalization can create the conditions for localization, various kinds of efforts to create bounded entities or communities in the face of their erasure through global flows.

For example, under conditions that cause groups of people to live in **diasporas**—that is, the breaking up and scattering of a group of people throughout the world so that those displaced from their homeland need to find other places to live—those people living in new places can become increasingly "ethnicized." This means that they place increasing importance on being seen as members of a group of people who share an identity based on certain distinctive cultural traits, especially a common origin, language, and history. "Ethnicization," as anthropologist Jonathan Freidman (2003) suggests, allows people to construct a common identity across great distances, thereby creating and reinforcing transnational economic, cultural, and social relations.

Focusing on one group's shared cultural traits in comparison to other groups helps solidify the idea that members of an ethnic group are "one people." Such representations of unity, however, often have more to do with contemporary global political, economic, and social arrangements than historical and cultural factors. Ethnicization can also be seen at work in the United States where members of historically distinct groups from around the globe find common identification as "Latinos" or as "Asians," for example.

Deterritorialization can also have repercussions for the sense of place held by people who have not moved from their original homeland. It can break the illusion of some supposed natural relationship between people, culture, and place. For example, as Europe experiences the influx of more and more people from Britain's former colonies—India, the Caribbean, and Nigeria—the notion that some people belong in some places and not others is stirred up as Europeans must make their own adjustments to the arrival of these immigrants (see Gupta and Furguson 1997). Often the disruption of

this sense of "rightful" belonging results in virulent, racist attacks on people seen as intruders. There has been an increasing number of such attacks in European nations: in 2001, for example, Germany reported a 40 percent increase in attacks on immigrants, such as one by neo-Nazi skinheads that resulted in the death of a man from Mozambique (http://news.bbc.co.uk/1/hi/world/europe/1159888.stm, accessed 8/14/03). Racist violence exploded in France in 2002, too, where more than half of racist attacks were aimed at Jews (http://www.inreview.com/archive/topic/1470.html, accessed 8/14/03). At its extreme, this fear of outsiders, or xenophobia, can result in genocide, the systematic murder of an entire group of people.

People who move from their place of birth to establish lives elsewhere face a number of difficulties and challenges. For example, they must find ways to reproduce their way of life in settings that may be inhospitable to the maintenance of their cultural traditions. These circumstances, as Appadurai points out, can exert tremendous pressure on marriages and families (1997:44). They can be especially stressful for women who are more frequently than men given the responsibility of cultural reproduction, the passing on of traditions to the next generation. This situation is exacerbated in a globalizing world of interconnections where the desire for continuity and certainty is often frustrated by the continuous movement of people, ideas, and beliefs (see Appadurai 1997:43–44).

Deterritorialization has also affected people's and nations' very idea of belonging. This is evident in the number of ways in which what it means to be a citizen of a country is being refigured.

Close-Up

1.3: Globalization and Citizenship by Nell Quest

The increased movement of people across national borders has affected how people think about membership in a community. It has had legal, cultural, and political consequences for understanding what it means to be a citizen of a nation. A citizen is a native or naturalized person who owes allegiance to a government that grants the person certain rights and protection.

For some (usually poorer) countries, globalization results in an increase in the numbers of citizens whose primary residences are not within the nation in which they were born. Yet, these individuals often participate in their birth country's national economies. For example, migrants often send large sums of money back home to families in the form of remittances. Remittances are now second only to tourism as a source of revenue in developing countries. Many migrants also participate in national elections in their countries of origin. For other (usually wealthier) countries, globalization's influence is marked more by increases in the numbers of noncitizens and "minorities" physically present on national soil. Increased movement of people across national borders can have significant consequences for how governments create a sense of cohesive national identity, and for how minority populations are treated, and understand their roles in, their countries of residence and origin.

Anthropologists have increasingly come to understand citizenship as a complex and uneven category, and one that has different meanings and importance depending on local and individual contexts. Anthropologist Renato Rosaldo, who has done research among Latinos in the U.S., has attempted to expand the way we think of citizenship beyond simple legal categories. For Rosaldo, traditional notions of legal citizenship do not tell the whole story of how minorities create or understand their belonging in a nation. He has used the term "cultural citizenship" to refer to the ways in which minority noncitizens or "second-class citizens" create belonging or participate in a country's political processes without giving up their right to maintain an identity marked by cultural and/or racial differences (Rosaldo 1994). His efforts follow scholarship in cultural studies (see, e.g. Gilroy 1987), which argues that even legal citizenship does not guarantee minorities equal rights. Scholars of cultural citizenship argue that examinations of legal citizenship should therefore be complemented by studies of how minorities create belonging in other ways, such as through participation in church groups or strikes at work, or through their aesthetic choices.

Other anthropologists have demonstrated that minorities' legal citizenship, or lack thereof, and the perception others have of their legality, illegality, or criminality play a very important role in what rights they have, what problems they face, and what choices are available to them. Ana Yolanda Ramos-Zayas' (2004) work with Puerto Ricans in Chicago shows that a "right to citizenship" can be insecure and is certainly not enough to avoid stigmatization. Ramos-Zayas conducted research among Puerto Ricans in Chicago, who have historically been seen as radical, criminal, degenerate, welfare-dependent, and even as terrorists. Despite the fact that they are legally entitled to U.S. citizenship, she says Puerto Ricans still feel they have to prove that they are worthy of it, which they partially do through high rates of service in the military. In work she has undertaken with anthropologist Nick DeGenova, Ramos-Zayas also finds salient differences in the sorts of belonging available to these Puerto Rican Chicagoans, many of whom have U.S. citizenship, and Mexican residents, many of whom do not. They point out the ways in which Puerto Ricans deploy their identity as citizens to set themselves apart from "illegal" Mexicans and to challenge stereotypes of their community as criminal.

The rights granted to legal citizens, and particularly to minorities, can also be eroded under certain conditions. This danger may be greater under conditions of globalization, since one way in which nations and their majority citizens might respond to globalization is to further fear, stigmatize, and restrict ethnic and cultural minorities, regardless of citizenship status. French anthropologist Étienne Balibar has argued that as national borders recede in importance, internal boundaries within countries—such as those between racial majorities and

(continued)

minorities—may actually become more important (2004). For these reasons, anthropologists interested in citizenship and a politics that is respectful of equal rights and of difference continue to pay careful attention to understanding citizenship, its changing meanings, and the way conflicts over it play out in a globalizing world.

References

Balibar, Étienne. 2004. *We the People of Europe?: Reflections on Transnational Citizenship.* James Swenson, trans. Princeton: Princeton University Press.

DeGenova, Nicholas, and Ana Yolanda Ramos-Zayas. 2003. Latino Crossings: Mexicans, Puerto Ricans, and the Politics of Race and Citizenship. New York: Routledge.

Gilroy, Paul. 1987. There Ain't No Black in the Union Jack: The Cultural Politics of Race and Nation. Chicago: University of Chicago Press.

Ramos-Zayas, Ana Yolanda. 2004. Delinquent Citizenship: National Performances, Racialization, Surveillance, and the Politics of "Worthiness" in Puerto Rican Chicago. *Latino Studies* 2 (1):26–44.

Rosaldo, Renato. 1994. Cultural Citizenship in San Jose, California. *PoLAR Political and Legal Anthropology Review* 17 (2):57–64.

Globalization as Westernization/Modernization

Those people who understand globalization as Westernization focus on the spread of "modernity," a form of social life and economic organization that emerged in Europe around the seventeenth century. Modernity is conceptualized as a way of life based on industrial capitalism that produces large-scale urbanization—the formation and growth of cities—and bureaucratization—the development of a complex system of administrative agencies overseeing all aspects of people's lives. Modernization is made possible by a belief in rationalism, that humans are rational beings who make decisions in line with their own self-interest, and by secularism, the movement away from religious values and explanations of the world. Under colonialism, modernity came to be equated with cultural "advancement" and economic "development" and was violently imposed on colonized people. Today's globalization is seen as a continuation of these modernizing processes.

The continued dissemination of ideas, products, ideologies, and images from the United States and other nations of the Global North to the Global South is called "neocolonialism" by theorists of modernization. It is seen as a new form of colonization as countries of the Global North exert economic, political, and cultural domination over nations around the world. Those who view globalization as Westernization focus on the devastating effects it has on traditional societies and local self-determination. Whether the increasing spread of such ideas and products will result in the erasure of cultural differences or in its opposite is a topic of debate among both academics and policy makers, as we will see later in this chapter in the section called "Homogeneity or Heterogeneity?"

Debates over Globalization

Globalization: Old or New?

People not only disagree over how best to define globalization but also over whether globalization is a new process or one that has existed for hundreds, if not thousands, of years. Although it is doubtful that any anthropologist sees today's globality as totally disconnected from historical processes, some do point to important ruptures between old and new. We consider both sides of this debate in the following sections.

Continuing Patterns of Human Interconnections: Globalization Is Old

People have been moving around the globe exchanging genes, ideas, and material goods since the beginning of humankind. Indeed, the constant exchange of genes that has typified human existence is responsible for the fact that humans, unlike other widely distributed creatures, belong to a single species. The inability of certain human groups to move from one location to another due to physical barriers, such as mountains and oceans, has resulted in some local biological differences among human groups, but the isolation of particular populations has never been so complete, or for so long, that any one human group has diverged from all others in significant biological ways—that is, has speciated.

Vast trade networks tying human groups together also have historical depth: obsidian and salt circulated widely throughout Mesoamerica, for example, long before Columbus invaded the New World in 1492. Trade caravans spread Islam throughout the Middle East and Africa centuries ago. Few societies have subsisted without any kind of trade, and many societies have formed alliances with others for mutual benefit or protection. For example, Athens, Sparta, and other Greek city-states, which often battled each other, banded together to form the Delian League around 487 BC to protect each other from the mutual threat of invading Persians.

Colonial empires are not recent occurrences either. Many date far back into human history; around 2000 years ago, for example, the Romans conquered much of Europe, northern Africa, Asia Minor, and the Middle East, spreading their religion, code of laws, technology, and other customs. Anthropologist Eric Wolf has made a strong case for viewing the history of humans as one of interconnection in his influential book, *Europe and the People without History* (1997). Scholars use evidence of these kinds of historic economic and political interconnections to suggest that globalization is a process that has been occurring for centuries.

Widening Global Connections under European Colonialism. Even those scholars who suggest that globalization is not an entirely new phenomenon often concur that after Columbus's entry into the New World in 1492, the nature of the interconnections that had once existed among groups of people changed radically. The conquest and colonization of the Americas by Europeans led to the beginning of a *world*-system that laid the basis for today's globalizing world.

Before the fifteenth century, except perhaps for a few forays by the Vikings into North America, there had been no contact for thousands of years between Europe, Asia, and Africa, on the one hand, and North and South America, on the other. Therefore, the entire global population was not connected. With the increasing exploration, exploitation, and colonization of the world by European nations following Columbus's four voyages, contact between once widely dispersed peoples became more regular. Europe, which had not

even been a regional power, was now enabled by a growing capitalist economic system and a ruthless use of force to become a world center with the Americas, Africa, and Asia at its peripheries.

Colonialism, based on economic, political, and cultural domination, was rationalized by systems of knowledge: an organized set of ideas and ways of thinking about the world that creates a reality for a group of people, as we will see in subsequent chapters. The system of knowledge underlying colonial domination posited that conquered peoples were inherently inferior and that they thus deserved to be dominated and controlled. Non-European people were viewed both as savages in need of being "civilized" and as "heathens" in need of having their souls saved through conversion to Christianity.

Shifting Power Relations in the Twentieth Century. Much of the world remained colonized until well into the twentieth century. During this time the United States increasingly displaced Europe as the center of world power, while the Soviet Union struggled to exert its control over more and more of the world. Japan, too, moved toward becoming an important world economic and political power, contributing to the emergence of Asia and the Pacific Rim as a significant regional economic center. Consequently, the "North/South" axis became increasingly important in distinguishing power inequalities among major regions of the world. Even these relations have shifted with the Soviet Union's complete unraveling in the 1990s and Japan's economic decline during the same period. In the meantime, the United States became a postindustrial society as more and more of its factories that manufactured goods shut down. It went from having a primarily manufacturing economy to having an economy based on providing services. Even in this time of economic crisis, all these factors position the United States as the world's only economic and political superpower. But the U.S. faces strong competition with nations such as China, which are working hard to build their economic strength and political power.

Even though colonialism declined in the twentieth century, its legacy can still be strongly felt today. Countries historically on the periphery, often referred to by world-system theorists as "Third World," "underdeveloped," or "developing" nations, now struggle to be on equal terms with wealthier "First World" or "developed" nations. Nevertheless, they enter the global system on unequal terms. The significance of historic center–periphery relations to understanding today's globality can be seen in the work of anthropologist Ulf Hannerz (1996). He envisions globalization as the coming together of once historically separate cultures under the conditions of inequality established by the core–periphery configuration of European colonialism.

Novel Aspects of Human Interconnections: Globalization Is New

If people have been socially, politically, and economically intertwined historically through population movements, trade networks, and political domination, what, then, are the features that distinguish today's globality from earlier forms of interconnection? Those theorists who believe that we are witnessing something new today often focus on very recent changes in the *kinds* and *extent* of human interconnections and their effects on identity, consciousness, and a person's experience of the whole world. They argue, for example, that more and more people no longer consider themselves simply members of a single territory, nation, or cultural group, but see themselves as citizens of the world. But critics of this view suggest that it is only a small group of elite people from around the world who have the privilege of viewing themselves as "world citizens," or "cosmopolitans," free from the constraints of local economic, political, and social forces.

Perhaps a more persuasive argument for the novelty of today's global condition is the suggestion that people everywhere are becoming increasingly conscious of the world as one entity. Most people, for example, realize that weapons are now capable of mass, if not worldwide, destruction and that local governments or corporate choices can have worldwide environmental consequences. This growing awareness of environmental interconnectedness explains why so many people worldwide responded negatively when in 2000 George W. Bush, during the first 100 days of his presidency, reneged on his campaign promise to support the 1997 Kyoto Protocol. This agreement calls for a reduction in carbon dioxide emissions suspected of quickening global warming, an environmental circumstance with potentially devastating ecological consequences for people all over the world.

The United States' participation with other countries to improve and protect the environment became an important issue in the 2008 U.S. presidential election as more and more people within the United States came to recognize the role of U.S. society in such environmental destruction. Another example of global awareness can be found in the concept of "human rights," which depends on an understanding of all people as "one people," sharing a basic set of entitlements. (Human rights will be discussed in more detail in chapter 3.)

Some theorists argue that today's globality can also be distinguished from earlier forms of interconnection in terms of its centrality to people's lives. They suggest that although various kinds of global connections have existed for centuries, now, for the first time in human history, mobility, communication, and connectedness are at the *center* of people's lives. Today, more and more people experience cultural difference as part of their everyday lives. For example, it is not unusual for many of us to learn and work alongside people from different geographic areas of the world. Before September 11, 2001, for example, there were people from more than 50 countries working together at the World Trade Center in New York City.

For those theorists who focus on the unique aspects of contemporary globalization, what distinguishes the world of today from the world of the past are the extent, intensity, ease, speed, and regularity of the interconnections linking people. These theorists view the changes not just in the context of degree but also as a matter of producing a qualitatively different kind of experience of life, of place, and of self. As we have seen, anthropologist Arjun Appadurai believes that today's global interconnections have profound effects on the imagination. Pointing specifically to the proliferation of electronic media and the mass movement of people around the world, Appadurai points to the possibilities they open up for "the construction of [new] imagined selves and imagined worlds" (1997:3). Many of the theorists who see something new in the contemporary world suggest that it feels profoundly different to live today than it did in ancient times, a few centuries ago, or even 50 years ago.

Globalization: Good or Bad?

There is also disagreement among people about whether globalization is a force for good or whether it has had primarily negative consequences for most people around the world, especially those in poorer nations. Those who see globalization as a positive force argue that economic globalization is necessary for undoing the unequal relations among nations and regions of the world established centuries ago. They argue that with increasing wealth, more and more investments can be made to develop the economies of poor countries, which will raise living standards and lessen the long-standing unequal conditions produced by colonialism. This will put all nations on more equal footing, producing worldwide equality.

But will globalization bring an end to worldwide inequalities? Many theorists think not. They point to economic indicators to make their case. For example, between the 1960s and the early 1990s, as global economic connections grew, the gap in *per capita* income between the industrial and the developing worlds tripled. Such theorists suggest that the increase in economic inequality between wealthier and poorer nations over the last few decades is due to the neoliberal policies instituted during that period.

Neoliberalism is an economic philosophy based on the idea that, if left alone, economic markets will naturally lead to technological innovation and progress. Government regulations of the market are seen as having negative consequences. In neoliberal thinking, it is assumed that corporations will be able to make large sums of money if left on their own, and a portion of these profits will eventually reach poorer countries. This is referred to as "trickle-down" economics, an idea that has become central to the philosophy of large-scale organizations such as the International Monetary Fund and the World Bank, which

lend money to poor countries for economic development. Their trickle-down policies, however, have not reduced inequalities but instead have increased them, resulting in devastating consequences for both women and men living in poor countries.

A belief in the power of the market to produce equality is also contradicted by evidence of growing income differences within many countries. In the last decade of the twentieth century in the United States, for example, the gap between "haves" (wealthy people) and "have-nots" (poor people) widened, despite an economy that grew at record rates. Data from 2007 show that the wealthiest 300,000 Americans enjoy almost as much income as the total earned by the bottom 150 million Americans (Johnston 2007). As we will see in chapter 7 when we discuss neoliberalism in more detail, this has had particularly harmful effects on women. In response to such statistics, some writers and policy makers argue that we have not given globalization enough time. Although globalization is in a phase that reinforces worldwide economic inequalities, they do not see this consequence as inevitable or bound to continue over the longer term. However, the recent collapse of the global economy is to a large extent a result of neoliberal policies that are based on an

Shanty shacks along the rail tracks in Pakistan present a sharp contrast to the home of a successful U.S. businessman.

unregulated market. In the United States, in particular, deregulation is tied to the excesses of a financial system that has nearly bankrupted the economy.

Most anthropologists agree that globalization has had various effects, some positive, some negative, depending on where and on whom our focus turns. For example, in an era of global demand for nurses, Indian women nurses from the state of Kerala have been able to migrate to the United States, becoming conduits for the international migration of their entire families. In the process, however, their husbands, often stigmatized as inferior by a U.S. system of racialization, have been unable to use their education and skills in this new context and consequently suffered downward mobility. They have simultaneously lost their traditional standing in the home and the prerogatives associated with it, as described by Sheba George in the Ethnography in Focus. Both men and women can be winners and losers in a world characterized by change on a global scale.

Ethnography in Focus

"Dirty Nurses" and "Men Who Play": Gender and Class in Transnational Migration by Sheba George

The liberalization of immigration, specifically the Immigration and Nationality Act of 1965, was an attempt to respond to [post-World War II health-care] labor shortages. The third preference category in this act allowed for the entry of skilled professionals who were needed in the United States. Because this act also increased immigration quotas for formerly restricted areas, it helped to induce increasing immigration of nurses from Asia, and in particular from India. [p. 154]

***

The incorporation of Kerala Christian nurses into the Indian labor force created a reservoir of migrant workers for a global market. As families began to depend on the incomes of their pioneering daughters, many Kerala nurses accepted financially lucrative nursing opportunities in other countries. No sooner did they occupy their new immigrant jobs than they became stepping stones to further migration for the family members they sponsored. [p. 153]

***

While their nurse-wives and sisters experienced upward economic mobility and increased status, Kerala immigrant men faced the prospect of perhaps never making as much money or gaining equivalent professional standing. Although many of the women had worked in India and had contributed financially to the household income, they had not been the primary breadwinners they became in the United States.

Immigrant men also lost status with respect to their previous social and economic positions. As immigrants they had limited access to the political and social structures of the wider American society. Low incomes and unstable employment in secondary labor market jobs left men with few opportunities for civic participation and access to leadership positions. The difficulty in transferring Indian academic degrees, credentials, work skills, and experience to the United States often meant that men had to start their careers all over again. [p. 155]

***

Since the women were the primary agents of immigration, their husbands and male kin were dependent on them when they joined them. The dependence of the men on the women often went beyond the financial aspect to include all manner of adjustments to American society. The downward mobility of the men raises questions about what happens in the domestic sphere. . . . [One woman I interviewed, Mrs. Papi,] believes that to keep up tradition she must not let her husband cook. Given the lack of auxiliary support from relatives or servants, even Mrs. Papi is sometimes forced to ask her husband for help, and he has no alternative but to acquiesce. [pp. 156–158]

***

The men I interviewed talked about their involvement in childcare as one of the major changes relative to their own fathers' roles in the household. Mr. Elias exemplified this view when he bemoaned the loss of a past where mothers were the exclusive caretakers of children.

> Back home, even if the father and mother are there, mother stays at home and father works outside. Mother takes care of the kids. Mother is the one who forms the character of the kids. Here, the mother works outside the home and so that is left to the father. That is the biggest difference here. Back home it is the mother's sole responsibility. Isn't it? Mother gives baths, and tells them to study, since she is the one at home. Here it is the opposite. [p. 158]

Additionally, in Kerala, the role of the disciplinarian [parent] was [traditionally] the jurisdiction of the father. It appears that the mother has now taken this over. In an informal discussion with four immigrant nurses, disciplining children became a topic of discussion. All the women agreed that the kids came to them for permission to do things, creating conflict with husbands who were consistently more conservative, especially when it came to daughters. One woman thought that perhaps mothers were better able to relate to their American-born children because they had studied American psychology for their registered-nurse licensing exams. . . . At the same time that they face greater responsibilities for childcare, [the immigrant husbands of nurses] discover that they have lost their prerogative as patriarchal disciplinarians. [pp. 158–159]

***

In addition to housework and childcare, I asked the couples about how they divided up the work around financial decision-making. . . . Despite Mrs. Thambi's concerted effort to leave financial matters to her husband, he and most of the other men whom I interviewed were all aware that the fact that their wives worked outside the home changed the balance of power. . . . Unlike their fathers, men like Mr. Cherian had to recognize their wives' financial contributions and take their opinions into consideration even if their wives chose not to sign their own paychecks. [pp. 159–160]

In summary, immigration has brought in its wake changes in the household division of labor. In a way their fathers would never have imagined, Kerala Christian men contribute to housework, cooking, and childcare, while at the same time sharing financial decision-making with their wives. [pp. 160]

From: Michael Burawoy, Joseph Blum, Sheba George, Zsuzsa Gille, Teresa Gowan, Lynne Haney, Maren Klawiter, Steven Lopez, Sean O'Riain, and Millie Thayer, *Global Ethnography: Forces, Connections, and Imagination in a Postmodern World*. Copyright © 2000. Permission granted by University of California Press.

Global processes, however, tend to reinforce traditional social inequalities based on such factors as gender, race and class. Although women are not *inevitably* more victimized by globalization than men, as we will see throughout upcoming chapters, they bear the brunt of its negative consequences.

Globalization: Heterogeneity or Homogeneity?

The United States solidified its position as the world's superpower through its constant involvement in world politics and through its increasing export of goods, services, and images around the world. This position has led some observers to equate globalization with "Americanization." Such observers see Americanization as a new form of colonization.

Theorists who construe globalization in terms of the spread of America's capitalist consumer culture often emphasize the homogenization they see resulting from Americanization, a process leading to the development of what Benjamin Barber calls a "McWorld" (1995). In this view, political occurrences such as the rise of ethnic nationalism in Serbia or fundamentalist governments in Israel or Iran are understood as local reactions to globalization, especially to **commodification,** which increasingly turns once-personal relations and objects into products to be bought and sold. These reactions are understood primarily as attempts by many people of the world to resist cultural homogenization by tenaciously holding on to their traditional cultures.

Close-Up

1.4: A McWorld?

At the height of European colonialism, Britain's rule was so extensive that the sun always shone somewhere on British territory. Today, it seems, the same can be said for McDonald's: the sun never sets on the "Golden Arches." McDonald's established its first franchise outside of the United States in Canada in 1967. Since then, it has expanded so widely that today a McDonald's fast-food restaurant can be found in over 100 countries around the world. At its training headquarters, Hamburger University in Oak Brook, Illinois, classes are taught in more than 30 different languages (Watson 1997).

According to Eric Schlosser, author of *Fast Food Nation: The Dark Side of the All-American Meal* (2000), since the appearance of the first McDonald's outlet in the United States early in the 1950s, it has become the world's biggest owner of retail property and, in some countries such as Brazil, the largest private employer in the nation. Schlosser points out that the Golden Arches are now more widely recognized than the Christian cross and that Ronald McDonald is recognized worldwide more often than any other fictional character except Santa Claus.

In cities such as Beijing, Moscow, and Seoul as well as Baltimore, Salt Lake City, and Juneau, McDonald's is a popular location for personal rituals, family celebrations, and group activities. In China, where a child's birthday was not traditionally celebrated, families now go to a local McDonald's restaurant to commemorate them with "Aunt" and "Uncle" McDonald (Watson 1997). But McDonald's not only affects cultural practices; in response to differing cultural expectations, it has been affected by cultural practices. In Paris, for example, wine is served with Big Macs, while in Tokyo local culinary preferences are satisfied with the teriyaki burger (Ohnuki-Tierney 1997:163).

References

Ohnuki-Tierney, E. 1997. McDonald's in Japan: Changing Manners and Etiquette. In *Golden Arches east: McDonald's in East Asia.* James L. Watson, ed. Pp. 161–182. Stanford: Stanford University Press.

Schlosser, Eric. 2000. Fast Food Nation: The Dark Side of the All-American Meal. Boston: Houghton Mifflin.

Watson, James, L., ed. 1997. Introduction. In *Golden Arches East: McDonald's in East Asia.* James L. Watson, ed. Pp. 1–38. Stanford: Stanford University Press.

Other theorists suggest that instead of producing homogeneity, globalization does the opposite, producing more diversity or heterogeneity. They point to the complex intersection of cultural ideas and practices throughout the world, an intersection that not only results in the presence of McDonald's in Russia and Disney World in Tokyo but also of Mexican egg rolls in Los Angeles, Asian wraps in London, and the tango craze in Japan. This view acknowledges the important influence of non-Western cultures on the West.

Theorists who focus on heterogeneity also argue that what may appear to be an assertion of, or return to, traditional forms of identity and practices on the part of people contesting globalization's effects is actually a creation of new identity forms. Fundamentalist religious movements today are an example. To be effective, religious fundamentalists cannot simply turn to ancient myths and rituals to counter worldwide secularization; they must adapt older religious ideas to a modern world dominated by scientific rationalism (Armstrong 2000).

Regardless of whether responses to globalization are based in tradition or not, it is clear that many people around the world not only adapt and contribute to global forces but also actively resist them. Resistance can take the form of quiet opposition or overt political revolts, such as the 1998 riots in Jakarta in which large numbers of Indonesians took to the streets to protest what they saw as stringent conditions placed on them by the International Monetary Fund (IMF). They accused the IMF of acting as the world's financial policemen, diverting Indonesia's scarce resources, and those of other poor countries, to creditors in some of the richest countries in the world.

Global News

1.2: American Culture Goes Global or Does It?

[T]he cultural relationship between the United States and the rest of the world over the past 100 years has never been one-sided. . . . [A]s a nation of immigrants from the 19th to the 21st centuries, and as a haven in the 1930s and 40s for refugee scholars and artists, the United States has been a recipient as much as an exporter of global culture. . . . Americans . . . did not invent fast food, amusement parks, or movies. Before the Big Mac, there were fish and chips. Before Disneyland, there was Copenhagen's Tivoli Gardens (which Walt Disney used as a prototype for his first theme park). [*The Chronicle of Higher Education*, 4/12/2002:B7]

Two Mozambican women embark on the road to the Mercado Municipale de Nampula to sell their goods and buy some staples to bring home at the end of the day.

Appadurai calls such resistances **grassroots globalization** or **globalization from below.** These terms refer to the various new social forms and organizations that have arisen to protest the negative effects of globalization, especially on the poor (Appadurai 2001:3). Many of these organizations, often referred to as Non-Governmental Organizations or NGOs, are transnational in nature and are themselves an important aspect of today's political globalization. Some NGOs have specifically protested the negative effects of conditions brought about by globalization and changed the lives of women who constitute the bulk of the world's poor. In Latin America, foreign banks, the IMF, and national governments have all been challenged through gender-based organizations in which women politicize their roles as mothers to protest the impact of economic crises on them and their families (Lind 2000:162). Chapter 2 provides a number of examples of grassroots resistance movements.

The increase in poverty worldwide due to globalization and neoliberal economic policies has also spawned movements for "development from below." After years of the failure of government-sponsored programs to create economic growth and alleviate the suffering of people in the Global South, new efforts seek to satisfy basic needs and increase human welfare

by focusing on the equitable distribution of income and other resources. One such effort, which has had particular importance to poor women, is the availability of microloans.

Microloans grant credit to people who would be unable to secure financing through traditional banks to start small businesses. According to one estimate, there are approximately 665 million clients at over 3,000 institutions worldwide offering financial assistance to emerging business owners (Christen et al. 2004). Overall, the evidence suggests that the process of adaptation and resistance makes it is hard to imagine that globalization will simply result in a homogenized world.

The Complex Effects of Globalization

Globalization is perhaps best understood as a dynamic process that both brings the world together and pulls it apart. Globalization universalizes and homogenizes some aspects of the world while simultaneously particularizing others, giving rise to differences. Globalization can foster an awareness of political difference at the same time that it develops an awareness of common identity. It can remove barriers to understanding or emphasize conflicts of interest (Pieterse 1995). On many college campuses in North America today, for example, students from a wide-range of Asian, African, and Latin American countries often come together as "people of color" to form student organizations based on a recognition of some shared elements of culture as well as common experiences of oppression and racism. Recognition of these commonalties does not necessarily negate the internal cultural, political, and historical differences among them, differences that often must be painfully negotiated within the group in the name of unity and a common cause.

Twenty-first-century anthropologists have documented the multiple, often-contradictory, nature of global transformations and its uneven and diverse effects. Their work calls into question simple claims about globalization and has led to a more nuanced understanding of its impact on women and men in different areas of the world. We explore much of this work in the chapters that follow.

The characteristics of globalization have posed challenges to anthropologists in their attempts to better understand and explain today's world, resulting in the development of new concepts, methods, and approaches. We will discuss some of the most significant of these in the section that follows.

Global News

1.3: Microcredit Pioneers Win Nobel Peace Prize

Bangladeshi economist Muhammad Yunus and his Grameen Bank won the Nobel Peace Prize on Friday for their pioneering use of tiny, seemingly insignificant loans—microcredit—to lift millions out of poverty. "Lasting peace cannot be achieved unless large population groups find ways in which to break out of poverty," the Nobel Committee said in its citation. "Microcredit is one such means. Development from below also serves to advance democracy and human rights." Grameen Bank was the first lender to hand out microcredit, giving very small loans to poor Bangladeshis who did not qualify for loans from conventional banks. No collateral is needed and repayment is based on an honor system. Anyone can qualify for a loan—the average is about $200—but recipients are put in groups of five. Once two members of the group have borrowed money, the other three must wait for the funds to be repaid before they get a loan. The method encourages social responsibility. The results are hard to argue with—the bank says it has a 99% repayment rate. Since Yunus gave out his first loans in 1974, microcredit schemes have spread throughout the developing world and are now considered a key to alleviating poverty and spurring development. Worldwide, microcredit financing is estimated to have helped some 17 million people. "Yunus and Grameen Bank have shown that even the poorest of the poor can work to bring about their own development," the Nobel citation said. Today, the bank claims to have 6.6 million borrowers, 97% of whom are women, and provides services in more than 70,000 villages in Bangladesh. Its model of micro-financing has inspired similar efforts around the world. [*USA Today*/Associated Press 10/13/06; http://www.usatoday.com/news/world/2006-10-13-norway-nobel_x.htm (accessed 7/7/08)]

Globalization's Challenges for Anthropology

How Does Deterritorialization Challenge the Concept of Culture?

Deterritorialization is of particular interest to anthropologists who have traditionally linked the idea of "culture" to particular geographic localities. People in Italy, for example, historically produced a unique cultural cuisine tied to local resources. But, today, Italian cuisine can be found in almost all nations, and it has been adapted and changed by people from many societies. As globalization increasingly dislodges particular cultural forms, practices, and ideas from their places of origin, anthropologists have had to rethink this basic notion of culture.

Culture has many definitions, but, in anthropology, it is often understood as a set of shared ideas, beliefs, and practices learned by members of a discrete group of individuals, generally occupying a particular territory or geographic space. In the past, many anthropologists treated the people they studied as though they lived in isolated and identifiably discrete entities called societies with a distinct and shared set of ideas, practices, adaptations, and beliefs called *culture*. Today, this conceptualization of culture has been questioned, not only because it oversimplifies the interconnections that have existed among people historically, but also because it is no longer viable in a world now characterized by global flows and worldwide interconnections. Ideas, practices, experiences, and identities have become increasingly disconnected from specific places and decreasingly shared by all people living in particular places.

Culture as a concept is being redefined to better capture a world in flux. Some anthropologists suggest we turn attention away from studying culture altogether and instead turn to such concepts as travel or borderlands as alternatives, which reflect a world in motion and the coming together of once culturally distinct people and ideas. Most anthropologists, however, continue to see **culture** as a useful concept, often defining it as a system of meaning through which people make sense of their lives, while still recognizing that these meaning systems may not necessarily coincide with a particular geographic locale.

How Does Deterritorialization Affect Where and How Anthropologists Work?

Deterritorialization has required anthropologists to rethink not only traditional concepts, such as culture, but also traditional approaches, including reevaluating where and how anthropologists do their research.

Until recently, most anthropologists traveled to one site to carry out their study of a people's culture, but now it might be necessary for them to visit several places, undertaking **multisited fieldwork.** For example, in the past, it may have been enough for an anthropologist studying the Hmong to travel to Laos to concentrate on the impact of traditional beliefs about marriage and kinship on women and men. Today, an anthropologist trying to understand the context within which more than 100,000 contemporary Hmong marry and have children would also have to travel to Sacramento, California, and Minneapolis, Minnesota. The U.S. government's involvement in Southeast Asia during the 1960s and 1970s resulted in this large-scale population relocation of Hmong from Asia to the United States.

Deterritorialization and New Areas of Interest in Anthropology

Deterritorialization gives rise to **hybridization**, the recombination of forms and practices no longer tied to local circumstances into new forms and practices. The severing of forms and people from traditional locations, therefore, has led many anthropolo-

gists to focus on hybridity, especially cultural ideas and practices that develop on borders.

Although hybridity has become an important area of study, some anthropologists warn against using the term to describe the cultural forms and practices that develop "on the borders," because of the connotations it might carry. "Hybridity" and "hybridization" are words that come from biology, where they have been used to describe offspring of "mixed" parentage, whether of animals or plants of different species or breeds. Anthropologist Kate Crehan is one anthropologist who warns against easy adoption of this term.

She points out that the implicit meaning in such terminology is that a hybrid is formed from the coming together of two forms that should have been kept separate; it is the product of "elements that somehow do not belong together" (2002:60). This connotation, when applied to groups of people, reinforces the idea that there is a natural distinction between them that should be kept intact, whether that distinction is understood as racial, ethnic, or religious. This worry over terminology is not a superficial argument about semantics. One challenge for twenty-first-century anthropologists is to find a new vocabulary and ways of talking that can capture and explain today's global processes and the forms and practices to which they give rise, without reproducing problematic ideas.

Despite this questioning of terminology, the enormous movement of populations accompanying globalization has led to a growing interest by anthropologists in studying migrations and diasporas. Many recent studies have focused on immigrants, exiles, refugees, and nomads as they come to occupy and produce transnational sites due to their voluntary and involuntary movement across traditional geopolitical boundaries.

A range of new issues is raised by today's population movements, given their differences from earlier ones. People and groups today, for example, are less likely than those in the past to come from one stable point of origin or to move to one clear and final destination. These circumstances make the development of coherent group identities difficult (Breckenridge and Appadurai 1989:i). As we have been discussing, they also produce opportunities for the creation of new identities and novel ways of practicing culture. Anthropologists today focus on the transnational mobility not only of people across local boundaries but also of things, such as commodities, images, and discourses.

Sites intensively involved in mobility, and in the encounter of people from different backgrounds, have been termed **translocalities**. Translocalities can also be networks of sites where people from particular locales interact. Cyberspace is one example of such a site; so too are multinational corporations that do business in more than two countries at a time.

Assessing Theoretical Orientations

There is no one way to study culture and difference. Anthropologists approach questions of inequality and oppression using a range of theoretical orientations with different underlying assumptions about how the world works and why humans behave the way they do. They employ different **theoretical orientations,** self-conscious, systematic, and formally organized bodies of knowledge. Theoretical orientations are based on a set of assumptions and accepted principles that provide a broad frame of reference for researchers and a general context for their investigations. Theoretical orientations guide researchers in choosing a subject, conceptualizing a problem, framing questions, investigating a topic, and interpreting and presenting results. Therefore, theoretical orientations profoundly influence the conclusions reached about a topic. Compare, for example, the conclusions about male aggression arrived at by investigators using the different theoretical orientations described below.

Many *sociobiological* investigators have theorized that men are naturally more aggressive than women. As we discuss in greater detail in chapter 5, the theoretical orientation within which they work assumes that complex human behaviors can be explained through the principle of natural selection: that individuals with traits best suited to particular environmental conditions are more likely to survive and pass on their genes to subsequent generations. This premise has led them to investigate the similarities between male aggression in humans and in nonhuman animals. They argue that if male aggression is found in many animal species, it must have played an important part in survival. Finding some such similarities, sociobiologists conclude that male aggression has a biological basis, one that has been selected for in the course of human evolution. But are these assumptions, forms of investigation, and conclusions the only viable ones?

Social learning theorists begin from the opposite premise from sociobiologists. They argue that biological explanations cannot account for the high degree of variation found in male aggressiveness in societies around the world. If men are more aggressive than women, proponents of this theoretical orientation argue, it is because in some societies boys learn to be aggressive from a very early age. They focus on how children learn gender role behaviors and argue that male aggression, like other human behaviors, is acquired through a process of socialization that prepares children for their adult roles. Parents, educators, peers, and popular culture all reinforce what they see as proper gender behaviors for boys and girls, leading children to imitate those of the appropriate sex, thriving on the rewards they get for doing so.

Social learning theorists argue that if boys are aggressive it is because this behavior is validated, even encouraged, through both obvious and subtle mechanisms. Rather than compare male aggression across animal species, social learning theorists compare across and within human societies. They attempt to correlate variation in male aggressiveness with other social and cultural factors. For example, anthropologists Melvin Ember and Carol Ember (1994) have shown in a number of studies that higher levels of aggression are found in societies that approve of, or glorify, violence—whether in war, sports, the movies, or on television—than in societies that do not.

Knowing the theoretical orientation out of which any particular knowledge arises is an important first step in analyzing particular explanations. That is why, throughout this book, we explore explanations of gender and difference in terms of the various theoretical orientations employed by anthropologists. Exposing the assumptions underlying theoretical orientations and the particular theories they produce enhances our ability to critically evaluate conclusions and choose between competing explanations.

The following chapters focus on multiple theoretical orientations used by anthropologists to investigate the nature of difference, power, and inequality. You will discover their starting premises and judge how well the conclusions they reach are substantiated by data. When analyzing these different approaches, consider the following questions:

- What are the intellectual and the political agendas of such an approach?

- How can those agendas be understood in terms of historical context out of which it arose or arises today?

- What are the strengths and drawbacks of any particular approach given the concerns of twenty-first-century anthropologists?

- How might understanding historical contexts of theorists' ideas help us understand our own assessments and commitments today?

WORD PORTFOLIO

anthropology: the study of human beings in all their diversity, both in the past and in the present, and in terms of biological, cultural, and linguistic similarities and differences.

class: people classified together into groups (classes) in a system of stratification based on a combination of factors, which most often include access to a society's means and modes of economic production, level of education, and cultural practices such as taste and style.

commodification: the process of commercializing objects and services, turning them into products, or commodities, that can be bought and sold in an economic market.

colonialism: a form of domination in which a nation extends its rule over territory outside of its boundaries by establishing settler colonies or by making that territory

culture: a system of meaning through which people make sense of their lives, which may or may not coincide with a particular geographic locale.

deterritorialization: the process by which the cultural, social, and political contexts that affect and define people's lives cease to be confined by territorial borders, boundaries, and distances.

diaspora: the breaking up and scattering of a group of people throughout the world.

difference: social factors such as gender, "race," and class that differentially position men and women in relationship to power, opportunities, and access to privilege and rewards.

feminist anthropology: a subfield of anthropology that studies the workings of gender, and other forms of difference, cross-culturally.

gender: the socially and culturally produced ideas about the differences between females and males in a particular society.

gender identity: the very idea of what it means to be a female or a male, feminine or masculine

gender role expectations: the social skills, abilities, and behaviors thought appropriate to members of a society or group depending on whether they are male or female.

gender stratification: a system of institutionalized inequalities that differentially grants access to resources, power, prestige, and opportunities on the basis of whether a person is female or male.

globalization: a term with no one simple definition but one that is often used descriptively to refer to a set of processes that have given rise to a widening, deepening, and acceleration of worldwide interconnections in all aspects of contemporary life. It is characterized by the worldwide spread of people, ideas, beliefs, goods, images, and technologies.

globalization from below: see *grassroots globalization*.

grassroots globalization: new social forms and organizations that have arisen to interrogate and protest the negative effects of globalization on behalf of the poor. Also called *globalization from below.*

hybridization: the recombination of forms and practices no longer tied to local circumstances into new forms and practices.

multisited fieldwork: anthropological research that is conducted in more than one place.

neoliberalism: a set of social values, ideologies, and economic policies that champions business deregulation and the privatization of social services.

power: the ability to act effectively and the capacity to exercise control over oneself and others.

race: a social category that uses arbitrary external physical characteristics to categorize humans into what are mistakenly thought to be biologically distinct human groups.

racialization: the social and political process of race making. The process by which social significance is attached to certain features based on a set of assumptions and stereotypes about a certain race. This organizes people who share these features into distinct groups, imposes a "racial character" on individuals thought to belong to that group, and is used as the basis of assigning rights, resources, power, prestige, privileges, and other social rewards.

scapes: dimensions of cultural global flows. Arjun Appadurai has identified five such scapes: financescape, ethnoscape, technoscape, mediascape, and ideoscape.

sex differences: the traits a society or group assumes differentiate males and females.

sexual diversity: a term used to acknowledge the multiple ways in which individuals experience their sexuality.

theoretical orientation: a self-conscious, systematic, and formally organized body of knowledge.

translocalities: sites intensively involved in mobility and in the encounter of people from different backgrounds.

transnational: interconnections across national boundaries.

twenty-first-century anthropology: a phrase encompassing the subfields of feminist, black feminist, and LGBT anthropology as well as other approaches that forefront not only cultural difference but also differences based on such factors as gender, race, ethnicity, or sexual diversity.

RECOMMENDED READING

Anti-Racist Feminism: Critical Race and Gender Studies, edited by Agnes Calliste and George J. Sefa Dei. 2000. Black Point, Nova Scotia: Fernwood.

Rethinking the relationship between gender- and race-based discrimination, Agnes Calliste and George J. Sefa Dei further develop antiracism approaches and practices. Tracing this approach through a variety of examples, readers will find new ways of using antiracist and feminist lenses to transform their own scholarship and practice.

The Kitchen Spoon's Handle: Transnationalism and Sri Lanka's Migrant Housemaids, by Michele Ruth Gamburd. 2000. Ithaca, NY: Cornell University Press.

Michele Ruth Gamburd examines how the migration of women from the coastal village of Naeaegama, Sri Lanka, to the Middle East has challenged ideas about gender, class, and caste. Looking at everyday practices, and the meanings embedded within them, Gamburd provides an ethnography of women's experiences of globalization, focusing on how large-scale economic changes shift local power dynamics.

Mayan Visions: The Quest for Autonomy in an Age of Globalization, by June C. Nash. 2001. London: Routledge.

June Nash draws on her long-standing fieldwork in Mexico to demonstrate how the Chiapas Mayan community is negotiating the changes created by globalization. Examining "indigenous culture" on the regional, national, and global levels, Nash argues that indigenous communities can offer alternatives to the destructive effects of globalization and are creating new visions for coexistence in a globally integrated world.

Gender in Transnationalism: Home, Longing and Belonging among Moroccan Migrant Women, by Ruba Salih. 2003. New York: Routledge.

Examining the lives of Moroccan migrant women and their families living in Italy, Ruba Salih offers a window onto the complex practices of moving and living between national spaces. Salih focuses on how the meaning of home and self are transformed by moving across borders, and how this also changes understandings of tradition, modernity, and difference.

Flexible Citizenship: The Cultural Logics of Transnationality, by Aiwha Ong. 1999. Durham: Duke University Press.

If you are interested in further exploring debates over what the consequences of globalization are, you should take a look at this book by anthropologist, Aiwha Ong. Focusing on Southeast Asian and Chinese economic elites, Ong moves away from the perspective that transnational flows of people, goods, and ideas have undermined the sovereignty of nation-states. Ong also argues that the majority of academic work on globalization ignores the role of human agency. Her analysis of transnationalism, governmentality, and agency contributes to our understanding of complex global flows both within Asia and beyond.

2

A History of Gender and Difference

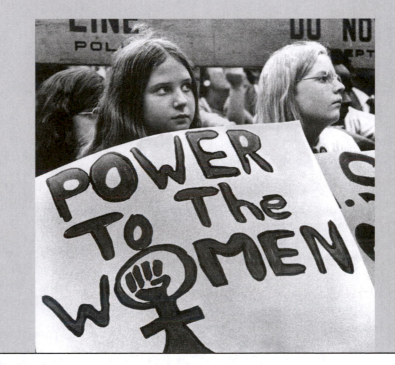

The study of gender and difference in contemporary anthropology—as well as in many other academic disciplines—grew out of the same context in the 1960s and 1970s from which images such as the following are drawn:

- Martin Luther King intones "I have a dream" to 200,000 civil rights activists gathered at the base of the Lincoln Memorial in Washington, D.C., in August 1963.

- On Friday evening, June 27, 1969, a crowd of several hundred people erupts in protest over a police raid of the Stonewall Inn, a gay bar on Christopher Street in New York City's Greenwich Village.

- Thousands of bedraggled, long-haired young men and women frolic through muddy fields in upstate New York in August 1969, creating a "Woodstock Nation" of peace and "free love" as Jimi Hendrix's guitar screams out "The Star-Spangled Banner."

- Shock registers on the terrified face of a young woman in bell-bottom jeans as U.S. national guardsmen gun down four students during student demonstrations at Kent State University in Ohio in May 1970.

This time of active political protest fuelled social movements throughout the world. Students demonstrated against authoritative government policies and actions not only in Ohio, Washington, D.C., and New York City but also in Paris, Tunis, and elsewhere around the world. People of color marched for civil rights in the United States while their counterparts throughout Africa and Asia actively, and sometimes violently, resisted racial oppression and colonial domination. Many Native Americans across the United States and Canada joined together in the American Indian Movement, waging a struggle against discrimination and racism and for the recognition of their right to native lands, protection from brutality, and human dignity. It is out of this context of struggle that many women began to recognize gender as a source of oppression. They joined together to protest and actively struggle against gender inequalities, resulting in the formation of a number of feminist movements.

This was not the first time that Western women came together to protest inequality. During the late nineteenth and early twentieth centuries in the United States and Britain, **first-wave feminism** developed as women fought for rights equal to those of men, especially the right to vote. In Canada, for example, women of color drew on a long history of resistance to colonial domination to question immigration and settlement policies and their lack of access to democratic rights (Dua 1999:11–12).

Although these efforts were critical precursors to those of the 1960s and 1970s, in this chapter we focus on women's experiences and political engagements during **second-wave feminism,** the period beginning in the 1960s. It is out of this period that a large-scale rethinking of the discipline of anthropology emerged, ultimately leading to the development of the anthropology of gender and difference. This reconceptualization was at first perhaps most rigorously undertaken in the United States.

A discussion of the second-wave U.S. women's movement can provide a sense of the context for a feminist rethinking of the discipline of anthropology and can help us confront some widespread stereotypes about women's political activism and its causes and meanings. **Stereotypes** are standardized mental pictures that represent an oversimplified or exaggerated opinion or uncritical judgment about a person or group. Because gender stereotypes are based on prejudiced attitudes, they can diminish women's political efforts and the struggle for gender equality. We will assess some widespread stereotypes of feminists and feminism in order to help dismantle long-standing but prejudiced characterizations of them.

The chapter ends with a discussion of early feminist anthropology, which at first focused on analyzing women's oppression and then on systems of oppression based on gender, racial, sexual, and class stratification cross-culturally. The chapter also concentrates on feminist anthropology's central concerns about women's oppression and it efforts to become more inclusive by focusing on difference more broadly.

Women's Global Activism

During the 1960s and 1970s, women throughout the world fought in social movements against oppression and for the liberation of men, women, and children. Many women, however, became increasingly aware of sexism in such movements, as they were assigned to traditional female tasks that were seen as less central to the group's political efforts. For example, in 1971, Chicanas, tired of being relegated to support roles in the Mexican American protest movement of the period, gathered in Houston, Texas, to hold a national conference to articulate their particular concerns as Mexican women oppressed by race, class, and gender, leading to the development of a number of Chicana liberation movements (see Garcia and Garcia 1997). In many other circumstances, too, women not only fought alongside men in movements for freedom, but they also joined together as *women* to contest male domination and sexism, struggling on multiple fronts for social, political, and economic equality.

Women in many European nations lobbied for such rights as equal pay, easier divorces, legal abortions, and widespread access to contraceptives. Working-class women, in particular, were at the forefront of seeking equal access to jobs. Women in Italy developed feminist organizations to protest a forced division of labor in the home and the workplace and called for an end to authoritarianism in the family and the larger society (Evans 1995:683). Over several decades, women throughout Latin America have come together to protest rape, battering, and reproductive control and to fight for improvements in housing, food, land, and medical care (see Stephen 1997). From the U.S. South to rural India, from Iran to Okinawa, women have protested war and militarization, fighting political domination (see Waller et al. 2001).

Whether in Asia, Africa, the Middle East, Europe, North America, or Latin America, women organized and protested in multiple ways: as workers seeking better working conditions and freedom from sexual harassment in the workplace, as members of international organizations mobilized to fight domestic and state-sanctioned violence, as participants in local and global environmental movements, as activists seeking gay and lesbian rights, and as mothers protesting the murder of their family members by dictatorial regimes. Bonnie Smith describes the range of women's activism this way:

> Women have carried guns, written diatribes, used shaming and bodily gestures of ridicule against those who would oppress or exploit them. Women have acted heroically on their own, banded together informally, formed national and even transnational groups, and disagreed with one another, sometimes venomously, over politics and social goals. . . . Women's activism is consistently rich, complex, and vast. [2000:9]

Women's activism is a truly global phenomenon. But this does not mean that there is, or has been, a single global women's movement in which one issue, form of protest, or proposed solution has arisen, joining women in a singular cause. Instead, women's political activism has taken various forms as people across the globe have adapted their causes to very different and complex local circumstances. In both the United States and China, for example, women have struggled for expanded reproductive choices. In the United States, however, women have fought for the right to limit family size through access to birth control and abortion. In China, by contrast, women, especially in rural areas, have struggled against a policy of "one child per family." The Japanese circumstance differs from both of these situations (Tolbert 2000). There, the government offers women financial incentives such as monthly cash subsidies for each child, to increase the number of children because of falling birthrates, which reached a record low in 1999.

Some Roots of the U.S. Women's Movement

By the 1960s, many U.S. women had begun to feel the extent of their inequality with men, whether within political organizations or the larger society. Although women were increasingly expected to function as full economic, social, and political participants in the nation, they confronted barriers in many aspects of life: they were denied equal opportunities and rights as activists, wage earners, spouses, parents, students, and citizens (Baxandall and Gordon 2000:3). The existence of these widespread inequalities and discrepancies between men and women in many areas of society sparked the rise of the women's movement in the United States in the late 1960s and early 1970s.

Rigid Gender Expectations

Despite increasing expectations, narrow gender roles were the rule during the middle decades of the twentieth century in the United States and other Western countries. The roles assigned to men and women were restricted in comparison to those that are available today. It was typical then to define men almost exclusively by their roles as breadwinners and leaders, that is, by their activities outside the home in the socially valued spheres of business and politics. In contrast, women were expected to remain at home and to be satisfied by their roles as housewives and mothers, roles that were not viewed as having economic significance. In truth, this option was open to only a limited number of women who could afford to do so. Many working-class women and women of color who had no choice but to enter the labor force were unable to attain this cultural ideal of the female role. Consequently, working women were often seen by the larger culture as inferior, inadequate, and less feminine and desirable than other women. Professional working women were often viewed as less competent than their male counterpoints.

Rigid gender expectations went largely unquestioned because almost every segment of U.S. society seemed to conform to them, making them appear natural and normal. On television, the *Ozzie and Harriet Show* provided a picture of the ideal American family, one composed of a hard-working father and a homemaker mother who had freshly baked cookies ready for her sons when they came home from school. From the pulpit, clergy such as the Reverend Billy Graham preached the sanctity of a wife's obedience to her husband. In Washington, D.C., an almost all-male Congress passed laws for the entire U.S. population while military bases housed a fighting force made up of men ready to "ensure the safety of democracy" at the height of the cold war. On the campuses of elite higher educational institutions in the United States, many privileged women were sent to college to receive not only an advanced education but a "Mrs." degree. Men from elite all-male institutions of higher education, such as Harvard and Yale, often traveled on the weekends to school-sponsored events at all-female "sister" institutions such as Vassar and Wellesley looking for the "right type" of woman to date and possibly marry.

For many women, especially women of color and women from working-class backgrounds, earning any type of college degree was not an option, and any aspiration they might have toward a higher education was frequently seen as misplaced and impractical. Women who felt dissatisfied with the limitations such restrictive expectations imposed were frequently labeled neurotic or abnormal, and magazine articles at the time even cautioned them that a college degree might make finding a husband more difficult (Martin 1987:186).

Women's Rising Dissatisfaction with Inequality

It was this social environment of limited expectations for women that Betty Friedan analyzed in her 1963 best-selling book, *The Feminine Mystique*. Focusing primarily on white, middle-class women, Friedan uncovered a pervasive discontent among them, a malaise that books and magazines told them was attributable to their own personal shortcomings. Friedan, by contrast, identified narrow societal definitions of gender roles that confined many women to the home as the reason behind many women's dissatisfaction.

Cold War Politics

Such restricted definitions did not arise in a vacuum. They were part of a widespread anticommunist political ideology arising out of the Korean War

(1950–1953) and the cold war (1945–1989). This ideology used gender arrangements to justify and rationalize U.S. international policy. According to Baxandall and Gordon, "Anxiety about the Soviet threat made family stability seem critical and linked women's domestic roles to the national security" (2000:3). U.S. images depicted women living in communist societies as drudges who wore babushkas on their heads and colorless and shapeless dresses or uniforms on their short, squat, heavily muscled, and mustached bodies. This depiction was meant to portray the inferiority of the sociopolitical systems under which Soviet women lived and toiled. It was compared to images of neatly coiffed, smiling U.S. housewives in freshly ironed dresses and high heels, standing in front of gleaming kitchen appliances.

Idealizing the middle-class woman's role in the home, the U.S. anticommunist ideology praised women for their role in shaping and maintaining the family and the domestic realm and for providing the bedrock for U.S. institutions. If women moved outside the sphere of the home, the message implied, the family and nation would disintegrate, and the result might be a lot like that of the despised Soviet system. Deviance from traditional male and female behaviors was thus considered suspect and even unpatriotic.

It may not be coincidental that the historic meeting on July 24, 1959, of Soviet Premier Nikita Khrushchev with Vice President Richard M. Nixon took place in front of a replica of a suburban American kitchen at a U.S. trade and cultural fair in Moscow. During these talks Nixon vigorously extolled the merits of the U.S. economic system, implying that the modern luxury commodities on display were a direct result of a superior capitalist political-economic system. As Baxandall and Gordon summarize:

> Far from interpreting [U.S.] women's obligations as constraints, cold war American culture regarded them as freedoms. That American middle-class women did not seem to need jobs and enjoyed an expanding array of household appliances demonstrated the superiority of American institutions over Soviet society. [Baxandall and Gordon 2000:3]

White Middle-Class Women and The Feminine Mystique

The Feminine Mystique documented many women's dissatisfaction with the social arrangements arising out of both traditional gender expectations and cold war politics. Along with the example set by civil rights activists and others demonstrating against U.S. social policies, Friedan's book was influential in sparking many women's awareness of inequality. At the same time, many women reexamined earlier works that helped them understand their situation, most notably, as we discuss in more detail later in the chapter, French philosopher Simone de Beauvoir's *The Second Sex*.

The women's movement of this era also inspired President John F. Kennedy's establishment in 1961 of the Commission on the Status of Women, which wrote several reports documenting women's secondary status in the United States at the time. Dissatisfied with the lack of progress made on commission recommendations, many women involved in these commissions became the nucleus of women who joined Betty Friedan in 1966 to found the National Organization for Women (NOW), an organization still active today in advocating women's rights (Freeman 1971).

During the 1960s and 1970s, many white middle-class women were prepared to undertake the critique of traditional notions of femininity and masculinity and to fight for autonomy and equality because the situation outlined and protested by Friedan and others created a complex context for them. For example, more and more women were being educated, but their position within the job market was declining; there was increased segregation of the job market into male and female jobs with the number of women in professional and technical jobs decreasing. This circumstance led to a decline in women's income and resulted in the creation of a class of highly educated, underemployed white women who began to protest their circumstance (Freeman 1971:1).

Recognizing Oppression by Class, Race, and Sexual Diversity

Despite cold war ideology, some feminists drew on earlier communist and socialist writings for inspiration and critiqued capitalism as the source of women's oppression. They saw women's subjugation as a product of the class structure that formed the basis of capitalist societies, a topic we explore in detail in chapter 6. But these "socialist feminists" criticized traditional socialist thinking, exposing how sexism within it undervalued women's work. This undervaluation, they argued, set women apart from the rest of the working class, thereby undercutting the very class consciousness that socialists believed was necessary to revolutionize capitalist societies. They argued for the rights of women as workers, and therefore called for the dissemination of

Close-Up

2.1: How Relevant Is *The Feminine Mystique* Today?

The relevance of Western feminism to women in other parts of the world has been a long-debated topic. Kornelia Slavova (2006), for example, has argued that Betty Friedan's *The Feminine Mystique* has limited value in Eastern Europe where socialist states prior to 1989 required women to work and claimed to have liberated them through communism. She describes the inapplicability of Friedan's work to her students in Bulgaria this way:

> One such example of failing to transmit Western knowledge across cultures is Betty Friedan's feminist agenda in her work, *The Feminine Mystique*, which has been heralded as having paved the way for the contemporary feminist movement. When I teach this book, my Bulgarian students complain that the concerns of middle-class suburban housewives, that are articulated in the outcry "I want something more than my husband and my children and my home," in other words, "I want a career," sound outdated and irrelevant. . . . Of course, Friedan's conclusion that being a housewife creates a "sense of emptiness and non-existence" is important in historical terms, but, from the perspective of women in Eastern Europe, it provides thin ground for them to identify with. (p. 4)

Does Friedan's agenda continue to have resonance for you or does it seem irrelevant and outdated?

Reference

Slavova, Kornelia. 2006. Looking at Western Feminisms through the Double Lens of Eastern Europe and the Third World. In *Women and Citizenship in Central and Eastern Europe*. Jasmina Luki, Joanna Rugulska, and Darja Zaviršek, eds. Pp.121–140. Hampshire, UK: Ashgate.

birth control and for women's right to abortion, maternity leave, child care, and equal pay. These measures were seen as necessary for establishing women workers' equality with male workers. Socialist feminists viewed women's work in the household as unpaid work that benefited capitalist business interests, and they called for the payment of housework (Sacks 1989).

Many women of color took their inspiration for challenging unequal gender arrangements, not from Friedan's book, but from a long history of oppression grounded in the experience of racism in the United States (McClaurin 2001). Women in the civil rights and black power movements organized with men against racial discrimination and racism; they also came together as women to dispute the secondary role they were often asked to play by male leaders of those organizations. According to anthropologist Leith Mullings, "the experiences of women within these movements became a touchstone for reflections on the deconstruction of gender and the need to assess, critique, and rethink the roles African American women played" in these movements (1997:2).

Women fighting for liberation from colonial regimes in many places in Southeast Asia and Africa during the same time period often found themselves in a similar circumstance. Such experiences provided a basis for a transnational awareness of women's oppression. As Bonnie Smith has pointed out, "during these struggles U.S. and colonized women came to discuss how the sexist ways they were treated by men in their own movement were paralleled by the racist ways they were treated by whites" (2000:3).

Looking for alternatives, other women turned to the work of Lithuanian-born activist Emma Goldman

(1869–1940). Goldman immigrated to the United States in 1885. As a proponent of anarchism she actively defended labor rights, free speech, women's emancipation, and their right to birth control. She also critiqued marriage as an institution that oppressed women and was an early defender of lesbian rights. Her work was a resource for feminists at the time who were searching for the development of a lesbian-feminist politics as the basis for the liberation of women. They drew on her work and that of other earlier activist women writers to protest the idea that lesbianism was only a sexual choice and reframed it as a political choice. They expanded the definition of a lesbian to include any woman who committed herself to other women for political, emotional, physical, and economic support (see Bunch 1972). These women argued for a range of goals, including women's personal liberation and growth, the establishment of strong relationships among women, and the need for women to break loose from limiting social and psychological patterns.

With the widespread recognition of women's oppression, a women's liberation movement began to form. With it was unleashed a political force that had broad reverberations throughout the United States. Over the next few decades, almost every aspect of U.S. society was questioned in terms of its assumptions about the "natural" differences between men and women that restricted women's opportunities and caused women to be seen and treated as inferior to men. With such questioning of the social arrangements that maintained gender discrimination, more and more people began to fight against the social injustices that plagued women's lives.

The Backlash

A backlash against the feminist movement arose in the United States almost immediately after it coalesced. Women's claims and demands were renounced as unwarranted and even as immoral (di Leonardo 1991:18). Susan Faludi explores this situation in her widely read book, *Backlash: The Undeclared War Against American Women* (1991). As Faludi shows, one tactic in the fight against claims for women's rights was to caricature and stereotype feminists in unsavory ways, especially career-minded women. As part of the backlash, conservative opponents also negatively stereotyped single mothers and lesbians and gay men. These groups were, and often continue to be, portrayed as dangerous to American "family values," specifically as a threat to the nuclear family based on father-mother-child and the way of life built on it. The passage in California in 2008 of "Proposition 8," forbidding gay marriage, indicates this ongoing opposition.

Negative portrayals of feminists and other activists acted, and continue to act today, to degrade and demonize them, thereby discounting their claims and struggles. Combating myths and working to portray feminist political activism positively, whether such action is labeled "feminist" or not, are important political efforts themselves because stereotypes and caricatures of political activity can reduce the effectiveness of women's struggles for equality. We take up this project briefly in the next section.

Characterizing Feminism: Myths and Realities

Negative Stereotypes of Feminism

Negative portrayals of women activists have plagued the women's movement in the United States since its inception. One early and persistent stereotype of feminist activity is of "women libbers" as a mob of angry women burning their bras as a symbol of their desire for freedom. One problem with this image is that it is not entirely accurate; there is no evidence that women tossed their undergarments into the flames en masse during a protest rally in the United States or elsewhere for that matter. What they did do was stage a protest at a Miss America beauty pageant. They threw constricting clothing—bras, girdles, and high-heeled shoes, for example—into a "freedom trash can" to symbolically protest how women's bodies were controlled, not just through bras and codes of fashion, but also through ideal notions of femininity and beauty, forced sterilization, abuse, and rape (Evans 1995:685).

These women linked such supposedly trivial concerns as clothing and expectations concerning beauty to more obviously problematic areas of control of women through violence. By doing so, second-wave feminists exposed the political nature of the personal realm of life and made this recognition into an anthem for the women's movement: **"the personal is political."** This slogan of second-wave feminism underscores the understanding that everyday life—even seemingly small and private aspects of it—is embedded in, and affected by, the larger power relations of a society.

Although the "bra-burning" image of feminists attracted media attention, providing feminists with publicity for their cause, it also "pigeonholed women's liberation as a fringe activity" (Evans 1995:686). Such stereotypic images suggest that the struggle for gender equality is frivolous. While the political movements of the 1960 and 1970s were linked, and each changed the face of U.S. society and other societies around the world in important ways, only the women's movement lacks a strong, memorable, positive image signifying its social and political importance. This lack of a positive image is odd given the movement's enormity: the women's liberation movement was the largest social movement in the history of the United States (Baxandall and Gordon 2000:1). It profoundly changed U.S. society and influenced many struggles for women's freedom around the world. Nonetheless, there are still mixed feelings about feminism. In the United States in 2000, for example, after decades of struggle against discrimination, only 51 percent of people believed feminists are helpful to women, only 53 percent felt that feminists are "in touch with the average American woman," and only 65 percent thought that black feminists help the black community (Baxandall and Gordon 2000:1).

Negative portrayals of feminists continue to saturate popular culture today, especially in the United States. Women who protest their objectification as sex objects are often portrayed as "man haters." Women who struggle to be on par with men in the workplace, rebelling against a **glass ceiling** that unfairly limits their advancement in their careers, or who contest unequal pay for equal work, are depicted as cold-hearted, calculating manipulators eager to get ahead at all costs or as whiney, bitter shrews who complain about inconsequential injustices. These images distort women's claims and actions. They also erase the presence of the men who have been involved in the struggle for men's and women's equality.

Such U.S. images are exported worldwide through a global media in the form of films, books, and television shows, perpetuating caricatures of U.S. women. Just as unfair representations of Soviet women were used during the cold war to maintain and rationalize U.S. women's claims for equality, so, too, can these negative depictions of U.S. women operate around the world to undermine local women's own claims for liberation.

Claiming Feminism

Despite such negative characterizations of feminists, many women who have taken part in the political struggles outlined above have used the label "feminist" to describe themselves and their activities. For example, many young women born in the United States after 1970, who have grown up with the ideas of feminism, have taken up the term, even as they work to define what it means for them. In a collection of essays entitled *Colonize This!: Young Women of Color on Today's Feminism* (Hernández and Rehman 2002), contributors draw on the insights of an earlier generation of women of color to fashion their own ideas and lives (also see Baumgardner and Richards 2000). This movement is often referred to as **third-wave feminism.** This term is used to distinguish these young women's experiences, concerns, and goals from both first-wave feminism and second-wave feminism. As we have seen, first-wave feminism of the late nineteenth and early twentieth centuries was largely a struggle by European women for equal rights, which in the United States culminated in women gaining the right to vote in 1920. In the United States of the 1960s and 1970s, second-wave feminism took the form of the women's liberation movement.

Like other women around the world, contemporary young women show, through their commitments and actions, that the best definition and understanding of a feminist is someone who opposes gender oppression and other forms of domination and discrimination.

Rejecting the Feminist Label

Other politically active women have rejected the term "feminist." Some women of color, for example, argue that the term is frequently associated with the concerns of white women alone. They have thus sought alternative terms. African American novelist Alice Walker prefers the term "womanist" as a way to signal that black women's struggles differ from those of white feminists who primarily protested sexism, not the oppression of women also based on race and class.

Some women in the United States reject the term "feminism" because of other associations. As Marianne Marchand and Anne Runyan suggest, "Today there is increasingly little political space for women to define themselves as feminists due to the association of feminism variously with Westernization, secularism, liberalism, state socialism, and/or sexual/social license" (2000:227). At the same time, they argue that due to globalization self-conscious analyses of gender oppression have increased, even when they are not termed "feminist." Globalization has increased both "the needs of and opportunities for women to struggle against the economic, social, cultural, and political oppressions that arise from it or in reaction to it" (Marchand and Runyan 2000:227).

Another reason a number of people today reject feminism is that they feel no need for it. So many people in the United States today seem to be accustomed to seeing women in positions of authority, and pursuing careers and options once closed to them, that they often take women's rights for granted. They forget the immense efforts that were necessary just a few de-

Close-Up

2.2: Opposition to the Equal Rights Amendment

In 1923, the U.S. Congress received the Equal Rights Amendment. The proposed 27th Amendment to the U.S. Constitution states that "Equality of rights under the law shall not be denied or abridged by the United States or by any State on account of sex." The ERA was developed in 1921 by the National Woman's Party (NWP), an organization founded by Alice Paul and a small group of her supporters as a vehicle for advancing women's rights beyond the achievement of suffrage and to highlight and eliminate the many inequalities that deprived women of equal citizenship with men (Sklar 1998). The controversial amendment, which proposed to establish the full legal equality of women as a fundamental principle of the American government, was finally passed by the U.S. Senate in 1972. It was then sent out to the states for ratification by three-quarters (38) of the states; it has yet to pass into law. By contrast, in 2001, Brazil approved a legal code meant to eliminate gender bias, making women equal to men under the law (Rohter 2001).

Opposition to legislation aimed at equal rights in the United States remains an active pursuit of a number of organizations that were originally established in opposition to the ERA. Concerned Women for America (CWA), for example, was founded in 1979 to campaign against the ERA, arguing that it would "break down God-given roles in families." Today, members travel to Washington, D.C., monthly for an event on Capitol Hill where they lobby members of Congress and their staff to urge them to vote for "family values" legislation. CWA describes itself as "the nation's largest public policy women's organization with a rich 29-year history of helping our members across the country bring Biblical principles into all levels of public policy. Its mission is to protect and promote Biblical values among all citizens—first through prayer, then education, and finally by influencing our society thereby reversing the decline in moral values in our nation" (http://www.cwalac.org).

References

Rohter, Larry. 2001.Brazil Passes Equal Rights for Its Women: After a Long Battle Patriarchy Yields. *New York Times* (August 19), A9.

Sklar, Kathryn Kish. 1998. Who Won the Debate over the Equal Rights Amendment in the 1920s? In *The Reader's Companion to U.S. Women's History.* Wilma Mankiller, Gwendolyn Mink, Marysa Navarro, Barbara Smith, and Gloria Steinem, eds. Pp. 176–178. Boston: Houghton Mifflin.

cades ago to get women to be taken seriously as leaders, thinkers, bosses, athletes, or as workers in traditional male-defined occupations such as fire fighting or construction work. As Rosalyn Baxandall and Linda Gordon put it, today the achievements of the women's movement—"the broad range of work women do, the equal treatment they expect, the direct way women express themselves—have become the very air we breathe, so taken for granted as to be invisible" (2000:2).

Nonetheless, it is important to remember that gender continues to differentially structure men's and women's experiences and opportunities throughout the world. There is still a long way to go before gender equality is attained in most countries. Even in the United States, where many people assume women to be on equal par with men in many areas of life, widespread discrepancies exist. Women and children continue to comprise the majority of people living below the poverty level; women's wages continue to lag behind men's for comparable work; women continue to hit a "glass ceiling" that constrains their opportunities for advancement in many careers; women are more likely than men to experience the double burden of working outside the home while simultaneously having responsibility for work in the home; and women continue to be physically battered by boyfriends and husbands at an alarming rate. Women in the United States still do not have their rights protected by a constitutional amendment, even though such protection has been granted to women in other countries, often in nations far less identified by U.S. citizens with the values of equality and democracy than their own

The Politics of Knowledge

Linking Activism to Scholarship

The same political commitments that brought people into the street and on to the battlefield in the 1960s and 1970s influenced scholars in colleges and universities around the world. Scholar-activists recognized the connection between ideas and power. They began to link their intellectual work to their political beliefs. They started to interrogate what has come to be known as the **politics of knowledge.** This term refers to the understanding that ideas are not the impartial products of unbiased minds. Instead, ideas arise from the minds of thinkers who are "situated" in a

particular time and place and embedded in relations of power. Prior to this time, it was not uncommon to treat ideas as objective. Recognizing how the politics of knowledge worked, scholar-activists argued that thinkers often produce ideas that are offered as objective truths, but that are often only partial truths at best. Such ideas can act as rationalizations for the maintenance of the status quo and perpetuate devastating inequalities. Traditional knowledge came to be seen as political, as implicated in maintaining unequal power relations. It was therefore in need of serious questioning and revision.

Women were at the forefront of this reconceptualization. Drawing energy from the developing women's movement, they developed far-reaching critiques of traditional forms of knowledge. They were greatly influenced by the work of earlier thinkers, such as Simone de Beauvoir who decades before had exposed the political nature of ideas in her book, *The Second Sex* (1949). As we discuss in more detail in later chapters, de Beauvoir argued that the subordinate position of women in Western society could be linked to the assumption that men were seen as "mind," as producers of ideas, but women were seen as "body," as producers of children, but not of knowledge. Her text provided an important foundation in the late 1960s and early 1970s for questioning the different attitudes about, and expectations of, men and women as thinkers both inside and outside academia.

Scholars influenced by the political questioning of this time period sought links between the limitations placed on women in their daily lives and how women were characterized and treated as subjects in scholarly thinking. They began to demonstrate that most academic fields had overlooked and denigrated women's experiences, perspectives, and contributions, producing ideas that maintained women's subordination.

The lack of women in areas of society where knowledge is produced and institutionalized, such as on college and university faculties, was one important factor contributing to this situation. Indeed, women were not even encouraged to aspire to graduate work, and those with undergraduate degrees at this time were often relegated to the three "Ts" in terms of occupation: typing, teaching, and "temperature-taking." This job segregation was maintained partly through advertising categories used well into the 1960s in the United States: employment advertisements in the daily newspapers were segregated into "Help Wanted—Males" and "Help Wanted—Females," and the female

Global News

2.1: The Latest Way to Discriminate against Women

Why does one of the biggest, sweetest lawsuits imaginable—colleges routinely discriminating against women in their admissions policies—go unfiled? Recently *U.S. News & World Report* laid bare the evidence. In desperate attempts to keep their campuses from swinging hugely female, as far more women than men apply to college these days, straight-A girls are told to look elsewhere, while B-average boys get the fat envelope. . . . As [Thomas G. Mortenson] wrote in a *USA Today* op-ed article, "Addressing the growing gender imbalance in college through affirmative action for young men addresses the symptoms but not the causes. It insults the efforts and accomplishments of young women." Far worse, it leaves many boys in the same confused condition they are in now. And it lets parents—especially fathers—and schoolteachers off the hook for their failure to raise and educate boys to be as accomplished, goal-oriented, engaged, and responsible as young women are today. [Richard Whitmire, *The Chronicle of Higher Education* 7/20/2007:B16]

category was filled with clerical, teaching, and nursing positions. When women were able to break into traditional male professions they were often given what were seen as "women-related" jobs. Women journalists, for example, were expected to focus on topics such as family, food, fashion, and home furnishings. These structural attitudes and practices resulted in barriers to women's advancement in terms of career, education, and financial gains (Anderson 1995). Women of color experienced even greater employment discrimination both inside and outside academia because of racial discrimination. As Global News 2.1 indicates, discrimination against women in higher education continues today, if in a different form.

It was not just knowledge that was being questioned by activist-scholars, however, it was also the manner of transmitting knowledge. Prompted by the political upheavals of the day, some professors changed their teaching methods from lecture monologues, which positioned students as passive recipients of knowledge, to active dialogues, or interactive "teach-ins," which empowered students to participate actively in the construction of knowledge.

The Development of Women's Studies

The questioning of accepted ideas, based on the recognition that knowledge is political, fundamentally changed traditional academic fields of study ranging from literature and anthropology to medicine and management. It also gave rise to the development of women's studies, an entirely new academic discipline, and to women's studies programs, which linked the academic study of women to larger social, economic, and political concerns. In 1970, the first women's studies program in the United States was established at San Diego State University in California. Today, there are more than 730 women's studies programs, centers, or departments at academic institutions across the country.

The development of such programs was not only a North American phenomenon linked to women's political activism in the United States during the 1960s and 1970s, it was a global one as well. Women's activism in many places across the globe has led to the development of programs that explore the relationship between everyday experiences of inequality and knowledge about women. At the prestigious center for gender studies in Russia, for example, scholar-activists advocate and strategize for change while simultaneously describing and theorizing economic and political subordination based on gender (Racioppi and See 2000).

The Development of "Minority" Studies

The challenge to traditional knowledge during the 1960s and 1970s was not confined to women's concerns and issues. At the same time that women's studies courses and programs were being developed, scholars and activists across college and university campuses fought for the institutionalization of minority studies programs as well. Just as many white women from a range of backgrounds protested their exclusion from the production of knowledge, so both women and men of color argued that traditional disciplines failed to take into consideration, or account for, their contributions and experiences.

Many women of color began to question how both gender and racial bias worked together to ignore them as subjects of interest in academic scholarship

and as producers of ideas. The particular situation of African American women was vividly reflected in the title of the groundbreaking collection of essays that helped set the agenda for black women's studies for a decade to come: *All the Women Are White, All the Blacks Are Men, but Some of Us Are Brave: Black Women's Studies* (Hull et al. 1982). The exclusion of not only African American women, but also of Latina, Asian American, Native American, and lesbian women was exposed in the award-winning collection, *This Bridge Called My Back: Writings by Radical Women of Color* (1983) edited by Cherrie Moraga and Gloria Anzaldúa, a book that helped give women of color a voice in academia.

The Development of Lesbian and Gay Studies

Like women's and minority studies, gay and lesbian studies emerged from a struggle for civil rights: the gay liberation movement that formed after the riots at the Stonewall Inn in 1969. In 1988, the City College of San Francisco developed the first program in the United States dedicated to the study of issues of

Close-Up

2.3: The Stonewall Riot and Its Aftermath

On Friday evening, June 27, 1969, the New York City tactical police force raided a popular Greenwich Village gay bar, the Stonewall Inn. Raids were not unusual in 1969; in fact, they were conducted regularly without much resistance. However, that night the street erupted into violent protest as the crowds in the bar fought back. The backlash and several nights of protest that followed have come to be known as the Stonewall Riots.

Prior to that summer there was little public expression of the lives and experiences of gays and lesbians. The Stonewall Riots marked the beginning of the gay liberation movement that has transformed the oppression of gays and lesbians into calls for pride and action. In the past [forty] years we have all been witness to an astonishing flowering of gay culture that has changed this country and beyond, forever. [Ken Harlin, Cases 1 & 2, Starr East Asian Library, Columbia University, http://www.columbia.edu/cu/lweb/eresources/exhibitions/sw25/case1.html (accessed 7/14/08)]

A month after the Stonewall Riots, the Gay Liberation Front (GLF) was formed. Radical and leftist in orientation, the GLF was but one of many politically focused lesbian and gay organizations that formed in the wake of the riots, both in the United States and around the world.

historical, cultural, and political importance to lesbians and gay men. Gay and lesbian studies questioned the knowledge that had been produced on sexual orientation and same-sexed relationships and brought homosexuality to the forefront of academic studies. Gay and lesbian studies scholars recovered the history and culture of homosexuality, reclaimed forbearers, challenged the invisibility of homosexuality in society, and investigated lesbians and gay men's experiences of oppression and struggles for recognition (Love 2003).

1970s Gay Pride rally.

More recently, gay and lesbian studies has broadened its scope to focus on other groups of people who experience sexual oppression such as bisexuals and transgendered individuals; this expanded focus is referred to as lesbian, gay, bisexual, and transgendered studies (LGBT Studies). A new approach to studies of alternative sexualities, known as "Queer Studies" has developed even more recently, as we'll see in chapter 11.

Programs in women's, minority, and gay and lesbian studies, along with the revised scholarship of traditional fields of study, have been instrumental in expanding our knowledge of humankind. They have transformed how people outside of academia have come to understand the influence of gender, race, sexual diversity, and power on their own experiences and options.

The Development of Feminist Anthropology in the United States

The inattention to gender in traditional academic disciplines was particularly ironic in anthropology given its goal of understanding humankind, not just men, within the context of their culture. Until the advent of the women's movement, anthropology had largely treated women as invisible and ignored issues of gender. Through comparing practices and beliefs in many different societies, anthropologists have demonstrated repeatedly how aspects of a particular society that are assumed to be universal and natural are really specific to it.

When similar insights about gender roles and inequality emerged in the 1970s due to influences from the women's movement, the subdiscipline of feminist anthropology was born. It arose as a special subfield within anthropology, one committed to understanding sex roles as a social construct and to exposing and explaining systems of sexual stratification. Feminist anthropologists focused on exposing sexism in both scholarship and the larger culture; questioning widespread assumptions about women, men, and society; reclaiming the work of earlier women anthropologists whose ideas had been downplayed or forgotten; and rethinking women's active roles within their own and other societies. We discuss each one of these efforts in the following sections.

Exposing Gender Bias

Feminist anthropologists set out to document and explain the contribution women made, and the significant roles they played, in societies all over the world, past and present. A first step in this endeavor was to interrogate the gender bias that permeated the discipline, which had caused women's contributions and roles to be overlooked or dismissed as unimportant (di Leonardo 1991). Concerned with the view of women produced by traditional anthropology, feminist anthropologists exposed biases in earlier anthropological studies and exposed how male-centered, or **androcentric,** perspectives had helped create a distorted picture, one that seriously underestimated the importance of women's work and place in society. For example, as we discuss in chapter 4, until recently in the scientific literature the very evolution of humans was attributed to the actions of men while women were portrayed as passive baby makers.

In the past, **ethnographies,** books or accounts written by anthropologists about a society, were primarily written by males, or by females trained by males, who collected information largely from and about men in other societies. Anthropologist Alice Schlegel, remarking about the consequences of this situation noted:

> One gets the impression from many ethnographers that culture is created by and for men between the ages of puberty and late middle age, with children, women, and the aged as residual categories; women are frequently portrayed, at best, as providing support for the activities of men. [1977:2]

Such data were frequently presented as the reality of a society rather than as representing only part of the cultural whole.

This kind of bias was not specific to anthropology. Psychologist Carol Gilligan, for example, reveals in her groundbreaking study, *In a Different Voice* (1982), that the widespread idea in the United States that women are less morally developed than men was based on analyses that used men as the norm and failed to include women as research subjects. It was also shown that men were routinely used as the standard in experiments in medical studies. The exclusion of women as research subjects in medical studies often had devastating consequences for women. Since the 1980s, research in the United States has increasingly included women as subjects.

The situation surrounding medical research studies done on women still has consequences for women today, if in a different way. Women in the Global South are used in experimental drugs trials that cannot be undertaken in the United States itself for ethical and legal reasons, even though U.S. and European women are the beneficiaries of these studies as Global News 2.2 describes.

Global News

2.2: U.S. Drug Tests on Third World Poor Leave Some to Die

Drug researchers are increasingly heading for the developing world to carry out trials on people with little understanding of their rights, some of whom are left without treatment for the disease under study, critics allege. They fear this practice will go on unchecked because, they suspect, the World Medical Association talks opening today may end up diluting the guidelines under which medical trials are meant to take place.

The issue has become highly contentious in the U.S., where public health doctors are privately agonising over the impossibility of reconciling President Clinton's call to help the millions dying of AIDS in Africa with the fact that babies in Uganda and elsewhere have been left by researchers to contract HIV. These are the babies of mothers in the section of a trial group that were not given drugs to stop HIV transmission. Such trials would not have been allowed in the U.S.; in western countries the different test groups in a trial must each be given some form of treatment.

In a recent study of HIV and sexually transmitted diseases in Uganda antibiotics were given to half the subjects and nothing to the others. In China, people were deliberately infected with malaria to see whether this reduced the level of HIV infection—another study that would not have been permitted in the U.S. The ethical battle has split the medical and scientific community, and today's WMA meeting in France is trying to reach a compromise by starting work on a new draft of the Declaration of Helsinki. This contains the guidelines—drawn up between 1953 and 1964, in the light of Nazi medical experimentation—on how doctors should treat patients involved in clinical trials.

Public Citizen, the U.S. watchdog leading the protests against the current test regime, says researchers are exploiting woolly wording in the Helsinki document. It says: "In any medical study, every patient—including those of a control group, if any—should be assured of the best proven diagnostic and therapeutic method." But in the developing world there is often nothing available to give those in the control group.

A row about the ethics of trials in the developing world on pregnant women with HIV, which broke out three years ago, led to the decision to rewrite not only the declaration but also the more detailed Cioms (Council for International Organisations of Medical Sciences) guidelines, which effectively interpret it. But Peter Lurie and Sidney Wolfe of Public Citizen believe that the institutions are just moving the goalposts: "Rather than bringing their behaviour in line with the guidelines, they have set about changing the guidelines to conform to their behaviour," Dr. Lurie said.

The controversy was stoked up in March by a study in 10 Ugandan villages to find out whether people who had sexually transmitted diseases such as syphilis were more likely to contract HIV. Marcia Angell, editor in chief of the *New England Journal of Medicine*, wrote of her doubts about publishing the study's findings. "It meant that for up to 30 months, several hundred people with HIV infection were observed but not treated," she wrote. Five villages were supplied with antibiotics to cure any sexually transmitted diseases, but those in the other five got no treatment beyond being advised to go to a government clinic. The effects when it came to HIV were compared.

The uproar broke out in 1997, when Dr. Lurie and Dr. Wolfe denounced as unethical 15 U.S. government-funded HIV studies in developing countries. Researchers wanted to find out if giving low doses of the drug AZT to pregnant women could reduce the chances of the baby being infected. Half the women got the drug, the other half got nothing. In the U.S. they would have been given longer courses of AZT and caesarian sections, and told to breast-feed—techniques known to reduce transmission.

Hundreds of infants needlessly contracted HIV, Dr. Lurie and Dr. Wolfe said. The early stages of drafting new guidelines for the WMA, Cioms and Unaids—the World Health Organisation's AIDS organisation—were directed by Robert Levine, a professor at Yale University School of Medicine, who takes the opposite view to the two men. He says that research on what works best and most cheaply in developing countries cannot be done without comparing new drugs with what there is at the moment in such places—that is, no other treatments at all. "My reaction and that of many other people is that it is all well and good to create something in Uganda that simulates London or New York [by giving various treatments to all the groups in a trial], but what you get out of that is data that is no good anywhere other than London or New York."

(continued)

He argues that babies in the AZT trials, for example, would have had to be bottle-fed under the sort of regime they would have in the west. If those arguing for western testing practices in the Third World wanted to be coherent and consistent, he said, "they would have to change the prenatal care programme in the country and clean up the water supply. Now you begin to see the absurdity of the position."

Delon Human, secretary general of the WMA, strongly hinted that the changes to the Declaration of Helsinki would be minimal. "Without any doubt the message from the WMA is that we want as little as possible change to the document and that research participants should be protected and given as much treatment as possible," he said. [Sarah Bosley, *The Guardian*, 5/4/2000]

Based on new knowledge about women all over the world, feminist anthropologists also began to "rewrite" many classic ethnographies that had neglected to consider the role of women or gender in their descriptions and analyses. For example, in *Women of Value, Men of Renown: New Perspectives in Trobriand Exchange* (1976), Annette Weiner showed that women as well as men traded objects in the complex exchange system known as the "kula ring" that characterized Trobriand Island society. Her analysis offers a correction to one of the most well-known ethnographies in anthropology, Bronislaw Malinowski's *Argonauts of the Western Pacific;* Jane Goodale questioned the view of Tiwi women as passive objects in a male system of marriage in *Tiwi Wives: A Study of Women of Melville Island, North Australia* (1974); and Yolanda Murphy and Robert Murphy returned to their own site among the Mundurucú of Brazil to pay attention to the position of women and wrote *Women of the Forest* (1974). Numerous other ethnographies were written, providing rich documentation of the role gender plays in societies around the world.

Excerpts from feminist and other twenty-first-century ethnographies that have transformed how anthropologists understand societies all over the world can be found throughout this book. Presented in this chapter is an excerpt from Marjorie Shostak's *Nisa: The Life and Words of a !Kung Woman* (1983), which tells the story of the life of one woman, a member of the !Kung, a group of hunter-gatherers from the Kalahari desert in Africa who today are called Ju/'hoansi. This ethnography broke ground with its juxtaposition of Nisa's own words about her life with those of the ethnographer, Marjorie Shostak. The excerpt begins with Shostak's generalized description of women's subsistence activities and ends with Nisa's words (presented in an indented format), describing her memory of a hard-learned childhood lesson.

Questioning Assumptions

Feminist anthropologists used the new cross-cultural data they were producing not only to correct the ethnographic record but also to question unproven assumptions about the causes of women's subordination. In particular, they challenged the widespread supposition that women's inequality was due to women's "natural inferiority."

By putting gender at the center of their analyses, feminist anthropologists were able to view many different societies, ancient and contemporary, with fresh eyes. In doing so, they uncovered a wide range of variation in gender constructs, in the value placed on activities performed by men and women, and in men's and women's access to important societal resources. They argued that variation in the roles and status of men and women uncovered by their studies suggests that gender is not a result of natural causes but is culturally constructed. They provided evidence that gender affects interactions with children from the moment of birth until their death, and sometimes even after that (see Andriolo 1998).

The work of early feminist anthropologists demonstrated that individuals across societies interpret sex differences within a framework of social meanings of gender. It showed that in all parts of the world cultural ideas about femininity and masculinity influence how people think about their children, how these children come to think about themselves and others, and what

Ethnography in Focus

Nisa: The Life and Words of a !Kung Woman
by Marjorie Shostak

!Kung women are recognized by men and women alike as the primary economic providers of the group. They gather vegetable foods from the wild about three days a week, providing the majority of the daily diet of their families and other dependents. Their economic activity is an autonomous undertaking. Men do not regulate women's schedules, do not tell them which foods to gather or where to go, and do not control the distribution of gathered foods. Women tell their husbands when they plan to be gone for the day, but this is as much a courtesy as a potential restraint, and it is what men usually do as well. If a husband were to forbid his wife to go, saying that there were chores to be done near the village or that they should go visiting together, she would probably listen to him. But men cannot afford to restrain their wives much, since they also depend on the women's efforts for food. [pp. 240–241]

***

Although women occasionally gather alone, most prefer the company of others. For social reasons as well as safety. Even the few miles between villages should preferably be traveled in groups. Fear of occasional predators, strangers, or even encounters with familiar men who might suggest romance, make solitary travel a moderately anxiety-provoking experience. [p. 241]

***

As a subsistence strategy, gathering for a living is quite satisfying. It can be energetically engaged in, no matter what the size of a woman's family. The schedule is flexible, the pace is self-determined, and the work is accomplished in the company of others. Although each woman basically gathers for herself, this does not isolate her from other women. Women present choice findings to each other as offerings of good will and solidarity. [p. 242]

***

When a woman returns to the village, she determines how much of her gatherings, if any, will be given away and to whom. She sets aside piles of food for those she feels inclined to give to, and places the rest in the back of her hut or beside her family's fire. The food she and her family eat that night, the next day, and perhaps even the next, will consist primarily of the things she has brought home. From start to finish, her labor and its product remain under her control. [p. 242]

***

We lived and lived, and as I kept growing, I started to carry my little brother [Kumsa] around on my shoulders. . . . [p. 69] One day we followed Mother when she went out gathering klaru bulbs. She had gone first and was soon way ahead of us. We were walking along behind looking for klaru. But one time, when I looked for her, I couldn't see her. I called out, "Mommy!" She didn't answer. I called out again, louder, "Mommy!" She still didn't answer. I called out again and again and again, but each time it was the same. We didn't know that she wasn't answering because she was

(continued)

hiding near a tree waiting for us. Meanwhile Kumsa and I followed her tracks calling out to her. When we came near to where she was hiding, she jumped out suddenly, yelling loudly, "What were the two of you doing? What were you looking for way back there? Why were you staying so far behind? Stay in front of me!" She surprised us! We were so scared, we trembled with fright. She went on, "If you two continue to walk like that, I'll go ahead digging klaru, but when I'm finished, I'll just go home. Then things of the bush will come and kill you. What's the matter with the two of you that you stay so far behind when I'm gathering?"

We all sat down and rested. Soon we began to talk again, then, to laugh about things. After that, we kept up with her. [pp. 70–71]

Reprinted by permission of the publisher from *Nisa: The Life and Words of a !Kung Woman* by Marjorie Shostak, pp. 69–71, 240–242, Cambridge, MA: Harvard University Press, Copyright © 1981 by Marjorie Shostak.

Nisa.

American parents with their newborn infants shows that sons are described more often as strong, healthy, and alert, and daughters as soft, delicate, and passive. These descriptions persist today even though they have been shown to fly in the face of evidence that males are more vulnerable physically than females, dying at a higher rate than females at all ages, except during a woman's childbearing years.

Feminist anthropologists documented how different behaviors and attitudes toward girls and boys do not stop at birth, but continue throughout a person's lifetime. They showed how gender constructs could mean the difference between happiness and misery in many societies and even between life and death in others. A young man living in the Soviet Union during the 1940s, for example, was at an extreme disadvantage in comparison to young women in terms of his chances of losing his life: more than 20 million Soviet people, the vast majority of them military men, died during the Second World War. During the same time period in rural China, it would have been more perilous to be born female than male due to a strong cultural preference for boys, a situation that still exists in many rural areas of China today.

Thus, all societies differentiate between males and females in some way, assigning different meanings to the behavior of boys and girls, allotting different roles to them, and often having different expectations for what they can become. One of the most significant aspects of feminist anthropological studies was its documentation of the great variation in these expectations that existed across societies and at different points in time. Feminist anthropologists have even shown that there is variation across societies in the number of gender categories into which sex differences are grouped.

inds of experiences and opportunities are open to them as they grow into adults.

Studies reveal how gender meanings are assigned to males and females at the moment of birth in the United States and Canada. Videotaped research of

Close-Up

2.4: Are Females the "Weaker Sex"?

The belief that boys are stronger and hardier than girls has a long history. For centuries in the Western world, "woman" has been seen as the "weaker sex," as more vulnerable than a man due to a supposed inherent physical fragility. This idea has at various times been used to rationalize certain women's exclusion from participation in the public sphere, whether the political arena, the job market, or educational institutions. In the nineteenth century, for example, attending college was thought to pose a danger to white women's health: many scientists argued that the intellectual effort required for thinking would tax these women's fragile systems, draining them of vital energy and making them incapable of motherhood, their "true calling." The view of woman as weak has not always been extended to all women. For example, for centuries African American women were not seen as vulnerable, but as capable of harsh physical labor, a convenient view for those who wished to exploit them as slaves or servants. The conceptualization of woman as the weaker sex has also had profound effects on men: large numbers of men have lost their lives in war and during periods of civil unrest due to perceptions of them as physically strong and able.

Despite the persistent stereotypic depiction of women as more delicate and frail than men, when life expectancy—one important measure of strength and hardiness—is compared, women have an advantage over men. In the absence of sociocultural factors detrimental to women, a woman's life expectancy today is higher than a man's in all regions of the world. Several countries of the former Soviet Union have the largest gender gap in life expectancy with women outliving men by as many as 10 or more years. Men and women living in wealthy countries such as the United States, Japan, and Canada live the longest, but even in these places women outlive men: the average life expectancy for a woman in the U.S. is 80.5 years, and for a man it is 74 (United Nations 2000:53). Older American women are, however, twice as likely as older men to find themselves living below the poverty line during their later years (Cattell 1996:92).

Race and class background have differential effects on men's and women's chances of living long and prosperous lives. It is estimated that an African American female born in the United States in the year 2000 can expect to live to an average age of 74.7, almost six years fewer than a white female whose average life expectancy for the same time period is 80.5 years. Similarly, an African American male born in 2000 can expect to live on average to 64.6, almost 10 years fewer than a white male whose life expectancy for the same time period is 74.2 years. These statistics mean that a white female born in the year 2000 can expect to outlive an African American male by an astounding 16 years (U.S. Bureau of Census 1998:94). Poverty has a lot to do with such differentials. It is a risk factor for both men and women in terms of life expectancy. For women living in poor nations, mortality during childbirth is a leading cause of death for women of reproductive age. The World Health Organization (WHO) estimates that a woman's lifetime risk of dying from maternal causes is 1 in 16 in Africa, dramatically higher than a European woman's risk, which is 1 in 1,400.

(continued)

References

Cattell, Maria G. 1996. Gender, Aging and Health: A Comparative Approach. In *Gender and Health: An International Perspective.* Carolyn F. Sargent and Caroline Brettell, eds. Pp. 87–122. Upper Saddle River, NJ: Prentice-Hall.

United Nations. 2000. *The World's Women 2000: Trends and Statistics.* New York: United Nations Publication E.00.XVII.14.

U.S. Bureau of Census. 1998. *Statistical Abstract of the United States.* 118th edition. Washington, DC: Commerce Department.

One of the best known cases of this variation in gender categories is described by anthropologist Serena Nanda (1990, 2000). She focuses on "hijras," a religious community in north India composed of individuals whom others see as men but who dress in women's clothing and act more like women than men. They are considered by members of their society to be neither male nor female. In worship of the Mother Goddess, they not only dress and act like women but also undergo a surgical operation in which their genitals are removed. These eunuchs occupy an alternative gender category, one that gives them a special place in Indian society. Other societies that recognize more than two gender categories are discussed in chapter 10.

The diversity in the treatment, roles, tasks, opportunities, and rewards accorded girls and boys, women and men, around the world gave Western feminists a basis from which to question the idea that women are naturally suited to the roles allotted them in their own societies. For example, they asked questions such as these: If Mende women in Africa could be long-distance traders, then isn't the assumption in Western societies of the naturalness of women's position as stay-at-home caretakers subject to question? If Ju/'hoansi (!Kung) women of the Kalahari Desert were the primary "breadwinners" in their society and Ojibwe women of the Great Lakes region of North America were active warriors, then is it not possible that cultural assumptions, not inherent causes, might explain women's supposed inability to contribute to the economic and political spheres in the United States, Canada, and a number of European societies?

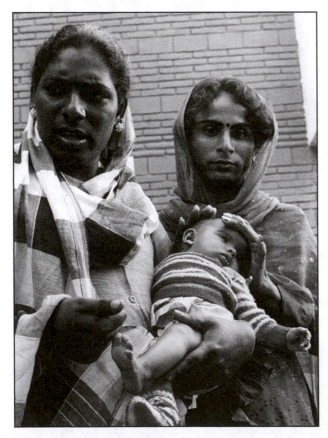

Hijras: "neither man nor woman."

Reclaiming Foremothers

Recognizing that many of their ideas had been anticipated by an earlier generation of women anthropologists, feminist anthropologists began to reclaim the work of pioneering anthropologists whose focus on gender had been ignored or dismissed for too long. They read and rethought the work of women anthropologists such as Elsie Clews Parson (1874–1941), Phyllis Kayberry (1910–1977), and Zora Neale Hurston (1891–1960) who, in the first half of the twentieth century, wrote ethnographies forefronting women's voices. Parson's focus on Pueblo women (Lamphere

1995) and Kayberry's on native women in Western Australia revealed the significant role of women in the lives of their groups. In her 1939 *Aboriginal Woman Sacred and Profane,* Kayberry discussed the absence of a focus on women in academic scholarship and made an important case for including their life experiences in anthropological studies. She put it this way:

> Until recently, aboriginal woman has occupied rather an obscure place in Australian anthropology; and in popular imagination, at least, she has too often been lost to view beneath the burdens imposed upon her by her menfolk. There has been little attempt to analyze the extent to which she participates in religion, the nature and importance of her contribution to the tribal economy. [*Aboriginal Woman Sacred and Profane* is my attempt] to portray aboriginal woman as she really is—a complex social personality, having her own prerogatives, duties, problems, beliefs, rituals, and point of view; making the adjustments that the social, local, and totemic organization require of her, and at the same time exercising a certain freedom of choice in matters affecting her own interests and desires. [1939:xix–xxii]

Perhaps the best known of these early pioneers was Margaret Mead (1901–1978), who popularized anthropology and made significant contributions to the study of gender. She was one of the first to debunk simplistic claims about the biological causes of sex differences with such ethnographies as *Coming of Age in Samoa* (1949) and *Sex and Temperament in Three Primitive Societies* (1935). Feminist anthropologists have written prodigiously about Mead and the significance of her work not only for the discipline of anthropology but also for U.S. society more broadly (see, for example, Lutkehaus 1995). For example, Mead wrote a regular column for *Redbook* magazine, was interviewed on radio and television frequently about social issues, and was a committed anti-Vietnam War activist.

The work of reclamation remains an important part of feminist anthropology as articles on a range of early women anthropologists suggest. This includes work not only on Hurston, Parson, Kayberry, and Mead but also on Ruth Benedict (Babcock 1995), Ruth Landes (Cole 1995), and Barbara Myerhoff (Frank 1995).

Black feminist anthropologists have directed particular attention toward reclaiming a black intellectual tradition in anthropology. Anthropologists Faye Harrison and Ira Harrison have shown how the ideas and contributions of African Americans to anthropology have been marginalized, pushed to the periphery of the discipline. Their book, *African American Pioneers in Anthropology* (1999) reclaims such peripheral or **subjugated knowledge** by providing the intellectual biographies of thirteen black anthropologists, both women and men. In *Black Feminist Anthropology* Irma McClaurin specifically focuses on recovering the subjugated knowledge of black women. She provides a timeline of selected black women/feminist anthropologists working from the 1930s to the present to rescue a history of anthropological work that has been "reduced, marginalized, and erased" because of "pervasive biases" in the discipline (2001:2).

Perhaps the most celebrated black woman in feminist anthropology is Zora Neale Hurston, an anthro-

Close-Up

2.5: Zora Neale Hurston

Zora Neale Hurston wrote ethnographies, short stories, novels, and an autobiography. She studied anthropology with Franz Boas, often considered the founder of American Anthropology, at Columbia University. She was also a part of the Harlem Renaissance—a hugely influential literary and African American cultural movement of the 1920s—collaborating with such writers as Langston Hughes with whom she coauthored the play, *Mule Bone* (1931), and writing for *Fire!*, a literary magazine associated with this movement. Her first novel, *Jonah's Gourd Vine* (1934), was

(continued)

followed by the highly praised novel, *Their Eyes Were Watching God* (1937), and her autobiography, *Dust Tracks on a Road* (1942). In anthropology she is best known for her ethnographic work, *Mules and Men* (1935), which focuses on the folklore, traditions, and social life of three African American communities: Eatonville, Florida, where she was born; Loughman, Florida; and New Orleans, Louisiana. This book has been hailed by a range of anthropologists as innovative in its focus, structure, and style, a forerunner of approaches that have recently become central in anthropology. Hurston, however, was largely forgotten until African American novelist Alice Walker rediscovered her and wrote about this foremother in "In Search of Zora Neale Hurston."

To learn more about on Zora Neale Hurston's contribution to anthropology, consult the following sources:

Gordon, Deborah. 1990. The Politics of Ethnographic Authority: Race and Writing in the Ethnography of Margaret Mead and Zora Neale Hurston. In *Modernist Anthropology: From Fieldwork to Text*. Marc Manganaro, ed. Princeton: Princeton University Press.
Hernández, Graciela. 1995. Multiple Subjectivities and Strategic Positionality: Zora Neale Hurston's Experimental Ethnographies. In *Women Writing Culture*. Ruth Behar and Deborah Gordon, eds. Pp. 148–165. Berkeley: University of California Press.
McClaurin, Irma, ed. 2001. *Black Feminist Anthropology: Theory, Politics, Praxis, and Poetics*. Piscataway, NJ: Rutgers University Press.

Reference

Ms. Magazine, March 1975:74–79, 85–89.

pologist and novelist who focused her work on both African American women and men; her work has been reclaimed not only in anthropology but also in literature. It is out of this black intellectual tradition that black feminist anthropology has emerged today (see Bolles 2001:25). Black feminist anthropologists have had to confront the male bias of traditional anthropology as well as the exclusion of black women's contributions in feminist anthropology. Their work has been critical in exposing racist bias in the discipline and the complex intersections of gender, race, and class oppression in black women's lives, both in the United States and elsewhere. Feminist anthropologists have also worked to reclaim other subjugated knowledges. For example, Janet Finn has focused on Ella Deloria (1889–1971), a Yankton Sioux, who, like Hurston, drew on women's experiences to write both powerful fiction and insightful ethnographies (see Finn 1995).

Black feminist anthropology recovers the contributions of a black intellectual tradition. Furthermore, it also reveals and analyzes structures of oppression while simultaneously showing how women of color have resisted these structures and creatively constructed meaning in their lives in the face of multiple

Zora Neale Hurston.

systems of domination. Black feminist anthropologists merge their scholarly agenda with a commitment to equality and social justice and today address many of the world's most pressing problems, turning attention to questions ranging from the impact of global neoliberal economic policies on women workers in Jamaica (Bolles 1996) to the global politics of feminism (Rodriquez 2007). Black feminist anthropologists—as well as other feminist anthropologists of color—have also made critical contributions to our understanding of the politics of ethnographic fieldwork, which will be discussed in greater detail in chapter 3 (see Perez 2007).

Focusing on Negotiation and Resistance

Many traditional anthropological accounts tended to focus on societies as static, unchanging, closed systems. Many feminist anthropologists contested this conceptualization because it failed to recognize that both women and men make choices and act within their societies in ways that can influence change. Arguing that systems of oppression are never all-encompassing, this "interactionist" or "practice" approach focuses on how people act upon, negotiate, and resist the social categorizations that define and constrain them. Feminist anthropologists became particularly interested in how people, as the active interpreters of symbolic gender meanings, work within the constraints imposed by their societies to negotiate and resist unequal power relations.

In some of the earliest practice studies, feminist anthropologists examined women's actions in societies that excluded them from official decision making. Anthropologists found that women often maximized their interests and gains privately by influencing the decisions of their father, husband, and sons (Collier 1974) or by creating alliances with women from other households, influencing opinions through informal discussion (Lamphere 1974). Later work of this type focused on how different groups of women negotiate and contest the way society constructs the categories of male and female and the meanings associated with them (see Ginsburg and Tsing 1990:2). A study by Kathleen Stewart (1990) revealed that Appalachian women use an argumentative dialogue and storytelling to dispute dominant definitions of gender and to produce a world in which they can "speak for themselves." Other studies focused on more overt forms of women's political negotiations and protest, such as the social organizations women formed in Belize to resist and challenge male dominance (McClaurin 1996).

The "practice approach" will be discussed in much more detail in chapter 8.

Competing Assumptions in Feminist Anthropology

Are Women Universally Subordinated to Men?

Second-wave feminist anthropologists shared a concern with exposing gender bias in anthropology, questioning traditional assumptions, reclaiming foremothers, and understanding people as active participants in the construction of social life. These shared concerns, however, did not mean that there was agreement among them about how best to conceptualize and understand gender roles and inequality.

One of the most significant debates during this period focused on whether or not women were subordinate to men in all societies, past and present. Theorists who claimed that they were argued that since there is no known society in which women are superior to men, and there are many in which they are not, it is appropriate to view women as universally the "second sex." Explanations for this situation tended to focus on those traits shared by women such as their role in childbirth and child rearing. Some theorists, most notably many writers who contributed to the groundbreaking collection *Woman, Culture, & Society* (Rosaldo and Lamphere 1974), argued that because of these functions, women were relegated to the private sphere of society, a realm that was devalued in comparison to the public sphere occupied by men. These writers showed that it was societal *interpretations* of women's role in childbearing and rearing that placed them in a devalued position, not some natural inferiority as was widely believed both inside and outside of academia at the time. The work of these feminist anthropologists was widely read outside of anthropology and contributed significantly to rethinking the causes of women's oppression.

Theorists who argued that women are not universally subordinate to men pointed to the variation in women's status around the world (see, for example, Reiter 1975a). Many of these researchers were influenced by a Marxist perspective that claimed that women had not always been dominated by men but came to be so when certain conditions associated with capitalism arose historically. These researchers often compared different societies, some in which women's position was higher than in others, hoping to isolate those factors that could account for this difference. We discuss these studies in chapter 6.

Are Women a Unitary Group?

Today, many feminists challenge the notion of **gender essentialism,** that women share an "essential" nature, situation, set of experiences, or status that is different from each of those shared by men. This critique of gender essentialism has led many feminists to question the very category "woman" and to question the assumption that "women" share a universal secondary position. Now, similarities and differences among women are rarely just assumed to exist. Instead they are considered important areas of investigation. Indeed, most feminists assert that essentializing "woman" fails to consider how other factors such as class, race, ethnicity, religion, sexual diversity, and physical ability intersect with gender to produce widely different experiences and positions for women both within a society and around the world.

Theories that assume that women can be treated as a single, unified category have thus been widely challenged by ones that take into account how other systems of oppression intersect with gender discrimination, differentially excluding and burdening women from different backgrounds (see, for example, Lugones and Spelman 1983; Mohanty et al. 1991).

Treating subgroups of women as though they are a homogenous group is also problematic. For example, there is no uniform group that we can refer to as "third-world" women or "indigenous women." One important compromise position between theorizing diversity and "sisterhood" suggests that women are oppressed as a group in many places around the world but that not all women are equally oppressed. Differences within gender are also used to subordinate women differentially:

> When men deny women rights, the category woman applies to all who are clearly embodied female, but when men offer privileges, the very entitlements that appear to be rooted in female anatomy can be shown to emerge from the grounds of race and class, heterosexual orientation and physical ability. [Conboy et al. 1997:5]

Changes in Feminist Anthropology

The Anthropology of Women

The early phase of feminist anthropology that we have been describing was largely concerned with "setting the record straight" about women, whether this meant focusing on women in non-Western societies, on women in the anthropologist's own society, or on women in the discipline of anthropology itself. In this initial phase, anthropologists were largely concerned with describing and analyzing women's lives, status, roles, activities, and contributions to society around the world in order to overcome the traditional exclusion of women as subjects of anthropological interest. This early form of feminist anthropology is called the **anthropology of women.**

Despite differences among researchers on women's universal subordination, feminist anthropologists did agree on the following:

- that it is essential to take gender into account when attempting to understand how a society operates or how an individual's identity and life experiences are shaped, and
- that such analyses must necessarily consider how power operates within societies since power shapes gender and other social relations of inequality.

The Anthropology of Gender and Difference

Feminist anthropology has not been a static field, but a dynamic one. It has responded to changing political, social, and intellectual conditions over the last three decades. During this time, feminist anthropology has increasingly focused on how gender affects both men and women. With this recognition, the anthropology of women has been transformed into the anthropology of gender. At the same time, anthropologists have increasingly explored the **politics of difference,** which focuses on how gender, race, class, ethnicity, sexual diversity, and physical ability, for example, produce different degrees of privilege and experiences of oppression for different groups of people. This scrutiny has included how gender and race politics have worked within the discipline of anthropology itself, marginalizing and erasing "the contributions of Black anthropologists in general, and U.S. Black women anthropologists specifically" (McClaurin 2001:2). Anthropologists who study the politics of difference are committed to uncovering and fighting social injustice and inequality wherever it exists.

The study of sexual diversity has been central to the development of a feminist anthropology focused on difference. Lesbian and gay anthropology has explored the intersection of culture, gender, sexuality, and power revealing a wide range of variation in gay and lesbian identities and desires across cultures. It has also documented the impact of anthropologists' lesbian or gay identities on their fieldwork and of "coming out" on their standing within the discipline of anthropology (Lewin and Leap 1996, 2002). It has also broadened its scope to include investigation of bisexual and transgender identities and lives.

In a globalizing world restructured by transnational processes (discussed in chapter 1), the focus on gender and other forms of difference leads feminist anthropologists to ask not only "where are the women and where are the men located in global processes?" but also "which women and which men are located where?" (Marchand and Runyan 2000:226). This latter question acknowledges that different women and men are privileged and subordinated in different ways; they experience and respond to their worlds in a range of ways. In a globalizing world, gender must be understood in terms of *multiplicities*—the many forms of "manhood" and "womanhood" found around the world (see Connell 1987).

The Politics of Location

Another important and related recognition that has grown over the last few decades is that Western feminist anthropologists are themselves "situated thinkers" in a globalizing world of power differentials. Just as early feminists demonstrated that prevailing ideas about gender arose out of the position of privilege afforded (some) men as producers of knowledge, so contemporary scholars have shown that Western feminist ideas must be understood in terms of the context out of which they are produced. That a person's position in a system of power affects one's perspective and way of thinking is known as the **politics of location.** This recognition has meant that feminists—anthropological and otherwise—have had to scrutinize the effects of their own location or of where they are situated on the ideas they produce.

Recognition of the politics of location has important implications for the production of knowledge. It means that all thinkers need to acknowledge their place in a global history of ideas, perspectives, and claims. They must challenge themselves constantly to question their own assumptions and conclusions. It is to these kinds of questions that we turn in the next chapter:

- How is it possible to be politically engaged in a world of difference where no one scholar or group of scholars can "speak for" and represent other women unproblematically?

- How does the anthropological commitment to understanding another culture on its own terms conflict with a feminist commitment to social change?

- How do anthropologists position themselves in debates that contrast human rights with cultural rights and both with women's rights?

- How might the unequal power relations inherent in anthropological fieldwork be addressed?

Conclusions

Understanding how ideas are produced, how they are embedded in the political and historical situation out of which they arise, and how they change over time in relation to changing conditions is an important tool for all anthropologists. For this reason, whenever possible in this book, ideas are presented in terms of the historical context out of which they arose and shown in terms of how they have changed over time. This focus will make you more aware of your own place in a history of ideas. Even though it may not be obvious, place is connected to a history of national and global relationships that privilege and empower some people, some countries, and some regions of the world over others.

In providing a historical contextualization for anthropological ideas about gender and difference, I do not mean to imply that there has been a simple linear progression in anthropology from older, less adequate theories, ideas, and approaches to newer, better ones. To depict the anthropological study of gender and difference in this way would be to gloss over a more complex reality. As feminist anthropologist Micaela di Leonardo asserts, behind any facade of progress in anthropological studies of gender is "a complex history of roads traveled and then abandoned, new starts and alliances and fissures across disciplines and among anthropological subfields" (1991:1). The chapters in this book constitute but one map of this complex territory.

WORD PORTFOLIO

androcentric: dominated by, or emphasizing, male-centered interests or a male-centered point of view.

anthropology of women: an early form of feminist anthropology concerned with describing and analyzing women's lives, status, roles, activities, and contributions to society around the world in order to overcome the traditional exclusion of women as subjects of anthropological interest.

ethnographies: the descriptive accounts anthropologists write about their work in other cultures based on fieldwork. (The research anthropologists conduct during fieldwork is often referred to as "doing ethnography.")

first-wave feminism: the equal rights movement of the late nineteenth and early twentieth centuries in the U.S and Europe. In the U.S., this movement culminated in women gaining the right to vote.

gender essentialism: the belief that women as a group share an "essential" nature, situation, status, or set of experiences that distinguishes them from men as a group who themselves share similar essential traits and characteristics.

glass ceiling: the invisible, artificial barriers that prevent qualified individuals from advancing within their workplace organization. This term is usually used to describe the limit beyond which white women and people of color are not promoted, limiting their advancement.

politics of difference: the understanding that differences of gender, race, class, ethnicity, sexual preference, and physical ability produce different degrees of privilege and experiences of oppression for different groups of people.

politics of knowledge: the understanding that ideas are not the impartial, objective product of unbiased minds, but of thinkers "situated" in a particular time and place who often have the power to validate their ideas as "truths" in the service of maintaining the status quo.

politics of location: the understanding that one's position in a system of power that produces inequalities affects one's perspective and way of thinking.

second-wave feminism: the women's liberation movement that emerged in the late 1960s and 1970s.

stereotypes: standardized mental pictures that represent an oversimplified or exaggerated opinion, prejudiced attitude, or uncritical judgment about a person or group.

subjugated knowledge: ideas and traditions that have been reduced, marginalized, and erased because of pervasive biases such as sexism and racism.

"the personal is political": a slogan of second-wave feminism that underscored the understanding that everyday life, even seemingly small and private aspects of it, is embedded in, and affected by, the larger power relations of a society.

third-wave feminism: a feminist movement comprised of young women born in the United States after 1970 who have grown up with the ideas of feminism and wish to define what feminism means for them on their own terms.

RECOMMENDED READING

Women, Activism and Social Change: Stretching Boundaries, edited by Maja Mikula. 2005. New York: Routledge.

If you are interested in the many women who are working for social change and fighting to transform the worlds around them, you will want to take a look this book. It explores activism across a variety of social, geographical, and political contexts, including Asia, Europe, Latin America, and Australia. This volume speaks to the importance of women as agents of change, their experiences as part of activist movements, and the centrality of women to political and social transformation.

Black/Feminist Anthropology: Theory, Politics, Praxis, and Poetics, edited by Irma McClaurin. 2001. Piscataway, NJ: Rutgers University Press.

This volume of essays draws our attention to the often-overlooked contributions of black and non-Western feminist anthropologists and to the critical ways in which they have shaped the field of anthropology. Topics include such themes as black feminist influence on anthropological practice in Africa and the Caribbean, the historical invisibility of black feminist work, and how theoretical interests and methodological choices are affected by the particular experiences of being a black feminist anthropologist.

Dear Sisters: Dispatches from the Women's Liberation Movement, by Rosalyn Baxandall and Linda Gordon. 2000. New York: Basic Books.

This compilation of original sources dating from 1968–1977 offers a new perspective on the U.S. women's movement through the lens of rare documents often overlooked by historians. Such documents include leaflets, position papers, drawings, and articles produced and circulated among a wide range of feminist organizations during this period. Appealing to both a scholarly and popular audience, this collection offers a rare glimpse into the ideas, passion, and collective efforts that underpinned this critical moment in feminist history.

Global Feminisms since 1945: Rewriting Histories, edited by Bonnie Smith. 2000. New York: Routledge.

This edited volume explores similarities and differences among feminist movements across a variety of geographic spaces. The authors analyze the development of multiple feminisms in the twentieth century. Looking to the importance of class, race, and colonialism as part of feminist movements, this collection addresses the issues that have shaped feminist movements on a global scale, including in the economic, political, sexual, reproductive, and ecological spheres.

I, Rigoberta Menchú: An Indian Woman in Guatemala, by Elisabeth Burgos-Debray; Ann Wright, trans. 1994. London: Verso.

This is a personal narrative of Rigoberta Menchú, a Quiché-speaking woman from the highlands of Guatemala that details her experiences as she fought against government and corporate interests in order to protect the land of her community and people. Deeply affected by the devastating violence that ensued, Menchú emerged as a leader in the struggle for indigenous autonomy within Guatemala and has since become an internationally recognized advocate on behalf of marginalized indigenous groups. This moving testimony is the story of her personal struggle and her vision for justice on behalf of those facing similar situations throughout the world.

3

The Politics of Anthropology

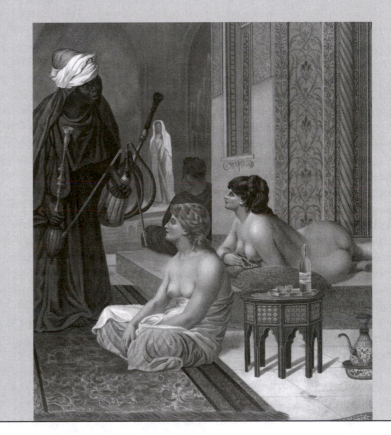

In this chapter you will . . .

examine some of the ethical dilemmas feminist anthropologists confront in their work • discuss how ethnocentrism blocks our understanding of another society • learn how cultural relativism can help combat ethnocentrism • explore cultural practices such as veiling and female genital cutting to investigate tensions between cultural relativism and feminist political engagement • discuss the postcolonial critique of anthropology and how anthropologists address it • explore power relations inherent to fieldwork, and ask whether there can be a truly feminist ethnography

As we saw in chapter 2, knowledge is a form of power. What any of us knows about gender, and other forms of difference, is affected by the political, historical, and cultural circumstance of both the knower and the known. How knowledge acts to create and maintain inequalities is one of feminism's central concerns. As we also discussed, because feminism arose in a political context conscious of differences in power between and among social groups, feminist and other twenty-first-century anthropologists are committed to both studying and overcoming political domination. Linking theoretical knowledge with an active search for social change in society is a form of **engaged anthropology.** The commitment to engaged research, however, is not without its ethical and political difficulties, especially in a globalizing world of conflicting interests and ideas. This has required feminist and other twenty-first-century anthropologists to think about the following questions:

- How do we balance anthropology's commitment to cultural relativism with feminism's commitment to engagement? In other words, how do we understand and interpret the beliefs and behaviors of another culture on its own terms without judgment as we simultaneously take a stand against forms of oppression that may exist within that culture?

- Can anthropologists avoid reproducing in their fieldwork the power relations that exist between them and the people they study? Can they similarly avoid this in the description, or ethnography, they write about them?

In this chapter the tension between cultural relativism and engagement are explored by examining two vexing issues: the veiling of women in Muslim societies and the widespread practice of female genital cutting. Next, is a review of how ethnographic writing, and other forms of representation, can objectify other people and cultures—rendering them as the exotic "other" in contrast to the European "self." The chapter then turns to an investigation of anthropological fieldwork and the debate over whether there can ever be a *truly* feminist ethnography and the implications for anthropologists of being members of the group they study. Throughout this chapter, some alternative ways of thinking and writing about these issues, which have been proposed to overcome these problems, are assessed.

Ethnocentrism vs. Cultural Relativism

In the first few decades of the twentieth century, the founder of American anthropology, Franz Boas—and many of his students such as Margaret Mead and Zora Neale Hurston—was concerned with the bias of earlier anthropological accounts of other cultures. As we will see in chapter 5, the European and American anthropologists known as social evolutionists thought of their own European society as superior and used it as a yardstick against which to judge other societies as inferior. Boas wished to overcome this **ethnocentrism,** the use of one's own societal values to judge those of another society. Boas argued that to comprehend an unfamiliar culture requires understanding that culture on its own terms. In other words, anthropologists must study the context that gives rise to the ideas and behaviors of other people. Although Boas himself never used the term, this idea is known as **cultural relativism.** One way to become culturally relative is to live with people of another culture for an extended period of time, carrying out **fieldwork** or "doing ethnography." Boas advocated that anthropologists conduct fieldwork so that they could learn the language of a people and get to know them intimately.

Fieldwork is the hallmark of anthropological training; it is one of anthropology's distinguishing characteristics, differentiating it from other social science disciplines such as sociology or political science. In the beginning decades of the twentieth century many anthropologists joined Boas in believing intimate knowledge of another culture could be gained only through the process of **participant-observation.** This required anthropologists to live with, take part in, and observe firsthand the society they studied.

But what does cultural relativism entail? We can understand the difference between judgment or ethnocentrism, on the one hand, and cultural relativism, on the other, by thinking about the cultural practice known as **infanticide,** the intentional killing of an infant usually through abandonment, exposure, or neglect. This practice might strike you as outrageously cruel and inhumane, one that should be condemned and stopped wherever it is found. If so, you may be using your own culture's beliefs about right and wrong to judge the beliefs of people in other cultures where infanticide is practiced.

Anthropologists who have studied this practice have discovered the context in which infanticide is most often practiced: often in societies where there is not enough food for everyone to survive. If the birth of another child means a mother must stop breast-feeding a child she already has, risking that child's life through malnutrition, the killing of the newly born infant might be a way to protect the older child and cope with life's difficult realities. This interpretation provides a culturally relative view. It understands the practice of infanticide within the context of the society under study, and it requires suspending one's own feelings about the issue to discover the meaning of this practice in those societies in which it takes place.

Yet, anthropologists also know that in many societies that practice infanticide, it is infant girls, not boys, who are most likely to be killed. Just as in the first case we described, there may be economic reasons for this: if after marriage the new couple goes to live with the husband's family, it makes sense, if a choice has to be made, to help sons survive, since they will stay near their parents and support them as they grow too old to work.

The practice in which a newly married couple goes to live with or near the husband's family is known as patrilocal residence, which is discussed in more detail in chapter 11. Patrilocal residence may be based on assumptions about the differential importance of males and females in a society to begin with. This means that female infanticide may be just one more strike against girls in an androcentric society. What position should feminist and other twenty-first-century anthropologists take on this issue?

Cultural Relativism vs. Political Engagement

Veiling

The practice of purdah poses similar kinds of political, moral, and ethical questions, making feminist political engagement complicated. **Purdah** refers to the practice found in some Muslim societies of secluding women from men to whom they are unrelated based on the belief that both men and women should be modest. Purdah can include the physical segregation of women from men as well as the requirement that when women appear in public spaces they cover their hair or other parts of their body. In some societies when a woman leaves the domestic domain, she is required to wear an outer garment that may cover her entire body, sometimes with mesh used as an eye covering to allow her to see. Such a covering is called a burqa or chadri. In other societies, purdah may only require a woman to wear a veil or head scarf, called a niqāb. The word "veiling," however, often refers to the practice of purdah in general. Veiling has been opposed by many North American and European feminists who deem it oppressive to women.

The repugnance some feminists have for the veil is recorded by Margaret Atwood in her best-selling dystopian novel, *The Handmaid's Tale* (1985). The book's plot focuses on the takeover of U.S. society by right-wing Christian extremists who institute a totalitarian regime that includes the control of women's reproduc-

This Afghan Muslim woman wears a burqa to experience piety.

tive freedoms as well as mandatory veiling. The book is written as a social critique and cautionary tale, meant to alert women to the danger of the feminist backlash that denounced women's struggle for equality in the United States in the 1980s and that came largely from the Christian right. That the book was so effective speaks to the horror with which many women in the United States view veiling. It is no sur-

prise then that after the events of September 11, 2001, President Bush used the veil as a symbol of Muslim women's oppression in Afghanistan and their need to be liberated or "saved." But the idea of "saving" Muslim women suggests that the U.S. is superior because of its enlightened knowledge about freedom and about how *all* women should live (Abu-Lughod 2002a:783).

There is no consensus among Muslim women about veiling; some protest it and invoke Western feminist thinkers in their efforts (see Abu-Lughod 1998). Others voluntarily take up the veil even as they actively reinterpret other aspects of Islamic law on their own terms. The right of Muslim women to wear the head scarf has been especially contentious in France, where a law was passed in 2004 prohibiting the wear-

Allegra Beck, daughter of Donatella Versace, at her 18th birthday party, is dangerously thin.

ing of any religious symbols in public schools. Although the law bans religious symbols of any type—such as a conspicuous Christian cross, for example, or a Jewish yulmake (skull cap)—many Muslims see the law as specifically targeted against Islam.

Muslim women have contested the interpretation of veiling as oppressive, and, as a result, many North American and European feminists have softened their objections, taking into account more fully the importance of Muslim women's cultural beliefs. Today, some Muslim women have chosen to wear the veil as a way to show their devotion to Allah, as anthropologist Saba Mahmood (2001) has recently documented among women in Egypt. Studies such as Mahmood's add an important dimension to our understanding of the significance of cultural practices to a woman's sense of meaning, identity, and value. For these

Bahraini Muslim girl protesting the French government's ban on Muslims wearing head scarves. Her sign reads, "Hijab is the symbol of our pride."

Global News

3.1: Thousands Protest against Head Scarf Ban in France

PARIS, Dec 21 (MASNET & News Agencies)—Thousands of protesters, including many young women in Muslim head scarves (**hijab**), demonstrated on Sunday against the French government's plan to ban overt religious symbols in schools.

The protest from a rarely heard section of French society was the first in Paris against President Jacques Chirac's announcement Wednesday that head scarves and other conspicuous religious symbols, including Jewish skullcaps and large Christian crosses, should be banned from schools to protect French secularism, reports the Associated Press (AP).

The predominantly Muslim demonstrators brandished French identity cards or the national flag as they marched in a boisterous column hundreds of yards long through rain to the Place de la Bastille, carrying banners that read "My veil, my voice" or "Veil, cross, kippa, leave us the choice."

Protesters sang the Marseillaise, the French national anthem, waved French tricolors—red, white and blue—and shouted "Beloved France, where is my liberty?" Some pinned enlarged photocopies of their voter cards on their chests to show their French citizenship, reports the AP. [http://justaskamuslim.blogspot.com/2006/11/thousands-protest-freedom.html (date posted: 12/22/03)] women, the veil is a symbol of a woman's modesty, much as it is for Catholic nuns, who have traditionally worn a "habit," a similar covering of the body.

From the perspective of many Muslim women, veiling signifies respect for Muslim women, something that women in the North American and European nations could be argued to lack. It is doubtful whether many Muslim women would trade their sense of their bodies' piety for that of U.S. teenagers who experience their bodies as a prison and try to escape its confinement and limitations through self-starvation or anorexia nervosa (see Mascia-Lees and Sharpe 1996–1997).

Given the discussion in chapter 2 about bra-burning as a symbol of liberation for U.S. women, it is not surprising that many feminist activists see having to wear a head scarf or other garments to cover one's body as a symbol of lack of freedom or of oppression. On the other hand, it is not hard to imagine that Muslim women might view the desire by some Western women to be sexually attractive as an indication of women's oppression. For example, Muslim women may react as negatively to the cultural pressure for such procedures as surgically augmented breasts as some Western women react to the veil.

Yet, if thousands of Muslim women came together to insist that breast surgery be banned in the United States because breast implants are an indicator of U.S. women's enslavement to notions of beauty, involve risks (see Close-Up 3.1), and maintain women's position as second-class citizens through making them sex objects, many U.S. women would think that a basic freedom was being taken away: their right to control what happens to their own bodies.

Female Genital Cutting

Let's look at another example that creates tension between a commitment to cultural relativism and also to political engagement, which many feminist anthropologists find particularly difficult to resolve: **female genital cutting** (FGC), also called "female genital mutilation," "genital surgery," and "female circumcision" (Gruenbaum 2001:3–4). These terms refer to a range of operations in which the genitals of young girls are surgically altered. The procedure that involves the removal of a young girl's clitoris or the hood of her clitoris is called **clitoridectomy.** When the small external lips (labia minora) of the vagina are also removed, the term "excision" is applied. In its most extreme form, called "infibulation" or "pharonic circumcision," the large external lips (labia majora) of the vagina are also removed and the girl's vulva is stitched together, leaving only a tiny hole for urination and menstruation (Gruenbaum 2001:3).

Female genital cutting is a widespread practice found in many African countries, such as Ethiopia, Egypt, Somalia, Sudan, and Mali, and some countries in the Middle East, such as Saudi Arabia, Yemen, and Jordan. Although it is primarily found among Muslims, some Jewish and Christian people have also performed it (Gruenbaum 2001:33). It is now practiced all over the world as people migrate to new places, taking the practice with them. The operation is often performed on girls too young to give their consent, is unhygienic and painful, and can cause a range of serious health problems (Gruenbaum 2001:4–5).

Feminist anthropologist Ellen Gruenbaum (2001) has studied these practices for over two decades, investigating their meanings for the people who perform FGC. She finds that there is a range of reasons given both across and within societies. Some people see it as a rite of passage—a ritual that indicates that a young girl is now a woman or that she is "clean, smooth, and pure" (Boddy 1997:313). Others give religious reasons for its use, and still others suggest that it is used to indicate that a girl is a virgin and therefore marriageable. For example, in the village of Hofriyat in Sudan, it is thought that if a woman is not purified through surgical alteration of her genitals, she may not marry (Gruenbaum 2001:313). In societies in which a woman's economic well-being is directly tied to her ability to marry, and her status to her ability to have children, ensuring virginity can become a matter of survival. Feminist anthropologist Janice Boddy suggests that FGC socializes female fertility:

> By removing the external genitalia, women are not so much prevented their own sexual pleasure . . . as enhancing their femininity. Circumcision as a symbolic act brings sharply into focus the fertility potential of women by dramatically deemphasizing their inherent sexuality, thereby asserting women's social indispensability. [1997:314]

Like some alterations women make to their bodies in the United States, such as breast augmentation or liposuction, FGC is understood by some as an aesthetic practice, required to make a woman beautiful and appealing.

There has been fierce debate over FGC for many years, with some North American and European feminists often leading the charge against FGC and some members of the societies in which it is performed de-

Close-Up

3.1: Breast Enlargement in the United States

"Increase Breast Size . . . Guaranteed! #1 Seller in America" announces an advertisement for Bioussant Breast Enhancing Tablets in a recent issue of *Vogue*.

"Breast Enlargement through Hypnosis" claims *The Body Contouring Programme*™ offered on the Internet.

These ads, like hundreds of others in popular magazines and on the web, have hit a real nerve with U.S. women. Dissatisfied with the size of their breasts, women in the United States have spent millions of dollars on creams, lotions, devices, and techniques for breast enlargement in the last few decades. For those women suspicious of claims that such products will have the intended effect, Victoria Secret came up with another answer. It offers a new twist on the old push-up bra: the Miracle Bra® has silicone-filled cups meant to mimic the shape and feel of breast tissue. Until recently, silicone was also used for surgically inserted breast implants, still the only way to ensure a permanent increase in breast size. Today saline implants are used. Nearly 400,000 U.S. women opted for surgical breast enlargement in 2007. This number has increased by 476% since 1992, despite the procedures considerable expense ($892,490,535 total expenditure in United States in 2007) and the health risks it poses.

In May 2000, the FDA approved saline breast implants as a safe and effective means of achieving breast augmentations. But despite this approval, there are risks from breast augmentation surgery. The most common ones include the following:

- Deflation
- Detection of breast cancer becomes more difficult because implants increase the difficulty of taking and reading a mammogram
- Capsular contracture
- Calcium deposits
- Infection
- Delay of wound healing
- Neuroma
- Additional surgeries to replace or remove the implant

- Hematoma
- Changes in breast sensation, including the nipple and breast
- Implant shifts
- Bleeding
- Breast asymmetry
- Excessive scarring
- Reactions to anesthesia

References

http://www.breast-augmentation-resource.com/html/risks_benefits.html (accessed 5/22/08).
http://www.cosmeticplasticsurgerystatistics.com/statistics.html#2007-HIGHLIGHTS (accessed 5/22/08).

fending it. The different terms that are used by differently positioned groups to describe the operations reveal this tension: Amnesty International, for example, refers to these practices as "female genital mutilation" and has called for its abandonment. Local people have their own names for the practice, sometimes referring to certain forms as "sunna circumcision." "Sunna" means "tradition" and refers to the practices that Mohammed approved during his lifetime, which Muslims are obligated to perform (Gruenbaum 2001:2).

Those people who understand the practice as traditional and religious argue that to think that parents would purposely "mutilate," harm, or torture their daughters is highly offensive and racist, reinforcing the stereotype of Muslims as evil, primitive, and barbaric (Gruenbaum 2001:3–4). This ideology rests partly on the idea that such practices are unique to these "backward" people (Sheehan 1997:325). Yet, clitoridectomies were performed in Britain during the latter part of the nineteenth century to treat "excessive" masturbation, and women's ovaries were removed, in a procedure known as ovariotomy, to "cure" women's emotional disorders (Sheehan 1997:326).

What stand can or should feminist and other twenty-first-century anthropologists take on this practice? Is FGC a violation of a girl's rights, a product of a patriarchal culture that oppresses women, against which feminists should protest? Or is it ethnocentric and imperialistic to take this view, and is the desire to stop FGC just one more instance of the West claiming its own moral values as transcendent—having to do with all humans—rather than as culturally specific?

Some people who answer yes to the second question are deeply critical of U.S. power and argue that FGC should be seen as a cultural response to the increasing encroachment and dominance of Western beliefs and images. From this perspective, practices such as FGC are forms of cultural resistance within a global context of American imperialism. These practices, in other words, are an attempt by some groups of people to maintain, and fight for the right of, cultural self-determination. The situation is further complicated by the fact that when white women intervene in such matters "on behalf of" women of other societies, ethnic groups, or nations, the very practices they protest can become a symbol of that group's distinct identity, which the group then emphasizes in its anticolonial or nationalist struggles.

Are feminists who oppose FGC essentializing gender, failing to consider how meaning is shaped and lives are affected by a range of factors, including ethnicity, class, nationality, and religion? Does your own view of FGC change if you know that women, not men, are most frequently the ones who insist on the operations for their young girls? Or that some Muslim women have sought to protect it as a cultural right while others, even some Muslim men, have opposed it (Boddy 1997:312)? In the case of both veiling and FGC, cultural rights may be in conflict with human or women's rights.

Human Rights, Cultural Rights, and Women's Rights

These examples are not meant to suggest that North American and European feminists or feminist and other twenty-first-century anthropologists cannot take a moral, political, or ethical stand on issues of oppression. Indeed, to claim that, is to confuse cultural relativism—the suspension of judgment in order to come to understand a society on its own terms—with **moral relativism.** Moral relativists argue that since all moral beliefs are culturally bound there is no basis on which to critique the beliefs and values of any other society.

Accepting a morally relative position unquestioningly might conflict with your commitment to **human rights,** your belief that all people have an equal entitlement to dignity that is "inalienable," that is, cannot be taken away. By adopting a strict moral relativist position, you would have no basis on which to oppose such practices as slavery or **genocide,** the attempt to destroy, or the destruction of, a national, ethnic, racial, or religious group. The extermination of European Jewry by the Nazis in the twentieth century is an example of genocide; so is the deliberate extermination of black Africans by the government-supported Arab militia, Janjaweed, in Dafur, Sudan, which began in 2003 and continues to this day.

The dilemma is deciding what to do when your own belief in human rights conflicts with your belief in **cultural rights,** that is, with your conviction that groups of people, not just individuals, have a right to preserve their customs, language, and way of life from extermination. This act of destruction of a group's culture is known as **ethnocide** and can include any action that is intended to deprive a group of people of its integrity as a people, whether through using physical force to take their land and other resources, or using legal and administrative measures to displace them from their homeland. The destruction by the U.S. government of many Native American cultures over the last several centuries is an example of ethnocide: native peoples were not just killed (genocide) but were also forcibly removed from their land and displaced onto reservations. They also had their children taken from them and placed in boarding schools so that they would **assimilate,** that is, so they would learn and adopt the customs and attitudes of U.S. society, rather than maintain those of their native culture.

In the last half of the twentieth century, the United Nations has emphasized the protection of the cultural rights of indigenous peoples such as Native Americans. **Indigenous peoples** are nations or communities of people who are historically related to societies prior to the invasion or colonization of their territories and who consider themselves distinct from other groups of those societies now occupying those territories (International Work Group for Indigenous Affairs, http://www.iwgia.org/sw310.asp, accessed July 29, 2008). The 1994 "United Nation's Draft Declaration on the Rights of Indigenous Peoples," supports the right of self-determination. "By virtue of that right," indigenous peoples can freely determine their political status and pursue their economic, social, and cultural development (Study Guide 2003).

Women's rights abuses occur when women are deprived of human dignity and other basic rights for no other reason than their gender. Care must also be taken when trying to reconcile cultural and women's rights: as Carole Nagengast cautions, cultural relativism can be used "to excuse, rationalize, or explain women's differential treatment before the law" (1997). Anthropologists have not found a moral theory that provides the basis for making crosscultural value judgments. This has led some scholars to suggest that the tolerance that relativism calls for "should constitute our default mode of thought; it should govern our moral position in the absence of persuasive arguments to the contrary" (Hatch 1997). What do you think?

Taking a Stand

This discussion suggests that taking a moral and political stand against others' practices and beliefs requires deep consideration of the complexity of such issues, especially the unequal power relations that may underlie them, such as that between the Global North and the Global South. It requires a serious appreciation of differences among women, one that takes into account women's diverse histories and circumstances and that recognizes that women's desires are also different (Abu-Lughod 2002a:785). In addition, it alerts us to how cultural rights may conflict with women's rights.

Nonetheless, North American and European feminists should not assume that third-world or indigenous women cannot speak for themselves on such issues. Instead, becoming involved requires working with, and alongside, those women who also seek change, but on their own terms. Caren Kaplan and Inderpal Grewal (1999) refer to this as **coalition work in the service of resistance:** coming together to work on issues that link oppressed groups. They argue that an approach focused on complex and linked inequalities around the world, rather than on supposed similarities among women, provides an alternative to traditional notions of solidarity based on essentialism. Linkages can be made without declaring "sisterhood" or assuming sameness.

The Postcolonial Critique of Anthropology

As we have seen, the decades of the 1960s and 1970s were marked by the struggles of colonized people to resist colonial domination and seek self-determination. These movements for independence began to break down traditional power relations. As a consequence, dominant European ways of seeing the world and the place of different societies within it were questioned by newly liberated people who revealed those ideas to be ethnocentric, racist, and oppressive.

Traditional colonialist explanations of social relations were criticized for the role they played in maintaining differential power between the colonizers and the colonized. The ways in which colonized people were portrayed by colonizers—whether in literature, painting, colonial documents, scholarly works, travel accounts, or journalism—also came under attack for their **objectification** of colonized people, viewing them as depersonalized objects, instead of as individuals. This scrutiny of the images and depictions of non-Western societies by European writers was greatly influenced by Edward Said, a literary critic of Middle Eastern descent. Said is one of the founders of **postco-**

Close-Up

3.2 Women's Rights Abuses

Millions of women throughout the world suffer the abuse of their rights just because they are women. According to Human Rights Watch (http://hrw.org/women/, accessed August 13, 2007) "abuses against women are relentless, systematic, and widely tolerated, if not explicitly condoned. Violence and discrimination against women are global social epidemics, notwithstanding the very real progress of the international women's human rights movement in identifying, raising awareness about, and challenging impunity for women's human rights violations." Human Rights Watch lists the following examples of such abuses:

- "Sierra Leone, Kosovo, the Democratic Republic of Congo, Afghanistan, and Rwanda, have raped women as a weapon of war with near complete impunity.

- Men in Pakistan, South Africa, Peru, Russia, and Uzbekistan beat women in the home at astounding rates, while these governments alternatively refuse to intervene to protect women and punish their batterers or do so haphazardly and in ways that make women feel culpable for the violence.

- As a direct result of inequalities found in their countries of origin, women from Ukraine, Moldova, Nigeria, the Dominican Republic, Burma, and Thailand are bought and sold, trafficked to work in forced prostitution, with insufficient government attention to protect their rights and punish the traffickers.

- In Guatemala, South Africa, and Mexico, women's ability to enter and remain in the workforce is obstructed by private employers who use women's reproductive status to exclude them from work and by discriminatory employment laws or discriminatory enforcement of the law.

- In the U.S., students discriminate against and attack girls in school who are lesbian, bi-sexual, or transgendered, or do not conform to male standards of female behavior.

- Women in Morocco, Jordan, Kuwait, and Saudi Arabia face government-sponsored discrimination that renders them unequal before the law—including discriminatory family codes that take away women's legal authority and place it in the hands of male family members—and restricts women's participation in public life."

lonial studies, the academic discipline that developed in the 1980s and 1990s to study the many facets of the experiences of oppressed peoples under colonial rule. Postcolonial studies scholars analyze the structures of power that kept colonial rule in place, shaping both the West and non-West; study colonial struggles for self-determination; and seek to understand the lives of once-colonized people in the postcolonial moment after independence.

Orientalism

In his best-selling book, *Orientalism* (1979), Said reveals how Western writers have created "the Orient," producing images of Asia, the Middle East, and

North Africa as exotic, mysterious, and "other." Since its publication, many other postcolonial studies scholars have shown how a Western "*self*" was constructed by contrasting it with the "Oriental other," a process that created a Western identity based on racial and cultural stereotypes about non-Western peoples. These contrasts included viewing the West as progressive, enlightened, familiar, and racially superior and the "Orient" or "East" as backward, primitive, exotic, sexual, and racially inferior, ideas that were used to justify Western imperialism.

But, according to Said, "the Orient" has never actually existed. It is a fabrication based on Western fantasies, one that turns Eastern societies into objects for consumption by Western spectators. Indeed, the Western fascination with the Orient was so intense that from 1800 to 1959, an estimated 60,000 books were published in the West on the Arab "Orient" alone (Hoodfar 1997:254). We will return to a discussion of the development of the self through the construction of an "other" in subsequent chapters.

Global News

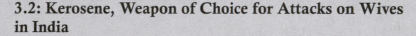

3.2: Kerosene, Weapon of Choice for Attacks on Wives in India

Every day, year after year, women grotesquely disfigured by fire are taken to Victoria Hospital's burn ward here in India's fastest-growing city. They lie in rows, wrapped like mummies in white bandages, their moans quieted by the pain-obliterating drip of morphine.

Typically, these women and thousands like them have been depicted as victims of disputes over the ancient social custom of dowry and as symbols of the otherness of India, a place where lovely young brides are doused with kerosene and set ablaze for failing to satisfy the demands of their husbands' families for gold, cash and consumer goods that come as part of the marriage arrangement.

But most women on the ward never mentioned dowry when explaining why they were burned. . . .

. . . The use of fire as a weapon, which seems so exotic, is simply expedient: kerosene, a ubiquitous cooking fuel here, is a cheap, handy weapon, much like a gun or a baseball bat in an American home. . . .

Violence against wives is a common problem in India, as it is in many societies.

More than half of married women justified wife-beating in a recently released survey of 90,000 women sponsored by India's Health Ministry, most commonly for neglecting housekeeping and child-rearing duties, showing disrespect to in-laws, going out without a husband's permission or arousing a husband's suspicions of infidelity. . . .

Women's groups are pushing for new laws to combat domestic violence. The government is considering a bill that would enable a woman to initiate civil proceedings against an abusive relative and obtain a court order of protection. [Celia W. Dugger, *New York Times* 12/26/2000:A.1]

Feminist Postcolonial Theory

Postcolonial studies have sought to understand the relationship among imperialism, colonialism, race, and power. Feminist postcolonial scholars have once again pointed out that understanding the colonial moment is not possible without asking how gender figures into other relations of power. They have thus called for the "gendering" of postcolonial studies. Feminist postcolonial scholars have also argued that feminist theory cannot fully understand gender relations and inequality without recognizing how groups of people are ascribed a racial identity through processes of racialization, like those described in chapter 2. This requires recognition that gender is always a racialized category (Lewis and Mills 2003:4). In the Ethnography in Focus, feminist anthropologist Ann Stoler describes how race and gender interacted in colonial Indonesia.

Ethnography in Focus

Carnal Knowledge and Imperial Power: Race and the Intimate in Colonial Rule by Ann Stoler

The colonial politics of exclusion was contingent on constructing categories. Colonial control was predicated on identifying who was "white," who was "native," and which children could become citizens rather than subjects, on which were legitimate progeny and which were not. What mattered was not only one's physical properties but also who counted as "European" and by what measure. Skin shade was too ambiguous. Bank accounts were mercurial. Religious belief and education were crucial markers but never clear enough. Social and legal standing derived from the cultural prism through which color was viewed, from the silences, acknowledgements, and denials of the social circumstances in which one's parents had sex. . . . Ultimately, inclusion or exclusion required regulating the sexual, conjugal [married], and domestic life of both European colonials and their subjects. [pp. 42–43]

***

The East Indies Company [which ruled many Asian colonies] regulated against female migration by selecting bachelors as their European recruits and by promoting both extramarital relations and legal unions between low-ranking employees and imported slave women. . . . [Because there were often few if any white women in the colonies], colonized women living as the concubines [unmarried sexual partners] of European men . . . formed the dominant domestic arrangement in colonial cultures through the early twentieth century . . . *Concubinage* ambiguously covered a wide range of arrangements that included sexual access to a non-European woman as well as demands on her labor and legal rights to the children she bore. . . . Critics were openly disdainful of these liaisons on moral grounds—all the more so when these unions became sustained and emotionally significant relationships. Such affective ties defied the racial premise of concubinage as no more than an emotionally unfettered convenience. . . . The tension between concubinage as a confirmation of racial hierarchy and as a threatening compromise to that order was nowhere more visible than in reactions to the progeny [children] that it produced. Mixed-bloods, poor Indos, and abandoned *métis* children straddled the division of ruler and ruled as they threatened to blur that divide. [pp. 47–51]

***

The arrival of large numbers of European women coincided with new bourgeois [middle class] trappings and notions of privacy in colonial communities. And these, in turn, were accompanied by new distinctions based on race. . . . Women were claimed to have more delicate sensibilities and therefore needed sensible quarters—discrete and enclosed. . . . Segregationist standards were what women "deserved" and, more importantly, what white male prestige required that they maintain. . . . [p. 55]

[But] if the gender-specific requirements for colonial living imposed specific restrictions on women, they were also racialized assessments of danger that assigned a heightened sexuality to colonial men. . . . Allusions to political and sexual subversion of the colonial system went hand in hand. The term "Black Peril" referred to sexual threats, but it also connoted the fear of insurgence, and of perceived nonacquiescence to colonial control more generally. Concern over protection of white women intensified during real and perceived crises of control—threats to the internal cohesion of the European communities or infringements on its borders. . . . The remedies sought to alleviate sexual danger [therefore] embraced new prescriptions for securing white control. These included increased surveillance of native men, new laws stipulating corporal punishment for the transgression of sexual and social boundaries, and the demarcation of new spaces that were made racially off limits. These went with a moral rearmament of the European community and reassertions of its cultural identity. Charged with guarding cultural norms, European women were instrumental in promoting white solidarity. But it was partly at their own expense, for on this issue they were to be almost as closely policed as colonized men. [pp. 58–60]

From: Ann Stoler, *Carnal Knowledge and Imperial Power: Race and the Intimate in Colonial Life.* Copyright © 2002. Permission granted by University of California Press.

It is interesting to note the interplay of gender and race in the role that the veil has played in constructions of "the Orient": then, as today, the seclusion of "Oriental" Muslim women was signified by the veil, seen as an extension of women's seclusion in the harem, or zenana. The harem refers to the living quarters of a man's wives and other female relatives, especially during the time of the Ottoman Empire (1299–1922). However, the harem was repeatedly depicted in Western representations as a brothel-like prison, within which Muslim men enslaved their wives, who had nothing to do but beautify themselves and fulfill their husband's sexual desires (Hoodfar 1997:254), just as in the representation of the harem that opens this chapter.

Harem women were portrayed as passive, oppressed, secluded, and imprisoned as well as sexually promiscuous. This representation excited Western spectators, suggesting the allure of forbidden sexuality (Lewis and Mills 2003:14). Thus, the harem, and by extension the veil, came to stand not only for forbidden female beauty but also for the mysteriousness of "the Orient" itself, its strangeness, its "otherness" (Lewis and Mills 2003:14).

This depiction also depended on images of white woman as modest, pure, and sexually moral and as in need of protection from the men of the "barbaric" and "backward" dark-skinned races and their animal-like sexuality. This idea linked the protection of white women's sexual purity to the maintenance of the colonizer's racial purity.

Harems, however, were not brothels but the space of women and children and the site of the family, places in which women played important roles in the lives of their society (Micklewright 1999, cited in Lewis and Mills 2003:15–16).

Anthropology and Self-Critique

Influenced by postcolonial and feminist studies, anthropologists in the 1980s began to analyze how ethnographic descriptions like Orientalist ones objectified the people anthropologists study, perpetuating inequalities between the "West and the Rest," contributing to colonial and racial domination. This response resulted in the formation of self-reflexive anthropology. Reflexive anthropologists think critically about how political disparities have contributed to anthropological depictions of non-Western societies in the past and in the present. Self-reflexivity is at the heart of feminist and other twenty-first-century anthropology.

The Problem with Culture

One aspect of this critique has been to interrogate the idea of culture for its "othering" tendencies. Like the concept race, critics have argued, culture categorizes people into discrete groups based on perceived similarities while at the same time contrasting that group with others. But many believe that grouping people based on shared traits simplifies the complexity of social identities (Abu-Lughod 1990).

To address the problematic nature of the term "culture," the concept of "travel" has been offered as an alternative to culture. In her ethnography, *In the Realm of the Diamond Queen,* Anna Lowenhaupt Tsing, for example, argues that "in defining itself as a science that can travel anywhere, anthropology has classically constituted its object—'cultures'—as essentially immobile" (1993:123). She suggests that the metaphor of "travel" might provide a more complex understanding of people's experiences in a world characterized by the movement of people between places and identities (Clifford 1997, Kaplan 1996).

The concept of "borderlands" has also been suggested as a replacement for "culture." This idea emerged from ethnic studies in which many researchers wrote "from the border" between different ethnic identities (Anzaldúa 1987, Ortner 1996). As with "travel," the idea of "borderlands" focuses attention on intersocietal relationships and interaction, rather than on societies as static entities bounded in space (see, for example, Behar 1994, Rosaldo 1989).

Global News

3.3: Stop Trying to "Save" Africa

Last fall, shortly after I returned from Nigeria, I was accosted by a perky blond college student whose blue eyes seemed to match the "African" beads around her wrists.

"Save Darfur!" she shouted from behind a table covered with pamphlets urging students to TAKE ACTION NOW! STOP GENOCIDE IN DARFUR!

My aversion to college kids jumping onto fashionable social causes nearly caused me to walk on, but her next shout stopped me.

"Don't you want to help us save Africa?" she yelled.

It seems that these days, wracked by guilt at the humanitarian crisis it has created in the Middle East, the West has turned to Africa for redemption. Idealistic college students, celebrities such as Bob Geldof and politicians such as Tony Blair have all made bringing light to the dark continent their mission. They fly in for internships and fact-finding missions or to pick out children to adopt in much the same way my friends and I in New York take the subway to the pound to adopt stray dogs.

This is the West's new image of itself: a sexy, politically active generation whose preferred means of spreading the word are magazine spreads with celebrities pictured in the foreground, forlorn Africans in the back. Never mind that the stars sent to bring succor to the natives often are, willingly, as emaciated as those they want to help.

Perhaps most interesting is the language used to describe the Africa being saved. For example, the Keep a Child Alive/"I am African" ad campaign features portraits of primarily white, Western celebrities with painted "tribal markings" on their faces above "I AM AFRICAN" in bold letters. Below, smaller print says, "help us stop the dying."

Such campaigns, however well intentioned, promote the stereotype of Africa as a black hole of disease and death. News reports constantly focus on the continent's corrupt leaders, warlords, "tribal" conflicts, child laborers, and women disfigured by abuse and genital mutilation. These descriptions run under headlines like "Can Bono Save Africa?" or "Will Brangelina Save Africa?" The relationship between the West and Africa is no longer based on openly racist beliefs, but such articles are reminiscent of reports from the heyday of European colonialism, when missionaries were sent to Africa to introduce us to education, Jesus Christ, and "civilization."

There is no African, myself included, who does not appreciate the help of the wider world, but we do question whether aid is genuine or given in the spirit of affirming one's cultural superiority. My mood is dampened every time I attend a benefit whose host runs through a litany of African disasters before presenting a (usually) wealthy, white person, who often proceeds to list the things he or she has done for the poor, starving Africans. Every time a well-meaning college student speaks of villagers dancing because they were so grateful for her help, I cringe. Every time a Hollywood director shoots a film about Africa that features a Western protagonist, I shake my head—because Africans, real people though we may be, are used as props in the West's fantasy of itself. And not only do such depictions tend to ignore the West's prominent role in creating many of the unfortunate situations on the continent, they also ignore the incredible work Africans have done and continue to do to fix those problems.

Why do the media frequently refer to African countries as having been "granted independence from their colonial masters," as opposed to having fought and shed blood for their freedom? Why do Angelina Jolie and Bono receive overwhelming attention for their work in Africa while Nwankwo Kanu or Dikembe Mutombo, Africans both, are hardly ever mentioned? How is it that a former mid-level U.S. diplomat receives more attention for his cowboy antics in Sudan than do the numerous African Union countries that have sent food and troops and spent countless hours trying to negotiate a settlement among all parties in that crisis?

Two years ago I worked in a camp for internally displaced people in Nigeria, survivors of an uprising that killed about 1,000 people and displaced 200,000. True to form, the Western media reported on the violence but not on the humanitarian work the state and local governments—without much international help—did for the survivors. Social workers spent their time and in many cases their own salaries to care for their compatriots. These are the people saving Africa, and others like them across the continent get no credit for their work.

Last month the Group of Eight industrialized nations and a host of celebrities met in Germany to discuss, among other things, how to save Africa. Before the next such summit, I hope people will realize Africa doesn't want to be saved. Africa wants the world to acknowledge that through fair partnerships with other members of the global community, we ourselves are capable of unprecedented growth.

Authorizing Anthropology

Another aspect of anthropologists' critical self-reflection has been to understand how anthropology has legitimated itself as the speaker of the "truth" about other societies. One primary way of doing this has been by calling anthropology a science. In Western societies, scientific objectivity is understood as a higher way of knowing, one that produces the "truth" about what something is and how it operates. The mantle of science positions anthropologists as objective and knowledgeable experts who produce accurate accounts of other people's lives.

The conclusion that ethnographic observations are objective is based on the assumption that a human researcher, like a scientific instrument, can collect data in a way that is unaffected by subjective concerns. This task, of course, is impossible. No human being can stand completely outside of the cultural context that has given rise to his or her own identity and sense of personhood. Anthropologists' perceptions and conclusions are filtered through their own cultural lenses, even if they strive to be culturally relative.

Nonetheless, for the most part, traditional anthropological accounts have been taken as accurate representations, and many anthropologists have seen their work as just that. Early anthropologists even claimed scientific objectivity as a means of distinguishing their efforts from other forms of crosscultural encounters that they claimed were less accurate. For example, travel to other societies was portrayed as a personal experience, and travel writing was seen as a subjective account of that personal experience. Anthropologists were able to legitimize anthropology as an academic discipline by claiming their own practices as scientific and objective in comparison to travel and other types of crosscultural interaction, which were seen as subjective (Pratt 1986).

The image of the anthropologist as an objective instrument of knowledge, as we will see in the next sections, has been achieved through different mechanisms: denying the subjective experiences of ethnographers and obscuring their presence in ethnographic texts through particular writing techniques.

Denying Subjective Experience

The appearance of impartiality in anthropological accounts has traditionally been established by suppressing the anthropologist's identity as a person with bodily and psychological characteristics that might affect his or her ethnographic description. Thus, traditionally anthropologists have been expected to make no reference to their own desires in their ethnographic writing and to deny emotions and disregard the sensuous aspects of life in another society—its smells, sounds, and flavors. This is based on a belief that objectivity is possible, that it is possible to split mind and body. Ideas are seen as capable of being detached from a particular knower and therefore beyond the limits of experience, making them transcendent.

As we discuss in more detail in chapter 9, the body and its associated feelings have traditionally been associated with the feminine in Western thinking and disparaged. But with the advent of feminism and postcolonialism, categories such as mind/body and objective/subjective have broken down. Many anthropologists now see their fieldwork as a subjective experience and also such topics as emotions (Behar 1997, Rosaldo 1989), unconscious desires (Mascia-Lees and Sharpe 1994), and sensual experiences (Stoller 1997) as appropriate areas of investigation.

Writing Culture

Establishing a veneer of objectivity has traditionally also been accomplished through writing techniques that anthropologist Renato Rosaldo has called "classic norms of description" (1989). These norms include the rejection of using the first-person personal pronoun "I" in anthropological writing and the expectation that an ethnographer speak in generalities about the people being studied. In the former case, "I" is avoided to distance writers from the content of their texts and to make it appear objective. In the latter instance, descriptions of the behavior or thoughts of particular people in other societies are written about as though they describe the behavior of a whole people, "the Iroquois" or "the Ashanti," for example. This technique distances the reader from the actual people with whom anthropologists interact in the field.

Several correctives have been offered to make it clear that ethnographies are subjective accounts of individual anthropologists. These include "putting the anthropologist in the picture," whether through using first-person narratives or through inserting into ethnographies the anthropologist's assumptions, background, and personal story. These mechanisms "situate" researchers. They reveal where particular anthropologists are located in terms of power relations in comparison to those they study.

Using dialogue as a form of writing has also been offered as a solution to old problems, showing that anthropological conclusions are really the result of interactions between individuals, not the product of distanced observations of a whole group. This reconceptualization shifts attention away from the idea that ethnography is an accurate portrait written by "us," primarily people from Western cultures, about "them," primarily people from non-Western societies. Instead it encourages us to recognize ethnographies as the product of cultural interactions that involve people from two or more societies. It thereby breaks down the concepts of self and other.

Shortcomings of the Writing Culture Critique

Renato Rosaldo (1989) cautions that although new concepts and writing techniques may be helpful in overcoming some problems with traditional ethnographic representation, no concept or writing style is entirely neutral. He urges anthropologists to go beyond the search for new concepts to develop measures for assessing ethnographic representation. One criterion might be to ask what effect ethnographic descriptions have on the reader. Do forms of description distance the reader of ethnographies so much that the people depicted in them appear unfamiliar and exotic? If the same language of description were used to represent the culture of the anthropologist or reader, would it seem valid and accurate? Another approach is to allow the people anthropologists write about to evaluate the ethnographies written about them and to take their critiques seriously (Rosaldo 1989:50–51).

Other critics argue that this "writing culture" critique shifts attention away from the people anthropologists study to the ethnographies they write. Although recognizing the important impact Western representations have had on non-Western people, these scholars suggest that it is essential that feminist and other twenty-first-century anthropologists remain committed to such forms of political practice as teaching, activist research, and solidarity work (Enslin 1994:559). Elizabeth Enslin warns that if feminist and other twenty-first-century anthropologists focus too much attention on ethnographies, they will have little hope of transforming the politics of research. Quoting Claudia Salazar, she argues that "by focusing our politics on textual innovation or critiques of them, we elude the more critical task of 'democratizing the social relations of research'" (Enslin 1994:545). This involves scrutinizing how power relations are reproduced in anthropological fieldwork, not just in texts.

Close-Up

3.3: Sexuality, or Being LGBT, in the Field by Nell Quest

Sex, desire, and fantasy make up regular parts of the lives of most adults. Although anthropologists have always devoted attention to the sexual lives of their "native" research subjects, sometimes problematically exoticizing them in the process, the role played by anthropologists' own erotic desires and sexual identities went largely unexplored until recently. As Esther Newton (1993) has pointed out, this lack of attention to anthropologists' sexual selves long served to bolster the discipline's claim to scientific objectivity. It made it seem as though the sexual and gender identity of the heterosexual male anthropologist was either unproblematic or unimportant.

Feminist, and LGBT, anthropologists have challenged the idea that a heterosexual male fieldworker's identity does not affect what he observes and how he writes about another group of people, by reflecting on the differences made by gender in their own fieldwork encounters. They have raised questions about their own sexualities, erotic subjectivities, and sexual identities. But anthropologists who do not identify as straight are often perceived as less credible by

(continued)

their colleagues. This has, as Esther Newton points out, suspended them between their urgent sense of difference and their justifiable fear of revealing it (1993:4).

Nonetheless, some scholars openly and candidly discuss the importance of anthropologists' erotic sentiments and encounters in the field (Kulick and Willson 1995, Newton 1993). Such scholars argue that anthropologists' intimate and emotional involvement with their research subjects, whether it is explicitly sexual or not, is central to the kinds of research questions they are able to ask and data they are able to collect. For twenty-first-century anthropologists interested in gender, sexuality, and difference, it is essential to recognize how anthropologists' desires, repulsions, or erotic sentiments inform their work. This is an issue that should be studied and carefully considered rather than avoided or denied.

Gay and lesbian anthropologists have also reflected on the ways their sexual identities enter into and affect their fieldwork experiences. Lewin and Leap (1996), for example, and the contributors to their volume have pointed out that, for many gay and lesbian anthropologists, "managing" their sexual identities is already a fraught process before they ever step into the field, given that they often face stigmatization in their own cultures because of their sexual orientation. For them, the issues of how to present their sexual or gender identity to research subjects in ways that neither get in the way of research nor are personally unsatisfactory can be an extremely complicated process that has important repercussions for the data they collect.

On the other hand, some LGBT anthropologists have argued that their sexual identities have allowed them to be accepted into and to conduct research among other stigmatized sexual minorities, including among drag queens (Newton 1979) or transgendered prostitutes (Kulick 1998; see Ethnography in Focus in chapter 10). These researchers argue that the communities among which they have conducted research would not have been able to trust them so easily if it weren't for their own identification as gay men or as lesbians. Furthermore, depending on the context, some lesbian and gay anthropologists find that in their fieldwork, their sexual identities are less problematic than they are in their home societies, a fact that denaturalizes the difficulties they face with discrimination at home. This can even lend them new strength in political projects and stances against discrimination when they return.

For feminist, LGBT, and other reflexive anthropologists who have devoted attention to these questions, sexuality has been shown to have varying effects on fieldwork encounters and the ethnographies that come out of them. What is certain is that sexuality cannot simply be assumed to be a nonissue. For anthropologists interested in power, gender, or sexuality, it is important not to take sexuality for granted. Instead, they continue to devote attention to the formerly taboo subject of anthropologists' sexual encounters and erotic desires in the field and attempt to hold frank discussions about how fieldworkers' manage their sexual identities and desires while also conducting responsible research.

References

Kulick, Don. 1998. Travesti: Sex, Gender, and Culture among Brazilian Transgendered Prostitutes. Chicago: University of Chicago Press.

Kulick, Don, and Margaret Willson, eds. 1995. Taboo: Sex, Identity, and Erotic Subjectivity in Anthropological Fieldwork. London: Routledge.

Lewin, Ellen, and L. Leap, eds. 1996. *Out in the Field: Reflections of Lesbian and Gay Anthropologists.* Chicago: University of Illinois Press.

Newton, Esther. 1979. *Mother Camp: Female Impersonators in America.* Chicago: University of Chicago Press.

Newton, Esther. 1993. My Best Informant's Dress: The Erotic Equation in Fieldwork. *Cultural Anthropology* 8 (1):3–23.

Power Relations in Fieldwork

Feminist and other reflexive anthropologists probe the context of fieldwork, raising questions about the inequality inherent in most fieldwork situations and the impact of gender and sexuality on the field experience. In Peggy Golde's *Women in the Field: Anthropological Experiences* (1986), women anthropologists explore how their gender affected their perceptions of their field experience and how it influenced the perceptions and behavior of members of the culture being studied. Lesbian and gay anthropologists have been particularly concerned with the impact of alternative sexualities on the ethnographic work they do.

Can There Be a Feminist Ethnography?

If anthropologists are predominantly privileged individuals from Western societies while those they study are often oppressed people from non-Western societies, can there ever be an equal relationship between researcher and research subject? Feminist anthropologists have framed this issue by asking whether there can be a truly "feminist ethnography." Can any study of the "other" be compatible with a politics of equality (Abu-Lughod 1990/91, Stacey 1988)?

Feminist sociologist Judith Stacey (1988) argues that feminist ethnographers may come close to producing fully feminist ethnographies but will never be able to completely do so. She asserts that no matter how much collaboration there is between ethnographers and the people they study, it is the ethnographer who ultimately controls the final ethnographic account, granting anthropologists the power to represent a culture, which their research subjects do not have.

Other feminists have argued that truly feminist research may be possible. They suggest that the moment feminist researchers begin to address the experiences of women and other oppressed people in their work, their investigations will necessarily become concerned with questions of power and political struggle, and their research goals will be defined by that struggle. Sandra Harding argues that this focus on the political is almost inevitable because

> the questions an oppressed group wants answered are rarely requests for so-called pure truth. Instead, they are questions about how to change its conditions; how its world is shaped by forces beyond it, how to win over, defeat or neutralize those forces arrayed against its emancipation, growth or development. [1987:8]

According to this viewpoint, anthropologists can produce feminist ethnographies if they design their research questions according to what members of the oppressed groups they study want and need (Mascia-Lees, Sharpe, and Cohen 1989). Nancy Scheper-Hughes (1995) has suggested that *all* ethnographers move in the direction of a "militant" anthropology that is morally engaged and openly committed to aiding the people being studied in their political struggle against oppression.

It has also been argued that because women are themselves "other" to the Western male, they are in a position that allows them to be especially sensitive to the problems with traditional ways of knowing. As people who have themselves been objectified, women may be better able to recognize the limitations of a concept that objectifies other people. This claim is based on the assumption that a feminist anthropology can be based on identification with those studied, rather than on differences and distance from them (Behar 1997). But feminist and other twenty-first-century anthropologists have also questioned the assumption that any one dimension of identity—such as gender—gives the anthropologist special, intimate knowledge of the group they study.

"How Native Is a 'Native' Anthropologist?"

These issues have been addressed in a discussion of **native anthropologists**—also sometimes called "insider" or "indigenous" anthropologists—who study groups of which they are seen to be a part. As feminist anthropologist Kirin Narayan points out the double bind for "native" anthropologists is that, on the one hand, they are seen as being able to represent the authentic insider's perspective, while, on the other, they are not considered "real" anthropologists, since they do not have an "objective perspective." But, Narayan asks in the title of her widely read article, "How Native Is a 'Native' Anthropologist?" (1993). She points out that in a world of increasing interconnections among people, no one is part of just one group; anthropologists identify as part of many communities simultaneously, and today no one speaks from a position totally outside the world of anyone else.

Yet, native anthropologists are often perceived as insiders regardless of their multiple identifications and complex backgrounds (Narayan 1993:677). The fact that "native anthropologists are often distanced—by factors as varied as education, class or emigration—from the societies [they] are meant to represent," Narayan writes, tends to be underplayed and their inclusion in the group defined primarily by a shared ethnicity emphasized: "the darker element in our ancestry serves to define us" (1993:677). Feminist and other twenty-first-century anthropologists have stressed how anthropologists must be mindful of the multiple insider/outsider positions they occupy when doing their fieldwork (Perez 2007). Narayan urges an "enactment of hybridity" in the texts anthropologists produce: "writing that depicts authors as minimally bicultural in terms of belonging simultaneously to the world of engaged scholarship and the world of everyday life" (1993:672).

LGBT anthropologists have faced a particular challenge in terms of being "insiders," since it is often assumed that when it comes to doing fieldwork with sexually diverse groups, only "native" anthropologists, that is, persons with a nonnormative sexuality, can provide an authentic perspective. But LGBT anthropologists have challenged such unquestioned assumptions. LGBT anthropologists are caught in the same ethical situations as other anthropologists and must, themselves, ask: Who has the authority to speak for the LGBT communities we study?

Who Can Speak?

Just as anthropologists were first motivated by the people they studied to question the power relations embedded in field research, so many feminist ethnographers, white and privileged, have been encouraged to scrutinize their research efforts because of criticisms raised by some women of the Global South (Trinh 1989). These critics have tended to agree with Stacey's position rather than with Harding's, arguing against the possibility of equality in ethnographic investigations. They have viewed white feminist efforts to study and write about non-Western people as exploitative. Western writers, they claim, "speak for" the oppressed instead of allowing the oppressed to "speak for themselves."

Some white feminists who have replied to this criticism argue that their work actually gives voice to many people around the world who are otherwise silenced by oppression. In addition, there is a danger in not trying to give voice to others. The postcolonial writer Gayatri Spivak argues that for the Western writer, choosing "not to speak" may be just another alibi for ignoring oppression. She encourages Western researchers to learn to identify with the position of the "other," rather than simply saying, "O.K., sorry, we are just very good white people, therefore we do not speak for the blacks." She argues that this stance just allows "business to go on as usual" (Spivak 1990:121).

Whether ethnographers silence or enable the non-Western people about whom they write is part of the complicated debate that has no single "right" answer. The complexity of this situation does suggest, as did our discussion of veiling and FGC, that researchers committed to feminist goals must be ever-vigilant in their self-reflection about their own motivations for undertaking research and their research goals.

Conclusions

Feminist and other twenty-first-century anthropologists encourage researchers to question how the concepts and the political commitments that frame and motivate their research might not be beneficial to the people they study. The significance of self-reflexivity to feminist and other oppositional projects lies in the constant evaluation and reevaluation it calls for and in its recognition of how power relations continue to operate not merely in anthropological research and writing but, more importantly, also in the larger world. If this process helps each of us to be more aware of power differentials in our daily interactions with different people, feminist and other twenty-first-century anthropologists' commitment to fighting oppression becomes more realizable.

WORD PORTFOLIO

assimilate: to learn and adopt the customs of a dominant culture rather than one's own native culture.

clitoridectomy: the surgical procedure that involves the removal of a female's clitoris or the hood of her clitoris.

coalition work in the service of resistance: the coming together of people, organizations, or social movements based on common oppression rather than on supposed similarities, to fight inequalities.

cultural relativism: understanding and interpreting the beliefs and behaviors of another culture on its own terms.

cultural rights: the rights and freedoms to which cultures are entitled, enabling the group to preserve its own customs, language, and way of life.

ethnocentrism: using one's own societal values to judge those of another society.

ethnocide: any action that is intended to deprive a group of people of its culture, or integrity as a people.

engaged anthropology: anthropology committed not just to studying but also to overcoming political domination of the people anthropologists study.

female genital cutting: a range of operations in which the genitals of girls or women are surgically altered.

fieldwork: the research anthropologists undertake with the people they study, usually based on participating with and observing those people in their own society.

genocide: the attempt to destroy, or the destruction of, a national, ethnic, racial, or religious group of people.

hijab: the Muslim practice of dressing modestly usually associated with the wearing of a veil or head scarf.

human rights: the belief that all people have an equal entitlement to dignity that is "inalienable," that is, cannot be taken away.

indigenous peoples: nations or communities of people who are historically related to societies that existed prior to the invasion or colonization of their territories, and who consider themselves distinct from other groups now occupying those territories.

infanticide: the intentional killing of an infant usually through abandonment, exposure, or neglect.

moral relativism: understanding and interpreting the moral beliefs and values of another culture on its own terms.

native anthropologists: also called "insider" or "indigenous" anthropologists, they study groups of which they are seen to be a part.

objectification: the act of treating a person as a depersonalized object instead of as an individual.

participant-observation: living with, taking part in, and observing a society firsthand as the means for anthropologists to gain intimate knowledge of another culture.

postcolonial studies: an academic approach to understanding the structures of power that kept colonial rule in place, the colonial struggles for self-determination, and the lives of once-colonized people in the postcolonial moment after independence.

purdah: the practice of preventing men from seeing women to whom they are not related, either through physical segregation of women and men or by requiring women to cover and conceal their bodies from men.

women's rights abuses: when women are deprived of human dignity and other basic rights for no other reason than their gender

"writing culture critique": part of the self-critique of anthropology that focuses on how certain writing techniques and styles maintain power relationships between anthropologists and the people they study.

RECOMMENDED READING

Women's Rights. 2006. Human Rights Watch, http://hrw.org/women.

Human Rights Watch is an excellent resource for finding out more about human, cultural, and women's rights as well as children's, health, LGBT, and migrants/refugees rights.

Burning Women: A Global History of Widow-Sacrifice from Ancient Times to the Present, by Joerg Fisch. 2006. Kolkata, India: Seagull Books.

"Widow burning" or "sati" has long been practiced in India, but little attention has been paid to its occurrence elsewhere. This book provides not only an excellent understanding of sati as an Indian Hindu custom based both on strong spiritual beliefs and contemporary secular power struggles, but also a history of widow-burning across the world.

The Female Circumcision Controversy: An Anthropological Perspective, by Ellen Gruenbaum. 2001. Philadelphia: University of Pennsylvania Press.

If you are interested in finding out more about female genital cutting, take a look at this text, which provides the most comprehensive description and analysis of the debate over this custom by an anthropologist.

Reading National Geographic, by Catherine Lutz and Jane L. Collins. 1993. Chicago: University of Chicago Press.

For decades, *National Geographic Magazine* was a primary source for readers in North America interested in finding out more about peoples in other parts of the world. The authors show how the magazine acknowledged and even celebrated cultural difference, while simultaneously creating an image of non-Western people as primitive and backward and how this worked to produce a sense of the reader's culture as more advanced and superior.

Politics of Piety: The Islamic Revival and the Feminist Subject, by Saba Mahmood. 2005. Princeton, NJ: Princeton University Press.

This ethnography of the Mosque Movement in Egypt provides an excellent case study of the tension between Western liberal feminist ideas about Islam's oppression of women and those of Muslim women themselves who adopt practices such as veiling as a means of demonstrating their reverence of and devotion to God.

Fictions of Feminist Ethnography, by Kamala Visweswaran. 1994. Minneapolis: University of Minnesota Press.

If you want to find out more about feminist anthropologists' concern with the representation of non-Western people in traditional ethnography, this text is an important resource. The author addresses issues that a feminist anthropologist must confront when writing about other women's lives and she provides an experimental approach to writing feminist ethnography.

Naturalizing Gender and Difference

[D]on't squat down to play marbles—you are not a boy, you know; . . . this is how to make a good medicine for a cold; this is how to make a good medicine to throw away a child before it even becomes a child; . . . this is how to bully a man; this is how a man bullies you; this is how to love a man, and if this doesn't work there are other ways, and if they don't work don't feel too bad about giving up; . . . this is how to make ends meet; always squeeze bread to make sure it's fresh; but what if the baker won't let me feel the bread?; you mean to say that after all you are really going to be the kind of woman who the baker won't let near the bread?

—Jamaica Kincaid

4

Sex Differences
Nature and Nurture

In the global marketplace today, biotechnology is big business. Companies have mapped the human genome. They have identified all human genes in an effort not only to find cures for diseases but also to gain huge profits from the biotechnologies developed to treat them, such as pharmaceutical drugs or therapies using such techniques as gene-splicing.

Although many people applaud these efforts, such research is not without its detractors. Some bioethicists, for example, worry about the use of biotechnologies to create "designer babies," infants developed from fetuses that are genetically altered to have desirable traits ranging from enhanced physical prowess, such as lightning speed, to increased mental capabilities in intelligence. Among the concerns these ethicists raise is that only the socioeconomically privileged—be they individuals or nations—will be able to afford these new technologies, paying large sums to choose those characteristics that will allow their children to surpass others in the global race for privilege, power, prestige, and wealth.

Francis Fukuyama (2002) has argued that the development of biotechnologies should be openly debated and discussed, as well as governmentally controlled because of their potentially dire consequences. He claims these new technologies will enable societies to control the behavior of their people in new ways; will change human personality and identity; will disrupt existing social hierarchies and affect the rate of what Fukuyama sees as intellectual, material, and political progress; and will have significant consequences for global politics. Is Fukuyama being an alarmist, envisioning a twenty-first-century "brave new world" no more likely to materialize than Aldous Huxley's (1932/1998) twentieth-century dystopian vision? It is, of course, impossible for us to tell right now. But what we can say is that fear of Fukuyama's predictions may be irrelevant since his concerns are based on the assumption that there is a simple link between genes and behavior.

In this chapter, we will investigate assumptions like Fukuyama's. Particular attention is paid to those assumptions underlying the debate over whether human behaviors and traits are the result of biology or society. A brief history of Western ideas about gender and racial differences as being natural is presented first, followed by contemporary scientific claims for biological gender differences. Understanding science as a cultural activity allows you to be in a better position to assess the evidence for assertions about gender differences, whether you encounter such arguments in your textbooks or in the larger society.

The Nature/Nurture Debate

Fukuyama's assumptions about the biological basis of human behavior, however, are not uncommon

Global News

4.1: Intelligence Genes Prove Hard to Map

Despite widespread predictions that parents would use new genetic tools to select for smarter children, scientists haven't been able to identify genes that would tell whether a child is going to be highly intelligent. . . . Some genes that play a role in mental retardation have been isolated. . . . But researchers are finding the genes that influence overall intelligence to be more elusive and complex than had been expected a few years ago. [*Star Tribune* 2/18/02:A1]

ones. In the history of Western ideas, such assumptions have fuelled one side of what has come to be known as the **nature/nurture debate.** This debate is concerned with whether humans think or act in certain ways because of some inherent nature (they are "born" that way) or because of the social and physical environment in which they are reared and nurtured (they are "made" that way). A seemingly endless stream of articles on the topic that appear on a nearly daily basis in popular magazines, newspapers, academic journals, and on Web sites attests to the fact that this question continues to be a central preoccupation. One recent example in the popular press left no doubt that it would take up the issue of the nature/nurture controversy. The headline printed on the front page of the "Science Times" section of *The New York Times* on March 14, 2000, nearly screamed its concern with this issue; it asked, "Human Nature: Born or Made?" (Goode 2000).

Nature and Nurture in the History of Western Ideas

In the history of Western ideas, the nature/nurture debate has been framed and addressed by many individuals from a variety of backgrounds and with varying interests. Western philosophers, for example, have tended to ask whether human concepts exist in the mind prior to experience (nature) or are derived from experience (nurture). Today, in both the academy and the wider society, the focus is not only on

questioning the basis of human thought but also on how people behave. For example, we often hear debates about whether humans are basically aggressive, whether killing, for example, is a natural quality or a learned behavior. Some who deem killing as a natural part of "humanness" base their presumptions on religious beliefs.

In the Judeo-Christian story of Genesis, for example, Adam and Eve are expelled from the Garden of Eden when they disobey the word of God. Although made in the image of God, they are now sinners capable of evil actions. It is their son, Cain, who commits the first act of aggression in the Bible: he kills his brother Abel. As his decedents, all humans thus carry the "mark of Cain," the ability and perhaps desire to commit murder. Others who see aggression as natural claim biological causes—the need for evolving humans to be "killer apes" in order to survive.

Although religious explanations for such supposed innate brutish human propensities still exist, it is much more common to find biological explanations proffered by scholars and the popular press. Those scientists debating the question, "human nature: born or made?" in the *New York Times* article mentioned above are a case in point: they are interested in whether aggression may have developed through the process of natural selection. Those who suggest that it did arise this way seek to explain how aggressive behavior was adaptive in human evolution. The belief that human behaviors are caused by biological factors is often referred to as **biological determinism.**

The Problem with the Nature/Nurture Debate

There is no doubt that human behavior is the complex outcome of both biological and social factors. The problem with the "nature versus nurture" debate is that proponents on both sides often do not take this complexity into account. On the one hand, strict adherents to the nurture argument overlook evidence that at least some human behaviors have a biological substrate: for example, it is likely that some mental illnesses, such as schizophrenia, have an underlying genetic component. That does not mean, however, that individuals with a genetic predisposition to the disease will express symptoms. That is because elements of the social environment in which an individual lives interact with the propensity for a disease, altering its external manifestations in symptoms or behavior. Yet, many researchers on the nature side of the debate describe behavior in a language that suggests that the presence of a particular gene inevitably causes a behavior, even though we actually know little about the relationship of biological mechanisms, such as the gene, and behavioral expressions, such as schizophrenia in humans.

As biologist Marlene Zuk (2002) points out, we do not yet know how a gene, which produces proteins, creates a response in the nervous system generating a complex behavior. What we do know is that even if two individuals share a genetic makeup, such as identical twins do, the social environment interacts with these individuals' genetic makeup in different ways. For example, identical twins, especially as they get older, tend to look different, enabling people to tell them apart: their faces change, one may grow taller

The physical characteristics that make these identical twins hard to tell apart will change as they encounter different experiences throughout their lives.

Global News

4.2: A Tragic but Telling Legacy

You couldn't design a grimmer experiment. A Nazi blockade of the western Netherlands in September 1944 and an early winter triggered a famine. . . . The "Hunger Winter" had killed 20,000 by Liberation Day . . . scarring an entire population—including, scientists later found, generations yet unborn. . . . [Scientists] Zena Stein and Mervyn Susser . . . discovered that fetuses exposed to the famine early in gestation . . . had an increased chance of central-nervous-system defects like spina bifida. . . . Other scientists found that a fetus starved early in development during the famine had a high risk for adult obesity. . . . [F]etuses who received poor nutrition early in gestation were twice as likely to develop schizophrenia in adulthood. [*Newsweek* 9/27/99:53] than the other, and so on. This difference in physical characteristics is the result of environmental influences. If even physical characteristics are affected by environment, there is little doubt that behaviors are as well. Thus, when a behavior is considered genetic, it does not mean that the existence of a particular form of a gene in an individual always leads to a particular behavior (see Zuk 2002:10–14). It may, instead, mean only that the potential for the behavior exists. We are far from being able to make claims for the simple biological basis of any human behavior.

Human Nature vs. Woman's Nature

What is particularly interesting about the *New York Times* article, however, is not its focus on a biological explanation for a complex human behavior. As we will see in the next chapter, this focus is a common one. What is noteworthy in this article is an interesting slippage, one that exists in many discussions of human nature but that is not often remarked on: the so-called human behavior being addressed is one much more often attributable to one sex than the other. The phrase "human nature" in the article's title suggests that it will concentrate on something all humans share, but it does not. Instead, it focuses on the debate over a recently published book entitled, *A Natural History of Rape: Biological Bases of Sexual Coercion* (2001), in which authors Randy Thornhill and Craig Palmer propose an evolutionary explanation for why males rape females. Thus, the question in the headline is misleading. The article is not about human nature at all, but about male behavior. This focus accurately reflects the central concern of the nature/nurture debate since the late nineteenth century: it has been preoccupied less with human nature—what all humans share by virtue of being a member of the species, *Homo sapiens*—than with human differences, even when the terminology of the debate suggests otherwise.

Woman's Nature as Inferior

Arguments that focus on human differences have tended to claim that there is a distinct "woman's nature." By contrast, one rarely hears talk about "man's nature" when referring to males alone, although certain supposed male behaviors like aggressiveness are

Close-Up

4.1: Is Rape Genetic?

Although there is little scientific data supporting consistent gender differences in behavior, isn't it obvious that males are more violent than females? Official statistics of crime recorded in all countries in the world today underrepresent actual levels of crime; nonetheless, in every nation, men overwhelmingly commit more violent crimes than women. When women do commit crimes, they are often motivated by economic hardship or the need for self-defense; women are often imprisoned for charges resulting from protecting themselves or their children against abuse (Mikkelsen 2000:217).

Does this suggest that violence has a genetic basis? That such behaviors as assault and battery have been selected for because the males exhibiting them won out in a contest of the survival of the fittest? Some scientists have proposed explanations like these, but as with most such accounts, there is little sound evidence to support their claims. Take the recent explanation of

(continued)

rape proposed by Barry Thornhill and Craig Palmer (2001). They argue that men assault women to maximize their reproductive potential. In other words, they propose that male sexual violence occurs because sexually unsuccessful men rape women to impregnate them in order to perpetuate their genes. Unable to attract females and pass on their genes legitimately, they resort to rape as a means of making sure their genes will be represented in the next generation. The evidence? The behavior of male scorpion flies and some other animals who engage in what Thornhill and Palmer interpret as forceful sexual intercourse with females of the species. How do Thornhill and Palmer know that rape is taking place among such animals? They observe that male scorpion flies have so-called "'genital claspers' (a pair of clamplike structures, one on either side of the penis)" that are used when male scorpion flies fight with one another (Thornhill and Palmer 2001:63). Males also employ them during copulation to hold on to what Thornhill and Palmer claim is an "unwilling female." Even though these appendages have other purposes, Thornhill and Palmer insist that these body parts are specialized appendages for rape. They support their claim for the prevalence of rape in the animal kingdom by pointing out that such appendages can also be found in other insects such as sagebrush crickets and in one species of water spiders.

This reductionist argument contains several flaws: in addition to being based on a model of heterosexual sex, it assumes behaviors found in insects and other animals are the same as those observed in humans so that their biological deterministic claims are justifiable. But is a male scorpion fly that mates assertively really involved in the same behavior as the Pakistani men who gang raped a teenage woman as punishment for the behavior of her brother? He was accused of interacting with a woman from a tribe with a higher social standing. A Pakistani tribal jury determined the sentence (Agence France-Presse 2002).

Biological explanations of rape also ignore the fact that one-third of rape victims are either children or postmenopausal women who are incapable of reproducing (Rose and Rose 2000:3). They similarly fail to account for homosexual rape, which obviously cannot lead to impregnation. Moreover, men also rape their wives, women to whom they have sexual access. Suggesting that rapists are sexual "losers" trying to increase their genetic fitness obscures the reality of rape: single men rape, married men rape, young and old men rape; poor men rape and wealthy men rape. *But, in not all societies do men rape.* Are we to believe that this is because there are no "sexual losers" in such societies?

In her pioneering cross-cultural study, anthropologist Peggy Sanday (1981) analyzed the differences between what she calls "rape-free" and "rape-prone" societies. She discovered that in rape-free societies both men and women are involved in public decision making and are integrated relatively equally into everyday activities. In contrast, Sanday found rape-prone societies to be more violent in general, emphasizing male competition and strength; women in rape-prone societies are held in low esteem and are often not treated as equal to men. Her results indicate that societies with widespread male dominance, which undervalue women's contributions, encourage male sexual violence. Sanday concludes that rape is not biologically determined but instead is a product of cultural selection.

A great deal of other work over the last 35 years supports the notion that rape and a culture of male dominance are linked. For example, Susan Brownmiller's research on the history of rape in the United States, published in *Against Our Will: Men, Women and Rape* in 1975, demonstrated that rape could be understood only within the context of the oppressive sexual culture in the United States in which women were disenfranchised. Women continue to be undervalued in the United States today, despite advances in the last few decades. For example, as of

June 2007, 185 nations have ratified a women's bill of rights first proposed in 1979 at the United Nations' Convention on the Elimination of All Forms of Discrimination against Women (CEDAW). Nearly 30 years after the original convention, the United States is the only industrialized nation that has not adopted CEDAW. Other countries that have not signed include Iran and Sudan (Doriss 2007). If women are denied the right not to be discriminated against, how can they be equally valued?

In turn, the legitimization of male violence supports male dominance and women's subservience in many nations throughout the world. Such violence is often embedded in socioeconomic, religious, and political institutions. In Papua New Guinea, for example, the Parliament has failed to prohibit wife beating because its members believe such a law is contrary to "traditional family life" (Altman 2001:7). Many societies view marital rape as socially acceptable; until fairly recently in the United States a husband's forceful rape of his wife was not considered a crime. Indeed, according to the United Nations, women are more at risk for violence inside their own homes than outside of them (UNICEF 1999:77). Male violence is often implicitly legitimized: in many countries, for example, where women represent the honor of a family or group, reporting her rape may mean a woman's social or physical death. For example, in Pakistan, female rape victims are sentenced to stoning to death in accordance with the interpretation of Qur'an-based law, known as *hudood*, which does not distinguish between forced and consensual sex (Mydans 2002:A3). For women who are victims of sexual assault, sometimes silence has been the only way to survive. In such circumstances, women's behavior may be judged as passive, but it is no more of an innate behavior than male aggression.

Biological explanations may be faulty due to poor scientific reasoning and lack of supporting data, but they are also dangerous. What are the implications of claiming that innate biological drives cause men to act violently? If a society does not recognize rape as culturally based sexual violence but rather views it as a genetic imperative or a form of Darwinian selection, are we not in danger of perpetuating a culture of rape and violence in which females continue to be victimized?

References

Agence France-Presse. 2002. Council in Pakistan Orders Gang Rape. *New York Times* July 2: A12.

Altman, Dennis. 2001. *Global Sex.* Chicago: University of Chicago Press.

Brownmiller, Susan. 1975. *Against Our Will: Men, Women and Rape.* New York: Simon and Shuster.

Doriss, Tanya. 2007. Crib Sheet: The United Nations Convention on the Elimination of All Forms of Discrimination Against Women, http://www.campusprogress.org/tools/1768/crib-sheet-the-united-nations-convention-on-the-elimination-of-all-forms-of-discrimination-against-women (accessed August 3, 2008).

Mikkelsen, Lene, ed. 2000. *Women and Men in Europe and North America 2000.* New York: United Nations Economic Commission for Europe.

Mydans, Seth. 2002. In Pakistan, Rape Victims are the "Criminals." *New York Times* May 17:A3.

Rose, Hillary and Steven Rose, eds. 2000. *Alas, Poor Darwin: Arguments against Evolutionary Psychology.* New York: Harmony Books.

Sanday, Peggy Reeves. 1981. The Socio-Cultural Context of Rape: A Cross-Cultural Study. *Journal of Social Issues* 37 (4):5–27.

Thornhill, Randy, and Craig Palmer. 2001. *A Natural History of Rape: Biological Bases of Sexual Coercion.* Cambridge: MIT Press.

UNICEF. 1999. *Women in Transition.* The Monee Project, Regional Monitoring Report. No. 6. Florence, Italy: United Children's Fund.

often attributed to natural causes. What supposedly characterizes the nature of women has varied historically, although some supposed traits have had strong staying power. The ideas that women are by nature more nurturing, emotional, patient, and less intelligent than men, and that women are physically the weaker sex, have a long history. Such traits have been deemed necessary because of what has been assumed to be women's primary purpose in life: to reproduce. Men, by contrast, are assumed to have the characteristics that allow them to succeed in their complementary roles of "production" and protection of women: physical strength, intelligence, and courage.

The belief that women and men are fundamentally and necessarily different has not been value-free and, in fact, has included a belief in women's inherent inferiority to men. This idea found expression in many areas of society; philosophy, religion, literature, art, the social sciences, the natural sciences, and the media have all made claims about the inborn, inferior nature of women. For example, Christianity's biblical creation tale portrays Eve as a derivative of Adam, from whose rib she was formed, and as a temptress whose moral weakness and disobedience to God led Adam to sin, resulting in the human fall from grace and expulsion from paradise.

Eve, the temptress, offers the forbidden fruit to Adam.

Belief in Women's Natural Inferiority in Western Philosophy and Religion

A belief in women's inherent inferiority has even deeper roots: over 2000 years ago, the Greek philosopher, Aristotle, saw women as defective men; "woman," for him, was a deformity (see Aristotle 1943). He claimed women were naturally inferior to men in their capacity to think rationally due to a physiological deficiency: they were understood to have less "vital heat" than men, an unidentifiable substance supposedly linked to the ability to shape ideas. Aristotle's ideas were reintroduced into Western societies during the Middle Ages when Muslim, Christian, and Jewish theologians used them to rationalize the idea of female inferiority that underpinned these religious systems (Yanagisako and Delaney 1995:8).

Belief in Women's Natural Inferiority in Western Science

It was not philosophers and religious thinkers alone who developed ideas granting men an exalted status in relationship to women. Scientists, too, contributed to this endeavor. For example, in the 1800s some scientists downplayed women's importance in reproduction, arguing that men formed new human life: they believed that every sperm cell held a tiny human being that merely matured in a woman's womb. In other words, men were seen as creators of life, and women as little more than incubators (Friedman 2001). Such ideas seem ludicrous today, but physiological differences, according to most scientists at the time, explained women's secondary position to men in Western societies.

With the rise of the biological sciences in the nineteenth century, even more attention was turned to documenting the physiological differences between the sexes and to searching for explanations of women's supposed inferiority. It was widely argued during the time that since biological differences were natural, so, too, were the differences in the social position, opportunities, and prestige accorded men and women based on these biological differences. Since women's inferiority was "natural," it was asserted, it should not be changed.

The Nature of Race

The preoccupation with finding scientific explanations for gender differences during the nineteenth century often was paralleled and linked to a search for explanations of so-called "racial" differences among humans. The developing field of biology played a par-

Global News

4.3: Lithuania: Gynecology and Driving

The gender ombudswoman had ruled that a regulation requiring women to have a gynecological examination before obtaining a driver's license is discriminatory. An investigation was begun when a 24-year-old woman complained the rule was unfair because men were not required to have a urological examination as part of their medical check-ups before getting licenses. Some Lithuanian medical officials argued that the requirement for women . . . should be kept, saying some gynecological diseases can cause sudden pains and even temporary loss of consciousness. [Agence France-Presse 1/11/02, Late Edition-Final, Section A, p. 6]

ticularly central role in these endeavors, as it did in the search for inherent gender differences. Many prominent biologists searched for anatomical, physiological, and evolutionary factors to explain the supposed natural basis of racial differences, making race a category of focused analytical attention.

Early Meanings of Race in Western Thinking

Prior to the nineteenth century in Europe, the word race had expressed a vague sense of difference among groups and was often conflated with other concepts such as "peoples" and "nations"; differences among races were even seen as nonintrinsic and reversible (Malik 1996:80). The shift from a focus on human *unity* to one on human *difference* and from understanding differences as *changeable* (due to nurture) to seeing them as *fixed* (due to nature) has been chronicled by Cynthia Russett:

> It had been characteristic of social theory in the late eighteenth century to stress the commonalities shared by all human beings. Humanity was one, in essence, however varied its particular manifestations might be. Eighteenth-century theorists did not deny the existence among races and national groups; they did not even deny that some groups were better, or more advanced, than others. But in the main, they did reject the notion that such differences were inborn or hereditary, and hence permanent. . . . This congeries of ideas gradually gave way in

the nineteenth century to a stress on differentiation and hierarchy. Environmentalism lost favor; categories were hardened and made permanent. . . . [This] shift . . . fractured the assumption of human unity; thereby encouraging invidious comparisons among groups; because it fostered typology at the expense of individual particularity; and because the new stress on measurable dimensions gave priority to just those physical attributes least amenable to change. [1989:6–7]

Race became understood as a fixed biological category, and people were classified into discrete groups based on a few observable physical traits such as skin color and eye shape. But as we saw in chapter 1, race has no biological validity, although it certainly has significant social meaning.

Race and Biological Inferiority in Western Thinking

Ethnocentric assumptions about race have traditionally equated the dark-skinned people of the world with animalistic "savages," believed to be incapable of higher thinking, of controlling their behavior, and of producing civilized societies. Such constructions justified slavery in the United States and, as we will see in the next chapter, the colonial subjugation by European nations of non-Western peoples throughout the world. Ethnocentric assumptions about race have not disappeared today and are evidenced on many fronts in North American society. In her ethnography, *Bad Boys: Public Schools in the Making of Black Masculinity* (2000), Ann Arnett Ferguson analyzes the impact of such pernicious stereotypes on young black male students in U.S. elementary schools. In the selection from her book reprinted here, she shows how some teach-ers, drawing on widespread and intersecting cultural images of childhood and race, view their young black male students as *inherently* bad.

Differences among social classes within European societies were also explained in terms of race during the nineteenth century: like the non-Western peoples of the world, individuals from the lower classes within

Ethnography in Focus

Bad Boys: Public Schools in the Making of Black Masculinity
by Ann Arnett Ferguson

The behavior of African American boys in school is perceived by adults at Rosa Parks School through a filter of overlapping representations of three socially invented categories of "differ-ence": age, gender, and race. These are grounded in the commonsense, taken-for-granted notion that existing social divisions reflect biological and natural dispositional differences among humans: so children are essentially different from adults, males from females, blacks from whites. At the intersection of this complex of subject positions are African American boys who are doubly displaced: as black children, they are not seen as childlike but adultified; as black males, they are denied the masculine dispensation constituting white males as being "naturally naughty" and are discerned as willfully bad. Let us look more closely at this displacement.

The dominant cultural representation of childhood is as closer to nature, as less social, less human. Childhood is assumed to be a stage of development; culture, morality, sociability is written on children in an unfolding process by adults (who are seen as fully "developed," made by culture not nature) in institutions like family and school. On the one hand, children are assumed to be dissembling, devious, because they are egocentric. On the other hand, there is an attribution of innocence in their wrongdoing. In both cases, this is understood to be a tem-porary condition, a stage prior to maturity. [pp. 80–81]

***

Historically, the existence of African American children has been constituted differently. . . . This difference has been projected in an ensemble of images of black youth as not childlike. In the early decades of this century, representations of black children as pickaninnies depicted them as verminlike, voracious, dirty, grinning, animal-like savages. [pp. 81–82]

***

Today's representation of black children still bears traces of these earlier depictions. The media demonization of young black boys who are charged with committing serious crimes is one example. In these cases there is rarely the collective soul-searching for answers to the question of how "kids like this" could have committed these acts that occurs when white kids are involved. Rather, the answer to the question seems to be inherent in the disposition of the kids themselves. [p. 82]

***

As black children's behavior is refracted through the lens of these . . . cultural images, it is "adultified." By this I mean their transgressions are made to take on a sinister, intentional, fully conscious tone that is stripped of any element of childish naïveté. . . . Adultification is visible in the way African American elementary school pupils are talked about by school adults. [p. 83]

***

There is a second displacement from the norm in the representation of black males. The hegemonic, cultural image of the essential "nature" of males is that they are different from females in the meaning of their acts. Boys will be boys: they are mischievous, they get into trouble, they can stand up for themselves. This vision of masculinity is rooted in the notion of an essential sex difference based on biology, hormones, uncontrollable urges, true personalities. . . . As a result, rule-breaking on the part of boys is looked at as something-they-can't-help, a natural expression of masculinity in the civilizing process. [p. 85]

***

African American boys are not accorded the masculine dispensation of being "naturally" naughty. Instead the school reads their expression and display of masculine naughtiness as a sign of an inherent vicious, insubordinate nature that as a threat to order must be controlled. Consequently, school adults view any display of masculine mettle on the part of these boys through body language or verbal rejoinders as a sign of insubordination. In confrontation with adults, what is required from them is a performance of absolute docility that goes against the grain of masculinity. . . . According to the vice principal, "these children have to learn not to talk back. They must know that if the adult says they're wrong, then they're wrong. They must not resist, must go along with it, and take their punishment," he says. [pp. 86–87].

From: Ann Arnett Ferguson, *Bad Boys: Public Schools in the Making of Black Masculinity*, 2000, University of Michigan Press. Reprinted by permission of University of Michigan Press.

European society were deemed an "inferior race" of people. To make this point, author Kenan Malik quotes Philippe Buchez who, in an address in 1857 to the Medico-Psychological Society of Paris, asked his French colleagues to consider

a population like ours, placed in the most favourable circumstances; possessed of a powerful civilization; amongst the highest ranking nations in science, the arts and industry. Our task now, I maintain, is to find out how it can happen that within a population such as ours, races may form—not merely one but several races—so miserable, inferior and bastardised that they may be classed below the most inferior savage races. [quoted in Malik 1996:82]

The shift to scientific explanations of difference occurred at the time that science was increasingly gaining prestige, partly because of its link to the great technological achievements of the nineteenth century.

During this time, science was granted more and more authority to pronounce the "truth," not only about the physical world, but about the social world as well. Scientific ideas about the supposed superiority of white upper-class men were used to explain, justify, and rationalize a hierarchical social order in which (some) white men within Western societies had differential access to power and resources in comparison to white women and to women and men of color within those societies. They also had increasing control through colonial expansion over non-Western peoples, who were deemed naturally inferior as well.

Naturalizing Power

Because explanations that assert natural causes for the differences between groups of people have so often served to justify unequal treatment of the group deemed naturally inferior, feminists and most anthropologists have been wary of them. They have investigated and revealed how arguments that assert a natural basis for the differences in behavior, motivation, and aptitude among people have operated historically to naturalize power. **Naturalizing power** entails making the unequal distribution of power, privileges, and resources among social groups appear as the natural and inevitable outcome of supposed inherent differences.

Because science has so often been used in the service of the subordination of white women and of men and women of color, revealing its biases has been an important feminist goal in the last century. As biologist Ann Fausto-Sterling puts it: "our debates about the body's biology are always simultaneously moral, ethical, and political debates about social and political equality and the possibilities for change" (2000a:255). The stakes are high in debates over the causes of gender and racial difference, because ideas about what is natural can act to make power differentials appear justifiable.

Questioning Traditional Scientific Assumptions

Despite easy and widespread claims for distinctions between men and women, clear substantiating evidence of universal and innate differences is difficult to come by. Just as race has been shown to have no biological validity, so, too, are the existence of universal biological differences between men and women highly questionable. Even finding physiological and anatomical traits that differentiate all males from all females is more complicated than is often acknowledged. Some individuals have anomalous chromosomal makeup and anatomical sex organs, and consequently defy traditional classification as male or female. Such people are said to be **intersexed.**

Differences in the behavior, aptitude, desires, and motivation of women and men have also been difficult to substantiate, and many studies that have claimed such differences have been revealed as faulty. No clear, unambiguous evidence for a biological mechanism or entity determining gender differences has been identified. When differences are found, it is just as likely that they are the result of social and cultural influences as of biological causes or that they are some combination of biological and environmental factors that is difficult to discern.

Understanding the overblown role biological arguments have played historically prompted feminists to question the belief in a fundamental and inferior nature of white women, and of men and women of color and to study science itself as an activity affected by cultural assumptions. The following sections contain a summary of the state of the biological research on gender differences to date and examples of how cultural assumptions have affected scientific investigations of biological gender differences.

The Data Are Inconsistent

Even though just about every personality trait and behavior imaginable has been studied in the hopes of revealing gender differences and their causes, almost no trait or behavior has been *consistently* shown to be differentiated along gender lines. For example, studies conducted in the United States are unable to substantiate that males and females differ significantly in terms of any of the following traits: intellectual aptitude, memory, cognitive styles, creativity, temperament, achievement motivation, verbal skills, quantitative ability, assertiveness, submissiveness, vanity, or the capacity for empathy, nurturance, altruism, and moral fortitude (see Basow 1992).

The preponderance of research on gender differences in behavior and traits, whether in anthropology, sociology, or psychology, does not provide substantiation for the existence of most *presumed* differences. Many times, a particular study may show a gender difference, but when studies of gender differences are analyzed as a group, they show no constant pattern of difference that holds across age, culture, ethnicity, and class.

Context Needs to Be Considered

Research also suggests that supposed innate gender differences in behavior are context dependent. That is, what people say and what they do differ considerably depending on the circumstance in which individuals find themselves. Developmental psychologist Eleanor Maccoby (1998) has shown that gender differences in children cannot be accounted for by personality traits but rather by the gender composition of a group in which the child interacts. She demonstrates, for example, that girls are not passive in all situations, although they may act passively when boys are around. This research suggests why studies that at-

Close-Up

4.2: What Makes Someone Male or Female?

Sex differences are defined as those physical traits that differentiate females and males. That such traits exist seems so self-evident that it might surprise you to find out that there is no one set of universal, biological sex differences that differentiate all females from all males. And yet gender differences are often presumed to arise from such sex differences.

For centuries, the difference between women's and men's genital organs was seen as an obvious way to distinguish a woman from a man and, certainly, in most cases this is so. But we know today that a number of people throughout the world have "ambiguous" genitals, which look neither distinctly male nor female. Such features include larger-than-typical clitorises, absent vaginas, smaller-than-typical penises, and irregularly shaped scrota and labia (see Kessler 1998). Some individuals, such as so-called "true hermaphrodites," are born with both ovaries and testes, making any clear designation of their sex, let alone their gender, on the basis of anatomical characteristics alone impossible.

The modern biological definition of men and women has shifted recently from one based on external genitalia to one focused on chromosomes: an individual with two X chromosomes is designated a female, an individual with one X and one Y chromosome, a male. Here again there are a number of anomalies that make the distinction between males and females based on this characteristic problematic. For example, some "genetic males" with an XY chromosomal complement have a mutation of the Y chromosome resulting in the lack of male genitalia. These individuals look typically female including having fully developed breasts at puberty. Other people have such chromosomal combinations as XO, XXY, XXX, and XYY, making their clear assignment into the category "male" or "female" difficult. It has been estimated that approximately 1.7 percent of all births in the United States today are intersexed, a rate that would result in a city of 300,000 having 5,100 of these individuals in its population, not an insubstantial number (Fausto-Sterling 2000:53–54).

Intersexed individuals may even undergo "clarifying" surgery to bring their external appearance in line with social expectations about masculinity and femininity. Intersexed individuals and people with ambiguous genital organs are assigned to one sex or another by physicians and parents based on cultural assumptions about gender. This process of labeling reveals that cultural interpretations, not some unambiguous biological definition, are at work in the designation of gender categories. Recently, in the United States, an "intersex movement" has emerged, composed of individuals who protest clarifying surgery claiming that it is a form of genital mutilation that ruins future sexual pleasure (Lorber 2001:228).

References

Fausto-Sterling, Anne. 2000. Sexing the Body: Gender Politics and the Construction of Sexuality. New York: Basic Books.

Kessler, Suzanne. 1998. Lessons from the Intersexed. Piscataway, NJ: Rutgers University Press.

Lorber, Judith. 2001. Gender Inequality: Feminist Theories and Politics, 2nd ed. Los Angeles: Roxbury.

tempt to measure sex differences in terms of individual traits or abilities are often quickly refuted: a change in experimental conditions produces changes in behavior.

Variables Need Better Operationalization

Many studies of gender differences also suffer from problematic assumptions and conceptualizations that render the broad conclusions derived from them questionable. It has not been unusual for studies of aggression to conceptualize this behavior in gendered-biased ways. Studies of aggression have, for instance, often looked for evidence of it in terms of overt, physical behavior. Given this understanding, it makes sense to observe the number of times research participants yell, hit, push, or use physical intimidation toward another. Studies that operationalize aggression in this way have found that boys are more aggressive than females. But are they? More recent work has begun to reveal that girls' aggression may take a different form than that of boys' aggression. For example, boys may show more physical aggression than girls, but girls may be more psychologically aggressive than boys. When aggression is defined broadly as "harm to others," the difference between female and males tends to disappear.

In the wake of the shootings in 1999 at Columbine High School in Colorado, and other rampage killings across the country and world, researchers have begun to study the relationship of bullying to aggression and violence. In the process, they discovered that girls do indeed bully, but in much less observable ways than boys. Although boys might openly tease, push, or taunt others, girls tend to use their interpersonal relationships to hurt another child. Girls in interaction with other girls, for example, have been shown to use a quiet, but effective form of ostracism and gossip to exclude and isolate some girls from the group. Victims of such treatment have reported the devastating consequences of such aggressiveness. Many previous studies of gender differences in aggression had not accounted for these differences in styles of aggression, thereby underestimating its occurrence in females.

It should be noted that evidence of female aggression in best-selling books such as *Queen Bees & Wannabes,* which advises mothers on how to help their daughters "survive cliques, gossip, boyfriends, and other realities of adolescence" (Wiseman 2002) and *Odd Girl Out* (Simmons 2002) focused on "the hidden culture of aggression in girls" is itself being characterized as unreliable and as failing to consider the behavior of girls who do not conform to this pattern. Soon after these two books were published, for example, the headline on a *Newsweek* cover read "In Defense of Teen Girls—They're Not All 'Mean Girls' and 'Ophelias.'" Inside, Susannah Meadows's story profiled not "alpha" girls—young women who use cutthroat tactics to remain popular—or "beta" girls—those who hurt others in their quest to become part of a popular clique—but "gamma" girls: resilient girls "who may not be 'popular,' but aren't losers either" and who do not use harmful tactics to gain popularity (2002:46–47). It is clear that much more extensive research is needed before conclusions are drawn about the extent and basis of aggression, whether in males or females.

Direct Evidence Is Lacking

Not only is there little reliable evidence that gender differences consistently exist across time and space, but there is also no clear evidence for the biological basis of gender differences in behavior, aptitude, and disposition. Although claims about inherent differences among groups continue to find their way into scientific journals, textbooks, and the popular media, there is no unequivocal data today that demonstrate that any complex human behavior—gendered, racial, or otherwise—is unquestionably biologically determined, whether by hormones, genes, or differences in brain structure and function.

As discussed earlier, although human behavior has both a biological and a social basis, the relative influence of these two factors in affecting behavior is extremely difficult to discern, despite new sophisticated technologies for isolating genes or for observing brain activity. When scientists make claims for the biological basis of human behavior, then, they are putting forth hypotheses and theories that are open to question, not asserting proven truths.

Nonetheless, it is not uncommon for people to believe that biology and, increasingly, that genes, in particular, hold the key to understanding human behavior. Indeed, there is so much faith in genes today that Dorothy Nelkin and M. Susan Lindee (1995) suggest that the gene is the new cultural icon of North American society. References to DNA and genes now dominate popular culture. "Gene talk," Nelkin and Lindee demonstrate, "has entered the vernacular as a subject for drama, a source of humor, and an explanation of human behavior" (1995:1–2). As they point out, in supermarket tabloids and soap operas, in television situation comedies, and in talk shows, genes appear to explain everything, including obesity, criminality, shyness, directional ability, intelligence, political leanings, and even preferred styles of dress. Nelkin and Lindee suggest that DNA and the gene function today in many respects as the secular equivalent of the Christian soul; they are seen as independent and immortal, as fundamental to identity, to the moral order, and even to human fate (1995:2). They point out that geneticists refer to the genome, the totality of human genetic material, as the Bible, the Holy Grail, and the Book of Man (Nelkin and Lindee 1995:8).

But, again, attempts to measure the relative influence of genes versus culture on human behavior, and to substantiate the genetic basis of a complex behavior, are highly problematic. Quoting the evolutionary biologist, Stephen J. Gould, Nelkin and Lindee write that

> genes may influence many aspects of human behavior, but we cannot say that such behavior is caused by genes in any direct way. We cannot even claim that a given behavior is, say, 40% genetic and 60% environmental. . . . Genes and environment interact in a non-additive way. [Gould quoted in Nelkin and Lindee 1995:10]

Indirect Evidence Is Weak

Genes are not the only data on which scientists have depended to make their claims about the biological basis of gender differences. Many instead have turned to indirect evidence, arguing, for example, that if a gender difference occurs in newborn babies, exists in all societies, or can be found in both humans and nonhuman animals, it must have a biological basis. But these conclusions are questionable. For example, some studies in the United States have revealed that baby girls tend to smile more than baby boys. But this observation does not necessarily lead to the conclusion that this difference is caused by a biological mechanism, as some have suggested. The parents of newborns have been shown to respond differently to their male and female infants from the earliest moments after their birth; thus, what researchers may be observing are different responses elicited by those differential parental behaviors. Studies of infants in other societies support this possibility. Research on differences between male and female babies in Britain, for instance, shows less difference between infant girls and boys than do studies in the United States, suggesting that different cultural assumptions about gender in Britain and the United States may indeed be operating

on parents who treat their children differently because of them.

Researchers have also suggested that if a gender difference can be shown to exist in all societies, then it must have a biological basis. Even if a behavior is universal, however, we need not conclude that it is due to innate causes. It may instead be a social and learned response or solution to a circumstance or problem all humans share. Some form of marriage, for example, exists in all societies, but few would argue that there is a physiological factor that causes humans to marry, although some sociobiologists, as we will see in the next chapter, have done so. What perhaps is more to the point is that no gender difference in behavior has been shown to exist in all societies, although difference in aggressiveness between males and females is the one trait most consistently found. As we have seen, however, this disparity may reveal more about how aggression has been defined and measured than about a fundamental gender difference.

Evidence from nonhuman animals is also sometimes used to suggest the existence of an innate trait or behavior. The assumption here is that if a gender difference appears in some species of nonhuman animals as well as in humans, they must share this characteristic because of a shared biology. Because nonhuman primates, especially monkeys and apes, are more closely biologically and evolutionarily related to humans than are other animals, they are most frequently studied for what their behavior might reveal about the biological basis of gender. But, here again, assumptions about the cause of a shared cross-species behavior can be weak. Just because a behavior exists in both humans and, let's say, chimpanzees, does not mean it has a biological basis: both species may have learned the behavior. But the assumption that such a shared behavior must be biologically based is not surprising since there is a tendency to underestimate the degree to which many animals *learn* to adapt and survive.

Science as a Cultural Activity

Given the shaky nature of the evidence on biologically based gender differences, why do so many people believe that there are fundamental differences in the behavior, personality, aptitude, and motivation of men and women? Indeed, why, as one popular U.S. news commentator has put it, has talk about gender difference become a popular American sport?

As we have seen, the belief in natural differences between men and women has deep historical roots going back as far as the Greeks whose ideas exerted considerable influence on Western thinking. Most of the major world religions similarly contend that men and women are naturally and fundamentally different. Western culture is thus infused with such ideas. These ideas have been shown repeatedly to influence scientists, who like all human beings cannot escape the cultural milieu of which they are a part. Although we are often taught that science is the unbiased, objective pursuit of truth, studies of science have repeatedly shown how cultural ideas affect scientific work, especially work in the biological sciences related to questions concerning humans. This bias begins with the very questions deemed worthy of study and of funding.

For example, researchers almost always focus on questions related to differences between men and women, a circumstance that often reflects social and political agendas. This interest in difference is so deeply embedded in Western society that suggesting that the study of gender differences might be misguided tends to strike most people as absurd. But, why? Today, most scientists believe it is wrong-headed to look for biological explanations of many other kinds of difference. And yet it was not that long ago that learned cultural differences between Jews and non-Jews, for example, were attributed to biological causes by leading scientists of the day. This assumption found its most hideous expression in the notion in Nazi Germany that Jews were so different from non-Jews that they were, as the Nazis phrased it, "life unworthy of life" and therefore in need of extermination. Today, such ideas about difference rightfully strike most people as ludicrous. Might this not be true for ideas about gender as well?

Alison Wylie has pointed out that we need not look to extreme examples of bias such as those found in Nazi science in order to make the case that cultural context affects the practice of science: "it is by now well established," she points out, "that the gendered standpoint of practitioners has had a profound impact on the content of the social sciences and many life sciences" (1997:45). Indeed, cultural assumptions have been shown to affect scientific investigations not only at the level of the question asked, but at every stage of the research process as well. Emily Martin has shown how the scientific language in both popular and scientific accounts of reproduction use gendered stereotypes. For example, sperm are almost always described as active; they "attack, "bind," "penetrate" and enter the egg (1991:493); they actively deliver their genes to, and activate the development of, the egg (1991:489). By contrast the egg is depicted as passive; it does not move on its own but is "transported" or "drifts" along the fallopian tubes (1991:493). Such language creates imagery that reinforces and perpetuates deeply embedded stereotypes of men and women in the United States.

The history of brain research on gender and racial differences, and of hormonal studies of gender differences, also clearly reveals stereotypical assumptions and demonstrates the often subtle ways researchers are influenced by preexisting gender assumptions.

Cultural Biases in Brain Research

The claim that men and women have different brains, and therefore, necessarily think differently, has been a long-standing one in Western society. Such supposed natural brain differences have been used historically to rationalize and further systems of oppression, and to determine social policy. For example, toward the end of the nineteenth century it was erroneously concluded that white men were naturally superior to women in intelligence because of the larger size of their brains. This assumption was used to justify women's exclusion from higher education and political participation. Skull measurements were also taken of African Americans and Native Americans, two other groups assumed to have intelligence levels inferior to those of white men, and a similar conclusion was reached: their smaller brain size was taken as evidence of their lower intelligence.

We know now, however, that the size differential noted by these scientists was based on biased measurement techniques affected by preexisting cultural assumptions about the supposed inferior intelligence of white women and of men and women of color. Craniometrists consistently underestimated the cranial capacity of these groups by knowing ahead of time whether a skull belonged to someone other than a white male and calculated the weights of skulls differently based on this knowledge. Even if such measurements had been correct, they would have no significance today, since it has been repeatedly shown that variation in human brain size is not related to intelligence.

Today, it is not brain size but differences in brain structure and in the way men and women use their brains, which supposedly explain gender differences in thinking and behavior, and questions of measurement are still an issue. Men and women have been studied to discern whether they use the left or right hemisphere of the brain for certain functions. The focus of such studies has been on differences in the *corpus callosum*, the band of white matter connecting the left and right lobes of the brain, which supposedly produce gendered styles of thinking. In the wake of one study conducted in 1982 that reported a difference in size in one area of this structure in 14 individuals—nine men and five women—a virtual industry of brain lateralization research has arisen (Fausto-Sterling 2000a:118).

But as molecular biologist Anne Fausto-Sterling has detailed in her book, *Sexing the Body* (2000), this research is not as straightforward as we might suppose. The corpus callosum is so complex and irregularly shaped that it is impossible to define it with certainty. "The *corpus callosum* is a structure that is difficult to separate from the rest of the brain, and so complex in its irregular three dimensions *as to be unmeasurable*" (Fausto-Sterling 2000a:120–121, final emphasis added). This has not stopped scientists from trying, although the results of this research indicate the intractability of the corpus callosum as an object of study: Fausto-Sterling's review of 34 scientific papers written between 1982 and 1997 found that there is no consensus on sex differences in the corpus callosum (2000a:130–135).

Given the highly inconclusive results of corpus callosum research, conclusions about how and why men and women think differently may be as faulty today as those of the craniologists who measured people's skulls to determine intelligence a century ago. Nonetheless, scientists and popular culture alike have made broad claims for the significance of brain function differences in males and females. In 1992 alone, as Fausto-Sterling has documented, *Newsweek, Time, Elle*, the *Boston Globe*, and the *New York Times* each featured stories about gender differences in the brain, claiming that they were responsible for everything from women's supposed intuition and difficulties with physics to women's stronger verbal skills and more holistic way of thinking, differences that have not been clearly substantiated (2000a:116–117).

Nor has the search for brain differences today concentrated on questions of gender alone. Just as craniometrists in the nineteenth and early twentieth centuries sought explanations for racial differences in varying brain size, so contemporary thinkers have searched for them in brain functioning; it is not unusual to hear now, for example, that Native Americans

or Asians think more holistically than Europeans (Fausto-Sterling 2000a:119).

Cultural Biases in Hormone Research

The view that differences in men's and women's behavior can be explained in terms of the presence of differing sex hormones in their bodies is also a widely accepted assumption, one that is often difficult to dislodge. It has, for example, become commonplace to blame complex human behaviors such as male aggression on the supposed male hormone testosterone or women's discontents on fluctuating levels of the supposed female hormone, estrogen. In the past, some critics of women's participation in politics argued that female hormonal fluctuations might cause erratic thinking and behavior, which would preclude responsible decision making. During the cold war, it was not unusual to hear that women could never be entrusted with the presidency of the United States since such supposedly biologically based erratic thinking might lead to nuclear disaster. How hormones are invoked to explain behavior is also gendered:

> Although male hormones are used to account for general masculine proclivities (such as aggression) only rarely is any individual man's behaviour explained in these terms. When a man loses his temper we seldom hear anyone say "It's just an excess of androgen," yet how often women's anger is explained in terms of the "time of the month." [Jackson et al. 1993:364]

But do hormones provide the key to the differences between men and women? Fausto-Sterling's work has shown that research on hormones has been no less burdened with unproven assumptions and misinterpretations than brain research discussed above: the choices endocrinologists (scientists who study hormones) have made about what to name a particular hormone, how to measure it, and how to interpret its effects have been so greatly influenced by cultural ideas about gender that it renders the very assumption that sex hormones *exist* questionable (see Fausto-Sterling 2000a:170–194).

As Fausto-Sterling points out, the primary role of hormones in the body of both men and women is not to control behavior but instead to work at the cellular level to govern cell growth, cell differentiation, cell physiology, and cell death. Hormones may be present in different quantities in males and females, and might affect the same tissues differently, but all hormones operate throughout the bodies of both men and women (Fausto-Sterling 2000a:179). There is, in other words, no hormone specific to either men or women.

Despite this, scientists have labeled some of these chemical secretions "male" hormones (*androgen,* meaning "to create a man") and others, "female" hormones (*estrogen,* meaning "to create estrus," which itself means "crazy," "wild," or "insane"), thus gendering them and infusing them with cultural assumptions about men and women (see Fausto-Sterling 2000a:188). The results of research on the activities of these substances in the bodies of men and women have been similarly affected by preexisting gendered assumptions, leading some biologists to call for abandoning the organizing metaphor of the sex hormone in endocrinology studies altogether.

Does this problematic history of endocrinology mean that there are no hormonal differences between men and women? Not at all; but it does suggest that claims presently made for such differences have been so clouded by faulty research assumptions that they are premature at best, dangerous at worst.

This history of brain and hormonal research makes clear how scientific work is affected by widespread cultural assumptions about difference. These studies, in turn, often reinforce deep-seated and widespread popular beliefs about gender differences. This feedback mechanism is further fuelled by the tendency of the popular media to report studies that suggest the existence of biological differences more often than reporting studies that do not. This differential reporting lends credence to the popular belief that biology holds the key to understanding men and women. Many people are eager to accept such ideas not only because they are familiar and comfortable but also because of their faith in scientific authority. When science offers simple answers to complex questions about human social behavior, it allows people a belief in certainties that can make their life in a complex world seem easier.

Conclusions

Studies of gender research often reveal that scientific questions, findings, and conclusions reflect the social order of which they are a part as much as, and maybe even more than, some hard, observable reality. Today, perhaps the most that can be said is that despite large amounts of time and huge sums of money spent in the pursuit of identifying the kind, extent, and causes of differences between women and men, we continue to be fairly ignorant.

In the absence of knowing for sure, does it matter how you think about sex, gender, and race difference? I argue that it does. I suggest that erring in one direction is more serious than erring in another. For example, we might assume that a gender difference is socially produced and then find out sometime down the road that it is innate. What would we have lost in making the wrong assumption? Perhaps money spent to improve the opportunity of those disadvantaged by their difference. But that is only if we assume biological differences are unchangeable, an idea that is itself unfounded, as was pointed out earlier.

If, however, we wrongly assume that a social difference has a biological cause, we might make a mistake that has devastating consequences. At least, we know that this has repeatedly been the case in the history of the Western world: white women, men and women of color, and people of the working classes, as we have seen, have all too often been seen as innately, naturally inferior, and their unequal treatment has been justified on this very basis. Knowing this history, it is hard to sit back and accept that in the absence of knowing the truth about difference, it matters little what we think. Indeed, it may matter quite a bit.

If new advances in biological research do, however, reveal a biological basis to some human behaviors, then another set of ethical and political questions arises, such as the ones voiced by the bioethicists discussed at the beginning of this chapter. How, for example, will we protect against the use of biotechnologies in ways that will constrain human choices and reduce human creativity? How will we ensure that these techniques are not used to create even bigger differences in the world between the "haves" and the "have-nots"? These are the kinds of questions we can only hope we will not have to confront in the globalizing world of the twenty-first century. But given the recent and rapid growth of biotechnology industries, that seems unlikely.

WORD PORTFOLIO

biological determinism: the belief that human behaviors are caused by biological factors.

intersexed: individuals who, because of an anomalous chromosomal makeup and anatomical sex organs, make their clear assignment into the category "male" or "female" difficult.

naturalizing power: making the unequal distribution of power, privileges, and resources among social groups appear as natural and inevitable by attributing differences to innate factors.

nature/nurture debate: a controversy over whether humans think or act in certain ways because of some inherent nature or because of the environment in which they are reared and nurtured.

RECOMMENDED READING

Rape Warfare: The Hidden Genocide in Bosnia-Herzegovina and Croatia, by Beverly Allen. 1996. Minneapolis: University of Minnesota Press.

This is one of many books that analyze rape, not as a genetically programmed behavior, but as a complex social practice that sustains power hierarchies. The author analyzes the use of rape as a strategy of war, focusing specifically on the military policy of rape for the purpose of genocide that existed in Bosnia-Herzegovina and Croatia in the 1990s.

Sexing the Body: Gender Politics and the Construction of Sexuality, by Anne Fausto-Sterling. 2000. New York: Basic Books.

As you might have been able to tell from this chapter, this book is one of the most important resources available for understanding the cultural bases and biases of contemporary scientific thought about gender. Even though I have relied heavily on it in this chapter, it has much more information that you might find interesting and it develops a theory of sexuality that I have not discussed.

The DNA Mystique: The Gene as a Cultural Icon, by Dorothy Nelkin and M. Susan Lindee. 1995. New York: W. H. Freeman.

This book provides a fascinating analysis of how the "gene" has become the "star" of both popular culture and scientific discourse in contemporary theories of biological determinism in North American culture. If you want to learn more about how cultural popular images affect public perception about gender, sexuality, and eugenics and how they influence scientific research, you will want to take a look at this book.

Intersex and Identity: The Contested Self, by Sharon E. Preves. 2003. Piscataway, NJ: Rutgers University Press.

Based on personal interviews, this book chronicles the impact on anatomically ambiguous individuals of medical procedures designed to give them a clear gender assignment, showing how being intersexed is a social, not a medical, "problem." It focuses on the impact of medical imposition of gender assignment on people's identity and the effect identity-based social movements, such as the Gay Pride Movement, have had on the lives and experiences of intersexed people.

Naturalizing Power: Essays in Feminist Cultural Analysis, edited by Sylvia Yanagisako and Carol Delaney. 1994. New York: Routledge.

If you are interested in finding out more about how power differences come to be seen as natural, you'll want to take a look at this collection of essays by feminist anthropologists. In it, they analyze how power is naturalized in a range of U.S. cultural discourses, especially in cultural narratives about "the birds and the bees," kinship, the family, and national identity.

Sexual Selections: What We Can and Can't Learn about Sex from Animals, by Marlene Zuk. 2002. Berkeley: University of California Press.

This is an excellent book if you are interested in how feminism can contribute to the understanding of the natural world and the use to which animal behavior can contribute responsibly to our understanding of such topics as motherhood, the genetic basis for adultery, female orgasm, menstruation, and homosexuality.

5

The Evolution of Gender and Difference

In this chapter you will . . .

explore the development of evolutionary theories of gender and society from the late nineteenth century to today • analyze the relationship between gender arrangements and theories of human evolution • compare and critique "Man the Hunter," "Woman the Gatherer," and "Man the Provisioner" models of the evolution of humans and gender roles • examine sociobiology and evolutionary psychology explanations of "selfish genes," "the battle of the sexes," and gender differences • assess the validity of popular and widespread evolutionary explanations of gender roles and behavior

Who are we? Where did we come from? What does it mean to be human? These kinds of questions are asked by people in different societies all over the world. For many people, religion provides the answer to such questions about origins and meaning. Others turn to science for answers, and, in particular, to anthropology, which has been concerned with such questions since the inception of the discipline in the late nineteenth century.

Early cultural anthropologists asked how societies, and their institutions, beliefs, and practices originated. In their explanations, they employed evolutionary ideas, which had become fashionable in scholarly circles in Europe and the United States during this period. This first school of cultural anthropological theory is known as **social evolutionism.**

Among physical and biological anthropologists, both historically and today, the search for human origins has been a central concern. Contemporary biological anthropologists often employ sophisticated types of evidence and techniques to reconstruct the evolutionary connections among **hominids** (a group that includes modern humans and our immediate ancestors) and among our ways of life and theirs in the past. Hominid evolution is complex: there is no single line of development. Instead, various hominid species have arisen over the past three million years, most becoming evolutionary dead ends and others eventually leading to modern humans. Which species to include

A sculptor's rendering of the 3.2 million-year-old hominid known as Lucy.

in the direct human line is still, however, a hotly debated issue.

Nineteenth-century social evolutionists were interested in finding explanations not only for the evolution of society but also for the gender differences they observed in their own societies, including what they saw as women's natural inferiority. By the early twentieth century, however, social evolutionism was largely in disrepute, abandoned because of its problematic assumptions about Western superiority and its claim that societies were like species that had evolved through a struggle for survival. The rejection of social evolutionism has not meant that evolutionary explanations of gender have disappeared. To the contrary, as we saw in chapter 4 these explanations are again popular today. Although differences in societies are no longer attributed to how evolved they are, particular gender behaviors are now routinely explained by how they have supposedly helped early humans compete in their evolutionary struggle for survival.

Although there is considerable fossil evidence indicating what early human ancestors looked liked and how they moved through their environment, there is no direct evidence of how they behaved or what they thought. Our ideas about their behavior, motivations, and psychology are always inferences based on interpreting evidence through the lens of a particular theoretical model. Inference, and not direct evidence, is at the center of any attempt to reconstruct the gender behaviors and ideologies of past populations. Models proposed to explain the behavior, roles, and ideas of early men and women are necessarily speculative. However, not all reconstructions are equal: those that rely on multiple lines of evidence and that avoid ethnocentrism and androcentric bias have more validity and explanatory power.

This chapter traces the development of evolutionary thinking about gender from late nineteenth-century social evolutionism to contemporary explanations. We pay particular attention to those contemporary models developed in anthropology, as well as in the field of **sociobiology,** an academic discipline that gives Darwinian explanations for nearly all animal behavior, and the closely related field of **evolutionary psychology,** a discipline that attempts to explain human emotions and psychological characteristics in the same vein. It may be hard to believe that social theories proposed in the nineteenth century are worthy of study today, but the degree of similarity in the underlying assumptions of nineteenth- and twenty-first-century evolutionary explanations is surprising.

Although current approaches focus on differential reproductive strategies in ways nineteenth-century thinkers did not, like their nineteenth-century counterparts, contemporary theorists begin with the assumption that the gender roles that exist in their own societies are natural. They seek explanations for supposed gender differences in behaviors in the Darwinian concept of **natural selection,** what nineteenth-century thinkers would have called the "struggle for the survival of the fittest." The idea behind natural selection is that individuals who have adaptive biological characteristics will be better able to pass on their genes to subsequent generations than those who do not have such characteristics. Contemporary thinkers who invoke natural selection today are often just as interested as past researchers were in supporting prevailing gender arrangements, although current theorists focus on the differences found between the sexes in the way they attract a mate, form bonds, or behave within marriage, not on the natural inferiority of women.

The intent in this chapter is to examine contemporary models of the evolution of gender that contain problematic assumptions and that are based on scanty evidence. The focus is chosen because, as with the other "nature" arguments discussed in chapter 4, these evolutionary explanations are purported to be soundly scientific and get considerable attention in the popular press. "Infidelity: Is it in the Genes?," asks the headline on the front cover of *Time* (8/15/94). A researcher quoted in an article in the *Star Tribune* claims that women lie less than men because they are "wired to talk and consequently are less likely to keep secrets" (Cummins 2002:E8). But is cheating on one's spouse a genetic trait with deep roots to our evolutionary past? Is there a good reason to believe that lying granted some men increased chances of survival millions of years ago? "Yes," say many of the writers we discuss in this chapter. Scrutinizing theorists' assumptions and placing them in historical context should put you in a better position to assess the validity of their conclusions about gender roles and behavior, whether you encounter them from anthropology or psychology textbooks, from articles in *Newsweek* or the *Washington Post,* or from watching the Discovery Channel.

Social Evolutionism

Beliefs in Progress and Western Superiority

British and North American societies in the late nineteenth century were steeped in notions of progress and Western superiority. The West's progress was attributed to its exceptional scientific technology and social advancements, which had enabled the success of its far-flung military and economic expansion. Indeed, Great Britain had such vast dominion over colonies throughout the world that one could rightfully remark that the sun never set on the British Empire. Colonialism was rationalized by systems of knowledge that supported the notion that conquered peoples were inherently inferior.

One such system is still all too familiar to us today and, as previously discussed, bases assumptions of inferiority and superiority on the notion of race. Western racial classification systems claimed that the darker-skinned inhabitants of the world are naturally inferior to white, lighter-skinned populations. In the late nineteenth and early twentieth centuries, as we have seen, differences within British and North American society were also explained and rationalized by scientists through references to biological attributes, especially brain size: members of the lower classes, women, criminals, and other societal "outcasts" were all viewed as inherently inferior to white men because of this *presumed* biological difference (see Gilman 1985). Thus, those who were not privileged white men were thought to be rightfully excluded from their society's economic, political, and cultural resources and privileges.

The Emergence of Anthropology

Anthropology emerged as a distinct academic discipline during this time of Western expansion. It distinguished itself from other fields interested in human behavior and social organization by its study of non-Western societies. By the mid-nineteenth century, an ever-increasing amount of information about non-Western societies collected by missionaries, colonial administrators, and travelers had found its way into Victorian society. Faced with evidence of the wide-ranging differences between non-Western societies and their own, as well as among different non-Western societies, early anthropologists thought they could uncover general laws about human behavior that would help them make sense of this variation. They thought they found such laws in the evolutionary principles so popular at the time.

These social evolutionists argued that societies had evolved from the simple to the complex, the chaotic to the organized, and the homogeneous to the heterogeneous. These theorists were immersed in beliefs about the desirability of progress. They saw non-Western societies that did not possess or operate with the technological and economic mind-set or gadgetry revered by the West as less advanced or "simpler." Thus, it made sense to view non-Western societies as inferior (see, for example, Tylor 1871).

Social evolutionists claimed that societies evolved through a fierce struggle for survival in which a more fit society like their own had won out over less fit ones. They pointed to Western civilization's political, economic, and cultural dominance over the rest of the world as evidence that it was the fittest form of social organization and, thus, the most highly evolved (see, for example, Spencer 1884). They not only saw the social practices, customs, and institutions of non-Western societies as inferior and less evolved but also claimed that they represented earlier stages in Western society's evolution. Non-Western societies were used, in other words, as living examples of the West's primitive past, one that was left behind in the struggle for supremacy. The natural struggle of the "fittest" for survival could be equated with military efforts resulting in colonial domination.

Morgan's Ranked Societies

In his book *Ancient Society* (1877), North American anthropologist Lewis Henry Morgan proposed what became the most well-known evolutionary scheme and one that was influential in the development and recognition of the discipline of anthropology in the United States. His model emphasized that culture progressed through a series of stages marked by important inventions and that such stages were also associated with cultural patterns. Morgan divided human history into three major levels of development: "Savagery," "Barbarism," and "Civilization."

These designations were determined by the presence or absence of traits that were assumed to be most desirable, and, thus, most evolved. Societies that lacked the sophisticated technology that would allow them to produce their own food, for example, were at the bottom of the evolutionary scale, belonging to the stage that social evolutionists termed Savagery. Those people at the bottom of the socioeconomic scale within the social evolutionists' own societies, such as the urban poor, were also classified as savages. Many

Ethical Period	Family Formation	Identifying "Invention" Features
SAVAGERY	no family, indiscriminate mating	
lower savagery		invention of speech; subsistence on fruits and nuts
middle savagery		fishing; the ability to make fire
upper savagery		invention of bow and arrow
BARBARISM	communal marriages	
lower barbarism		pottery making
middle barbarism		domestication of animals in the Old World; cultivation of maize by irrigation and stone architecture in the New World
upper barbarism		iron tools and metallurgy
CIVILIZATION	monogamous marriages	
civilization		phonetic alphabet and writing

Figure 5.1   Lewis Henry Morgan's Classification of Stages of Cultural Evolutions

social thinkers viewed them, like their non-Western counterparts, as degenerate, bestial, and morally and intellectually bankrupt (Stocking 1987:213).

Non-Western societies that had risen above such supposed lowliness by producing their own food through the domestication of plants and animals but had not produced a phonetic alphabet were placed in the category of Barbarism. Not surprisingly, the Western society to which social evolutionists belonged was thought of as at the highest stage of social evolution, that of Civilization. It not only had an industrial base for food production and a system of writing but, according to social evolutionists, it also had a superior set of social institutions, which had enabled the development of these factors.

Spencer's Explanation of Evolutionary Progress

Highly evolved social institutions, according to the early social evolutionist Herbert Spencer (1884), included superior forms of family along with gender-role organization that ensured male rights and male dominance. What made these family institutions superior was **monogamy,** a marriage practice allowing a person to have only one spouse at a time, and **patrilineal descent,** a system of reckoning ancestry by tracing genealogical connections through men.

Spencer hypothesized, even though there was no evidence to support his claim, that the earliest societies were promiscuous and lacked any institution to regulate sexuality. This situation meant that knowledge of paternity, the father of a child, was obscured, so females and their offspring neither formed lasting bonds with their children's' fathers nor established a system of descent. Out of these chaotic conditions evolved societies that traced descent through the female line, giving a mother's kinship group rights to her children, thereby using a **matrilineal descent** system. Since matrilineality established some rights over progeny, social evolutionists classified societies that instituted it at a higher evolutionary level than promiscuous ones. Nonetheless, according to Spencer, matrilineal societies were inherently weak because men lacked control over women and paternal authority over children.

By contrast, any society that regulated paternity through monogamy or institutionalized it through tracing descent through the male line would increase the chances of its existence. In other words, institutionalized paternity would lead to institutionalized male protection, ensuring the vitality and survival of the entire society. A society that favored monogamy and accentuated the male line would be able to conquer those that did not, thereby increasing its size and strength. In the process, that society would become more complex and evolve to a higher stage of development (Spencer 1884:611–631).

According to Spencer, freeing women from productive labor would also increase a society's chances for survival, since it would allow women to devote all of their time and energy to being "fit" mothers. Due to the increased capacity of its industrial system, Spencer argued, Victorian England was able to accomplish this goal. Equating his own society's ideal notion of womanhood with evolutionary progress, Spencer praised women's exclusion from the public realm. He argued that women's exclusion was the natural consequence of a long evolutionary process that selected those women dedicated to their duties in the domestic sphere. The inability of women of the working classes to attain this position was taken as evidence of their less evolved status.

The evolutionary explanation that women were best suited for raising children was invoked to rationalize women's *continued* exclusion from the public realm. Many scientists at the time claimed that women had a limited amount of vital energy. To ensure that women had enough energy for their childbearing and child-rearing duties, it had to be channeled away from other functions, such as the development of higher mental abilities. The concentration of energy on reproductive functions was responsible for women's supposed inferior mental capabilities, causing women to lack "the power of abstract reasoning and the most abstract of emotions, the sentiment of justice" (Spencer 1884:374). Such inadequacies, which made women unsuited for important activities in the public realm, were seen as the natural outcome of the struggle for the survival of the fittest. Women's attempts at the time to advocate for equal rights, especially at the voting booths, were, therefore, discounted and their demands were viewed as unnatural and perilous. If women were subordinate to men in Western society, opponents of women's equality argued, it was because biological necessities rendered them physically and intellectually inferior. Male dominance was seen to have evolutionary origins grounded in the biological differences between the sexes, especially those related to women's reproductive functions.

The Critique of Social Evolutionism

Uncovering the questionable assumptions underlying social evolutionism is not difficult from the vantage point of the twenty-first century. Most obvious is the problematic starting point of these analyses. Social evolutionists set out to explain what they already assumed: that Western society and its gender arrangements were the result of an evolutionary process that produced forms of social organization superior to all others. Such assumptions were, however, not questioned or tested but merely asserted.

Our suspicions of using claims of superiority to justify political domination, whether of one society over another or one social group over another within the same society, have deepened considerably in the post-Holocaust, post-Vietnam, postfeminist world in which we live. For example, we have come to see how racism, rather than being an explanation of Western superiority, rationalized Western expansion and how assuming the inherent inferiority of women and members of other disenfranchised groups justified white male control of desirable resources. Similarly, we are no longer comfortable with the ethnocentric claim that Western society is unquestioningly superior to all others because of advanced technology.

We are all too aware of the profoundly detrimental consequences technology can wreak. The potential impact of nuclear weapons or chemical warfare on humans and the disastrous effects of chemical wastes and other industrial products on the environment are now cause for alarm, not celebration. Today, in our efforts to improve the health and the quality of life of individuals in highly industrialized societies, many people are increasingly turning back to the herbal cures, holistic healing, and the sustainable forms of agriculture associated with nonindustrialized societies.

Most social scientists no longer hold the belief that societies can be equated with biological organisms able to evolve through processes of adaptation. While it is clear that all societies change, there is no universal law governing the direction of that change. Instead, twenty-first-century anthropologists seek explanations for societal change by looking at complex historical, social, and environmental factors. Thus, the equation of evolution with a natural progression toward some ultimate state of perfection has lost its currency for most social scientists, as has the tendency to use living non-Western societies as representative of some past moment in time. Non-Western societies are not remnants of some earlier time; they are not living fossils. Each has its own past, present, and future.

Contemporary Evolutionary Arguments

More recent evolutionary theorists are less interested in the evolution of societies than in the evolution of our particular species, *Homo sapiens*. They compare human behaviors and traits with those of such nonhuman primates as monkeys and apes. The similarities found between humans and these other species are understood as general primate characteristics. Behaviors and traits that humans possess but monkeys and apes do not are seen as uniquely human and are attributed to natural selection. In other words, evolutionary theorists argue that traits found only in humans must have arisen because they allowed our early human ancestors to adapt to environmental conditions and survive.

Evolutionary thinkers generally agree that the most significant trait differentiating hominids from other animal species is **bipedalism,** or walking upright on two feet. Early theorists of this school of thought tended to focus on bipedalism's capacity to free the hands for such supposedly quintessentially human behaviors as hunting. Perhaps the most well-known explanation of this idea is the one proposed by Sherwood Washburn and C. S. Lancaster in their 1968 article, "The Evolution of Hunting." Robin Fox and Lionel Tiger (1997) developed a model of human evolution based on the importance of hunting.

Other theorists, such as C. Owen Lovejoy (1981), also focus on bipedalism, but they tend to emphasize a suite of biological and behavioral changes that enabled our hominid ancestors to evolve, as we will see later in this chapter. These theorists are especially concerned with the traits that they think might have allowed our species to procreate more successfully and have drawn explanations from the principles E. O. Wilson formulated from his research on the social behavior of ants. Wilson's explanations are outlined in his influential book, *Sociobiology: The New Synthesis* (1975), including his underlying assumption that the social behavior of animals, including humans, is largely genetically programmed. Sociobiologists are particularly concerned with what they see as the different strategies men and women have developed over the course of evolution to increase the likelihood that their genes will be passed on to later generations.

More recently, sociobiology has transmuted into evolutionary psychology, a field that claims to explain almost all aspects of human behavior, ranging from humans' possession of a "sweet-tooth" to the development of their moral systems (see, for example, Wright 1994) through universal features of human nature that supposedly developed deep in our evolutionary past.

Even though newer models of human evolution draw on information that was unavailable to Washburn and Lancaster in the 1960s, they, as we will see, still contain many of the same problematic assumptions about gender and employ much of the same questionable forms of reasoning. Washburn and Lancaster's model (1968) is a good starting point for understanding even the most current evolutionary explanations of gender roles and behaviors.

Man the Hunter

During the 1960s and 1970s, hunting was often presumed to be the distinguishing characteristic of early hominids. Models of human evolution were often based on the assumption that hunting was the primary force behind the evolution of humans. Since it was presumed that only men hunted, these models had significant implications for how gender roles were conceptualized. Here we look at two variants of this model that were influential inside and outside of anthropology.

Washburn and Lancaster's Man the Hunter

Washburn and Lancaster proposed what has come to be known as the **Man the Hunter** model of human evolution. According to them, "our intellect, interests, emotions, and basic social life . . . all are products of the success of the hunting adaptation" (1968:293). This scenario suggests that as a result of bipedalism, the hands of our hominid ancestors were freed, eventually leading to the ability of early humans to hunt large game with tools or weapons. This ability exerted a force over almost all aspects of human cultural behavior and social organization. For example, Washburn and Lancaster assert that language arose because it allowed successful communication among members of a hunting party, while the manufacture of tools for hunting resulted in increased brain size and the development of art. Washburn and Lancaster explain this relationship this way:

> There must have been strong selection for greater skill in manufacture and use [of tools], and it is no accident that the bones of small-brained men (*Australopithecus*) are never found with beautiful, symmetrical tools. If the brains of contemporary apes and men are compared, the area associated with manual skills (both in cerebellum and cortex) are at least three times as large in man. Clearly, the success of tools has exerted a great influence on the evolution of the brain, and has created the skills that make art possible. [1968:298]

The most significant aspect of the Man the Hunter model for understanding gender roles is Washburn and Lancaster's assumption that it was men who hunted large game, while women gathered vegetable foods and cared for dependent infants. This division of labor necessitated the sharing of food resources between women and their offspring and men. Food sharing provided the basis for the development of the human family. According to Washburn and Lancaster, the family is "the result of the reciprocity of hunting, the addition of a male to the mother-plus-young social group of monkeys and apes" (1968:301). Washburn and Lancaster admit, however, that there is no direct evidence that the human family arose deep in our evolutionary past.

In addition to bipedalism, the **loss of estrus** in human females suggests an additional basis for establishing families. **Estrus** is a period of a female's heightened fertility, when female animals ovulate, which is indicated by external signs. Nonhuman primate females have this moment of heightened fertility and receptiveness to sexual intercourse when they ovulate once or twice a year. During these moments, sexual intercourse is more likely to occur and result in conception. External signs, such as enlarged genitalia, signal a female's readiness to mate. In some animals, this is referred to as "heat." Loss of estrus, then, means that for human females, ovulation does not occur once or twice a year but instead once a month, and they have no outward signal they are ovulating. Furthermore, human females are receptive to sexual intercourse even when not ovulating. This difference between most primates and humans, Washburn and Lancaster contend, allowed human males to initiate intercourse with females at any time and led to the development of mechanisms to control women so that men could be assured of sexual activity whenever they wanted it.

Loss of an estrus period, according to this way of thinking, gives rise to pair-bonding, the development of long-term male–female bonds, which also contributed to the establishment of the family. Females acquiesced to male sexual desire to ensure that they and their children would be provisioned with the meat that males brought back from the hunt. This scenario is often referred to as the **food-for-sex hypothesis.**

Washburn and Lancaster also claimed that hunting exerted a profound effect on human psychology (1968:299). Since they saw hunting as essential to human survival, they reasoned that it must have been easily learned and pleasurable. Language facilitated the transmission of ideas about hunting and thus made learning easier, while immediate enjoyment from the hunt itself was the reward for killing. Washburn and Lancaster tell us that the satisfaction early men supposedly derived from the hunt is still evident today in the efforts made to maintain killing as a sport and in the pleasure men derive from participating in warfare (1968:299).

Tiger and Fox's Man the Hunter

Lionel Tiger and Robin Fox developed a version of the Man the Hunter scenario in their book *The Imperial Animal* (1997). Like many others at the time, they used evidence from nonhuman primates, especially monkeys and apes, to reconstruct early hominid ways of life. They turned specifically to savannah baboons, an African monkey, as the primate exemplar. They did so based on the assumption that since humans evolved on the open savannah of Africa, they would have faced some of the same pressures as these monkeys who live there.

From initial observations of baboons, they constructed a model of savannah baboon social organization and behavior. According to them, savannah baboon social life is hierarchical, with dominant males at the top having first access to resources, including estrus females. Juvenile males stay on the periphery, awaiting their chance to usurp a dominant male's position through aggressive behavior. Females and their young acquiesce to the demands of dominant males who protect them. This form of social organization, it was hypothesized, underlies human social groupings.

Tiger and Fox suggest that hominids diverged from this way of life when they began to hunt. Since hunting, they presume, would have required cooperation among males, they argue that, unlike baboons, our earliest hominid ancestors would have downplayed male competition for mates through pair-bonding based on a meat-for-sex exchange between individual males and females. Nonetheless, they argue that male competition and dominance over females was the template from which early hominids emerged, one that still finds its natural expression in contemporary human groups.

Lovejoy's Man the Provisioner

Newer evolutionary models no longer emphasize hunting as the prime mover in human evolution, yet they contain many of the same assumptions as those underlying the Man the Hunter scenario. A well-known example of this type of model is the one developed by Owen Lovejoy (1981). Lovejoy's account, often referred to as the **Man the Provisioner** model, grants the importance of gathering to early hominid development but posits that it was primarily males, not females, who acquired foods based on this subsistence technique (see Hager 1997:8). Lovejoy's ideas have been widely disseminated through the popular book, *Lucy: The Beginnings of Humankind* (Johanson and Edey 1981a) and in the multipart television *NOVA* series, "In Search of Human Origins" (Johanson 1997). It is also, as Lori Hager points out (1997:8), the model of hominid evolution frequently presented in textbooks and the popular press and therefore is worth discussing in detail.

According to Lovejoy, for a primate to stand up and run is a crazy thing to do, especially since bipedalism is an inefficient form of locomotion (see Johanson and Edey 1981b:45–49). Nonetheless, bipedalism arose. It evolved, according to Lovejoy, as part of a group of characteristics that solved what he calls the demographic dilemma of apes. This dilemma resulted from the reproductive strategy, referred to as **K-selection,** which is explained by Johanson and Edey in the chapter entitled "What's Sex Got to Do With It?":

> There are two fundamentally different ways in which an animal can function sexually: It can produce a great many eggs with an investment of very little energy in any one egg, or it can produce very few eggs with a large investment in each. These are known as the "r" strategy and the "K" strategy respectively. . . . "K" is obviously far more efficient than "r," but it too has its limits. Accidents, predation, seasonal food failure, illness—all take their toll on animals. Losing an infant to one of these hazards after an investment of five or six years is hideously costly compared with the loss of an egg by [an r strategy animal]. [1981b:46]

Lovejoy hypothesized that apes were dangerously K-selected; that is, they were dangerously close to extinction because they invested a large amount of energy in the rearing of a very few children. Such a focused investment could be disastrous for the group even if only a few infants died each year. According to Lovejoy, those females who have shorter intervals between children are able to produce more children, increasing their chances of their genes being represented in subsequent generations. With more offspring, the K-dilemma diminished for the group to whom these primates belonged, ultimately leading to the evolution of our hominid ancestors. This resulted in more overlap among children and required that mothers care for more than one baby at a time, which meant they needed to restrict their movements and become more sedentary so they could direct their energy to caring for children. Rearing more children required females to become dependent on males to provide food for them and their offspring. The reward for such sharing, Lovejoy argues, was sex.

Strategy	Characteristics	Practiced by	Advantages	Disadvantages
K-selection	• parents produce few offspring • parents invest large amounts of energy in caring for each egg	• relatively large organisms, such as humans and higher primates • organisms that reproduce more than once in their lifetime • organisms with long life expectancy	• each egg has a better chance of surviving to sexual maturity because of parental protection • offspring often live a long life and can reproduce more than once	• very vulnerable to environmental changes because the loss of any offspring is costly • usually successful only in stable environments
r-selection	• parents produce many offspring • parents invest little or no energy in caring for any particular egg	• relatively small organisms, such as fish and insects • organisms that usually reproduce only once in their lifetime • organisms that have short life expectancy	• eggs are so numerous that at least some are likely to survive, even without parental care • not especially vulnerable to environmental hazards • successful in unstable habitats	• most offspring die after short time • offspring must survive without parental care • less efficient than K-selection because eggs are considered "expendable," and so energy is wasted, especially in small animals

http://fig.cox.miami.edu/Faculty/Tom/bil160sp98/16_rKselection.html (accessed 7/22/03).

Figure 5.2   K-Selection vs. r-Selection

When males and females come together in primate species to copulate, at least according to Lovejoy, competition and fighting among males often occur. Thus, he reasons, mechanisms must have evolved in early hominids to reduce conflict. This reduction in male competition was accomplished through the loss of estrus, which made females sexually available to males year round, facilitating long-term pair-bonding. With the loss of obvious external signals of ovulation, accompanied by the loss of estrus, Lovejoy argues, a female began to depend on permanent features of her body, such as her hair, skin, breasts, and shape, to attract a male. As Johanson and Edey put it, the "estrus flag" no longer counts, since the female has permanent ones to keep her man—her hominid—interested in her all the time (1981b:48). Johanson and Edey summarize Lovejoy's model this way:

> There are always ways of defusing male [aggression due to competition for mates]. . . . One is to lower the competition for sex. If each male has his own female, *his own private gene receptacle*, he doesn't have to fight with other males for representation in succeeding generations. More parental care and food sharing become possible. As a result, the females can afford to become less mobile. If the primate becomes less mobile . . . it can become more bipedal. . . . Because it doesn't have to run as much, it can afford to be less efficient in order to do other things that begin to have survival value—like carrying the extra food needed to nurture extra children. If a male is now walking upright, he's better equipped to carry food and more likely to bring it to the female. [1981b:47–48, emphasis added]

Critiques of Man the Hunter and Man the Provisioner Models

The Man the Hunter and the Man the Provisioner models suffer from many of the same problems. In particular, androcentric bias and unsubstantiated assumptions plague both accounts. Such unsubstantiated assumptions are not uncommon. Depictions of our hominid ancestors, both in science and in popular culture, are influenced by a history of ideas about, and representations of, our hominid ancestors, as you can read about in Close-Up 5.1, which is excerpted from an article by anthropologist Judith Berman Kohn.

Exposing Androcentric Bias

What Were the Women Doing?   Sally Slocum provided one of the earliest and most complete responses to the Man the Hunter model in a 1975 article entitled "Woman the Gatherer: Male Bias in Anthropology." Slocum contested the androcentric biases in Washburn and Lancaster's model, especially its assumption that behavior exclusive to men resulted in the evolution of all that we have come to think of as uniquely human. Slocum quotes Jane Kephart, another critic of the Man the Hunter model, who has made clear the ramifications of its androcentric bias. The implications of the Man the Hunter scenario, according to Kephart, are:

> Since only males hunt, and the psychology of the species was set by hunting, we are forced to conclude that females are scarcely human, that is, do not have built-in the basic psychology of the species: to kill and hunt and ultimately to kill others of the same species. The argument implies built-in aggression in human males, as well as the assumed passivity of human females and their exclusion from the mainstream of human development. [in Slocum 1975:38]

To counter this androcentric viewpoint, Slocum provides the alternative model of **Woman the Gatherer.** Slocum demonstrates that the same aspects of human culture and social organization that Washburn and Lancaster attribute to the "hunting way of life" can be explained with reference to the "gathering way of life."

Slocum shows how gathering rather than hunting was more likely to give rise to the specific human activities Washburn and Lancaster attribute to hunting. Her argument is as follows: among nonhuman primates, males and females do not share food. Even mothers do not share food with infants, but feed them by nursing them. Once young nonhuman primates are weaned, they are able to obtain food for themselves. During the course of human evolution, the period of an infant's dependency on its mother increased, requiring a change in this pattern: now it was necessary for mothers to share food with their children in order to ensure their survival.

Thus, food sharing would have developed, according to Slocum, not because men shared meat with women, but because mothers shared gathered food with their children, both male and female. This behavior probably predated hunting, since gathering is the basis of the diet of all primates. Moreover, as Slocum points out, there is no solid empirical evidence to suggest that sharing would have arisen only with the development of a sexual division of labor, one in which women gathered exclusively and men hunted, as Washburn and Lancaster assumed.

Close-Up

5.1: Natural Man?: Bad Hair Days in the Paleolithic
by Judith Berman Kohn

From his first "scientific" appearance in 1873, the "Cave Man" seems utterly familiar. Although he has never been seen in the flesh, we instantly recognize him in illustrations, art, films, cartoons, and museum displays. His place in human evolutionary time is signaled by several attributes, most of which appear concurrently: he is found in or in front of caves, or in a wild setting confronting savage beasts. He is equipped with (and archaeologically best identified by) stone, wooden, or bone implements, usually associated with hunting or combat. In scientific illustration, he is often serious in demeanor, as seems to befit the arduous circumstances of his life. He is attired in fur, which is often draped in ways that shield the wearer neither from weather nor untoward gazes. Accessories, when they exist, consist of bone, antler, or claw jewelry. His hair is particularly noteworthy: he sports shoulder-length or longer, often unstyled and even unkempt, hair on his head and frequently is bearded. Significant body hair is often depicted. . . .

And yet our actual referents for this image are extremely scarce or are belied by the extant paleoanthropological record. . . . The image of the Cave Man is notably data independent, and is, I suggest, almost entirely based on a specific visual construct that has remained remarkably stable for three millennia and more. What then accounts for the persistence of this counterimage that powerfully negates paleoanthropological reality?

Visual conventions or stereotypes provide both artist and audience with a parsimonious mode of expression: a world of meaning through a single image. Conventions immediately, simply, and effortlessly convey the elements of a situation or story so that we can properly "read" it. The economics of popular images, such as cartoons, force reliance on visual shorthand, on a common iconographic vocabulary, in order to communicate with an audience. Without this shorthand, we would not be in on the joke. But although conventions appear *en face* to simplify and clarify, they contain complex and often contradictory messages. Readings of images are psychologically, culturally, and socially conditioned and may bear only a contingent relationship to reality. [p. 288]

. . .While the Cave Man is *visualized* stereotypically, both in scientific and popular culture, he is *read* in many different ways. These readings . . . reflect our views of ourselves in terms of our place in nature, our origins, and perhaps our destiny. The Cave Man's long, polemical pedigree is a product of centuries of debate about the origins of humans, "natural man," human nature, and primitive humans and comprises discourses about human evolution, human language, and the place of humans in the natural world. [p. 289] [Judith Berman Kohn. 1999. Bad Hair Days in the Paleolithic. *American Anthropologist* 101 (2):288–304]

Slocum also suggests that gathering could have been responsible for the aspects of human behavior Washburn and Lancaster attribute to hunting: the development of complex social organization, language, and tools. She argues that over the course of human evolution, longer pregnancies, more difficult births, and a lengthened period of infant dependency would have required "more skills in social organization and communication—creating selective pressure for increased brain size" (Slocum 1975:46). Early hominid procurement strategies also demanded specialized knowledge, including knowledge of the location and identification of plant varieties and of seasonal and geographic changes, knowledge more easily transmitted through language (Slocum 1975:47). Thus, Slocum argues, we need not look to hunting as an explanation for these aspects of human life. Furthermore, the first tools used by humans may not have been for hunting but for gathering food and caring for children: digging sticks, food storage containers, or slings and nets to carry babies. Such tools would have enabled more efficient food gathering and accumulation of food resources.

In sum, according to Slocum, "the emphasis on hunting as a prime moving factor in hominid evolution distorts the data." She argues that "it is simply too big a jump to go from the primate individual-gathering pattern to a hominid cooperative hunting-sharing pattern without [hypothesizing] some intervening changes" (Slocum 1975:48). Moreover, fossil evidence makes clear that hunting was a late development in hominid evolution.

What's Male Anxiety Got to Do With It?   Androcentric bias is also an element of Lovejoy's model. As in the Man the Hunter model, the Man the Provisioner scenario depicts women as necessarily dependent on males for their survival. Women are also characterized as sex objects, seen as attractive to males for the very traits that present-day Western men find desirable in women. Such conclusions are highly ethnocentric and androcentric. As paleoanthropologist Dean Falk has pointed out, this model may actually suggest more about present-day male worries than about early hominid behavior and evolution (1997). According to Falk, Lovejoy's model suggests that early male hominids suffered from a set of sexual anxieties that are lessened in the scenario he offers. Men need not worry, for example, about whether they will have children, if a woman's children belong to him, or whether "his" female will leave him for another man. A woman, this model suggests, will happily have sex

with a man, and form a life-long pair-bond with him, as long as he supports her (see Falk 1997:114–115). Contemporary gender roles, behaviors, expectations, and anxieties are projected back into the evolutionary past and seen as being at the foundation of the survival and evolution of humans.

Although Slocum's model provides an important alternative to widespread androcentric models of human evolution, some later researchers suggest that it, too, reproduces some problematic ideas about gender. Primatologist Linda Fedigan (1986), for example, argues that juxtaposing Woman the Gatherer with Man the Hunter merely inverts a Western gender system that opposes men to women. Feminist archaeologists such as Margaret Conkey (2005) and Joan Gero (1985) are working not only to call into question traditional assumptions about prehistoric gender roles but also to reveal the complexities involved in reconstructing gender relations in past societies, as we will see in chapter 7. Many feminist primatologists today use data from free-ranging primate groups to offer alternative evolutionary models that do not rely on the problematic assumptions so deeply embedded in the Man the Hunter account (see, for example, Fedigan 1982; Hrdy 1981; Morbeck et al. 1997; Tanner 1981).

Unsubstantiated Assumptions

Both the Man the Hunter and the Man the Provisioner scenario are loaded with problematic assumptions that are not supported by evidence. These include the following assumptions:

1. that early hominid females were sedentary, requiring them to become dependent on males for food and resulting in a strict division of labor between males and females, and

2. that loss of estrus created a radically new and different kind of relationship between males and females.

In addition, Lovejoy's model contains two more highly questionable assumptions:

3. that early hominids experienced a demographic dilemma, and

4. that female attractiveness was a key factor in the survival of the species.

The following assumption of Tiger and Fox is also highly questionable:

5. that baboons, with highly aggressive males dominating social life, provide the best model for understanding hominid evolution.

Assumption #1: Females Were Sedentary and Dependent. The assumption that early hominid females settled down and became dependent on males to bring them food is not supported by ethnographic evidence. Early hominids most likely lived a life based on a scavenging or foraging food-collecting strategy. Thus, comparisons with contemporary foraging societies are instructive for gaining insight into early hominid subsistence patterns. Among contemporary foragers, women are highly mobile; even with infants they often range over large areas in search of vegetable foods. They are anything but sedentary. Women in such societies tend to be the primary provisioners, often contributing the largest proportion of food to the diet of men, women, and children in the group. This consists primarily of vegetable foods, but can include meat from the small animals they routinely capture as they gather. Evidence from the archaeological record also contradicts the assumption that there is an inherent sexual division of labor. As Lila Leibowitz (1983) has remarked, "the artifacts and early detritus associated with early human groups . . . reflect the use of foraging techniques that are simple, involve both sexes and call for similar activities on the part of both" (p. 136).

Assumption #2: Loss of Estrus Was Central. Slocum was among the first to point to the problematic assumptions that the Man the Hunter model contains about female sexuality. She suggests that in most primate groups it is the female who initiates sexual intercourse, not the male. It is Western male bias, she claims, that infers that early male hominids both chose a female and maintained control over her and her offspring to ensure a man's sexual access to her. According to Slocum, the presumption that the long-term commitment of one male to one female as an old, established pattern is contradicted by evidence that shows that long-term monogamy is a relatively rare pattern even among modern humans (Slocum 1975:43).

Evidence from nonhuman primate societies also contradicts Lovejoy's claims that the reduction of male competition among our early hominid ancestors was accomplished through the loss of estrus, which made hominid females, unlike their primate ancestors, sexually available to males year round, facilitating long-term pair-bonding. Studies of the sexual behavior of nonhuman primates, however, reveal that sexual activity outside a female's period of maximum fertility is not an exclusive characteristic of human sexuality (see Burton 1972; Hrdy 1979; Manson 1986; and Rowell 1972).

Assumption #3: Prehumans Were in a K-Trap. Many anthropologists have questioned whether early hominids were in a K-trap, experiencing a demographic dilemma requiring an increase in birthrate and infant survivorship. They suggest that there is no solid evidence to support this contention (see, for example, Harley 1982; Isaac 1982; Wood 1982).

Assumption #4: Female "Attractiveness" Was Key. Lovejoy's model, as well as the sociobiology and evolutionary psychology accounts that we discuss in the remainder of this chapter, can also be critiqued for the underlying assumption that female attractiveness acted as the cement for long-term pair-bonds in our early hominid ancestors. This assumption is based on the idea that **sexual selection** has operated as a significant factor in the evolution of humans.

In *The Descent of Man* (1871), Darwin suggested that some traits, like the beautiful tails of male peacocks, could not have arisen due to natural selection because they did not confer a survival advantage to

To attract female mates, male peacocks display extravagant fans of brilliant feathers.

the individuals possessing them. He proposed, however, that they could nonetheless have provided a reproductive benefit if those individuals possessing such traits were seen as more attractive than those individuals without them, leading members of the opposite sex to seek sexual relations with them more often. He termed this process "sexual selection."

Although most animal biologists agree that sexual selection operates as an important evolutionary force in some species, there has been considerable controversy over its operation and significance for humans. Is it possible that those females who possessed rounded, enlarged breasts thousands of years ago, before marriage was instituted, would have had more frequent sexual relations with males who found them attractive, thereby passing on their genes for large breasts to subsequent generations? For example, did the "nice breasts" of some females or the shapely body of others form the basis of human pair-bonding in our evolutionary past, as Lovejoy and others suggest?

Because sexual attraction is emphasized so widely in contemporary Western societies, and traits like breasts and beautiful bodies are so frequently touted as the key to such attraction, it seems obvious that sexual selection must have been at work in our evolutionary past. But was it?

Close-Up 5.2 draws attention to the problem with such ideas and provides a model for the evolution of permanently enlarged breasts in human females that does not depend on viewing women as sex objects whose breasts evolved to attract males.

Close-Up

5.2: Are Women Evolutionary Sex Objects?

Since all mammals have breasts to nurse their young, it might seem odd to search the unique evolutionary past of humans for an explanation for their existence. Yet, there is a reason to do so. There *is* something different about human female breasts, leading scientists to develop theories about them: after the age of puberty, the breasts of a human female become "permanently enlarged," while this is not the case in other primates, our closest evolutionary relatives. Although the breast tissue of a female ape or monkey swells when she is pregnant and nurses her young, once she is done lactating, it typically recedes back to a flattened form. What accounts for this difference between humans and other primates?

Do modern women have breasts because sometime long ago in the human evolutionary past males became erotically aroused by them? Was male attraction to big-breasted women a key to the survival of early humans? In other words, are women evolutionary sex objects? (See Mascia-Lees 2008.) Many sociobiologists and evolutionary psychologists argue that they are. They suggest that hominid males became attracted to "chesty" females as sexual partners more often than their less-endowed sisters, resulting in the maintenance of this trait in modern human populations. That is, they claim that sexual selection best explains why women have breasts (see Cant 1981; Gallup 1982; Halliday 1980; Morris 1967; Potts and Short 1999; and Szalay and Costello 1991).

Can permanently enlarged breasts be explained without reference to assumptions about their erotic appeal? In 1986, Fran Mascia-Lees, John Relethford, and Tim Sorger provided a model to explain the evolution of permanently enlarged breasts that depends not on the problematic notion of sexual selection but instead on the more well-established theory of natural selection.

They argue that fat storage is the crucial element in terms of the selective advantage of permanently enlarged breasts: hominid females who were able to store fat would be more likely to survive under the conditions of resource fluctuation that characterized the early hominid environment. Hominid females with more fat would be able to convert fat to energy, increasing the likelihood that they could nurse their young in times of scarcity and bring them to reproductive maturity. They could also continue in the high-energy expenditure activity of food collection, as women do in contemporary hunter-gatherer societies, increasing their own, and thus their children's, chances of survival. Mascia-Lees and her colleagues do not assert that this selection depended on a male becoming attracted to the "right" type of woman based on her breasts. Instead, they draw on evidence of fat ratios in primates and humans, energy expenditure in contemporary hunter and gatherers, and endocrine studies to argue that permanently enlarged breasts were not selected for at all. Indeed, they argue that breasts are merely a coincidental by-product of the selection for fat.

Humans have more body fat than any nonhuman primate, and women on average have more fat then men per overall body weight. One important characteristic of fat is that it stores estrogen, the hormone responsible for breast development at puberty. With higher levels of estrogen in the body, breast growth would be stimulated. Since the breast tissue of nonhuman female primates swells during lactation and pregnancy when there is more circulating estrogen in the body, it is evident that a favorable hormonal background permissive of the eventual permanent enlargement of human female breasts is already present in nonhuman primates. Once estrogen levels increased in our hominid ancestors due to the selection for increased fat storage, the potential for permanent breast enlargement became an actuality.

Pawlowski (1999) expanded this scenario, arguing that fluctuating food resources were not the only selective pressure operating on early hominids. In addition, he argues, the large difference between daytime and nighttime temperatures characteristic of the open environment of early hominids might also account for the importance of fat storage to early hominid survival. Those individuals with decreased amounts of fur were able to withstand high daytime temperatures but would be vulnerable to the cold nights of this environment. Individuals with more fat were better able to withstand these hypothermic conditions. Like Mascia-Lees and her colleagues, Pawlowski argues that permanently enlarged breasts are a side-effect of fat storage. Under conditions of early hominid development, fat storage would increase the likelihood of the survival of individuals possessing this trait.

Whatever the exact selective advantage of fat, it is clear that the evolution of permanent breast enlargement in human females need not be explained through their erotic appeal to men. Natural selection does not operate merely on the male of the species who then makes choices about which females to copulate with based on their attractiveness, thereby selecting for female body features like permanently enlarged breasts. Fat storage and its by-products, including permanently enlarged breasts, serve survival purposes. Early hominid women need not be understood primarily as sex objects any more than their twenty-first-century counterparts.

References

Cant, J. 1981. Hypothesis for the Evolution of Human Breasts and Buttocks. *American Naturalist* 117:199–204.
Gallup, G. 1982. Permanent Breast Enlargement in Human Females: A Sociobiological Analysis. *Journal of Human Evolution* 11:597–601.
Halliday, T. 1980. *Sexual Strategy*. Oxford University Press.
Mascia-Lees, F. 2008. Are Women Evolutionary Sex Objects?: Why Women Have Breasts. *Anthropology Now* 1 (1):4–11.

(continued)

Mascia-Lees, F., J. Relethford, and T. Sorger. 1986. The Evolution of Permanently Enlarged Breasts in Human Females. *American Anthropologist* 88:423–428.

Morris, D. 1967. *The Naked Ape.* New York: McGraw-Hill.

Pawlowski, B. 1999. Permanent Breasts as a Side Effect of Subcutaneous Fat Tissue Increase in Human Evolution. *HOMO* 50 (2):149–162.

Potts, Malcolm, and Roger Short. 1999. *Ever Since Adam and Eve: The Evolution of Human Sexuality.* New York: Cambridge University Press.

Short, R. 1976. The Evolution of Human Reproduction. *Proceedings of the Royal Society of London* 195:3–24.

Szalay F. and R. Costello. 1991. Evolution of Permanent Estrus Displays in Hominids. *Journal of Human Evolution* 20:439–464.

Female gorilla during lactation (above) in contrast to a nonlactating female gorilla (left).

Sexual selection, however, does not simply mean that males and females have a sexual attraction to one another. It suggests that certain traits are the basis of increased sexual opportunities for some individuals over others, conferring on them increased reproductive potential. But is this a legitimate claim?

The ethnocentric basis of sexual selection scenarios is clear when we consider that all human societies regulate sexual relations between men and women, and often do so through the institution of marriage. Although in many contemporary Western societies, the choice of a marriage partner is thought best left to the individual, in most societies marriages have been, and continue to be, arranged by parents and other family members, seen more as an institution joining two families than merely two individuals. The sexual attraction felt between two individuals often has little, if nothing, to do with a family's choice of a suitable partner for their sons and daughters. Moreover, in most human societies, it is rare for an individual not to marry, since marriage is the mechanism by which individuals gain adult social standing in their group.

Thus, whether a woman has attractive breasts or beautiful hair does not determine whether she will marry and give birth to children. Despite the seemingly constant airing on The Learning Channel and PBS of one television show after the other claiming that "beautiful" faces, the practice of wearing lipstick, or fresh, clean skin have been sexually selected for in the course of human evolution, there are no data to support this claim. In other words, no one has yet proven that particular traits and behaviors such as these grant some women reproductive advantage over others.

Assumption #5: Baboons, with Highly Aggressive Males, Provide the Best Model. Nancy Tanner and Adrienne Zihlman (1976) were among the first to call for increased attention to the behavior of female primates for furthering our understanding of human evolution, and more particularly for rethinking which primate species might best hold the key to that understanding.

Instead of relying on baboons as models, they turned to chimpanzees to reconstruct hominid evolution because of the close genetic relationship and anatomical similarities between humans and chimps.

They brought together evidence based on chimpanzees with fossil and ethnographic data to reconstruct early human behavior (see Zihlman 1997:98). Based on fossil hominid dental evidence, for example, they proposed plant foods as the basis of the early hominid diet and hypothesized the need for the development of technological innovations for carrying and sharing plant foods, as Slocum had.

Based on evidence from extant societies of foragers, they also argued that early hominids would have had a flexible division of labor, allowing individuals, regardless of sex, to undertake a wide range of tasks. They saw little evidence from observations of chimpanzees to support the idea that pair-bonding and monogamy would have been the basis for early hominid social groupings (see Zihlman 1997:98).

Barbara Smuts (1985) has shown that highly aggressive males dominate baboon social life much less than previously reported. Indeed, as you can see from the Ethnography in Focus: *Sex and Friendship in Baboons* (on the following page), male–female relationships among baboons are complex. Females base their choice of a mate as much on "friendship" as on a male's fighting ability or place in the social hierarchy of the group, as hypothesized by Man the Hunter proponents.

Global News

5.1: Study Compares Human, Chimp Brains

As different as chimps and humans look, they share 98.7 percent of the same genes, researchers say. Most of the genetic differences seem to be in the brain, according to a new study. . . . Chimpanzees are more closely related to humans than any other primate. The two are thought to have shared a common ancestor 5 to 7 million years ago, although just what that ancient primate looked like is unknown. Since then, chimps and humans have evolved separately, with humans developing a brain about twice the size of a chimp's brain. . . . "The problem of developing an understanding of the molecular differences between humans and chimpanzees is both a fascinating and an enormous one," said [one researcher]. [The Associated Press 2002, http://1010wins.com/StoryFolder/story_1348732250_html (accessed 6/25/02)]

Ethnography in Focus

Sex and Friendship in Baboons by Barbara Smuts

I returned from the field with a suitcase full of data sheets and a number of questions about baboon friendship that I was eager to explore. My first task was to devise an objective definition of friendship. . . . My goal in the friendship study was to determine whether the type of long-term relationship a male and female had (the independent variable) was an important factor to consider when trying to understand behaviors like male protection of infants and female choice of mates (dependent variables). . . . I decided to use grooming and proximity to measure the affinity between adult male and female baboons. [pp. 37–38]

***

Throughout the day, I recorded grooming between females and males on an ad lib basis. . . . For each anestrous [nonovulating] female, I determined the percentage of all her grooming episodes with males that involved each of the 18 subjects . . . and found that] the vast majority of an anestrous female's grooming with males was typically restricted to 1 or 2 of the 18 possible partners. [pp. 38–40] For each female, I [also] plotted the distribution of the C scores [measures of a male's spatial proximity to the female] of all adult and subadult males. . . . If . . . females tended to associate with particular males, the distribution should be discontinuous: One or a few males should have much higher C scores than all the others. In general, [this] pattern held. . . . [My] results support the hypothesis that most anestrous females associated with one, two, or occasionally three males. [pp. 45–48]

***

Measures of grooming and proximity were used to differentiate male–female pairs with particularly strong bonds from all other male–female dyads. . . . Most anestrous females were . . . found in proximity to one, two, or occasionally three adult males considerably more often than they were found near any other males. These were usually the same individuals the female groomed with most often. [p. 55] The striking similarities between the ad lib grooming scores and the composite proximity scores provided the basis for the definition of friendship. [p. 48]

***

What made Friends special was, most of all, the unusual quality of their interactions. Female baboons, in general, are wary of males. This is understandable: Males sometimes use their larger size to intimidate and bully smaller troop members. Females, however, were apparently drawn to their male Friends, and they seemed surprisingly relaxed around these hulking companions. The males, too, seemed to undergo a subtle transformation when interacting with female Friends. They appeared less tense, more affectionate, and more sensitive to the behavior of their partners. [p. 61]

***

[An] analysis [of male baboon aggression] suggests that females form friendships in part because of their extreme vulnerability to males in general. A female baboon is continuously surrounded by males who could easily injure, or even kill, her or her offspring. Her most effective defense against these dangers is another male. But rather than relying on the possibility that *some* male will risk injury and come to her aid, the female forms a long-term bond with one or two males who are more reliable allies, presumably because they in turn receive benefits from their relationship with her. [p. 102]

***

First, a prior bond with an anestrous female significantly increases a male's chances of forming consortships with this female when she resumes sexual cycles. Second, males are able to use both female Friends and those females' infants as buffers during agonistic encounters with other males. Third, in many cases but by no means all, the male's relationship with the mother provides an opportunity for investment in his own likely offspring; this may include protecting the infant against aggression from other males during carrying interactions and in other contexts. [p. 198]

***

Why is male consort activity enhanced by previous bonds with females? The simplest explanation is that females sometimes prefer to mate with their male Friends, and that female preferences affect consort relationships. . . . Females frequently refuse copulations, and since copulations cannot occur without female cooperation, the female has final control over which males she mates with. [pp. 169–172]

***

[M]ale baboons do not have all the power in the male–female relationships. Although the male's large size and superior fighting ability clearly affect the nature of male–female relationships, female baboons ultimately determine whether a male becomes an accepted member of a troop, and . . . once a male enters a troop, female preferences strongly influence his mating success. [p. 199]

From: Barbara Smuts, *Sex and Friendship in Baboons.* Edison, NJ: Transaction Publishers, 2007. Used by permission of Transaction Publishers.

Sociobiology

Selfish Genes and the Battle of the Sexes

Rather than understanding human reproductive strategies to explain the evolution of the species of *Homo sapiens* as a whole, sociobiologists focus on the difference in male–female sexual relations and see them as a contest between men and women. This "battle of the sexes," as they call it, has arisen over the course of evolution because men and women must develop competing reproductive strategies to ensure that their genes will be passed on. These strategies are, in turn, the result of the differences in the biology of males and females. As sociobiologist Richard Dawkins explains, selfish genes motivate male and female gender behavior. That is, females and males have a genetic propensity to exploit each other, trying to force

the member of the opposite sex to invest more in their offspring in order to optimize the chances that their own genes will be passed down to future generations (Dawkins 1976:150).

Size Matters (or Does It?)

According to sociobiology, there is a disparity in the investment men and women must make in the rearing of children to ensure the child's survival and the survival of their own genes. Differing degrees of this parental investment arise because a female's egg, or ovum, is much larger than a male's sperm, requiring more energy investment for the egg's maintenance, and because women get pregnant and men do not. This means that a female *always* starts with a larger investment in a pregnancy because it has taken her more energy to maintain an egg than for the male to produce sperm. This prior investment, sociobiologists suggest, means she will have more to lose if an offspring does not survive. Dawkins emphasizes that all the other differences between the sexes stem from this one basic difference (1976:152).

Dawkins argues that men and women therefore develop different reproductive strategies. Sociobiological accounts propose that males can optimize their genetic fitness—the chances of passing on their genes—by impregnating as many females as possible. Males are genetically programmed, according to sociobiologists, for hypersexuality, a drive that encourages them to "cheat" and to have frequent sex with multiple partners.

Coy Females and Cheating Males

Women, so this scenario suggests, are chaste by comparison to men. Once pregnant, more frequent sexual relations will not increase a woman's chances of successfully passing on her genes, since she can only be pregnant once at a time. After her child is born, according to sociobiologists, a female increases the chances of her investment paying off by investing even more time and energy in the rearing of her child. To relieve some of this burden, sociobiologists argue, a woman attempts to encourage a man to help her care for her dependent child. Even with this help, it is not in the woman's self-interest to abandon her child to a male caretaker in order to be impregnated again by a different male. A female might fear that if she leaves her baby in a man's care, the relatively small investment (his sperm) he made in the child might not cause him to attend to it properly and eventually abandon it completely. Therefore, she risks losing her investment entirely. According to sociobiologists, a woman benefits from a man's help but must develop a means to keep the man interested in her so that he does not merely leave her in order to spread more of his own genes.

Sociobiologists claim that to keep the male around, women engage in a "domestic-bliss strategy," one that depends on her playing hard to get in the mating game. By being "coy" and holding out on sex, the female is likely to attract a male willing to wait. It is in the female's interest to find such a male, since he might also be more willing to stick around after the birth of a child than a male who wants sex without commitment. Long courtship periods also aid the male who is in less danger of being duped into believing that a child is his when a female has really been impregnated by another male. Having invested so heavily in courtship, the male optimizes the return on

his investment by remaining committed to his coy female partner.

Coy females, and more-or-less faithful males, are the ones most likely to rear children successfully and pass on their genes. What may have begun as an idiosyncratic reproductive pattern becomes stabilized in the population once enough females play the game. As Dawkins argues:

> When coy females increase in numbers so much that they predominate, the philanderer males, who had such an easy time with fast females, start to feel the pinch. Female after female insists on a long and arduous courtship. The philanderers flit from female to female, and always the story is the same. The net payoff for the philanderer male when all the females are coy is zero. [1976:164]

Nevertheless, since no system is perfect, "loose, fast" women will always exist, tempting men to increase their genetic fitness by copulating with them, even if the men are monogamously bonded to other women. Faithful wives and less faithful husbands are thus the product of natural selection. According to sociobiologists, the genes giving rise to these behaviors have been selected for during the course of human evolutionary history.

Critique of Sociobiology

As we have suggested, the characteristics associated with males and females in the selfish gene model are strikingly similar to those that exist in contemporary Western societies. Until the sexual revolution of the 1960s in the United States, for example, women were expected to be virgins at the time of marriage, a trait that was highly valued. Male indiscretions, by contrast, were not cause for alarm or disparagement. Even today in the age of Acquired Immune Deficiency Syndrome (AIDS) and sexually transmitted diseases (STDs), when any promiscuous sexual behavior is dangerous, highly sexually active women in North American society are often viewed more contemptuously than highly sexually active males. A man enjoys a double standard and need not fear being labeled a "slut," a "whore," or "loose."

Do men everywhere actually have a more active sex drive than women? According to Fatima Mernissi (1987), in Morocco women are viewed as more highly sexed than men are. There, men fear the intensity of female sexuality, seeing it as capable of distracting them from their dedication to God. The existence of societies in which men have sex more often than women does not provide proof of the naturalness of an intense male sex drive and a passive female one, as sociobiologists claim. Because women experience the consequences of pregnancy more directly, they may have stronger societal sanctions against frequent sex, not internal genetic mechanisms regulating it (see Mascia-Lees et al. 1989).

The sociobiological model can also be questioned for its assumption that there is differential investment in a child at the moment of its conception since female ova are bigger than male sperm. This assumption may be warranted for species in which the size of the female gamete is large in relation to total body size, but not necessarily in humans where the energy needed to produce male and female gametes is minimal. Moreover, human females are born with all of their ova, while men must continuously produce sperm. Sociobiologists have not yet produced studies measuring the differential energy required in the maturation of eggs versus the production of sperm, even though, as we have seen, they base their entire explanation of the evolution of gender roles and behaviors on this assumption (see Fedigan 1982 for a more detailed discussion of the egg–sperm fallacy).

The reasoning in sociobiological models is much like that found in nineteenth-century social evolutionary accounts. As social evolutionists used their own societies as the starting point of their analysis, assuming their inherent superiority, so sociobiologists today use themselves and the behaviors found in their own societies as a universal reference point. They make unwarranted and unsubstantiated generalizations about the universality of their own society's sexual norms, such as the coyness of females, and then suggest that because these traits are universal, they must have come about during the long evolutionary history of humans.

Unlike most cultural anthropologists, sociobiologists frequently take a behavior out of context. Sociobiologists observe animal behavior and apply it simplistically to humans, without providing evidence that the behavior of ants or of spiders has any direct relationship to human activity. They also take behaviors out of cultural context and assume that if a certain behavior in another culture looks the same as one in their own, it must mean the same thing. Anthropologists have repeatedly shown the pitfalls of this thinking. Even something as simple as a wink, for example, can have many different meanings associated with it in different societies; it may not carry the meaning of

flirtation that many Westerners attribute to it (see Geertz 1973).

Evolutionary Psychology

A Moral Agenda

Currently in vogue is the field of evolutionary psychology, an area of study descended from sociobiology. The stated aim of evolutionary psychology, according to one of its practitioners, is to generate "good theories of personality development" (Wright 1994:82). Evolutionary psychology, however, goes much further than this. As Dorothy Nelkin points out: "Evolutionary psychology is not only a new science, it is a vision of morality and social order, a guide to moral behavior and policy agendas" (2000:24).

The agenda of evolutionary psychologists is far-reaching, as the title of the widely read book by evolutionary psychologist Robert Wright clearly indicates: *The Moral Animal: Why We Are the Way We Are* (1994). For example, evolutionary psychologists suggest that the current U.S. legal system, based on the idea that humans are responsible for their acts, is outmoded and dangerous since it fails to recognize that humans are governed by uncontrollable biological urges; they argue that international violence is an adaptive strategy for males in acquiring mating partners and thus producing offspring; and they claim some nations and some races of people are naturally inferior to others, a claim all too reminiscent of nineteenth-century social evolutionism (Nelkin 2000:25–26). Nelkin quotes a 1995 *Boston Globe* article on the policy message of evolutionary psychology: "Moral codes and policy prescriptions that don't acknowledge human nature are doomed to fail" (2000:26).

More of the Same

Although evolutionary psychologists criticize earlier sociobiologists for their reductive reasoning—that is, for attributing all human behaviors to simplistic genetic mechanisms—their own models differ in only the slightest of ways. Their explanations for the evolution of gender behaviors, for example, are nearly identical to those proposed by earlier writers, such as Washburn and Lancaster, Lovejoy, Wilson, and Dawkins.

Robert Wright's model (1994) includes all the familiar references from sociobiology. He proposes a genetic basis for human social behavior; he draws on the female dependency/male provider concept; he points to women's use of their sexuality to attract and exploit men; he hypothesizes genetic payoffs for optimal mating strategies; and he invokes the "battle of the sexes" scenario. Thus, according to Wright, women, who must necessarily put all their eggs in one basket, have been selected to be choosy—that is, "coy"—in their choice of mates in order to "dupe" men into helping them raise their infants. Men, by contrast, have been selected to seek multiple matings with as many partners as possible, a strategy that requires risk taking and ambition, and thus explains the increased propensity of such behaviors in males in comparison to females in contemporary society.

Biologist Anne Fausto-Sterling, focusing specifically on the ideas of Robert Wright, summarizes the evolutionary model of gender behavior and its social and political implications:

> Modern evolutionary psychologists . . . [argue] . . . that females are supposed to have evolved to be more sexually reserved than males. One consequence of such reticence is deep confusion about sexual harassment: What seems like normal sexuality to a male registers in females as traumatic, unwanted attention. Wright, for instance, suggests that our legal systems should make adjustments to these evolution-bound sexual differences. He also proposes that women will never break the glass ceiling because, biologically, they have less of men's innate ambition and willingness to take the risks necessary for success. This particular version of evolutionary theory implies that affirmative action can only result in hiring or promoting inferior candidates. (Discrimination against equally qualified applicants, it seems, no longer happens.) [2000b:211]

Critique of Evolutionary Psychology

Since evolutionary psychology shares the assumptions of sociobiology, it is open to the same criticisms: its view of male and female sexual behavior is replete with Western bias; it is based on no hard data from the human evolutionary record or from physiological experiments confirming the greater energy expenditure of females in maintaining eggs than of men in producing sperm, and thus women's supposedly higher investment in their offspring than men's. There is also no evidence, as we saw in chapter 3, for the existence of the universal gender behaviors evolutionary psychologists purport to explain. Moreover, both sociobiologists and evolutionary psychologists underestimate the importance of variation to evolutionary survival, "the logic of natural selection suggests that individuals

should vary their reproductive behaviors as a function of the environments in which they find themselves" (Fausto-Sterling 2000b:221).

Most anthropologists would concur with Fausto-Sterling's point that evolutionary psychology's view of human behavior as genetically hard-wired and invariant "flies in the face of the evidence of the plasticity of behavior" (2000b:221). Indeed, one of the central lessons of anthropology, with its focus on human behavior across societies, is that it is highly variable and flexible.

Human survival has depended on this flexibility, which has allowed humans to adapt to almost every environment on the planet. Humans, for example, can survive in the coldest of environments because they have learned to harness energy to use as heat and to build houses and wear clothing for protection, not because they are genetically programmed to withstand the cold. Because human behavior is largely learned, it can be altered in the face of environmental changes. If humans were hard-wired for behavior, their ability to change and adapt would have been severely hampered, leading to extinction, not evolutionary success.

Evolutionary psychologists do tend to claim, or at least pay lip service to the idea, that there is more complexity in the genetic mechanisms underlying reproductive strategies than earlier sociobiologists recognized. For example, complex traits like human sexuality, Wright tells us, "result from the interaction of numerous genes, each of which, typically, was selected for its incremental addition to fitness" (1994:57). Rather than a simple selfish gene dictating human behavior, Wright envisions multiple genes coming together to "counsel" individuals in the behavioral strategies most beneficial to them. Indeed, he describes them as knights at the round table. Yet, Wright and other evolutionary psychologists are just as far from being able to identify a complex set of genes as sociobiologists are from finding that single selfish gene.

Conclusions

Evolutionary models have an important place in anthropology when evidence is used carefully and models are checked for problematic assumptions and faulty reasoning. Knowing how our early hominid ancestors adapted and survived can provide us with significant insights into questions concerning who we are, where we come from, and what it means to be human. As we have seen, cultural assumptions about human nature and gender can seriously color evolutionary reconstructions of past lifeways. This chapter has provided you with some tools for thinking critically about the assumptions underlying many evolutionary explanations of gender differences. The hope is that this knowledge will better enable you to assess such explanations for yourself wherever you encounter them, whether in textbooks or on the evening news.

WORD PORTFOLIO

bipedalism: walking upright on two feet. Among the primates, this form of locomotion is unique to humans and is often thought to be the central factor leading to the evolution of the human species, *Homo sapiens.*

estrus: a moment of heightened fertility when female animals ovulate, which is often marked with external signals. In some animals this period is referred to as "heat." Among primates, human and orangutan females do not have an estrus period.

evolutionary psychology: a recently developed academic field growing out of sociobiology that explains human emotions, human psychological characteristics, and almost every conceivable human behavior in terms of the adaptive advantage they confer to individuals possessing them.

food-for-sex hypothesis: the hypothetical scenario that posits that, in the evolutionary past, females exchanged sex for food provided by males, allowing for the evolution of the human species. This hypothesis is at the basis of both the Man the Hunter and the Man the Provisioner models of human evolution.

hominids: humans and their immediate ancestors.

K-selection: a reproductive strategy characterized by few offspring who are heavily invested in to ensure that they live and grow to reproductive maturity. It is in contrast to an "r" strategy in which a great many offspring are produced with an investment of very little energy in any one of them.

loss of estrus: the lack of a discrete moment in a female's reproductive cycle when she is sexually receptive to sexual intercourse because she is ovulating and therefore capable of becoming impregnated. The loss of estrus in human females is taken by "Man the Hunter" and "Man the Provisioner" theorists as a central event in human evolution, allowing females to have intercourse with males at any time during the year thereby producing enduring pair-bonds.

Man the Hunter: an explanation that posits male hunting as the central force in the evolution of the human intellect and emotions as well as in a wide-range of human cultural behaviors and aspects of human social organization.

Man the Provisioner: a model of human evolution that posits female/child dependency on foods gathered by males as the central force in the evolution of humans. In return for such food, a female would pair-bond with the male provider, offering sex in exchange. See *food-for-sex hypothesis.*

matrilineal descent: a system of reckoning ancestry by tracing it through the female line.

monogamy: a practice allowing an individual to be married to only one spouse at a time.

natural selection: a mechanism of evolutionary change that results from the differential survival of individuals with adaptive biological characteristics that allows them to pass on their genes to subsequent generations in higher numbers than those not possessing such characteristics.

patrilineal descent: a system of reckoning ancestry by tracing it through the male line.

sexual selection: a mechanism of evolutionary change that results from individuals choosing a mate based on the "attractiveness" of certain traits.

social evolutionism: the first school of anthropological theory. It proposed a hierarchical model for understanding similarities and differences among human societies in which those societies at the top were seen as more evolved than those at the bottom, having won out over them through a fierce struggle for survival.

sociobiology: an academic discipline begun by E. O. Wilson in the 1970s that posits natural selection as the force leading to the development of nearly all aspects of social behavior in animals, including humans.

Woman the Gatherer: an explanation that posits women's gathering of plant foods as the central force in the evolution of the human intellect and emotions as well as in a wide-range of aspects of human cultural behavior and aspects of human social organization.

RECOMMENDED READING

Women in Human Evolution, 2nd edition, edited, by Lori D. Hager. 2007. New York: Kindle.

This is an excellent collection of essays if you want to learn more about evolutionary models of gender differences and what the archeological evidence tells us about them.

The Caveman Mystique: Pop-Darwinism and the Debates over Sex, Violence, and Science, 2nd edition, by Martha McCaughey. 2008, New York: Routledge, Taylor and Francis Group.

You'll love this book if you want to find out why evolutionary psychology's ideas about sexual and gender difference have become so popular among American men. McCaughey shows the similarities between explanations offered by evolutionary psychology and those that exist in popular culture in such outlets as *Playboy*, Broadway, and self-help books for couples, all based on the myth of the "caveman."

The Evolving Female: A Life-History Perspective, edited by Mary Morbeck, Alsion Galloway, and Adrienne Zihlman. 1997. Princeton, NJ: Princeton University Press.

This is a collection of essays that examines how human's long evolutionary history has shaped the lives of women, including those in contemporary society. It concentrates on the stages of a woman's life from infancy to old age.

Alas, Poor Darwin: Arguments against Evolutionary Psychology, edited by Hilary Rose and Steven Rose. 2001. New York: Vintage.

This entertaining and highly informative book focuses on the misuse of Darwin's ideas in contemporary sociobiology and evolutionary psychology. The authors include biologists, social scientists, and philosophers who reveal the flaws, and lack of evidence, in contemporary biological determinist arguments.

III

Political Economy and the Production of Culture

In the good old days
My community lived in great prosperity
They fed and clothed themselves well
They controlled and ruled their lands
But a change in the world had changed them
Europe invented machines that changed life
Factories turned over goods in large quantities
Demand for market and raw material increased
Invasion of Africa had become a high priority
Science played a role to swallow my people
It transported new people, new cultures
Globalization started in the good old days
                              —Abdi-Noor Haji Mohamed

6

Production, Capitalism, Ideology, and the State

In this chapter you will . . .

analyze Marxist ideas about the evolution of private property and state societies and the rise of class and gender oppression • examine the relationship between a society's economic structure, political system, and system of ideas • assess the impact of a range of material factors on women's status • compare women's productive roles in foraging, pastoral, horticultural, agricultural, industrial, and postindustrial societies • explore the relationship between women's relegation to the private sphere of life and ideas about domestic labor • discuss thinkers who have used and reformulated Marxist ideas to understand women's oppression • focus on reformulations and critiques of Marx's concept of ideology • explore the idea of a moral economy

In the next two chapters, we focus on the political economy of gender and difference. We analyze the connections between a society's **political economy,** its economic system and political structures, and their relationship to the creation and maintenance of inequality and oppression. We thus explore how political factors influence the functioning of an economic system and how that economic system affects a society's political ideas and structures. We are particularly interested in investigating how political economic structures affect and shape ideas.

In this chapter, we focus specifically on materialist explanations of gender and class inequality and oppression. These explanations assume that the economic organization of a society is the prime mover in establishing unequal relations between women and men. We frame our discussion within the materialist model of Karl Marx and Friedrich Engels, which deeply affected feminist anthropological analyses of gender stratification during the 1970s. This chapter reflects the major concerns of that period by exploring the following questions:

- What is the effect on different women and men of the way that goods are produced and consumed in a particular society?

- What is the relationship of work to women's status?

- How does work produce inequality and structure relations of power?

- How are the conditions and forms under which people work created and how do they change over time?

- Is women's seemingly universal subordination a form not just of gender oppression but also of class oppression?

- What is the relationship of capitalism to the construction and maintenance of inequality?

- Does capitalism depend on women's labor being undervalued and invisible?

- How does ethnicity interact with class and gender to produce inequality?

- What are the moral values associated with labor?

A political economic approach continues to be an important tool for twenty-first-century-anthropologists concerned with understanding inequality and oppression. As we will see in chapter 7, it has been especially productive for understanding the impact of capitalism on inequality and oppression in the *global* economy.

Gendered Labor

Anthropological studies show that gender affects all aspects of work, including what work one will do, who works and for whom, whose labor is valued and whose remains invisible, who manages production and coordinates economic transactions, who consumes, and how much one is paid. Ideas about work and the appropriate activities that women and men should undertake are shaped by culturally and historically specific ideas and beliefs about what it means to be a woman and what it means to be a man. What in one location or moment in history may be considered "women's work" may in another place and time be thought of as a "man's job." Labor is affected by different ideas, beliefs, and values about gender in a given society or culture. This is what we mean when we say that work is gendered.

On both a national and a global scale, however, social expectations and stereotypes about gender and labor are constantly in flux. Indeed, an interesting phenomenon occurs in many societies: When women enter and come to dominate a profession that once was thought of as men's, those jobs can become feminized, linked ideologically to women. This feminization of certain jobs masks a simple paradox: these jobs rely on the fact that certain tasks seem naturally or necessarily linked to men or women, even though the same jobs may be feminized in one location or historical moment while never feminized in another.

Feminist anthropologists have asked why societies develop a sexual division of labor, such that it is rare to find women and men carrying out the same daily tasks across societies. As we will see, this question has been central to theoretical formulations about the origins of women's "inferior" status. Feminist anthropologists have also investigated how the sexual division of labor operates across nations, as we will see in the next chapter.

As we have seen, anthropological theory was greatly informed by significant social movements in the United States in the 1970s, including the antiwar, civil rights, gay and lesbian, and women's movements. This vibrant social and political climate promoted a great sense of doubt about preestablished social "truths." At the same time, an increasing number of women in the United States began to enter the labor market, creating a need to theorize women's participation in the workforce. Much of the feminist scholarship that focuses on the relationship of women's economic lives to inequality draws heavily on the ideas of Marx and Engels.

While Marx is best known for his analyses of class oppression, Engels is perhaps best recognized for his treatment of gender inequalities in his classic study, *The Origin of the Family, Private Property and the State* (1884), a book whose influence can still be felt today.

While the evolutionary model Engels used in this text, and some of the assumptions underlying it, have been rejected, his basic approach has not. Researchers today continue to focus on how the material conditions of people's lives and different forms of labor affect women and men around the globe and how economic factors produce gender, and other forms of, inequality.

The Basics of Marxist Theory

The social evolutionists discussed at the beginning of chapter 5 were not the only nineteenth-century thinkers to employ an evolutionary framework to explain differences in men's and women's roles and status. So, too, did Marx and Engels. Like the social evolutionists, Marx and Engels hoped to uncover universal laws governing historical change and proposed a sequence of societal stages. Unlike the social evolutionists who sought to support what they saw as Western civilization's naturalness and superiority, Marx and Engels searched to uncover the origins of its systems of oppression. They focused on the inequalities brought by the development of capitalism in the United States and Western European societies. They also rejected the idea that humans have an inherent and unchanging human nature.

Marx and Engels ([1848] 1967) proposed that societies evolved from one stage of social organization to another based on their economic structure. These stages were distinguished based on how a society "makes its living," or, in other words, how economic production is organized in a particular society. Marx and Engels referred to this economic system of production as a **mode of production.**

Marx and Engels identified several modes of production that have arisen in the course of human history; these include: primitive communism, ancient (or slave) mode of production, feudalism, capitalism, socialism, and communism. Each mode of production consists of the physical resources used in the economic activities of a society, including raw materials such as land and other resources such as tools, machines, and factories. Marx and Engels referred to these as the **means of production.** Different modes of production determine the form of social relationships that exist between groups of people, what Marx and Engels refer to as the **social relations of production.** Ownership of the means of production is the most important factor in determining these social relations.

For example, Marx and Engels hypothesized that in early societies the economic mode of production was based on the foraging, or gathering, of foodstuffs from the environment. The primary means of extracting foodstuffs from the environment was through human physical labor and simple tools. These productive resources were shared in common by the entire group. Under such conditions of "tribal ownership," as Marx and Engels called this form of ownership, social relationships among members were essentially egalitarian. With increases in population, however, societies grew into ones that eventually instituted private property ownership. Once ownership of such resources as land was no longer shared equally by all, class distinctions within these societies arose, thus replacing the egalitarian society with the **class society.**

This movement away from communal forms of property ownership toward private property ownership had reached its height, according to Marx and Engels, in the capitalist societies of their time. These societies were founded on an industrial base and were characterized by deep divisions that excluded a large portion of the population from access to resources and privileges. Under capitalism, two distinct classes had emerged: the **bourgeoisie,** who owned the means of production, and the **proletariat,** who worked for the owners and sold their labor to the bourgeoisie in exchange for wages.

Marx and Engels ([1848] 1967) viewed the exchange of labor for money in capitalist societies as unfair to workers—as exploitative. Owners never paid workers what their labor was worth, because if they did, they would not make a profit. The bourgeoisie used the surplus value produced by members of the proletariat to further their own position. Marx and Engels also criticized capitalist productive relationships for separating workers from the fruits of their own labor. According to them, productive work is pleasurable when workers are able to reap the benefits of it. Indeed, Marx and Engels saw productive labor as the very thing that differentiated humans from other animals. They contended it was responsible for the development of human consciousness. Toiling for wages, by contrast, divided workers from the products of their own labor, alienating them not only from their work but from themselves as well.

Marx and Engels ([1848] 1967) also argued that a society's economic base, or **infrastructure,** determined its **superstructure**—the ideas and beliefs of a society, as well as the legal, political, social, and cultural institutions, which develop to ensure the continuation of the economic *status quo*. The ideas and beliefs of a society constitute its **ideology** that is perpetuated by these institutions. The superstructure of a society, according to Marx and Engels, produces human consciousness, determining the very way people think about the world and themselves.

For example, the importance granted to the notion of "individuality" in Western European societies since the seventeenth century would be tied, in a Marxist analysis, to the demands of a developing capitalism. In order to sell their labor, people needed to think of themselves as distinct from a larger social group, able and entitled as individuals to make decisions based on their own interests alone. Becoming an autonomous individual thus became an ideal to which people aspired. They saw it as *the* right and desirable way to be. People who were not "individuals" or not individual enough were, and continue to be, disdained and seen as lacking or inferior. We can see this "cult of individuality" operating in the United States today as women and men strive to "be their own person."

Similarly, the increasing value in the United States and many Western European societies over the last century placed on having young couples start their own households after marriage can be understood from a Marxist perspective in terms of the advantages it creates for a capitalist economy. If every individual household must have its own refrigerator and washing machine, for example, more products can be sold than if members of an extended family live together sharing goods and expenses.

Thus, what we value, aspire to, and think of as the right way to live is a product of ideology. The important point here for Marx and Engels is that ideology conceals from the proletariat the reality of their own subordination, exploitation, and domination. They do not, for example, see the cult of individuality as something that perpetuates the very capitalist system that oppresses them. Engels called this **false consciousness.**

Marx and Engels theorized that once the proletariat became aware of their oppression as a group, or class, by shedding their false consciousness for a true understanding of their subordinate position, they would rise up against the bourgeoisie in a class struggle so severe that revolution would occur. This revolt would lead to the establishment of a system of shared ownership, or communism. Marx and Engels envisioned this communistic society as one free of all exploitation and oppression, one in which people were no longer alienated from their labor and themselves, and one in which an entirely new human consciousness would arise. Engels outlined how, with this new consciousness, women would no longer be viewed as merely a tool to be used in a system of production.

Engels' Evolutionary Account

Engels began his analysis of gender oppression with the premise that the roles and position of men and women varied in time and space depending on the economic relationships that characterized a particular society. He claimed that the movement away from the communal ownership of property found in early societies toward the private property ownership associated with class societies corresponded to the movement from higher to lower status for women.

Communal Society and Women's Position

According to Engels, in early communal societies in which everything produced was held in common, women enjoyed a high position. They performed important subsistence functions compatible with childbearing and child rearing, while men performed other necessary tasks. In a society in which people do not know who is the father of a child, descent was matrilineal, traced through women who were highly esteemed for their role as mothers. These were often called "mother right" societies.

Since what was produced in such societies was shared by everyone, the division of labor between women and men was reciprocal, not exploitative (Guettel 1974:11). Women were viewed as equal and productive members of society, performing domestic labor necessary for the functioning and survival of the group. Their participation in socially valued activities granted them political equality as well, since in communal societies, Engels proposed, those individuals who made decisions also carried them out. The participation of women in a major share of the significant labor needed for society's functioning, Engels theorized, gave them decision-making power commensurate with their contributions (Leacock 1972:34).

Impact of Private Property on Women

Engels ([1884] 1978) postulated that as the production of wealth in a society increased, private property ownership would emerge, and men would be-

come more important within the family. Men used their strengthened position to overthrow "mother right" and matrilineality in favor of patrilineal descent, which traces kinship connections through males. It also replaced preexisting polygamous marriage forms that allowed a person to have more than one spouse at a time with monogamous marriage. Monogamy allows a man or a woman to be married to only one spouse at a time.

Monogamy was instituted to ensure that a man's wealth and property would be passed on to his own children and to no one else's. This practice was enforced through patriarchal control of the family in which men were the most powerful family members able to control other members' actions and ideas. Engels claimed that under such conditions, women became degraded, the slaves of men's lust, and mere instruments for breeding children. The movement away from communal ownership and "mother right" to private property and patriarchy constituted nothing less, according to Engels, than "the world-historical defeat of the female sex" (p. 736).

Women were thus transformed from productive members of society, whose roles as mothers and whose participation in necessary and valued labor had once given them social and political equality, into wives dependent on their husbands' activities for survival (Sacks 1979). Under such circumstances, women's domestic labor was no longer viewed as an important contribution to the larger society. Instead, a woman's labor was seen as work done for her individual family, headed by a man whose role in the outside world granted him power and status.

Once women were no longer perceived as important contributors to society's economic functioning, they lost their status as valued members and, with it, their position of political equality. The development of this inequality between men and women, according to Engels, constituted the earliest form of oppression known in human societies. As he phrased it, "The first class antagonism that appears in history coincides with the development of the antagonism between men and women in monogamian [monogamous] marriage and the first class oppression with that of the female sex by the male" (Engels [1884] 1978:739).

Impact of Class Society and the State on Women

With the development of class society, according to Engels, the state arose. In a Marxist perspective, the

state is understood as a political mechanism that protects the interests of the privileged, or elite, class. The state protects these interests not only through using political force if need be but also through ideology, the shared ideas and beliefs that serve to justify the interests of dominant groups (Giddens 1990:583). An ideology of women's inferiority, many materialist theorists argue, did just that. Thus, with the development of class society, women's status, defined in terms of their equal rights, declined. The new social relations, brought about by an economic pattern based on private property ownership, was supported by state structures, making women economically and politically powerless and socially and culturally undervalued.

Influence of Engels' Theory

Engels' ideas have provided feminist researchers with a model for understanding women's position in particular societies in both the past and the present. One particularly early and clear example of the usefulness of Engels' model when applied historically is Fatima Mernissi's analysis of women's position in Morocco in *Beyond the Veil: Male-Female Dynamics in Modern Muslim Society* (1987). In it, Mernissi argues that the position of women in Morocco historically and at the time of her study is not based on a belief in women's inherent (biological) inferiority, as it has typically been in Western ideology, but on a belief in women's active and dangerous sexuality. Mernissi suggests that contemporary Islamic practices and laws and Muslim social structure can be seen as a defense against this belief in the disruptive power of female sexuality. Note that although Mernissi focuses on the control of female sexuality as the basis of women's oppression, she suggests that the need for this control arose under circumstances much like those Engels proposed (see Ethnography in Focus on the following page).

Engels' model has also provided feminist researchers with a number of productive areas of further investigation. It has led researchers to ask the following questions:

- Did ancient matriarchies or "mother right" societies, in which power was invested in the hands of women, actually ever exist?
- Do women fare better in societies that put them at the center of social organization by tracing descent matrilineally?

- What is the relationship between a society's mode of food production and sexual stratification?
- How does the existence of private property alter women's status?
- What effect does the separation of public and private spheres, which accompanies the rise of state societies, have on gender oppression?

The next sections in this chapter address each of these questions.

Matriarchies

Engels drew his knowledge of early communal societies from the work of social evolutionists such as J. J. Bachofen. Using myths that show women as once powerful as evidence, Bachofen's *Das Mutterrecht* ([1861] 1992) suggested that women in early societies were unhappy because there were no rules regulating sexuality, allowing a promiscuous social order. Women revolted against uncontrolled male lust, which enabled men to have sexual relations with many women. In its place, they instituted a new form of social organization based on "mother right," which sprang from the natural biological association of mother and child (Bamberger 1974:264). Ultimately, according to Bachofen, men became unhappy with a society based on "nature and sensuality" and revolted, establishing patriarchal rule and subordinating women in the process (Sacks 1979:53). This event produced a superior form of social organization, according to Bachofen, since transcending sensuality allowed men to create civilization.

Like other social evolutionists, Bachofen ([1861] 1992) proposed the existence of matriarchies somewhere in the West's evolutionary past based on scant evidence. He did so, however, not to praise mother right, as Engels did, but instead to point to its undesirability. By contrast, many feminists in the 1970s used such accounts much like Engels did, to argue that women in early societies had enjoyed power (Leacock 1972). They believed that women's current oppression was best explained in terms of social and economic factors, not in terms of some natural inferiority.

Today, assertions of the existence of matriarchal societies have become big business. Book after book claims that mother goddess religions emphasizing fertility are evidence of earlier societies that venerated women, ones in which the "female principle" was dominant and women had power. Each year New Age shops sell thousands of tiny replicas of what they presume to be fertility idols from mother-right societies in

Ethnography in Focus

Beyond the Veil: Male-Female Dynamics in Modern Muslim Society by Fatima Mernissi

It is a widely shared belief among historians in different cultures that human history is progressive, that human society, in spite of accidents and setbacks, moves progressively from "savagery" to "civilization." Islam too has a progressive vision of history. The year 622, the *hijra* is the year one of civilization. Before the *hijra* was the *jahiliya,* the time of barbarism, the time of ignorance. Islam maintains that one of the dimensions of society in which there was progress is human sexuality. Under *jahiliya* sexuality was promiscuous, lax, and uncontrolled, but under Islam it obeys rules. . . . But what is peculiar about Muslim sexuality as civilized sexuality is this fundamental discrepancy: if promiscuity and laxity are signs of barbarism, then only women's sexuality was civilized by Islam; male sexuality is promiscuous (by virtue of polygamy) and lax (by virtue of repudiation). [p. 46]

***

It is by examining Islam's *selective* attitude toward *jahiliya* sexual practices that we may grasp the new religion's stance toward relations between the sexes. That is my object here. [p. 65]

***

Early Islamic historians . . . held that the Muslim family marked a break with earlier practices. They acknowledged that the patriarchal marriage endorsed by Islam had been paralleled by many other forms of union that were clearly anti-patriarchal: there were unions in which the child did not belong to the biological father (and even polyandrous marriages in which the woman had more than one regular sexual partner) and there were unions in which the woman had the absolute right to send her husband away if she so desires. . . . But all these practices, though amply documented, were subsequently prohibited by Islam. . . . Islam banished all practices in which the sexual self-determination of women was asserted. [pp. 66–67]

***

[Robertson Smith] argued that the period of Islam's appearance had a multiplicity of sexual unions belonging to two trends: a matrilineal trend he calls . . . *sadiqa* marriage, and a patrilineal trend he calls *ba'al* marriage. . . . The two systems, which existed side by side down to the Prophet's time, were diametrically opposed to each other . . . *Sadiqa* marriage . . . is a union whose offspring belong to the woman's tribe. It is initiated by a mutual agreement between a woman and a man, and it takes place at the house of the woman, who retains the right to dismiss the husband. . . . *Sadiqa* marriage was characterized by sexual freedom for women. . . . It is evident that this kind of marriage could only be uxorilocal [matrilocal], since the woman remained with her tribe and depended on it. . . . In *ba'al* marriage, the offspring belong to the husband. He has the status of father as well as of his wife's *ba'al*, or "lord," "owner". . . . Robertson Smith concludes that Islam accelerated the transition from matriliny to patriliny by enforcing a marriage institution that had much in common with the patrilineal dominion marriage, and by condemning all matrilineal unions. [pp. 73–75]

(continued)

***

The panorama of female sexual rights in pre-Islamic culture reveals that women's sexuality was not bound by the concept of legitimacy. Children belonged to their mother's tribe. Women had sexual freedom to enter into and break off unions with more than one man, either simultaneously or successively. . . . The husband would come and go; the main unit was the mother and child within an entourage of kinfolk. [p. 78]

***

If we consider marriage as a "rearrangement of social structure" and social structure as "any arrangement of persons in institutionalized relationships," then a change in the marriage system would imply far-reaching socio-economic changes. A change in kinship implies a dislocation of old socio-economic structures, and the appearance of new networks based on new units. . . . [In the Arabia of Mohammed's time] insecurity and discontent were spreading because of the rise of a thriving mercantile economy which was corroding traditional tribal communism. Individuals engaged in trading were motivated by new mercantile allegiances which often clashed with traditional tribal ones. . . . Responsible members who were supposed to administer property for the communal good were now lured by individualistic pursuits and neglected their traditional role as protectors of the weak. Women and children were among those most directly affected by the disruption of the old networks of solidarity since they had no institutionalized access to property through inheritance.

. . . It has been argued that many of Islam's institutions were a response to the new needs that emerged with the disintegration of tribal communalism, a means of absorbing the insecurity generated by such disintegration. . . . The *umma* (or Muslim community) steered the tribes' bellicosity, usually invested in tribal feuding, in a new direction—the holy war. The old allegiance to the tribe was replaced by an allegiance entirely different in both form and content. The new form is the *umma* and the basic unit is not the tribe, but the individuals. The bond between individuals is not kinship but a more abstract concept, communion in the same religious belief. . . . There was a similar absorption of self-serving tendencies into the family structure. One of these channeling mechanisms was the concept of fatherhood and legitimacy. . . . Biological paternity had been considered unimportant in pre-existing systems, and the patterns of female sexuality made it difficult to establish who had begotten whom. Islam dealt with this obstacle in two ways . . . it outlawed most previous sexual practices . . . and institutionalized strict control over paternity in the form of the *idda*, or waiting period [during which widows and divorcées are forbidden from re-marrying until it is evident that they are not pregnant by their deceased or ex-husband]. The *idda* can be seen as the best proof both of the previous disregard for biological paternity and of Islamic curtailment of female sexual rights, since no equivalent period was instituted for men. [pp. 79–81]

***

The social order created by the Prophet, a patrilineal monotheistic state, could exist only if the tribe and its allegiances gave way to the *umma* [or male-dominated Muslim community or public sphere]. The Prophet found the institution of the family a much more suitable unit of socialization than the tribe. He saw the tightly controlled patriarchal family as necessary to the creation of the *umma*… The assumptions behind the Muslim social structure—male dominance, the fear of *fitna* [chaos or disorder], the need for sexual satisfaction, the need for men to love Allah above all else—were embodied in specific laws which have regulated male-female relations in Muslim countries for fourteen centuries.

the form of necklaces, earrings, key chains, and T-shirt logos.

Feminist archaeologist Sarah Nelson (1997), however, has pointed out the problem with interpreting archaeological evidence as a sign of the admiration, or veneration, of women. She suggests that the interpretation of Venus figures as ancient fertility symbols is not supported by evidence. Instead, it reproduces a Western male bias. As Nelson puts it, "underlying the description of the figurines as erotic and reproductive is a masculinist construction of the world, in which females are assumed to exist primarily for males, sexually or reproductively" (p. 70). Nelson suggests that it is just as likely that the figurines were used as teaching devices for young girls experiencing puberty (p. 71).

Similarly, Joan Bamberger's (1974) analysis of a constellation of myths about women-controlled societies from societies in Tierra del Fuego in South America and in the tropical rainforests of the Amazon suggests that these myths do not reveal an actual moment in the past when women had power (also see Murphy and Murphy 1974). To the contrary, she argues that they act to justify male dominance in these societies in the present. These myths begin with a discussion of an earlier time when women ruled. But they then move on to describe a moment when men took this control away from them. Men, these stories suggest, needed to do so because women could not handle power or use it in the proper way—in the way, that is, that men use it today. The myths thus reinforce the properness and desirability of male power. Bamberger concludes her analysis with the following warning: "The myth of matriarchy is but the tool used to keep woman bound to her place. To free her, we need to destroy the myth" (1974:280).

Paula Webster agrees with Bamberger that stories about the existence of past matriarchies, whether from our own society or from others, do not represent proof of the actual existence of mother right. Yet, she presents a conclusion that is diametrically opposed to Bamberger's. Webster suggests that the debate over whether matriarchies have ever existed can play an important role in our society:

It pushes women (and men) to imagine a society that is not patriarchal, one in which women might for the first time have power over their lives. . . . Thus even if feminists reject the existence of matriarchy on empirical and/or theoretical grounds, we should acknowledge the importance of the vision of matriarchy and use the debate for furthering the creation of feminist theory and action. [Webster 1975:155–156]

Whether one agrees with Bamberger or with Webster, it seems clear that there is little empirical evidence to substantiate claims that matriarchies ever existed. The stories of their existence, however, can act either to oppress women or to offer us a vision of a different world. When claims of ancient mother right are invoked, then, we need to listen carefully to the underlying message to decide why the myth of matriarchy is being used. We might question, for example, whose interest it serves. We might also wish to analyze the role it plays in women's actual lives. Does belief in matriarchy empower the women who buy "proof" of it from their local New Age stores to take action in the real world against oppression, or does it prevent them from doing so?

Matrilineality

Engels' claim that matrilineality accorded women high esteem in ancient societies has been a source of controversy for many years in anthropology. Engels' opponents argued that this was not the case since in matrilineal societies, women are still controlled by men. Now, the important men for a woman are her brothers, not her husband or father (Hobhouse 1924). Kathleen Gough, by contrast, argues that in matrilineal societies, "women tend to have greater independence than in patrilineal societies [even though] the ultimate head of the household lineage and local group is usually a man" (1975:54).

How Does Matrilineality Work?

To understand these seemingly contradictory statements, it is necessary to see how matrilineal descent systems work. In a matrilineal society, people's relatives are not determined by tracing relationships through both one's mother and one's father, as they are in the mainstream culture in the United States, Canada, and in many European societies. This system of tracing kinship is known as **bilateral ("two sided") descent.** In contrast, in some societies, **unilineal descent** determines who are, and who are not, a person's kin by tracing family connections though only one line—either that of the mother's side (matrilineal descent) or that of the father's side (patrilineal descent). In unilineal systems one's social identity and access to resources, as well as one's rights, duties, and obligations, are defined by membership in a descent group (see fig. 6.1).

In a matrilineal society, one's descent group would consist of all members related to a person through connections with a woman. If you lived in such a society, some of the individuals who would belong to your matrilineage would include your mother, her mother, your brothers and sisters (you share a mother with them), your mother's brothers and sisters (they share a mother with your mother), and your mother's sisters' children (their mother and your mother share a mother). Many people whom you think of as your relatives if you trace descent bilaterally would not be considered members of your descent group in a matrilineal society. These individuals would include your father and grandfather (your father belongs to his mother's group and his father to his mother's group), your mother's brother's children (they belong to the matrilineage of their mother), and your mother's father (he, too, belongs to his mother's group).

As you can see, while a woman's father and husband are not part of her matrilineage, her brothers are. Under such circumstances, men typically show stronger loyalty toward their mothers and sisters than to

their wives (Nielsen 1990:33). Yet a man frequently lives with his wife's family in a matrilineal society, a circumstance that can potentially give rise to conflicting duties and responsibilities between a woman's husband and her brothers. This possible tension can be eased somewhat by granting authority over women and children to a woman's brother (Nielsen 1990:33). This clarification should help explain Hobhouse's and Gough's seemingly contradictory statements. Just because women are the links in a matrilineal kinship system, this factor does not necessarily mean that they exercise power and authority. Their brothers might instead.

Domestic Authority in Matrilineal Societies

To investigate the role male authority plays in matrilineal societies, Alice Schlegel (1972) constructed a continuum of matrilineal societies based on who has authority in a woman's household. On one side of the continuum were societies in which brothers had total control over women, while on the other side were those in which husbands did. She found that at both ends of the continuum, women had little independence and little freedom to make their own decisions. In societies falling between the two extremes, where brothers and husbands shared domestic authority equally, however, women's independence, or autonomy, was much greater. This finding led Schlegel to conclude that when power is shared among different groups of men, their control over women in the domestic sphere lessens. The implication of Schlegel's study is that tracing descent through females alone does not guarantee women a high degree of autonomy. Instead, it is the pattern of domestic power relations in such societies that affects women's options.

The Advantages of Matrilineality for Women

Martin K. Whyte (1978) has also analyzed the relationship of matrilineality to women's position in society. His analysis, like Schlegel's, suggests that it is too simple to claim that women have a high status in such societies. He argues that we need to uncover the specific benefits of matrilineality for women. His cross-cultural analysis reveals that matrilineality is associated with several advantages for women. These benefits include women having greater control over property, greater domestic authority, and a higher value placed on their lives (Whyte 1978:133). But they do not include women being in control or being the most powerful members of the society.

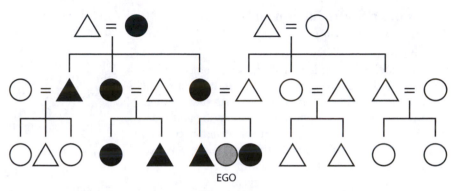

Matrilineal Descent

Members of "Ego's" matrilineage, which includes all people related to her through the female (her mother's) line, are marked in black.

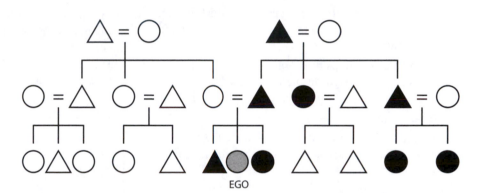

Patrilineal Descent

Members of "Ego's" patrilineage, which includes all people related to her through the male (her father's) line, are marked in black.

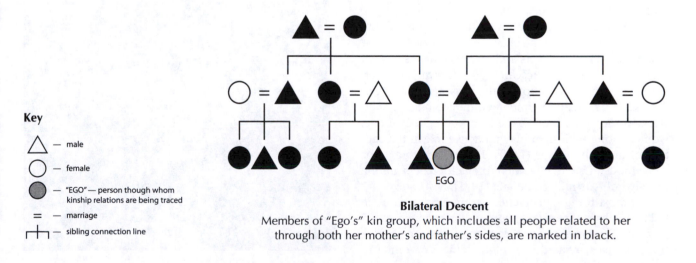

Key

△ — male

○ — female

⬤ — "EGO" — person though whom kinship relations are being traced

= — marriage

⊓ — sibling connection line

Bilateral Descent

Members of "Ego's" kin group, which includes all people related to her through both her mother's and father's sides, are marked in black.

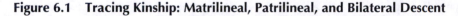

Figure 6.1   Tracing Kinship: Matrilineal, Patrilineal, and Bilateral Descent

Modes of Food Production and the Sexual Division of Labor

Engels' model is based on the assumption that in pre-class societies women's role in subsistence activities provided the basic necessities of life, ensuring them equal status with men. He asserts that women performed activities compatible with having and rearing children, while men undertook other necessary tasks. This sexual division of labor, however, was not exploitative, since both women and men performed tasks necessary for the group's survival.

This assertion has led many anthropologists to focus on the role that the sexual division of labor plays in societies with different subsistence strategies, or modes of production. These modes include:

- foraging (hunter-gatherer) societies in which food is obtained by hunting animals and gathering fruits and vegetables;

- horticultural societies that practice small-scale cultivation of plants based on the use of the hoe;

- pastoral societies that depend primarily on herd-animal husbandry; and

- agrarian societies that usually employ the plow in cultivation and use irrigation systems and fertilizers to increase yields.

Foraging or Hunter-Gatherer Societies

There is little stratification in foraging societies of any kind. There is almost no private property ownership. In general, in such societies, women enjoy an equal position with men, although certain exceptions do exist.

Among foragers, there is no universal form of division of labor by sex. Early studies assumed that women were the gatherers and men the hunters in such societies. Subsequent research has shown, however, that there is great variation in the subsistence tasks undertaken by men and women in different foraging societies. Among the Mbuti of the Ituri forest, for example, women along with men play an active role in the capture of animals in nets (Duffy 1996). Men forage for some foodstuffs while women forage for others among the Tiwi of Australia (Goodale [1971] 1994).

In most foraging societies, women contribute the bulk of subsistence foods, sometimes as much as 75 percent. Women's contribution to subsistence is, for the most part, related to a high status for women in foraging societies. In an analysis drawing on Engels, Eleanor Leacock (1978) suggests that this status is due

to several factors. Women's work in foraging societies contributes to the overall group, and there is no division in such societies between a public and a private sphere with men occupying the former and women the latter. In addition, individuals who carry out decisions tend to make them. These factors, according to Leacock, grant women a great deal of autonomy within foraging societies.

Horticultural Societies

Among horticulturists, women continue to play an active role in subsistence, although their contributions do not necessarily result in high status. This finding suggests that women's contribution to subsistence alone cannot account for their position within society. According to Joyce Nielsen (1990), kinship organization within horticultural societies is more significant for determining women's position than their subsistence contribution. In line with some researchers discussed earlier in this chapter, Nielsen suggests that the presence of matrilineality is the significant factor in-

Like many other women in Myanmar, this woman's job is in a rice field, helping to produce the main staple food crop.

fluencing women's lives in horticultural societies (pp. 32–36). She also points out, however, that there is variation in women's position in horticultural societies that practice matrilineal descent, suggesting this variation can be explained by differing residence rules that govern where or with whom a couple is expected to live after marriage (p. 29).

In matrilineal societies, two types of residence patterns generally dominate: **matrilocal residence,** in which a newly married couple lives with or near the bride's family, and **avunculocal** residence, in which the couple lives with or near the husband's maternal uncle. This latter pattern should make sense, given the previous discussion of the importance of a woman's brother to her and thus to her children in matrilineal societies.

In societies that practice matrilineal descent, Nielsen (1990) argues, women fare better in those with matrilocal residence than in those with avunculocal residence. With matrilocal residence, related women live together while men leave to live with their wives. With avunculocal residence, however, it is women who are dispersed. Drawing on the work of Kay Martin and Barbara Voorhies (1975), Nielsen suggests that matrilocal residence is found in horticultural societies in which food sources are abundant; there is little competition over resources, thus the threat of warfare is decreased; and there is no surplus production. Under such circumstances, related men need not be kept together (Nielsen 1990:33).

In societies with avunculocal residence, a woman is a member of a household in which the distribution of land and products is controlled by a man unrelated to her (usually her husband's maternal uncle). She will have less autonomy in decision-making opportunities and will be less valued by the group than if she resides with members of her own descent group. Thus, according to this analysis, subsistence contributions alone do not account for women's position in horticultural societies. Their status is mediated by kinship structures and residence rules.

Pastoral Societies

Pastoral societies involve animal herding and are noted for the importance placed on men. They are almost always patriarchal and patrilineal, and they establish **patrilocal residence** (a newly married couple goes to live with or near the husband's family). Women's contribution to subsistence is frequently low in these societies, although studies of some East African groups report that women occasionally herd large

animals and perform tasks related to the maintenance of animals, such as watering, feeding, milking, and caring for young livestock (Dahl 1987). The combination of a patrilocal residence pattern and a strict division of labor, not surprisingly, leads to a relatively low status for women in most pastoral societies, although there are exceptions.

In some pastoral societies today, women make direct and important contributions to subsistence. Dairy products are critical to the diet of the Afghan Registan Kuchi, for example, especially curd and buttermilk, which are produced by women, primarily at home (Gura 2006). Women also prepare food products such as cheese for sale in local markets. In Iran, women do more than 85 percent of the milking and 42 percent of the feeding, watering, and health care of livestock (FAO National Sectoral Report on Women, 1994, cited in Gura 2006). In Pakistan, women look after the herds during the summer, while men travel back and forth between pastures in alpine areas and base camp (Gura 2006).

Agricultural Societies

Several authors claim that the rise of plow agriculture corresponds to a decline in women's position due to the loss of their productive role. Martin and Voorhies (1975) suggest that with the adoption of intensive cultivation techniques, especially the use of the plow and irrigation, a sexual division of labor develops in which men take over women's position as primary producers. This change in women's productive tasks occurs, they argue, because such innovations require strength and prolonged absences from the household, a requirement incompatible with child rearing (see Brown 1970). Consequently, women are withdrawn from agricultural production and become isolated in the domestic realm where they are concerned primarily with child care. At the same time, ideologies develop to justify women's domestic isolation. According to Martin and Voorhies:

> The economic horizons of women are thereby gradually limited to the physical and social space of the domicile. Entirely new mythologies appear to redefine the innate aptitudes of the sexes with respect to domestic and extradomestic horizons. [1975:331]

Substantiating this claim is Matthiasson's (1974) finding that there is a relationship between women's participation in agriculture and public status. In societies in which women are heavily involved in agricultural production, such as in the Philippines and Cambodia, the status of women can be high. In places in which women participate little in such activities, as among the peasants of China, North and Central India, and Egypt, men tend to dominate public life (p. 433).

Ester Boserup (1970) has pointed to the detrimental effects of the adoption of plow agriculture on women's position in societies that were colonized. According to her research, due to population pressures on foraging groups, some societies adopted horticulture with shifting cultivation in which fields are used for a few years, but then left empty for many years to restore the soil's nutrients. Under such conditions, it was common for women to engage in more horticultural work than men and to enjoy a considerable degree of autonomy as well. However, with even greater population pressures, plow agriculture emerged, and with it, women lost their productive role. This change was primarily the result of colonial policies that en-

couraged men to take over farming by introducing cash crops and new farming technologies exclusively to men (see Quinn 1977:185).

According to Martin and Voorhies, the effect of colonial introduction of agricultural techniques on women's role and status is also affected by kinship. Colonial practices, which favored men's participation in agricultural labor, also encouraged the development of the nuclear family, which acted to isolate women from a larger social group. Furthermore, according to them:

> Colonial administrators and missionaries took the initiative in inculcating European institutions and value systems. Since the culture they brought with them had a strong patriarchal base, the social and economic horizons of the colonized male were characteristically broadened at the expense of women. [Martin and Voorhies 1975:297]

Colonial histories continue to influence women's labor today, as we will see in the next chapter.

Global News

6.1 Behind Roses' Beauty, Poor and Ill Workers

In just five years, Ecuadorian roses, as big and red as the human heart, have become the new status flower in the United States, thanks to the volcanic soil, perfect temperatures and abundant sunlight that help generate $240 million a year and tens of thousands of jobs in this once-impoverished region north of Quito.

This St. Valentine's Day, hundreds of American florists and catalogs are offering the roses of this fertile valley. Calyx & Corolla, for instance, bills it as a place "where Andean mists and equatorial sun conspire to produce roses that quickly burst into extravagant bloom, then hold their glory long after lesser specimens have begun to droop."

But roses come with thorns, too. As Ecuador's colorful blooms radiate romance around the world, large growers here have been accused of misusing a toxic mixture of pesticides, fungicides and fumigants to grow and export unblemished pest-free flowers.

As in other industries like garment production, bananas and diamonds, the poor worry about eating first and labor conditions later. They toil here despite headaches and rashes for the wealthier of the world, who in turn know little of the conditions in which their desires are met.

Doctors and scientists who have worked here say serious health problems have resulted for many of the industry's 50,000 workers, more than 70 percent of them women. Researchers say their work is hampered by lack of access to flower farms because of reluctant growers. But studies that the International Labor Organization published in 1999 and the Catholic University issued here last year showed that women in the industry had more miscarriages than average and that more than 60 percent of all workers suffered headaches, nausea, blurred vision or fatigue.

"No one can speak with conclusive facts in hand about the impact of this industry on the health of the workers, because we have not been able to do the necessary studies," said Dr. Bolívar Vera, a health specialist at the Health Environment and Development Foundation in Quito. "So the companies have been able to wash their hands of the matter." . . .

. . . Dr. César Paz-y-Miño, a geneticist at the Catholic University, said several pesticides used on a farm that was the setting for his research in the late 1990s were restricted as health hazards in other countries, including the United States, and labeled as highly toxic by the World Health Organization. . . .

Roses have become one of the top five sources of export revenue for Ecuador. The bloom boom has transformed this once sleepy region of cattle ranches, inhabited primarily by Indians. Much of the heartland has been hollowed out by illegal immigration to Europe and the United States, but the population in the flower regions north and south of Quito has soared. In Cayambe, the population has increased in 10 years, from 5,000 to more than 70,000.

Flowers have helped pave roads and built sophisticated irrigation systems. This year, construction will begin on an international airport between Quito and Cayambe.

The average flower worker earns more than the $120-a-month minimum wage. By employing women, the industry has fostered a social revolution in which mothers and wives have more control over their families' spending, especially on schooling for their children. . . .

Public/Private Spheres and the State

The review of ideas drawn from Engels' work suggests that while women's contribution to subsistence does not necessarily guarantee high status, it seems to be a prerequisite for it. Women tend to fare better in foraging and horticultural societies where their labor is significant to the group's basic needs than they do in pastoral and agrarian ones, although their higher position may also be related to the overall lack of stratification in general among foragers and horticulturists. Engels ([1884] 1978) contended that with the emergence of private property and the rise of the state, women were confined to the domestic sphere and reduced to a position of dependence and subservience. Several authors have expanded on this assertion, and, in the process, have offered important qualifications of Engels' position.

Martin K. Whyte (1978), for example, has tested the hypothesis that women have lower status in societies possessing significant private property rights to the means of production. His cross-cultural analysis suggests that the only strong relationship existing between private property and women's position is that in societies with private property, women's labor tends to be less valued than in those societies without it. Interestingly, Whyte has also found that women tend to have more informal influence in societies with private property, leading him to conclude:

There may be a modest tendency in cultures with private property for women to have somewhat lower status or more restricted roles in some areas of social life than in other cultures. The figures . . . do not lead us to believe, however, that the advantage of private property is in some sense the crucial change affecting women. [1978:38]

Furthermore, Whyte suggests that the existence of private property cannot itself explain why men take control of it in the first place, an assumption underlying Engels' analysis. Christine Gailey (1998) has raised a similar criticism. She calls into question Engels' assumption that there is a necessary relationship between private property and a desire on the part of men to transmit property to their biological children.

Rayna (Rapp) Reiter (1975b) focuses on the implications for women of the split between **public/private spheres** that accompanies the development of class society and the state. She argues that when states arose, kin groups lost their role as determiners of access to important societal resources. Instead, access was decided by membership in the class that consolidated control. Under such conditions, the bourgeoisie, or elite class, whose interests the state serves, developed a monopoly on force, not only to control and defend its territory but also to ensure its access to people's labor (in the form of taxes or the military draft, for example). But the use of repressive force is not a practical way to guarantee conformity. It is more effective to convince people through ideas of the value of their compliance.

One mechanism that enabled state control over people's minds, according to Reiter (1975b), was the separation of the public and private spheres of life. Superstructural institutions, such as educational and religious systems, perpetuated the view that work in the public sphere was valuable, but not in the private sphere. It did so by instilling the idea that labor in the public sphere was for the good of the state and thus for the good of all. By contrast, the work of the people who labored in the private sphere was seen to benefit only individual families. Because of women's roles in childbearing and child rearing, Reiter argues, they were confined to the domestic sphere in class societies, while men participated in public activities. Thus, in traditional state societies, the power and prestige associated with the private domain is extremely limited, and women's work within it is highly devalued. This also seems to be the case in industrial societies.

Industrializing Societies

The relationship of industrial labor to women's lives has been a central focus of feminist anthropology since its beginning. Ester Boserup's work focused not only on the impact of colonial relations on women within nations but also on how women fare under conditions of world or global capitalism. She ushered in a decade of work that investigates the marginalization of women in societies undergoing **modernization,** the transition from an agrarian to an industrial mode of production. This work has revealed the negative impact on women of a wide range of development programs instituted by various organizations to modify a nation's economic development and effect social change. Capitalism as a broad category, and its impact on "developing" nations, was repeatedly identified as having profound and detrimental effects on women's roles and position. These early studies helped develop the notion of dependency theory.

Capitalism and Dependency Theory.   Scholars invoking dependency theory focus on the relationship of First World core (developed) nations to Third World peripheral (developing) countries. **Third World** is a term that refers to a loose category of approximately 120 countries that are dependent technologically on highly industrialized, relatively affluent First World nations. Third World or developing countries are characterized by high population growth and low standards of living. A small, wealthy elite usually controls much of the nation's economy. Research using the dependency model focuses on how the position of women in Third World nations is affected adversely by an international exchange system that places developing nations in a position of dependency on more technologically developed capitalist societies.

Dependency theory asserts that economic development occurs within the context of a world system of international economic relations. This system extracts wealth from developing nations and transforms their economies in order to support the needs of "advanced" capitalist countries (Bossen 1984). "Dependent development" creates an international division of labor in which Third World countries must respond to the demands of industrialized capitalist societies. It also intensifies the sexual division of labor since, under such circumstances, men tend to be integrated into formal capitalist work relations while women perform precapitalist or domestic work, toiling in the home without pay to reproduce and maintain a labor force (Nash and Safa 1980). The introduction of this new division of labor, according to Laurel Bossen (1984), is accomplished by praising women's reproductive roles while looking down on their productive ones. The advantage to a capitalist economy of keeping women confined to the home is that it provides a reserve labor supply, one that can be called on to offset the demands of men for higher wages, which will be discussed in more detail in the next chapter.

Domestic Labor and the Informal Sector.   Although women's domestic labor was a precondition for the development of a capitalist mode of production, domestic work is viewed as "secondary" under capitalism. This situation has created unfair and exploitative relations in the private sphere (Sacks 1989:537). Women are usually not paid for the work they do in the home despite the fact that it is critical for maintaining capitalism, sustaining the present generation of workers, and reproducing social ties. Women's reproductive labor is also essential to capitalism: it produces and sustains the next generation of laborers. Just as unpaid domestic labor reproduces households and maintains capitalism, so too does childbearing. Feminist have thus insisted that having children cannot be understood simply as some inevitable and natural stage of women's lives. Instead, reproduction must itself be understood as a form of productive labor, requiring both physical and psychological work.

Feminist studies have also shown how women's role in reproduction often results in their working in the **informal economy,** the sector of a society's economy that is unregulated by societal institutions and the government and is not based on paid wages. Work in the informal economy is low paying. Informal labor sector activities include raising food for home use or for sale in local markets as well as work in small, unregulated businesses, often family-managed or self-employed enterprises that use labor-intensive methods (Qadeer 1983). The informal labor market absorbs most of the available unskilled and uneducated women in poor countries. Therefore, work in the informal sector is highly insecure, low paying, and unregulated. Many women undertake this kind of work as a strategy that allows them to simultaneously earn an income and take care of the home and their children (Fernandez-Kelly 1989:13–15).

Waged Work in the Formal Economy.   Studies of women working for paid wages in a society's official or **formal economy** show that women's domestic responsibilities do not decline even after they are fully employed. Instead of experiencing a decrease in the time and energy they must dedicate to carrying out household tasks and caretaking activities, they experience a "double shift" or **double burden:** they have responsibility for running a household at the same time that they are working for wages or tending subsistence

A Mayan woman makes decorative pot holders to sell as souvenirs to tourists in Mexico.

crops (Lewellen 2002:83). Because domestic labor is seen as "natural" work for women, women employed as domestic workers—positions overwhelmingly held by women of the Global South—are paid less. Devaluing women's work in the private domain stigmatizes women's work abilities in general.

Much of the feminist research in the 1980s on women's paid labor tended to focus on Third World women's work in multinational corporations, especially on the "global assembly line," where women work for extremely low wages, for extremely long hours, and in dismal conditions, primarily making electronics, clothes, and pharmaceuticals for First World consumers. By the 1990s, feminist research began to focus not only on women's work in multinational corporations but also on the impact of neolib-

Close-Up

6.1: Work in the Informal Labor Sector
by Martha Alter Chen, Joann Vanek, and Marilyn Carr

Although the informal economy is varied, it consists of labor in two main areas:

- People who are self-employed working in small unregistered enterprises, and
- Wage workers, laboring in insecure and unprotected jobs

The informal economy is characterized by a lack of economic security and legal protection. In every country, the informal economy is highly segmented by gender.

Much of the informal labor done by women in countries with developing capitalist economies takes place on the streets and in open-air markets, where women act as vendors, selling everything from vegetables, fruit, and meat to clothing, cosmetics, and electronic goods. Women in rural areas work on farms, raise livestock, and make handicrafts.

Women, called "homeworkers," work in the most "invisible" sector of the informal economy; they may process food, sew garments, make shoes, weave cloth, embroider textiles, or make handicrafts. Some also assemble garments and electronic components on a piece-rate basis. Informal workers also labor in factories or small workshops, where, among other jobs, they weave, dye and print cloth and embroider clothes. [Martha Alter Chen, Joann Vanek, and Marilyn Carr. 2004. *Mainstreaming Informal Employment and Gender in Poverty Reduction: A Handbook for Policy-makers and Other Stakeholders*; http://www.idrc.ca/openebooks/173-6/page_14 (accessed 5/27/08)]

eral economic policies on women across the globe. In the next chapter, we link neoliberal globalization to today's increasing feminization of labor, feminization of migration, feminization of poverty, and feminization of unemployment.

Postindustrial Societies: New Forms of Labor?

Since the 1970s, the manufacturing economy of some highly industrialized capitalist nations, such as the United States, has shifted to an economy that focuses on the production of services, work done for others as an occupation or business. This shift is often referred to as the **postindustrial revolution,** which has required new forms of labor.

In an industrial economy labor produces an actual product or good, such as a piece of furniture, a safety pin, or a T-shirt. In a postindustrial economy, labor generates intangible products such as information, analyses, and ideas. In service economies, emphasis is placed on theoretical knowledge and intellectual, creative labor rather than on practical "know-how" and manual, industrial labor (Lazzarato 1996). Developing a brand name slogan, for example, creating a new fashion "palette" for the Fall, and working as a consultant for a large company to produce a study of corporate work relations are all examples of the outcome of immaterial labor.

Service economies often also require **emotional labor,** feelings that a worker must publicly display to successfully complete a task. Because of this, workers may have to simulate feelings they may not feel and they may have to repress other emotions they do have in order to get a favorable response from a client or customer: the hospital patient nurtured and cheered up by a health care provider and the angry shopper soothed by a customer service representative are both buying not just a service but also emotional care. In each of these cases, the emotional style of offering a service becomes part of the service itself; emotion is turned into a product to be bought and sold. In other words, it becomes a **commodity** (Hochschild 1983:5).

For example, the cheerful, relaxed, and frequent smile on the face of a flight attendant is part of the package sold to airline passengers. This display comes to be representative of the company's disposition— "its confidence that its planes will not crash, its reassurance that departures and arrivals will be on time, its welcome, and its invitation to return" (Hochschild 1983:4). The exchange of emotional performances on the job, in other words, has a value, and that shifting value enters the market of exchange. In *The Managed Heart* (1983), Arlie Hochschild refers to this emotional manipulation as "management of the heart."

Researchers argue that when work in a postindustrial society entails this mobilization of intimate feelings for the purpose of production, workers become alienated from themselves, distorting their lives (Hochschild 1983:14). This issue is particularly significant for feminist anthropologists since women make up the largest percentage of service workers in a postindustrial society and are given far less emotional freedom than male workers who are overwhelmingly at the top of the employment hierarchy. Home and family, long relegated to the private sphere in industrial economies, are now no longer the only centers for emotional activity.

Critique of the Public/Private Dichotomy

The significance of the distinction between public and private realms and the importance of the rise of the state for women's position have been debated in the anthropological literature for some time. From the perspective of the 1990s, it is easy to see how U.S. women's fight for equal access to the public sphere of work in the 1970s influenced theorists like the ones discussed above.

But as Louise Lamphere suggests, "as appealing as this dichotomy [between public and private spheres] seemed in the abstract, it turned out to be difficult to apply when looking at examples of women's activities in other cultures" (2005:87). She feels that even in societies in which there is a clear association of men with the public sphere and women with the private, and powerful ideologies that maintain this distinction, these dichotomies are never that neatly arranged in actuality. Moreover, since production entails reproduction and since reproduction is a form of production, both types of labor can be found in "the factory and in the household," a trend that is becoming increasingly evident as emotional labor becomes more of a requirement for doing a job successfully (Lamphere 1986:119). Insights such as this moved feminist anthropologists beyond the public/private dichotomy to actively studying how the divide between work and family affects different women within a society as well as in different societies.

Another criticism of the validity of the public/private distinction has come from women of color. Aida Hurtado, for example, has argued:

> Women of Color have never had the benefit of the economic conditions that underlie the public/private distinction. . . . Welfare programs and policies have discouraged family life, sterilization programs have restricted reproduction rights, government has drafted and armed disproportionate numbers of people of Color to fight its wars overseas, police forces and the criminal justice system arrest and incarcerate disproportionate numbers of people of Color. There is no such thing as a private sphere for people of Color except that which they manage to create and protect in an otherwise hostile environment. [1989:849]

In general, a Marxist approach tends to essentialize women, treating them as a universal marginalized class. As Hurtado's quotation suggests, studies of the public/private must also account for differences along racial, ethnic, and national lines. This is also the case when theorizing the state: by conceptualizing the state as a singular entity, Marxism fails to do justice to the multiple ways in which "specific cultural histories, diverse social hierarchies, and systems of stratification affect gender relations and ideology" (Brettell and Sargent 2005:303). Thus some critics view Marxism as reductionist, claiming that a class-based analysis oversimplifies the relation between people and culture. Feminist anthropologists try to avoid making claims about *the* state and instead focus attention on a variety of state approaches to the institutionalization of gender relations. They study how specific groups of women are affected by particular state policies (Ferree et al. 1999:xxiii).

Regardless of these shortcomings, Lamphere (2005) reminds us of the strength of approaches focused on the material conditions of life, and even on the public/private dichotomy. She argues that this concept has been useful in showing how an ideology of "women's place is in the home" has operated in such countries as the United States, Great Britain, and France, the very kinds of societies Engels focused on in his analysis of oppression in industrialized capitalist states (p. 90). The focus on the division between the public and private spheres brought the importance of women's work within the domestic realm to scholars' attention and illuminated the significant role it plays in the overall functioning of capitalist societies, even though that work is unpaid.

Emphasis on public/private spheres has also led people in the United States to question the consequences of men's traditional lack of contribution to the domestic realm and to call for more equal participation by men in household duties and child-care responsibilities (see Rosaldo 1974). It is still the case, however, that in the workplace, mothers in the United States are negatively affected by their role in child care, while fathers generally are not.

Rethinking Ideology

Traditional Marxist approaches assume that material factors explain all aspects of stratification. But do they? While it is difficult to deny the crucial effect of economic factors on people's lives, the relative weight that can be given to them is an open and highly debated question. Although some theorists would argue that race and ethnicity are ideological constructs used to maintain the interests of a largely white, Anglo-Saxon class of owners, others contend that class alone cannot explain racism and ethnic prejudice. A similar argument has been made about gender. To account more fully for differences other than class, feminist and other twenty-first-century anthropologists today seek a reformulation of Marxist class theory, one that treats not only gender but also race as historically and culturally specific. They acknowledge that there is "no race-neutral or gender-neutral 'essence'" to people's lives (Sacks 1989:534).

Global News

6.2: Wedded to Work, and in Dire Need of a Wife

"The thing I most want in life is a wife. I'm not kidding," said Joyce Lustbader, a research scientist at Columbia University, who has been married for 29 years. "I work all day, sometimes seven days a week, and still have to go home and make dinner and have all those things to do around the house." It is not just the extra shift at home that is a common complaint. Working women, whether married or single, also see their lack of devoted spousal support as an impediment to getting ahead in their careers, especially when they are competing against men who have wives behind them, whether those wives are working or staying at home. . . . Married men and women, on average, earn more than those who are unmarried, with part of that possibly attributed to career and wage advancement as workers mature (and are more likely to be married). But the gap is significantly larger for men than for women. Married women make an average 17 percent more than unmarried women, according to 2005 B.L.S. data on the median earnings of full-time workers, while married men make 42 percent more than unmarried men. [Shira Boss, *New York Times* 8/11/07; http://select.nytimes.com/search/restricted/article?res=FB0D1FFD385F0C728DDDA10894DF404482]

To refine Marxist notions, many feminist and other twenty-first-century anthropologists have turned to reformulations of ideas about the relationship of ideology, the state, and domination. In the next section, we will examine the ideas of three thinkers whose work has been influential in understanding how ideology is not a simple reflection of class relations imposed by the state: Max Weber, the German political economist, writing around the turn of the twentieth century, who is considered one of the founders of modern sociology; the Italian political theorist Antonio Gramsci, one of the most influential Marxist thinkers of the early twentieth century; and Michel Foucault, the influential French philosopher whose work has had profound effects on how anthropologists and feminists conceptualize power and domination.

Max Weber's Protestant Ethic

In his famous book, *The Protestant Ethic and the Spirit of Capitalism* ([1905] 1958), Weber argued that it was not only material conditions that shaped the development of capitalism, but also religious beliefs and values. He was interested in how religion, specifically Protestantism, enabled a capitalist economy to grow and function.

Weber drew direct connections between aspects of Protestant beliefs, especially those of Calvinism—a strict form of Protestantism—and capitalist values. Although capitalism requires it, Weber argued that humans are not "by nature" motivated to work harder and harder to earn more and more money. Weber suggested that this motivation was provided by the **Protestant ethic:** a belief that toil, duty, efficiency, and order increase the glory of God. In other words, Weber believed that the Protestant religion, with its "work-and-save" ethic, gave capitalism its "spirit" or ethos, one based on self-sacrifice for future gain.

Like Marx and Engels, Weber claimed that capitalism required a strong state capable of organizing and coordinating economic activity; but he was less concerned than Marx and Engels with the role of the state in maintaining the power of the ruling class. Instead Weber emphasized how people's actions could also shape capitalist relations. He thus placed human action at the center of his model (Ortner 1984:147). This contribution opened the door to the idea that people are not only confined by ideology but may also resist it, as we will see in our discussion of practice theory in chapter 8.

Antonio Gramsci's Hegemony

Gramsci was himself a Marxist and, in line with Marx, believed that class struggle was the motor propelling society forward. He, however, differed from Marx in understanding how the ruling class rules. His analysis of this issue has made a major contribution to contemporary thinking by refining the Marxist notions of ideology and consciousness and their relationship to the state. In general, he sees ideology playing a more active role in politics and history than does traditional Marxism. For Gramsci, the oppressed class is not merely the passive victim of the dominant class's ideology. He is thus able to provide an understanding of how ideas and power relations can change.

Gramsci sees a society's superstructure as operating in two ways to maintain state power: through obvious means such as force and coercion—which he refers to as **forms of domination**—and through subtler forms of control and manipulation—which work to build consensus for ruling ideas. Gramsci uses the term **hegemony** to refer to this process in which a dominant group gains—for its own interests—the approval of a subordinate class through the use of intellectual, moral, and cultural encouragement. Hegemony has become a powerful idea in feminist and other twenty-first-century anthropology.

Hegemony operates culturally through various institutions, such as the educational system, the family, the church, the mass media, and popular culture (Strinati 1995:168–169). For example, ideas about gender identity based on notions of femininity and masculinity can be seen as hegemonic. The characteristics associated with hegemonic masculinity in the United States are ambition, strength, aggressiveness, and self-reliance. This is what most men strive to be and what most women are taught to desire in a partner. By accepting, or consenting to, these ideas, men and women reproduce gendered hierarchies. One of the most important points about hegemonic ideas, however, is that they can change.

Ideology encourages oppressed people to believe that what is in the interest of the dominant group is also good for them. We have already seen an example of this in chapter 4 when we discussed the process of naturalization. As you may remember, naturalizing power makes the unequal distribution of power, privilege, and resources within a society seem right and self-evident rather than as based on political ideologies and differential power. As a result, naturalized, ruling class values come to be seen as commonsense values.

Close-Up

6.2: It's Just Plain Ol' Common Sense by Chad Raphael

The dominant ideology in any society is a set of commonsense assumptions that legitimates the existing distribution of power. Ideology makes this structure of power seem "natural," "normal," or "inevitable," and therefore beyond challenge. Aspects of the reigning ideology might include such "common sense" sayings as: "The poor will always be with us" (despite the fact that there have been many societies in human history in which wealth was owned communally or divided more equally than in [capitalist societies]); "You can't fight City Hall" (despite the fact that people sometimes do take on government, and make changes); "Blacks are less intelligent and lazier than whites, so they need to be watched over" (despite the fact that slaves worked far longer and harder than their white masters, and there is no legitimate evidence that any [group of people] possesses more intelligence than another); "Asians are docile, so they don't make good leaders and managers" (despite the fact that Asians seem to have ruled themselves for quite awhile before white folks showed up on their shores); "America is the land of equal opportunity" (despite the fact that some people start out life in slums while others start out in mansions). [From: Chad Raphael, *Theory of Hegemony and Ideology;* http://www.dangerouscitizen.com/Articles/244.aspx (accessed 8/24/07)]

As we will see in the next chapter, such a hegemonic idea can be found in neoliberalism, which maintains the division between the "haves" and "have-nots" both within and across societies. A Gramscian perspective is important for pointing to the fact that cultural hegemony is just as significant in maintaining the inequalities of a capitalist state as are the institutions of government, the police and armed forces, and the legal system.

Gramsci's conception of hegemony and how the state gains legitimate authority over a population has influenced feminist thinking in a number of important ways. First, it focuses attention on the importance of struggles over ideas, ones that enable women and other oppressed groups to question the right of the dominant class to rule. This struggle requires the development of a counterhegemony, such as feminist thinking itself, which can sever the ideological connection between dominant and oppressed groups. Second, since the maintenance of hegemony rests on people's consent, the ruling class must constantly adjust

and readjust, negotiate and renegotiate hegemonic ideas. People's own experience of their material and social conditions remind them of their subordinate position and the contradiction between these experiences and the dominant ideology of their society. This contradiction produces "ideological seams" (Radway 1986): places of struggle where ideas can be contested and resisted, as we will explore further in chapter 8.

Lesley Gill (1993) has fruitfully applied Gramsci's notion of hegemony to show how hegemonic ideas can be protested and thus how they must be adapted to new conditions if they are to do their work of domination. She focuses on the relationship of "traditional" ideals of femininity to the maintenance of class differences in La Paz, Bolivia. Gill shows how an impoverished group of Aymara immigrants hired as domestic servants drew on symbols of the dominant class to contest depictions of them as racially inferior and socially backwards.

In La Paz the ideal "señora" or lady is submissive, devout, self-sacrificing, and sexually chaste. These were the characteristic attributed to a small, elite class of women. Following Bolivia's economic and political revolution of 1952, consumer goods expanded and Aymara immigrant women began to make use of commodities—from clothing to cars—to diminish sharp class and racial divisions between criollo (mostly "whites") and indios (indigenous Aymara women). The dress styles and conventions adopted by Aymara indios in the city reflected a newly acquired "urban sophistication" that closely approximated—and disturbed—middle- and upper-class criollo women in La Paz (p. 73). One consequence has been a new glorification of "traditional" rural Aymara women whose lifestyle, dress, and work distinguished them from the socially mobile Aymara urban migrants. Shifting the ideal of class femininity to rural women represents a way in which the upper class responded to threats upon hegemonic class and gender orders within Bolivian society.

For Gill, the practices of this class of Aymara domestic servants represent a hegemonic moment characterized by "conflict and accommodation" (p. 73). She asserts that maintaining hegemony takes a great deal of cultural work on the part of dominant groups precisely because of these frequent moments in which hegemony is undermined. Close-Up 6.3 describes how Penelope Eckert uses this idea to explain the relationship of high school cliques to class structure.

Michel Foucault's Governmentality and Critique of Ideology

Just as Gramsci is interested in how people consent to their own self-domination, so, too, is the French philosopher and historian, Michel Foucault, who may have adopted this idea from Gramsci. Foucault argued that with the rise of capitalism a new kind of power arose in which people became self-disciplining and self-regulating, thereby, participating in their own subjugation.

Unlike Gramsci, Foucault disputed several of the fundamental premises of Marxism, including the Marxist concepts of ideology and false consciousness. He offers the notion of "governmentality" instead, as we discuss below. Before moving to his specific ideas, however, it is important to acknowledge the importance of Foucault's ideas for feminist, and other twenty-first-century, anthropologists. His conceptualization of power and how power is maintained and perpetuated in contemporary societies has been of singular significance to the field.

Foucault, Anthropology, and Feminism

Foucault and anthropologists share several common concerns. Both are interested in understanding who "we" are. Like twenty-first-century anthropologists, Foucault does not suppose that there is a universal "human nature," which all members of our species

Close-Up

6.3: Hegemony in High School by Nell Quest

Antonio Gramsci's notion of hegemony is complex, but can help us understand a great deal about how social structures, power, and differences between groups are created and maintained in everyday situations. Remember, hegemony refers to the ways a dominant group gains the approval of a subordinate group through the use of intellectual, moral, or cultural influence. Anthropologist Penelope Eckert studied the everyday workings of hegemony by looking at the ways that high school students in the United States establish patterns of behavior, identities, and values about school, which then have an effect on their career options. More specifically, in the high school she studied in Detroit, she found that all of the students could be bro-

(continued)

ken up into two groups: the jocks, those who worked hard to participate in school life, and who accepted the school's authority and status as a major, all-encompassing social environment; and the burnouts, those who rejected the school's authority, did not believe that it could meet their needs, and felt that they were shut out of the system. Eckert found that the students not only recognized these categories, but used them to structure their other behaviors, whether dress, bodily comportment, musical choices, or uses of language.

More specifically, Eckert argues that, from elementary school, students demonstrate differences in how they dress, talk, and behave, many of which are based on differences in their families' economic status. However, she found that by the end of middle school, these differences become more marked and take on new meaning because they begin to be opposed to each other in terms of the two categories of "jocks" and "burnouts." From then on, students' social worlds are structured around demonstrating that they are either a "jock"—those who are engaged in school life, or a "burnout"—those who do not recognize the school's authority and do not believe it can meet their needs, and therefore do not fully participate. Largely, these differences corresponded to the economic class of individual students; those whose families were from lower economic classes were more likely to be burnouts and to feel shut out of the system. In Eckert's study, she found that the jocks and burnouts behaved in ways specifically designed to distinguish themselves from each other. For example, while the jocks wore pastels, the burnouts wore dark colors; while the jocks worked to speak politely and with proper grammar, the burnouts used improper grammar and cursed frequently; while the jocks used the school building in traditional ways by eating in the cafeterias, playing sports in the sports fields, and storing things in their lockers, the burnouts congregated in marginal areas like hallways, doorways, and the courtyard, and refused to use lockers. While the jocks "do well" in traditional school subjects, the burnouts are more likely to only consider vocational or art classes important. These behaviors are also dictated by students' economic means—jocks can afford to spend more money on clothes or sports equipment, for example, and are expected to do so.

For Eckert, this distinction functioned in a hegemonic way. The opposition between these two categories structured not only students' behaviors, but also what was expected of them, the options they had available to them, and the values they were assumed to hold. But by considering their behavior as a rejection of the school environment itself, burnouts "consented" to the school system functioning the way it did, even if they believed it could not do them any good. This meant that what school was supposed to mean, and what it meant to succeed, went unquestioned, and the jocks were the people more likely to succeed. The jocks, therefore, were the mainstream, while the burnouts were those who resisted the mainstream. The jocks could not exist without the burnouts, who structured their identity category, and vice versa. Eckert points out that these distinctions mirror the class distinctions present in larger adult society, where what clothes people buy, the way they speak, and their comportment can all demonstrate important things about their economic means and belonging to particular social groups. Her work provides a good demonstration of the way Gramsci's conception of hegemony can be applied to understanding power in everyday life.

Reference

Eckert, Penelope. 1989. *Jocks and Burnouts: Social Categories and Identity in the High School.* New York: Teacher College Press.

share. Like them, he argues that what it means to be human changes within different contexts. For Foucault, there is no such thing as the universal human, only different types of human beings who are created through the working of power at particular moments in history.

Foucault is centrally concerned with one type of human: the "modern" individual, which emerged in the seventeenth and eighteenth centuries to serve the needs of capitalism. In Foucaultian terms, we would say he is interested in the development of the "modern human subject." Foucault's focus on this time period has been particularly significant for our understanding of global capitalism and the neoliberal ideology that sustains it, as we discuss in more detail in the next chapter.

Unlike feminist and other twenty-first-century anthropologists, Foucault does not focus on how being a "modern human subject" differs within societies or across societies. As many critics have pointed out, when Foucault speaks about the "modern human subject," he is primarily referring to white Anglo-American men. This does not mean, however, that his work has been unimportant to scholars interested in difference. Indeed, his ideas have been central to the work of many feminists, not just the ones who have adopted, critiqued, and transformed his conceptualization.

Feminists and Foucault share certain primary concerns. First, both have placed the body at the center of their analyses. Since the 1970s the question of how the body is used as a site of domination and control has been central to feminist political struggles, particularly in the United States, as we discuss further in chapter 9. Feminists have focused both on direct forms of bodily control such as forced sterilization, abuse, and rape, as well as on less direct forms, such as codes of fashion and discourses about ideal notions of femininity and beauty. Foucault's work has had a tremendous impact on how we understand the working of these less direct forms of power. Second, feminists and Foucault share an understanding that the creation and uses of knowledge are always related to power. In his early work, Foucault focused on the politics of knowledge through his concept of the "knowledge/power nexus." In his later work he refers to it as "governmentality."

In this chapter, we focus primarily on how and why Foucault's ideas contrast with Marxist conceptualizations but we also introduce a number of Foucault's central ideas, which are elaborated in subsequent chapters in this book.

Governmentality

Foucault proposed the idea of **governmentality** (in French, *gouvernementalité*) to get at the multiple ways that control is exercised over people. Governmentality does not depend entirely on state and legal enforcement of a set of laws (government), according to Foucault, but also works using a wide range of ideas and ways of thinking (*mentalités*) that are collective and part of a society's culture. These ideas are instrumental in shaping how people behave and how they think about themselves and their society.

Although Foucault's idea of governmentality may sound a lot like Marx's and Engels' notion of ideology, Foucault has actively rejected the Marxist concept of ideology for several reasons. Ideology in a Marxist sense is thought to be a set of ideas that work to obscure reality, which is seen as the result of the material conditions of a society and the relationships of power established on them. Since the idea of "false consciousness" suggests that something is false, it implies that something else exists that is true. But for Foucault, as we discuss in more detail elsewhere, power creates reality and produces what we think of as true. It is not a given. For Foucault, there is no truth independent of power.

Foucault also rejects the notion of ideology because it is conceptualized in Marxist thinking as ideas that are imposed on people. In this framework, power is seen to operate from the top down, as constraining and regulating people by imposing itself on them from the outside in the interest of the state and the ruling class. Foucault argues that this is not the only way that power works; at least it has not been the primary way since the seeds for the development of capitalism were sown in the seventeenth century.

Modern power, Foucault argues, does not come exclusively from the state and it is not the property of a group of people such as the ruling class. It does not work from the outside in, but from the inside out. For example, a starving person who refuses to steal food does so not only because she or he may break a law and get caught but also because the person has internalized stealing as something that is wrong and immoral. Having inculcated society's ideas of the value of being a moral person, a starving individual is deterred from satisfying a basic human need. Through the combination of morality and governmentality, Foucault argues, oppressed groups reproduce their own domination, considerably expanding the reach of government.

Sovereign Power vs. Biopower

Foucault hypothesizes that before capitalism emerged in Europe, power emanated from a sovereign, a supreme ruler, usually in the form of a monarch such as a king or queen. But with the industrial revolution that fueled the development of capitalism in the nineteenth and early twentieth centuries, a new form of power came into play that exits alongside state or sovereign power. This new type of power is able to control people in ways that support and maintain a capitalist mode of production. Foucault calls this type of power **biopower.**

Biopower is literally having power over people by having power over their bodies. This kind of power is not centralized; its source is not a ruler or sovereign. Instead, Foucault conceptualizes biopower as diffuse. It molds people's bodies and minds through numerous and diverse techniques, which act to discipline people from the inside out. Just as children are "disciplined" to act in the correct way by their parents, so all people are controlled and made obedient through **disciplinary power.** But unlike children who may be physically punished by being paddled, with biopower people come to discipline themselves by thinking they are always being watched, as we will see in the next section.

The aim of disciplinary power is to produce populations of people who are obedient, passive, submissive, and compliant workers adapted to the requirements of capitalism, especially industrial capitalism (Dreyfus and Rabinow 1982). By organizing time and space, and by regulating the movement of their daily lives, workers adapted to work in the factory. This new kind of worker was efficient and reliable, could punch a clock, and work all day doing mind-numbing repetitive tasks. Capitalism required, in other words, people who were regimented and could be strictly controlled. It depended on, in Foucault's words, obedient and **docile bodies,** bodies whose energies were accustomed to regulation.

The Panoptic Gaze

Disciplinary power works from the inside out. It creates docile bodies and obedient people by controlling their consciousness and their very sense of who they are. What is significant about disciplinary power, according to Foucault, is that it works through *self*-regulation: people come to internalize and discipline themselves. Docile bodies, Foucault argues, are produced by a **panoptic gaze,** an invisible, but all-seeing "eye."

Foucault explained the panoptic gaze in his book *Discipline and Punish* (1979). In it, he focuses on how prisoners become their own "wardens," constantly monitoring themselves to behave in acceptable ways. His idea of the prison, however, is also meant to help

Panoptic view: U.S. Statesville Prison.

us understand how people under capitalism are imprisoned in their daily lives. He theorized that disciplinary power for all people today is panoptic.

Foucault based his notion of the panoptic gaze on a type of prison designed by British philosopher Jeremy Bentham in the late eighteenth century.

As you can see in the photograph, a central tower provides a prison warden with a place to watch prisoners without being seen. Thus, prisoners do not know whether they are being watched. The effect, according to Foucault, is to make prisoners presume that they are always under scrutiny or constant surveillance. As a result, they internalize "the gaze." They monitor and self-police their own behavior. Foucault referred to these forms of self-policing as "technologies of the self."

Foucault suggests that society itself can be understood as a system of surveillance through which all human bodies are trained to know their limits through an internalization of society's power. Just as people who are imprisoned come to act "correctly" in the absence of anyone watching them, so, too, do people who are not in an actual prison. As Foucault puts it, in a

system of surveillance there is no need for arms, physical violence, material constraints. Just a gaze. An inspecting gaze, a gaze which each individual under its weight will end by internalizing to the point that he [sic] is his [sic] own supervisor, each individual thus exercising this surveillance over, and against, himself [sic]. [Cited in Miller 1993:222–223]

Prisoners are also controlled through the precise regulation of the body in time and space. Their day is broken up into exact times when certain activities occur: they must get out of bed at six in the morning in winter; at a quarter to seven, they go down into the courtyard where they must wash their hands and faces, and receive their first ration of bread, and so on throughout the day (Foucault 1979).

Once again, the point for Foucault is that like prisoners, people in general became increasingly regulated by the clock and by demands that they sit still and listen, whether in schools, factories, hospitals, psychiatric institutions, or the military. The internalization of the panoptic gaze and this regimentation work together to produce docile bodies.

Discourses and Expert Knowledge.   Foucault is critical of Marxist approaches that focus primarily on the impact of government or state policies on groups of people, not only because of his conceptualization of biopower as diffuse, but also because the Marxist view

of power is that it is restrictive and negative. Foucault sees power as productive. The modern human subject, the very type of humans we are and think we are, according to Foucault, is created through power, specifically through discourses.

A **discourse** is a system of thought made up of ideas, attitudes, beliefs, and practices that creates a picture for people of what is true and what is not and it constructs their very sense of who they are. This system of thought is institutionalized; that is, it is the established way of thinking that creates our ideas about what is normal. It does this by constructing an object of knowledge. A discourse defines how this object of knowledge can be meaningfully talked, what can, in other words be said or not said about a topic at a particular moment in history. Discourses create people's very sense of what the world is and ideas about who they themselves are.

For example, sociobiology is a way of thinking that makes it appear normal that men have a stronger sex drive than women. Sociobiologists argue that they are uncovering a scientific truth about women's and men's natures, merely by uncovering the "truth of existence," that is, genetic, biological, and physiological differences between women and men. This so-called truth seems so obvious to people that they come to believe that men do posses a stronger sex drive than women. And many women and men come to think of themselves and others in these very terms: a sexually active woman, for example, may wonder if there is something wrong with her and she may be labeled by her society as promiscuous or a "slut," in other words, as abnormal.

Feminism is a counterdiscourse: as we've seen, it arose in opposition to the widespread and deeply embedded discourse about men's natural superiority over women. This superiority was presumed true, and this truth was "scientifically" supported and verified by social evolutionary thought. A discourse of male superiority defined the ways in which sex differences were talked about for centuries and how women and men thought about each other and themselves.

As discussed in the next chapter, the docile modern human subject is created through multiple discourses, in particular through professional knowledge, knowledge about people that is used by experts (for example, physicians, psychiatrists, and social scientists) to discipline them. Disciplinary practices, discourses, and the institutions in which they are embedded (for example, the hospital, the asylum, and the university), as well as expert knowledge, as we've seen, act to "normalize" men and women, bringing them into conformity with society's ideas.

Economy as Moral Order

The next example demonstrates how labor and economic relationships are embedded in a system of values. It shows how, in other words, labor and economic relationships are part of a society's **moral order**: its shared understanding of what is right and wrong, good and bad, fair and unfair, just and unjust. Ideas about work are tied to cultural notions of what constitutes a fair, just, and ethical exchange; what is considered a fair distribution of rewards; and what is believed about how individuals should behave in economic interactions (Collins 2002a:). These values and beliefs permeate culture, supporting the status quo, and therefore, can be understood as hegemonic. How people conceptualize a "good" society affects a range of relationships and behaviors that are treated not as economic issues but as moral ones.

If, for example, the idea of community is considered important by a society, and its people have a sense of responsibility for one another, then sharing and distributing resources equitably will be valued and seen as the right way to interact. In small-scale societies moral obligations involving "economic" exchanges are ordered by gender, age, and kinship affiliation. In such societies, those who cannot provide for themselves—such as the elderly—are not blamed for not being able to contribute an equal share to subsistence activities. Historian E. P. Thompson (1993) has suggested that these kinds of societies have a moral economy. Rather than working toward individual accumulation people in these societies work for the welfare of the "collective good."

Thompson applied the idea of a **moral economy** to small-scale societies. But anthropologists have shown that moral principles also guide ideas about economic production and distribution in capitalist societies and create particular obligations and feelings of indebtedness among various people. In capitalist societies, individualism and competition are highly valued; thus, moral rankings between people and understandings of justice are based on notions of individual gain and profit. The ideal society is seen as one based on competition in which resources flow to those who, through individual achievement, deserve them. People who cannot provide for themselves are seen as infe-

rior, and their position is often attributed to what they lack within themselves.

Derogatory names are often applied to individuals who break the shared understanding of a proper economic relationship. For example, in U.S. slang a person who lives on the fruits of someone else's labor may be called a "moocher" or a "free rider." Both terms suggest that an individual has accumulated goods or services without properly or morally fulfilling his or her role in the exchange.

Terms indicating moral deviance in economic transactions are often gendered. Consider, for example, the example of the "sugar daddy" and "gold digger." A sugar daddy is a man who supplies financial benefits to a supposedly undeserving and manipulative woman—the gold digger—who enters the relationship for economic gain. But "sugar daddy" and "gold digger" are not equally insulting labels. A sugar daddy is not condemned for entering into a relationship in which he pays for a woman's needs and desires. But a gold digger is looked down on for "only being after his money," profiting from a heterosexual romantic relationship, which in U.S. society is seen as a union that should remain *outside* the realm of strategic economic gain. Thus, these women are socially stigmatized as people who do not conform to U.S. society's social obligations of economic exchange. The equivalent term, "sugar mamas," circulates with far less frequency in the United States because women have not traditionally had the wealth necessary to support a man. The etymology "sugar daddy" may also bear the mark of race relations as well and may originate with the idea of wealthy sugar plantation owners able to lavish gifts and money upon women.

Much of what constitutes a moral economy goes unquestioned, yet it underlies people's attitudes toward a wide array of issues: minimum wage, taxation, welfare programs, regulation of private property, state ownership, regulation of the economy, affirmative action, and pension funds. Who is entitled to welfare? For how long? Should the state tax the wealthiest more than the poorest? Should the state limit gambling? Should certain individuals be promoted based on gender or race in order to diversify and redistribute educational opportunities?

Conclusions

Scholars interested in gender and labor now approach a world increasingly defined by border-crossing, swift exchanges, and a workforce not easily marked off by territorial boundaries. Recent scholarship is thus deeply affected by a new age of international interdependence and exploitation, the ideology of free market, and the hegemony of "flexible" labor, as we will see in the next chapter.

WORD PORTFOLIO

avunculocal residence: the practice in which after marriage, a newly married couple goes to live with or near the husband's maternal uncle.

bilateral ("two-sided") descent: a form of reckoning descent by tracing relationships through both the male and the female lines.

biopower: a form of power in the modern capitalist state that regulates people and controls populations through numerous and diverse techniques that produce docile bodies.

bourgeoisie: in a capitalist mode of production, the class of people who own the means of production.

class society: a form of society in which private ownership of resources distinguishes and privileges owners over non-owners.

commodity: an item, idea, or service that is assigned economic value and can therefore be bought and sold.

dependency theory: asserts that a system of international economic relations extracts wealth from developing nations and transforms their economies in order to support the needs of advanced capitalist countries.

disciplinary power: a type of biopower for the creation of docile bodies in which a form of surveillance is internalized so that a person comes to discipline herself or himself.

discourse: a system of thought made up of ideas, attitudes, beliefs, and practices that create a picture for people of what is true and what is not and it constructs their very sense of who they are.

docile bodies: bodies whose energies are habituated to external regulation.

double burden: the phrase that describes women's dual responsibility for running a household and at the same time working for wages or tending subsistence crops.

emotional labor: the feelings that a worker must display to successfully complete a task.

false consciousness: Marxist term for the misrepresentation or obfuscation of dominant social relations in the consciousness of oppressed workers in capitalist society.

formal economy: a society's officially recognized economy based on paid employment.

forms of domination: the maintenance of state through force and coercion.

governmentality: the multiple ways of exercising control over a population that depend on both state and legal enforcement of a set of laws (government) and the use of a wide range of ideas, knowledge, and discourses (*mentalités*) that discipline and shape people and their bodies.

hegemony: the process by which a dominant group, for the purposes of advancing its own interests, gains that consent of a subordinate class through the use of intellectual, moral, and cultural encouragement.

ideology: the shared ideas and beliefs that serve to justify the interests of a dominant group. In Marxist thinking, ideology is the system of ideas that obscures the truth of worker's oppression and serves the interests of the ruling class.

informal economy: the unofficial sector of economic activity in a society that is beyond a government's regulation.

infrastructure: a society's economic base.

matrilocal residence: the practice in which after marriage, a newly married couple goes to live with or near the wife's family.

means of production: the physical resources of a society used in economic activities, such as land and tools.

mode of production: the Marxist term for the economic system of a society that is made up of its productive forces and relations of production.

modernization: the transition from an agrarian to an industrial mode of production.

moral economy: the principles that guide ideas about economic production and distribution, creating particular obligations and feelings of indebtedness among various social actors.

moral order: a society's shared understanding of what is right and wrong, good and bad, fair and unfair, just and unjust.

panoptic gaze: an invisible, but all-seeing "eye" that is internalized by modern workers (and others) who self-monitor their behavior in compliance with workplace expectations, becoming docile workers.

patrilocal residence: the practice in which after marriage, a newly married couple goes to live with or near the husband's family.

political economy: (1) the interaction between political and economic systems, especially the impact of a society's economic system on politics and the impact of political events on economic systems; (2) a field of study that focuses on the interactions between political processes and economic factors.

postindustrial revolution: a productive system that depends on delivering services.

proletariat: in a capitalist mode of production the class of people who must sell their labor to the owners of the means of production (or the bourgeoisie) in order to survive.

Protestant ethic: the belief among Protestants that toil, duty, efficiency, and order increase the glory of God, which fueled the development of capitalism.

public/private spheres: the division between the realm of work and the realm of the family in state societies.

social relations of production: social relationships between groups of people that are structured by a society's mode of production. A capitalist mode of production produces different classes of people based on whether or not they own the means of production. Marx and Engels referred to the group of owners of the means of production in capitalist societies as the *bourgeoisie*, and the class of people who had to sell their labor to these owners in order to survive as the *proletariat*.

state: in Marxist theory, a form of political structure that protects the interests of the elite class.

superstructure: the legal, political, social, and cultural institutions that developed to ensure the continuation of the economic status quo.

Third World: refers to a loose category of 120 countries that are dependent technologically on highly industrialized, relatively affluent "First World" nations and are often characterized by high population growth and a low standard of living.

unilineal descent: a way of reckoning kinship by tracing family connections though only one line—either that of the mother's side (matrilineal descent) or that of the father's side (patrilineal descent).

RECOMMENDED READING

Factory Daughters: Gender, Household Dynamics, and Rural Industrialization in Java, by Diane Wolf, 1992. Berkeley: University of California Press.

Diane Wolf draws on her fieldwork in Java in the 1980s to examine the experiences of young women working in factories, including how working outside the home affects the practices of family, kinship, and gender. Drawing connections between young women's work, the changing landscape of agricultural production, and industrial capitalism, Wolf moves away from straightforward understandings of the economic strategies of poor households, offering instead a complex picture of the contradictory opportunities and constraints that such work holds for "factory daughters."

For We Are Sold, I and My People, by Patricia Fernandez Kelly. 1985. New York: SUNY Press.

In this pioneering book on the topic of women's work within the "global assembly line" Patricia Fernandez Kelly analyzes the lives of women who work in the textile and electronic industries (*maquiladoras*) in Ciudad Juarez, Mexico. Through a political economy analysis, she looks at the connections between globalization and local communities to examine the effects of economic outsourcing on women's everyday lives.

The Headman was a Woman: The Gender Egalitarian Batek of Malaysia, by Kirk Endicott and Karen Endicott. 2008. Long Grove, IL: Waveland Press.

Based on their fieldwork among the Batek of peninsular Malaysia, Kirk and Karen Endicott focus on how equality between men and women is produced through the egalitarian organization of hunting and gathering. The book is also accompanied by a 37-minute DVD (*The Batek: Rainforest Foragers of Kelantan, Malaysia*), further illustrating the social and economic processes explored in the text.

Living Rooms as Factories: Class, Gender, and the Satellite Factory in Taiwan, by Ping-Chun Hsiung. 1995. Philadelphia: Temple University Press.

Taiwan's recent "economic miracle" was in large part accomplished through the labor of wives, mothers, and daughters-in-law who brought factory work into their own homes. This formed a satellite system of home-based "factories" integrated within industrialized capitalism. Ping-Chun Hsiung analyzes the lives of women workers and the effects of state policy on gender and class stratification.

The Vanishing Hectare: Property and Value in Postsocialist Transylvania, by Katherine Verdery, especially chapter 4. 2003. Ithaca, NY: Cornell University Press.

Based on extensive fieldwork between 1990 and 2001, Katherine Verdery examines the transition from collective to individual land ownership in post-socialist Central and Eastern Europe. Concentrating on one Transylvanian community, Aurel Vlaicu, Verdery looks at the meanings associated with privatized property as a symbol of political change and also looks at the complex relationships that emerge between local groups and new owners competing over the value of land and its uses.

7

The Global Economy, Neoliberalism, and Labor

In this chapter you will . . .

learn how neoliberal ideologies shape the world economy and women's and men's experiences of their daily lives of transnational labor • confront the idea that the global economy is raced and gendered • examine the feminization of poverty, of the labor force, of international migration, and of unemployment • investigate the relationship of identity to work • encounter the impact of labor relations on relations between men and women within nations and among geopolitical regions of the world • learn about the global sex tourism industry as an example • look at new configurations of labor under conditions of globalization • investigate the production of culture in a globalizing world

In this chapter, we examine how the *global economy*—an immense network of exchanges of capital, goods, resources, people, and services across national borders—is raced and gendered. In today's globalizing world, economic inequality along these dimensions has increased both within particular societies and between nation-states. To get a sense of the widening gaps between those who have benefited little or none from the global economy and those who have amassed wealth beyond their personal needs, consider this: on a worldwide scale, each year some five million children die of hunger, and each day the number of people who go hungry ranges from 600,000 to over one billion. In 2001, 2.7 billion people lived on $2 per day (Edelman and Haugerud 2005:9). At the same time the wealth of the richest 200 individuals in the world was equivalent to the combined income of 41 percent of the world's population (UNDP 1999:38 in Edelman and Haugerud 2005:9). The distribution of wealth around the globe has been greatly affected by neoliberalism, which is discussed in the first section of the chapter. Understanding the effects of neoliberalism will provide a good basis for the topics addressed in the rest of the chapter.

Neoliberalism

Feminist and other twenty-first-century anthropologists have focused on neoliberalism as a set of social values, ideas, and economic policies that have had significant consequences for nations, groups, and individuals since the late 1970s. Current theories about the relationship of capitalism to inequality and oppression tend to focus on the particular form of capitalism that emerged under the influence of neoliberal theory and policies in the late 1970s. The notion of "neoliberalism" has its roots in classical liberal economic philosophy developed in the eighteenth century by such thinkers as Adam Smith and David Ricardo.

Liberalism is a philosophy based on the idea of *laissez faire* (a literal French translation would be "let do") capitalism. Laissez-faire capitalism opposes governmental interference in economic affairs. It promotes developing the economy through "free markets," entities that are self-regulating. Liberal ideology helped fuel the Industrial Revolution in Europe during the middle of the nineteenth century. This revolution, if you remember, was enabled by European colonialism—a period in which colonized countries provided European nations with raw materials and cheap labor to produce and sell manufactured goods and gain enormous wealth.

Proponents of liberalism argue that the government should not impose limitations on manufacturing, restrictions on commerce, and taxes or duties on manufactured goods. Instead they favor **deregulation**, the removal of governmental controls over commercial activities and markets. Advocates of liberalism argue that it eventually benefits all because free markets achieve a stable, unbiased, and thus fair and balanced, distribution of wealth. The fundamental ideology underlying liberalism, therefore, is that markets are efficient engines of technological innovation and progress and should be allowed to operate without government regulations and controls (Schneider 2002:64). In addition to deregulation, liberalist proponents of economic liberalism strongly support **privatization,** the transfer of governmentally owned enterprises to the private sector, including those social services that provide basic necessities such as education, health care, and child care.

As liberalism evolved in the twentieth century, it was given the name "neoliberalism" and was largely based on the ideas of the economists Milton Friedman and Friedrich von Hayek, both of whom helped spread the idea of neoliberalism in Europe and the United States (Berend 2006:275). Neoliberalism became the dominant economic ideology of the United States and Britain beginning in the late 1970s and early 1980s, and it remains so today. Below are the underlying values of neoliberal thinking (Martinez and Garcia n.d.):

- Freeing markets from any kind of interference
- Deregulating anything that can interfere with profits, such as environmental laws
- Privatizing a society's projects, goods, and services—whether electricity, toll highways, or the fresh water supply—by selling them to private investors
- Replacing the idea of a community or "public good" with one that values "individual responsibility"

Although many other industrialized nations have adopted the term neoliberalism, most people in the United States are not familiar with it. They are more likely to hear phrases such as "free market economics" or "free market economy." The word neoliberalism is somewhat confusing in the U.S. context, because in political discourse, the word "liberal" is understood as the opposite of "conservative." Yet, political conservatives, who have forged strong alliances with big business, are the strongest proponents of neoliberal ideas and agendas. Some of the most famous conservative political figures who have passed large-scale neoliberal policies and programs include former British Prime Minister Margaret Thatcher and U.S. President Ronald Reagan.

In the United States, neoliberal ideas are associated with neoconservatism and the Christian Right. As David Harvey (2005) has described, in the late 1970s the Republican Party allied itself with the Christian Right in order to expand its base, and today the Christian Right is an important voting bloc in the United States. Supporters of the Christian Right, referred to as the "Religious Right," saw themselves as a silenced "moral majority." They mobilized, along with the Republican Party, to oppose feminism, affirmative action, and homosexuality. They blame the people they call "liberals," mostly Democrats, for using the power of the state to create policies that they see as favoring black and white women and black men in hiring decisions. It is too early to tell whether the recent election of Barack Obama signals a major defeat of conservatism and the religious right, as some have suggested.

Neoliberalism is tied to the ideological assumptions that individuality and freedom of choice are natural inborn rights. In addition, neoliberal philosophy assumes the following (Schneider 2002:64):

- Motivation for economic gain is a fundamental element of human nature.
- If people are given a chance, they will instinctively welcome the opportunities for choices offered by markets and will make "rational" choices to maximize their individual advantage.
- Unregulated markets can deliver human happiness. Thus, economic inequalities are temporary and are due not to the system but to individual characteristics, such as laziness or having too many children.

Proponents of neoliberal policies say unregulated markets promote opportunities for more people to exercise their rights and better their lives. But neoliberal ideology and policies do not eliminate power imbalances; in fact, they go so far as to naturalize class differences and social inequalities. This situation especially affects women, since the world's have-nots are disproportionately women. As we will see in the following sections, the consequences, for women, of the development of a global economy under neoliberal philosophy and policies have been multiple.

Foucault's (1979) concept of governmentality, which we discussed in the last chapter, is useful for thinking about neoliberal ideology. For Foucault, neoliberalism is not an economic reality; it is a form of governmentality that structures power relations. According to Foucault, posited in neoliberalism is the idea that every person is an entrepreneur managing his or her own life; this extends into noneconomic areas of life as well. Individuals are rational and autonomous; they have the knowledge to assess the costs and benefits of their actions. The self is prioritized and specific individual values are prized.

Neoliberalism assumes that individuals have the necessary knowledge and drive to manage and solve their health, education, and other social problems on their own. Neoliberalism works to govern and shape the conduct of people by presenting them with a picture of the world as a free market in which the responsibility for dealing with social risks and problems fall to the individual, not to the government.

Consider the following as a concrete example of neoliberal governmentality. Shortly after the attacks on the United States on September 11, 2001, President George Bush asked U.S. citizens not to allow the terrorist acts that occurred that day, including the destruction of the World Trade Center, to affect their liberty and freedom. Americans were told that the U.S.'s commitments to freedom and democracy, enabled by a free-market economy, were at risk, necessitating a battle against the dark forces of "evil." Shopping was seen as a main front in this battle. Bush thus encouraged people to leave their homes and urged them to keep spending money as a patriotic duty (Zieger 2004). Shopping became a way for individuals not only to demonstrate patriotism and national pride but also to resist terrorists.

Foucault would consider this "call to shopping" a form of governmentality, because asking people to shop is not a legal mandate, but it nonetheless reinforces economic interests by appealing to the U.S. values of autonomy, liberty, and patriotism. The president's statement used a set of values that drove the particular practice of consuming products and services. President Bush did not have to repress or punish U.S. citizens for not engaging in shopping; rather, they were self-motivated to do so.

Structural Adjustment Policies

A critical factor in the development of the global economy under neoliberalism has been the establishment of important supranational institutions such as the World Bank (WB) and the International Monetary Fund (IMF). Both institutions, heavily dominated by the United States, have economic policies that countries must follow in order to qualify for loans that are essential to helping them repay debt and develop their economies. The widening divisions within, between, and across the Global North and South in the last few decades of the twentieth century are tied to WB and IMF policies.

The WB and IMF have been very influential in restructuring the global economy, particularly by imposing structural adjustment programs (SAPs) on borrower nations. Among other requirements, SAPs oblige countries to balance their national budgets by cutting government spending, resulting in deep cuts in social programs that provide education, health services, and social care (Edelman and Haugerud 2005:6–7). They must also remove subsidies designed to control the price of basic necessities such as food and milk, often resulting in extremely high prices that are sometimes three or four times more than they were prior to the imposition of neoliberal policies.

These programs have expanded poverty, radically reducing people's standards of living. They have devastated environments and greatly decreased employment opportunities. Since women and children constitute the highest proportion of the world's poor, SAPs have had devastating effects on their lives. In essence, then, in providing financial support to poor countries, the WB and IMF seek to reduce risks to international financial investors, accomplishing this by transferring the suffering to the ordinary citizens of these nations, and disproportionately to women.

Gender and Structural Adjustment

Valentine Moghadam's (1999) work on gender and globalization provides a clear picture of the differential burden placed on women by structural adjustment policies. She notes that:

- The poor and especially poor women shoulder the burden of structural adjustments.

- Women bear most of the responsibility of coping with increased prices and shrinking incomes, since in most instances they are responsible for household budgeting and maintenance.

- To survive higher prices and the withdrawal of government services for such basic needs as food, education, and health care, women must work more. This increases both their labor time and their reproductive burdens (they have to compensate in caregiving for cutbacks in social services).

- More work and fewer services increase vulnerability of women and their children, especially in households that favor men and other income-earning adults in terms of their consumption, health care, and education needs. But this also occurs in female-headed households.

- Structural adjustment policies and other forms of neoliberalism are said to be a major factor behind the "feminization of poverty."

- The poverty-inducing aspect of structural adjustment hits female-headed households with children particularly hard.

- Restructuring (downsizing) and privatization adversely affect women, who tend to be the first to be fired because of gender bias, but also because women workers tend to be concentrated in the lower rungs of the occupational ladder, in unskilled production jobs, or in overstaffed administrative and clerical positions.

- Structural adjustment policies that require the reduction in government expenditures through cutting social services disproportionately hit women's jobs, which tend to be in the caregiving and services professions: nurses, social workers, educators.

In addition, gender discrimination maintains a large gap in the income of women and men. Even though women play a central and essential role in the global economy, global restructuring often displaces large segments of the labor force, producing high rates of unemployment. The tendency for women to disproportionately lose their jobs due to cuts in manufacturing and service industries in countries, especially those hit by financial crises, has resulted in the **feminization of unemployment.** Women workers have been especially affected by this due to the gender biases of the free market, making the feminization of unemployment as much a characteristic of the global economy as the feminization of labor (Moghadam 1999).

As a result of industrialized nations seeking cheap sources of labor available in the Global South, a **global division of labor** has emerged in which the manufacturing of goods occurs in poorer nations while the vast majority of these goods are bought by people in nations with advanced capitalist economies. As we discuss in chapter 9, this has bloated the development of a consumer society in capitalist countries.

Neoliberal Policies in the United States

Although neoliberal programs have particularly affected the Global South (Mohanty 2002), the consequences and social costs of neoliberal labor regimes also affect countries of the Global North. As in the Global South, the neoliberal policies adopted in post-socialist societies have resulted in higher rates of women's unemployment and the dismantling of public services such as child care facilities and food kitchens (Gal and Kligman 2000). In wealthy nations, such as the United States, neoliberal ideology has also led to dramatically expanded poverty. One in five children in the United States, for example, lives under the poverty line (O'Hare 2001).

It is interesting to note how deeply neoliberal ideas shape thinking in the United States. A central and alluring ideology of neoliberalism is that individuals can "freely compete" for wealth and success if, and only if, the market is left unregulated from state intervention. The idea is that individuals in the United States can pull themselves up by the "bootstraps," enabling them to climb the social and economic ladder. Wealth is seen as something to which everyone has access, despite the harsh disparities of economic structures that favor particular racial, ethnic, and gender groups over others.

Given their impact, why have so many people in the United States supported neoliberal policies? One study suggests that support is related to the belief in neoliberal ideology as "truth." Another study showed that large numbers of college seniors believe that they will one day be rich. But this is far from the reality: the top 0.1 percent of the population shared 7.4 percent of the nation's wealth in 2002 (Johnston 2005:182). The wealth is disproportionate: for every dollar that the bottom 90 percent of the population earns, the top 0.01 earns $162 (Johnston 2005:186). In short, though an "open market" suggests equal opportunity, neoliberal ideologies mask the inequalities upon which such wealth is produced.

Racial Disparities

The global economy builds on differences that were established under colonialism in the nineteenth century and earlier. The racial and economic disparities that existed between the colonizers and the colonized in the nineteenth century did not disappear with the disbanding of colonies and colonization. Those countries that today are seen as wealthier and as having "advanced capitalist economies" are largely composed of white people and were the colonizers; the vast majority of people in today's Global South are people of color and live in countries that were colonized. The global economy is maintained by the hard work of men and women from the Global South who are increasingly crossing national borders in search of work.

Marable Manning has referred to this situation as **global apartheid:** "the racialized division and stratification of resources, wealth, and power that separates

Europe, North America, and Japan from the billions of mostly black, brown, indigenous, undocumented immigrant and poor people across the planet" (2004:2–3). Racialized divisions also occur among groups within nations; although millions of people in the United States are affected by increasing inequalities, African American and Latino youth bear the brunt (Manning 2004).

Manning draws the following picture: racial disparities in employment and the criminal justice system perpetuate disproportionably high levels of unemployment and mass incarceration for these populations. In 2004, one-quarter of the nation's entire population of black male adults was jobless for the entire year during 2002. Mass unemployment feeds mass imprisonment: about one-third of all prisoners are unemployed at the time of their arrests. This situation is compounded by the racial disparities that exist at all levels of the criminal justice system. For example, a higher percentage of young African Americans are arrested compared to the percentage of young white arrestees; black and white juveniles are treated in radically different ways by the criminal justice system. Youth offenders who are white are more likely than their black counterparts to be referred to juvenile courts, while black youth are often tried as adults. Mass imprisonment, in turn, leads to mass political disfranchisement. About 15 percent of all African American males nationally are either permanently or currently unable to vote due to criminal records (Manning 2004).

Racism and racialization maintain racial inequalities and have been perpetuated by wealthy nations' immigration policies for many years (Preibisch and Binford 2007). For example, Canadian immigration policy in the 1950s subjected Caribbean domestic workers, under the threat of deportation, to restrictions that did not apply to domestic workers from Europe (Preibisch and Binford 2007). In the 1960s, farm workers from the Caribbean were subject to different immigration policies than other groups based on the belief that their population would get progressively larger and cause social problems in the future.

In *Defining America through Immigration Policy* (2004), Bill Ong Hing analyzes how immigration policy at any particular time in the United States is tied to racialized notions of what an "ordinary American" is. He shows that although different minorities have been singled out for differential treatment over the course of the history of U.S. immigration policy, what has not changed is the mechanism by which immigrants are "de-Americanized": a long-standing dominant ideology that implicitly associates being white with being American and that both creates and exacerbates fears about "undesirable" citizens. Today, this process of "de-Americanization" tends to focus on individuals with Muslim or Arab ancestry and Latinos, but in the past it has concentrated variously on French immigrants, Germans, Asians, Eastern Europeans, Italians, and Jews, among others.

The Feminization of Labor

Across the globe, women and children make up the largest percentage of the world's poor living under harsh and highly unequal conditions. Even when women make up 80 percent of the labor force, produce 70 percent of food crops, and represent 30 percent of heads of household, as they do in rural areas in sub-Saharan Africa, they earn only 60 percent of what men do in wage labor, are rarely able to obtain credit in their own names, have much lower literacy rates, eat less, start working younger, and almost always carry the double burden: running a household while working for wages or tending subsistence crops (Lewellen 2002:83). In the Philippines, women work 61 hours a week to men's 41, while in Uganda women work twice as many hours as men (Lewellen 2002:83). The tendency for women to bear the burden of poverty is called the **feminization of poverty.**

During the last half of the twentieth century, U.S. multinational corporations (MNCs) looking for "cheap" labor moved their manufacturing plants to the Global South. It is not unusual for countries to compete to attract MNCs for the tax revenues and employment opportunities they produce, by providing incentives such as tax breaks and government assistance. Women are often seen by MNCs as "ideal" workers, not only because of their lack of social, economic, and political resources in comparison to men, making them more likely than men to accept lower wages and harsher conditions, but also because of assumed "natural" tendencies. Today, 80 percent of the employees of MNCs are women.

The "Ideal" Female Worker

The gendered global labor force is created through tying certain kinds of imagined and constructed identities to certain forms of labor. For example, data-entry jobs have become known as "feminine" work in Barbados, a characterization that is reinforced by, and relies heavily on, gender ideologies and stereotypes (Freeman 1993).

As stated above, MNCs tend to prefer women as workers because they are more likely than men to accept lower wages (Salzinger 1997). But as we have also discussed, the preference for women workers is often explained through discourses that make the choice of

Ethnography in Focus

High Tech and High Heels in the Global Economy
by Carla Freeman

Discipline and worker control have been central to the incorporation of women workers along the global assembly line. Their role in the management of the new "pink-collar" enclave is in some respects reminiscent of their role in other industrial settings and in other respects their role is strikingly different. The general expectation that offshore "office" workers conform to so-called traditional female stereotypes (i.e., that they be pleasant, loyal, courteous, well groomed if not attractive, cheerful, etc.) adds both the hidden dimension of "emotional labor" and expense to the explicit labor process. The discipline exerted in creating what virtually everyone in informatics refers to as a "professional-looking" workforce establishes the industry's most visible market. Like the hidden but potent sign of the computer, the impressive appearance of the informatics workers is noted with a degree of wonder by virtually every passerby. Together, the computer and the distinctly fashioned new pink-collar worker are vital ingredients in a process through which the status and position of this new sector and its employees are made strategically ambiguous. The ambiguity between whether informatics constitutes white-collar office work or blue-collar factory work and whether workers in the industry are assembly line workers or clerical workers is manifested in the following comment by the manager of one the smaller local data entry operations:

> When you see a group of the young ladies, like the ones from Data Air, you can see they're much better dressed than the ones from the assembly plant. That's my observation. They're probably not getting paid much better but their work environment is a cleaner one, a purer one, and they in fact live out that environment. . . . The Data Air is very plush, so the young ladies working in there perceive that they are working in an office and they dress like it and live like it. It's a very interesting phenomenon—it only got started when the data entry business got started—this new breed of office-type workers. They equate themselves with clerical staff in an office and they carry themselves in that way. [p. 214]

The manager's emphasis on women's "professional" presentation as bound up in a particular worker "mentality" implies that the way one looks reflects and shapes one's work ethic and productive capacity. The importance of this notion is expressed and absorbed in numerous ways. This subtle additional job requirement, while positively striking to every onlooker, becomes invisible as a form of labor. In the arena of the open office, dress and fashion become powerful metaphors of corporate discipline, as well as a form of individual expression and

(continued)

pleasure. In fact, the importance of dress can be compared with its significance in the 1920s, when the hats worn by cotton-ginning women reflected their superior status.

Rosie, a data processor at Multitext, in discussing the pros and cons of her job and the general atmosphere of this information enclave buzzing with computer keys and "plenty of gossip," emphasizes the importance of dress and appearance in maintaining the professional character of the workplace and touches on the misperception that some workers have about the true nature of the industry.

> They had to talk to one or two people in there already about the way that they dress, but I never had to be spoken to like that. You should dress in a place like that not like if you're going to a party or a disco or going to town [you should] dress as if you are working at an office . . . but if they were working in an office they would dress a certain way, so I think that if you think that way about working at an office, think that way about working at Multitext and dress to suit the occasion.

A few quotations from Data Air's employee-produced newsletter further illustrate the grave importance attributed to dress and appearance and the complex ways in which messages about dress are bound up in foreign corporate ideals as well as local cultural values. "What you wear is really who you are and how you feel about yourself. Clothing sends a message, a statement to others about you." [p. 215]

women seem natural. For example, women's supposed intuitive and natural caretaking abilities are often thought to make them great nurses. Women's small and "nimble" fingers are supposed to enable them to sew better than men.

To substantiate these kinds of claims, it is often necessary to make a **tautological argument.** This is a circular argument in which the existence of more women or men in a particular job or industry due to gender stereotyping is used as evidence for the existing preconceptions about women and men. For example, the majority of nurses and secondary education teachers in the United States have been women. This has been considered appropriate because women are seen as "natural" caretakers. But then when people look for evidence that women are natural caretakers, they often point to the fact that so many women have careers as teachers or nurses.

The global garment industry provides another example of tautological thinking. It employs nearly 29.3 million workers, the majority of whom are women. Women's participation in the garment industry is based on the gender ideology that views women as "nimble" and "docile." Given the detailed handwork involved and the monotonous working conditions,

these traits are assumed to be important to the job itself (Garwood 2005:21). Linking existing ideas about women's natural skills to the choice of women as the preferred labor pool then comes to seem natural and part of common sense. Once, again, however, assumptions like this vary from one place to another, demonstrating how ideas about femininity and masculinity are embedded in cultural assumptions.

A hospital patient learns about his new medications from a nurse.

More and more women have been drawn into labor-intensive and low-wage industries such as the garment, pharmaceutical, and electronics industries. As a result, these manufacturing jobs have come to be seen as "women's work," which men avoid, if at all possible. MNCs welcome this **feminization of labor** not only because it reduces labor costs but also because women traditionally have been less likely to form labor organizations, such as unions, to protest harsh conditions. MNCs are attracted to poorer nations where minimal labor regulations and environment standards reduce costs and increase profits. Women are thus often toiling for the lowest of wages under the worst of labor conditions, hesitant to speak out for fear of losing their jobs. At the same time, due to increasing poverty in such nations, household incomes have decreased, raising the number of women seeking employment and increasing the size of the female labor supply. Both of these factors keep women's wages low.

By contrast, men, on a global scale, occupy upper-level positions and are placed in the role of supervising female workers (Mills 2003). Because women fulfill the increasing demand for cheap, unskilled labor, they experience a higher risk of exploitation than men.

Close-Up

7.1: Maquiladora Factory Workers by Noelle Molé

The "maquilas" are "export-processing factories" found along the border between the United States and Mexico (Salzinger 2003). Though they were initially opened in the 1960s as a work alternative for male migrant workers, the hiring trends for women and men fluctuated in the 1980s, and women became the favored employee for maquilas and remain so today. Much of this was due to a cultural discourse that emphasized women's "natural" superiority as workers and led employers to prefer hiring women.

In maquilas women workers are often exploited for their sexuality by their male supervisors but not all in the same way. In her study of shop floor practices in maquilas, anthropologist Leslie Salzinger (2003) documents this. In one predominantly female factory, for example, she found that women workers are subject to the gaze of their male supervisors who monitor them as much for their appearance as for the quality of their work. Day-to-day gossip and social relations surround the extent to which women perform their roles as feminized and sexualized workers. These women fit the standard image of female laborer as docile and productive, one that multinational corporations favor.

This dynamic varies, however, depending on the percentage of female versus male employees who work at a particular shop. In another factory where both men and women work together and must wear uniforms that obscure differences and downplay gender, Salzinger found that women often display aggressive and competitive behaviors, more typically associated with men, in order to gain an advantage on a shop floor. Variation in maquila women's working styles, Salzinger suggests, is shaped partly by management style and policy.

Reference

Salzinger, Leslie. 2003. *Genders in Production: Making Workers in Mexico's Global Factories*. Berkeley: University of California Press.

The Transnationalization of Labor

Women supply inexpensive labor not only in their home countries but also in other nations, as they are forced to travel to find work. The global economy is made possible by, and depends on, a **transnational labor force.** In other words, it depends on the movement of people across national boundaries for the purpose of economic production. Women crossing borders to find work typically move from the Global South to the Global North and end up with low-paying jobs abandoned by citizens of the host country as too low-status, too boring, or too short-termed (Lewellen 2002:140).

The most common job for women is in domestic service, followed by health services and garment manufacturing. Women from a range of poor countries leave their families behind to pursue domestic work and other forms of low-wage labor in richer countries.

This includes women from the poorer countries of Asia, such as Sri Lanka, Indonesia, Vietnam, and the Philippines; Eastern Europe, such as Poland, Rumania, and Ukraine; and Central and South America, such as Mexico, Nicaragua, Peru (Parreñas 2001). Often women must leave their children behind, and the responsibility for their own children's care falls to other women, usually female relatives, since husbands who remain in their home country may be culturally restricted from engaging in child care because it is considered to be "women's work."

Even educated women who cannot find employment in their poor home countries often become caregivers of children in other countries. This practice of women from the Global South becoming caretakers of children of the Global North has developed into the phenomenon of **transnational motherhood** (Hondagneu-Stelo and Avila 1997). The money these women earn is often sent home for the care of their own children.

Global News

7.1: Many Nannies Leave Their Children Behind

The night that she left to become a nanny in America, Rowena Bautista knelt in the empty church of her Philippine farming village and lit a candle. "Please watch over my children," she prayed. "Bring us back together soon." More than six years later, Bautista and her children are growing further apart. Bautista, 39, cares for the daughter of a working mother in Washington, D.C. She hasn't seen her own son and daughter in more than two years. The last time she went home for a visit, her 8-year-old son refused to touch her and asked, "Why did you come back?" Bautista left the Philippines to support her children. Over a third of the residents of her village are unemployed. Most jobs in the Philippines pay less than $5 a day. She sends home $400 a month from her $750 monthly salary for her children's schooling, food, and clothes. Her salary also pays for a nanny in the Philippines, Anna de la Cruz, who cares for her two children. De la Cruz has a teenage son of her own, whom she leaves with her 80-year-old mother-in-law while she's caring for the Bautista children. As the global economy draws more Western women into the workforce, it is also pulling mothers from poor countries to take care of children in wealthier ones. Last year, 40 percent of the 792,000 private-household workers in the United States were foreign-born, not counting the large number of illegal immigrants who provide child care. [Robert Frank, *Star Tribune* 2/25/02:E4]

The tendency that there is a disproportionate number of women who move across national boundaries to find jobs is called the **feminization of international migration.** Indeed, women comprise the largest growing segment of migrations in all regions of the world (Brah 2003:614). Such transnational movement places particularly heavy burdens on poor countries and poor women.

The global economy also favors women's labor migration for employment in professional sectors such as law, banking, accounting, computing, architecture, information services, and nursing. These opportunities induce women to move transnationally (Moghadam 1999). As we saw in chapter 1, women from Kerala, India, come to the United States as nurses in large numbers. Moghadam describes the movement of women in search of labor this way:

> Mexican, Central American, and Caribbean women have migrated to the United States to work as nurses, nannies, or domestics; Filipinas and Sri Lankans to neighboring countries as well as to the Middle East to work as waitresses, nurses, nannies, or domestics; Argentine women to Italy to work as nurses; and an increasing number of Moroccan, Tunisian, and Algerian women migrating alone to work in various occupations in France, Italy and Spain. [1999:373]

The Global Industry of Sex Tourism and Trade

Perhaps no area of the world economy has been more affected by the loosening of border controls and migration than tourism. Tourism is the world's largest industry and has become a preferred way for many developing countries to improve their economies. Due to a scarcity of economic resources, growing economic insecurity, and a sector of the world's population with an ample supply of disposable income in today's world, there has been a large expansion of the sex industry worldwide. The sex tourism and trade industry is not a contemporary phenomenon, however.

For four centuries, tourism has been structured according to gender and racial hierarchies, and in many places it continues to be so. During the seventeenth century, the "Grand Tour" was seen as a rite of passage into manhood and proper upper-class society for white European males. Young, mostly wealthy British men were encouraged to travel in order to educate themselves about the rest of the world. During this time, as you may remember, the British colonial empire was at its height.

British male travelers often went to the colonies not only to increase their understanding of the world but also to gain access to women in "exotic" locations, feeling they were in a region where they could shed the constraints on their behavior that existed in their "civilized" home countries (Enloe 1989:28). Thus, the types of experiences once-colonized countries offered in the past have emerged to become a vital part of the tourism industry in these countries today. The expectations and stereotypes of today's male travelers often reinforce colonial ideas; under colonial domination colonized women were often seen and represented as sexually promiscuous, a representation that enabled such behaviors as rape to be rationalized.

An Indian sex worker sits outside her room to attract customers in a red-light district in Mumbai.

Sex tourism destinations are most often in countries with developing economies, but the male tourists who travel to them come predominantly from advanced capitalist nations. Many women now work in the sex trade industry in urban centers in their home country or abroad in "exotic" tourist locales to support their husbands and children at home (Brennan 2004). Thus, the tourist sex trade is a transnational industry, which transforms the daily lives of people living in tourist destinations in ways different from other forms of tourism. There may be as many as several million sex workers in Indonesia, Malaysia, the Philippines, and Thailand. The numbers have greatly expanded in many Eastern European countries too, such as Russia and Ukraine since the crumbling of communist regimes in 1989. This increase has also occurred in China and Cuba, but to a lesser degree (Lewellen 2002:141–142).

Many girls are sold by their families into sexual slavery and are forced to work in the sex trade industry. However, more and more women today choose to turn to sex work as an economic strategy and see themselves as professionals. They organize for better working conditions, health benefits, and increased wages. In Calcutta, India, sex workers have organized the Durber Mahila Samanwaya Committee, which represents 40,000 female, male, and transsexual sex workers (Lewellen 2002:142).

The Value of Flexibility

From Fordism to Flexible Accumulation

The nineteenth-century boom in industrialization and the mass production of goods created a labor market in the United States and European nations in which employers relied on stable, long-term employees who were able to adapt to working in a factory. This form of capitalist development is often referred to as **Fordist accumulation,** named for Henry Ford, the inventor who introduced assembly-line production in 1914 for the building of automobiles. Workers were trained to work along a production line and were expected to carry out monotonous and repetitive tasks. Things changed in the 1930s when the Great Depression hit, but the effects of the Great Depression were relieved after World War II. Consumption in the post–World War II period of the 1950s was flat, and it declined in the 1960s. In the 1970s, the U.S. and Britain battled a number of financial crises, which included inflation, stagnant business activity and growth, and increasing unemployment. The financial crises of the 1970s, heightened by international competition, spawned new methods for acquiring wealth and capital. Fordist accumulation was replaced with a strategy of "flexible accumulation," a strategy closely tied to neoliberal philosophy (Harvey 1989).

Flexible accumulation relies on networks of small-scale corporations or businesses that can smoothly and swiftly adapt to changing market needs and other economic shifts (Harvey 1989). This new flexibility of production allows for the downsizing of manufacturing plants (which means laying off workers) and the shrinking of inventories, both at considerable savings to pro-

ducers. It also allows manufacturers to respond rapidly to changing market demands and to sell their products to increasingly specialized consumer niches, as we will see in chapter 9 (see Harvey 1989). Corporations become more internationally mobile, due partly to globally connected communications networks and financial systems.

Flexible Labor

Flexible accumulation strategies place a high premium on reduced labor costs for business owners, increasing the trend of hiring women workers to keep costs down. A flexible economy needs a workforce whose size can be quickly adjusted through the rapid hiring and firing of workers to meet changing production demands. This is made possible by offering employees short-term contracts with few or no benefits, a process that contributes to the development of the individualization of labor. This individualization requires workers to manage a series of semipermanent jobs on their own, rather than develop a stable or dependable relationship with a single employer and institution for the long-term, which was the typical employer–employee relationship for white male workers in capitalist nations after World War II. Women's work in the informal sector not only renders them a cheap labor force but also a flexible one.

Today, MNCs often deploy strategies such as outsourcing to increase flexibility and maintain low labor and production costs. **Outsourcing** is the transfer to, or management of, some functions of a corporation to an outside party through subcontracting. For example, many information technology service jobs have moved from the United States to India. Such arrangements encourage the persistence of home-based, part-time, and temporary work (Boris and Prugel 1996). Due to existing gender ideologies regarding women's roles, especially as mothers, and the perception that women's work is less valuable, women are disproportionately involved in these forms of employment.

Neoliberal ideas have also contributed to the formation of risk societies or "risk regimes" in which the government of a society sees itself as centrally concerned with managing possible financial risks incurred by economic sectors, rather than unemployment incurred by its citizens. Individuals, not governments or corporations, must bear the risk that employment is not secure. This insecurity results in constant job loss and constant job seeking (Beck 2000). In line with neoliberal ideas, individuals working in risk regimes are expected to rely on their own resources to gain employment, provide for their families, and secure benefits, such as health care or pension plans.

A flexible economy requires laborers who have multiple and diverse skills. Feminist anthropologist, Emily Martin (1994) has pointed out that "flexibility" today is not only widely valued as a way of running a business, it is also the trait of the best employees. Flexibility has come to be considered so fundamentally important, natural, and normal that its value and desirability are rarely questioned.

Disciplining Workers and Sexual Harassment

It is not uncommon in today's workplace for employers to monitor their workers' behavior and pro-
ductivity. For example, computer programs are used to measure workers' output in a data-entry firm in Barbados, becoming an "unrelenting eye" (Freeman 1993:89). Internet filters and e-mail controls also restrict employees' behaviors. But disciplinary measures are rarely that high-tech: they can include dress codes, codes of conduct, and even placing workers in low-rise cubicles where their behavior can be seen and monitored. Disciplinary measures are also often gendered. For example, sexual harassment of women on the job may be used to discipline them. There are many pressures on women to accept or hide sexual harassment. One highly publicized case involving a large number of U.S. women military personnel suggests why (*New York Times,* 3/18/07).

While reports of sexual assault are high for the U.S. army, particularly during wartime (3,038 charges of sexual assault in 2004–2005), less than 10 percent

Close-Up

7.2: **Mobbing as a Form of Harassment** by Noelle Molé

Mobbing refers to the marginalization, isolation, or persecution of a worker by one or more same or upper-level worker, often with the objective of making an employee's work situation so intolerable that she or he will resign. Feminist anthropologist Noelle Molé (2007) has studied this new phenomenon in Italy, where mobbing (*il mobbing*) has led to the opening of mobbing clinics, where workers go to seek help by taking educational classes and speaking with professionals who specialize in resolving the problem. Despite the high numbers of women who believe they are being mobbed, it is often considered a gender-neutral form of harassment, and victims may receive public sympathy in addition to social, economic, and political resources as "compensation" for having been mobbed.

This can be seen in the 2003 film, *Mobbing: I Like to Work (Mobbing: Mi Piace Lavorare),* which tells the story of Anna, played by Nicoletta Braschi, who works in the accounting office of a corporation where, following a corporate merger, she begins to be isolated and marginalized. Her desk is overtaken by a colleague and she is moved to a shared office, ignored by her colleagues, demoted, and given solely photocopying assignments as work. Eventually, she is transferred to an all-male storage facility where she is asked to time the workers' completion of their daily tasks. Her assignment has been devised by her boss to elicit hostility and threats by the male workers, producing an untenable work environment for her. In one scene, the men scream at Anna and surround her until she flees from them and collapses in the bathroom. In

(continued)

Anna's case, her isolation among men is used as a tactic to mob her by creating a situation in which Anna would likely be and feel threatened. At the end of the film, Anna eventually sues the company for mobbing and wins her case of mobbing.

Because of the high-profile nature of mobbing and the public support that surrounds it, it is perhaps unsurprising that women have begun to prosecute sexual harassment offenses as cases of mobbing not only in Italy, but also in Germany (Zippel 2006). While on the one hand, such plaintiffs take advantage of the plentiful public resources dedicated to resolving mobbing, the lawsuits contribute to masking sexualized inequalities in the workforce, since attention is diverted away from understanding these cases as instances of *sexual* harassment.

References

Molé, Noelle. 2007. Protection and Precariousness: Workplace "Mobbing" and Gender in Neoliberal Northern Italy, PhD Dissertation, Rutgers University.

Zippel, Kathrin S. 2006. *The Politics of Sexual Harassment: A Comparative Study of the United States, the European Union, and Germany*. Cambridge: Cambridge University Press.

of perpetrators were punished to the full extent of army law. Women soldiers—who now make up 10 percent of the military—may also experience what has been termed "command rape," in which a higher-ranking officer demands sex upon penalty of humiliation or compromised safety of the lower-ranking soldier (*New York Times*, 3/18/07). This kind of rape received attention when Suzanne Swift filed charges against her commanding officer and, seeking to avoid redeployment, defended herself against charges of being AWOL (absent without leave).

The dangers of sexual assault that women soldiers face within the ranks of a male-dominated field are shaped by gender hierarchies and unequal expectations about the treatment men and women deserve. When service women report rapes or sexual harassment, they are often blocked by a more wide-reaching taboo on speaking against a highly male-dominated field and institution.

Legal protections for women against sexual harassment are not universal. Even when they exist, they are often violated because women lack the social, economic, and political support necessary to carry claims forward. In some places, women risk shame and familial isolation if they expose sexual harassment at work. Other times, women's claims of harassment may be made under a new guise. In Europe, for instance, a new form of harassment called "mobbing" has captured a great deal of public attention since the 1990s, as described by anthropologist Noelle Molé in Close-Up 7.2.

Labor Activism

Women who work under harsh conditions are constrained to remain in their jobs because of limited options for obtaining economic resources. Many women around the globe have begun to organize large-scale strikes and have collectively come together to improve working conditions. On March 8, 2004, the fifth annual Global Women's Strike took place in 60 countries all over the world, including Uganda, England, Argentina, Peru, Guyana, southern India, Spain, Trinidad and Tobago, and the United States. These women were fighting for payment for housework and more equal wages, among a number of other causes.

Women who come together to fight for their rights as workers often must negotiate gender expectations and stereotypes. In Thailand, for example, many young and unmarried women, who have migrated to cities to find work as industrial laborers, have, through strikes, challenged stereotypes of women workers as compliant and docile (Mills 2005). At the same time, they must consistently defend their respectability because of the sexual connotations that attach to women who leave the protection of their families to work in urban centers (Mills 2005:137).

Mary Beth Mills has shown that whether in Indonesia, Latin America, or elsewhere, understanding women's labor struggles requires close attention to participants' own gendered and place-based politics. For example, working mothers in certain communities may be

Global News

7.2: As Women Rise, Corporate Korea Corks the Bottle

In South Korea, managers and workers often engage in evening social activities that involve rigorous and copious consumption of alcohol. . . . In one case, a female graphic designer was threatened she would lose her job unless she drank. "One time, he told her that if she called upon a [male colleague to take her turn in a drinking game], she would have to kiss him. So she drank two glasses of soju. Another time, after she slipped away early, he called her at home and ordered her to come back. She refused." The designer eventually quit and sued the company. " . . . In the first ruling of its kind, the Seoul High Court said that forcing a subordinate to drink alcohol was illegal, and it pronounced the manager guilty of a 'violation of human dignity.'" . . . In Korea's male-dominated corporate world, women's entry signals a series of social, economic, and political shifts. "Many professional women manage to avoid much of the drinking. . . ."

"Still, at least 90 percent of company outings still center on alcohol, according to the Korean Alcohol Research Foundation. The percentage of women who drink has increased overall as they have joined companies." Companies have awakened to the potential dangers of bingeing: health threats, decreased productivity and, with more women working, the risk of sexual harassment. It is this fear of not being accepted as full members of the team that has led many women to drink to excess. [Norimitsu Onishi, *New York Times* 6/10/07]

criticized for not living up to their roles as mothers. At the same time, in other parts of the world, full-time work may be seen as the realization of *proper* motherhood. For example, Moldovan women who migrate to Turkey to work as domestic caretakers are ridiculed for not taking care of their own children, because mothering is seen as the key to the social order. They are often portrayed by others as "irresponsible mothers, immoral wives and selfish consumers" (Keough 2006:431–432). In Ghana, in contrast, Asante women working outside the home are seen as making the most valued contribution to their children's lives that an Asante woman can (Clark 2000).

Conclusions

The central objective of this chapter has been to expose the underlying gendered structures of global capitalism. Another has been to show that the effects of global processes are neither uniform nor predict-

able. Some women experience highly oppressive work situations while other women enjoy some benefits through increased employment. Work in the global economy has allowed some women to escape oppressive home situations by earning their own money. Some women have also experienced greater reproductive rights. As anthropologist Jane Collins puts it:

> Neither deterritorialization nor localization are [sic] unambiguously good or bad for workers. They are different strategies or styles of recruiting and managing labor and as such they constitute distinct environments within which workers must struggle for autonomy, labor rights, respect, and fairness. [2002b:153]

In other words, the global economy is not monolithic. It is an ongoing process, and many people work within their daily lives to shape it (Freeman 2001:1010). In the next chapter, we turn to a consideration of how women and men resist domination, especially through the creation of new forms of culture.

WORD PORTFOLIO

deregulation: the removal of government controls on business.

feminization of international migration: tendency for women to disproportionately move across national boundaries to find employment.

feminization of labor: relative growth in the use of female labor as a result of deregulation of labor markets.

feminization of poverty: the tendency of women to bear the burden of poverty.

feminization of unemployment: tendency for women to disproportionately lose their jobs due to retrenchment in manufacturing and services activities in countries hit by the crisis.

flexible accumulation: a form of capitalism arising out of the economic crises of the 1970s in which corporations developed more readily changeable, "flexible" forms of production, allowing manufacturers to respond rapidly to changing markets and to sell their products to increasingly specialized consumer niches.

Fordist accumulation: assembly-line production named for Henry Ford who invented it for the building of automobiles. Workers are trained to work along a production line and expected to carry out monotonous and repetitive tasks.

global apartheid: an international system of minority rule that promotes inequalities, disparities, and differential access to basic human rights, wealth and power largely determined by race, class, gender and geographic location. [http://www.google.com/search?hl=en&rlz=1T4ADBF_enUS239US242&defl=en&q=define:GLOBAL+APARTHEID&sa=X&oi=glossary_definition&ct=title (accessed 9/22/08)]

global division of labor: the organization of production across national borders such that corporations in advanced capitalist nations increasingly outsource manufacturing functions to countries with lower wages, resulting in manufacturing goods being produced in developing nations while the vast majority of these goods are bought by people in nations with advanced capitalist economies.

outsourcing: transfer to, or management of, some functions of a corporation to an outside party through subcontracting.

privatization: the transfer of governmentally owned enterprises to the private sector, including those social services that provide such basic necessities as education, health care, and child care.

tautological argument: argument based on circular reasoning.

transnational labor force: the movement of people across national boundaries for the purpose of economic production.

transnational motherhood: the practice in which women from the Global South come to be the primary caretakers of children of women of the Global North, who often seek higher paying employment outside of the home.

RECOMMENDED READING

Nightwork: Sexuality, Pleasure, and Corporate Masculinity in a Tokyo Hostess Club, by Anne Allison. 1994. Chicago: University of Chicago Press.

Providing a window onto a little researched world, Anne Allison offers an ethnographic account of high-end Tokyo hostess clubs designed to provide Japanese corporate men with a release from their job tensions. Working as a hostess at one such club, Allison details how women perform subservient roles with their corporate clients, such as lighting cigarettes, pouring drinks, and serving as the object of highly sexualized conversations. These performances provide a model of eroticized femininity that, in turn, reinforces culturally specific forms of masculinity.

After Revolution: Mapping Gender and Cultural Politics in Neoliberal Nicaragua, by Florence E. Babb. 2001. Austin: University of Texas Press.

Drawing on extensive fieldwork in Managua, Nicaragua, Florence Babb offers a unique analysis of the post-Sandinista transition to neoliberalism during the 1990s. Bringing together feminist, political-economy, and cultural analysis approaches, Babb focuses on how low-income residents negotiate the political transition to a market economy. She concentrates on how women have been forced to deal with the harshest effects of structural adjustment even as they demand change through the development of dynamic new social movements.

The Wages of Empire: Neoliberal Policies, Repression, and Women's Poverty, edited by Amalia L. Cabezas, Ellen Reese, and Marguerite Waller. 2007. Boulder, CO: Paradigm.

This edited volume offers critical perspectives on the effects of neoliberal policies on women's lives throughout the world. Tracing the links between economic policy, growing poverty, and increased militarization, these interdisciplinary analyses draw attention to the oppressive conditions in which many urban and rural women live and to the social movements that have formed in resistance to these devastating inequalities.

The Politics of Gender after Socialism, by Susan Gal and Gail Kligman. 2000. Princeton, NJ: Princeton University Press.

Susan Gal and Gail Kligman analyze the centrality of gender in the transition from socialism to capitalism in Eastern Central Europe after 1989. Broadly examining the transformation of political, economic, and social systems, they question the meaning of "democratization" in the context of gender inequality and argue that male and female citizenship is often imagined differently.

Desiring China: Experiments in Neoliberalism, Sexuality, and Public Culture, by Lisa Rofel. 2007. Durham, NC: Duke University Press.

Lisa Rofel looks at the changing meanings of Chinese citizenship, subjectivity, and social belonging in a postsocialist world. Referencing two decades of research in Hangzhou and Beijing, she argues that neoliberal subjects are formed through the production of desire in relationship to material and sexual self-interest. She examines the formation of desiring subjects in a variety of sites, including a television soap opera, a transnational network of lesbians and gay men, and a women's museum.

Free Trade and Freedom: Neoliberalism, Place, and Nation in the Caribbean, by Karla Slocum. 2006. Ann Arbor: University of Michigan Press.

Offering a nuanced understanding of the interrelationship between regional, national, and transnational spaces, Karla Slocum challenges commonly held understandings of globalization through her close examination of banana farmers in St. Lucia. Through a historical and ethnographic approach, Slocum helps us understand the many forms resistance to neoliberalism takes and draws attention to the often-overlooked work of growers to theorize globalization in alternative ways.

8

Producing Culture
From Structure
to Agency

In this chapter you will . . .

examine the structure/agency debate to find out if people are free to create their own ideas or whether ideas are determined by those in power • explore the foundations of structural anthropology and its limitations • focus on how feminist anthropologists have drawn on structural anthropology to explain women's oppression • examine the development of practice anthropology with its dual focus on meaning and practice • explore why the field of Cultural Studies focuses on popular culture and everyday practices • learn about recent studies on the impact of mass media on people of the Global South and immigrant groups

As Western goods and images increasingly circulate throughout the world in mass mediated forms, will local cultures be destroyed? Will globalization lead to the McDonaldization of the world? Or will people find ways to resist the loss of their traditional ways of life or creatively construct new worlds for themselves?

As we discussed in chapter 1, such questions are at the center of one of the most debated issues in discussions about globalization: will it produce cultural heterogeneity or homogeneity? Most anthropologists understand globalization as a dynamic process that has different effects on different groups of people: in some places globalization destroys local ways of life; in others it strengthens it. Global forces can fragment culture or bring people into wider cultural networks.

Anthropologists concerned with the worldwide proliferation of images, symbols, and modes of thought are particularly interested in how, given these forces, people produce meaning in their everyday lives. Anthropologists interested in this question often focus on how people attach meaning to the particular things they do every day, such as dress, eat, watch movies, and shop. Through these practices, people are involved in the production of culture.

But how are new meanings produced? And what are the obstacles that people face in producing local meanings in a globalizing world? To answer these questions, feminist and other twenty-first-century anthropologists have had to grapple with a fundamental tension in theorizing oppression: are oppressed people completely determined by a society's ideas, institutions, and structures, or are people free to make independent decisions?

This set of questions underlies the **structure/ agency debate** in anthropology. In this debate, **structure** is understood as the societal context that differentially constrains and enables people's actions based on their position in society due to such factors as gender, race, class, and ethnicity. It is a kind of "playing field" on which some activities are more likely to happen than others because of such structural arrangements. **Agency** is an individual's capacity to act independently of oppressive structures.

An example of an explanation of oppression focused on structure is Marxist theory, as we have seen. Marx argued that the material conditions of people's lives determine their position in relationship to power; the way people are organized into groups controls how they think and why they act the way they do. Early feminist arguments that portrayed women as victims of a pervasive and unchanging "patriarchy" were also focusing on structure. For them, this was a patriarchal structure, one that was based on male control and domination.

In contrast, theorists who conceptualize humans as actors focus on how people create, re-create, and give meaning to their lives. The theory based on the belief in the ability of humans to be meaning makers, or, in other words, to be agents of culture, despite the system within which they must operate, is called **practice theory** or a "practice approach."

Practice anthropologists hold that social structures influence human activities and that human actions influence social structures. For feminist and other twenty-first-century anthropologists understanding oppression has involved both exposing those factors that constrain people's lives and identifying ways in which oppressed people maneuver within constraints and resist gender, sex, racial, and class oppression. How, they ask, do oppressed people, whose very selves are created through a society's social structure, nonetheless transform themselves and their society? How do they resist the power of oppression and exert an oppositional force to domination?

In practice theory structure is understood as a field of social possibilities within which certain activities are more likely to happen than others. For example, it is more likely for white men and white women than it is for African American women to become highly paid leaders of major corporations because gender and race differentially structure the possibilities.

In this chapter we will trace the roots of the structuralist approach and its influence on feminist anthropology in the 1970s. This approach entered anthropology primarily through the work of the French structuralist anthropologist, Claude Lévi-Strauss. He focused on the structure of the human mind in looking for answers to how cultural meaning is produced. His ideas provided an important starting point for understanding how a society constructs meanings about being a man or a woman.

By the 1980s, however, feminist anthropologists who had been centrally involved in structuralism began to develop an understanding of how meaning is produced through people's everyday behavior. Sherry Ortner, as we will see, was a pivotal figure in switching from a structuralist interpretation of women's oppression in the 1970s to advocating practice anthropology in the next decade. The practice approach not only offers feminist and other twenty-first-century anthropologists a powerful theoretical framework for understanding structures as containing inequality and oppression; it also offers feminist researchers a way to understand how women and other oppressed people resist their oppression (Ortner 1989).

Structures of the Mind: Lévi-Strauss' Model

The basic premise of **structuralism** is that human behavior is determined by structures. A structure is an entity consisting of parts that conform to a set of intrinsic laws, which make that entity internally logical and consistent. Structures are self-regulating and are not dependent on anything outside of themselves. They also have the ability to incorporate new material, and thus, they can be transformed (Hawkes 2003:5–7). For example, language has a structure that we refer to as its grammar.

Anthropologist Claude Lévi-Strauss, a practitioner of structuralism, based his ideas on the work of the linguist Ferdinand de Saussure who, as we will see below, thought that meaning in language does not arise because of some natural relationship between a sound and what it refers to; instead, meaning is produced through the structure of a language, that is, a system made up of parts, such as words and sentences originating in the human mind.

Lévi-Strauss believed that culture, too, arises from structures, which lay deep in the human mind. He set out to uncover how the mind works and therefore how culture is produced. Because of this goal, Lévi-Strauss focused his efforts on uncovering the logic behind such human creations as art, myth, and social organization. Lévi-Strauss argued that myths, rituals, and even aspects of social organization, such as marriage and kinship systems, are like a language; all are reflections of the underlying structure of the human brain.

He argued that the human mind works the same way everywhere because the human brain is structured the same way everywhere. This structure, according to Lévi-Strauss, is binary: all human thought is dualistic, dividing the world into sets of oppositional categories like black and white, male and female, and nature and culture. Lévi-Strauss viewed cultural expressions like myth and kinship as efforts to resolve fundamental paradoxes set up by such **binary thinking.** One such paradox, according to Lévi-Strauss, is produced by the recognition that humans are both natural (are biological beings) and cultural (rely on a system of shared meaning that is learned).

Lévi-Strauss drew on linguistic models in his analyses and focused on symbolic systems, but he assumed that biological structures in the brain explain cultural forms.

Binary Opposition and Meaning

Lévi-Strauss drew his understanding of the particular form that thinking takes from Ferdinand de Saussure. Saussure claimed that language is a system that creates meaning by setting up binary oppositions between signs or sounds. A **sign** is something that stands for something else. Usually the meaning of a sign is straightforward to members of a society. For example, the word "vat" differs from the word "bat" by only one sound. In English, the sound associated with the sign (or letter) "b" carries meaning, just as the sound associated with the sign (or letter) "v" does. The meaning of the word "vat" is different from the meaning of the word "bat" because "b" is not "v" and "v" is not "b." Thus, meaning has been constructed through opposing "b" with "v." For Saussure meaning is found within the structure of a whole language and the relationships of its parts rather than in an analysis of individual words.

In discovering this system, Saussure felt he had discovered the deep structure of language and the underlying law governing it: meaning is produced through setting up oppositions between signs. Speakers of a language, however, are not necessarily conscious of this process; they do not need to know how the underlying structure of language produces meaning in order to speak it.

Drawing on Saussure, Lévi-Strauss claimed that the underlying structure of myths and kinship systems can also be explained in terms of this particular logical structure, even though this structure is not conscious. He sought to show how social institutions can be analyzed in terms of the binary oppositions set up by the mind. At the same time, he pointed to the problem inherent in all binary oppositions: they are arbitrary. Lévi-Strauss contended that, at some level, the mind recognizes this flaw and is dissatisfied. It knows that the binary oppositions it has established are not real but are the product of how the mind operates. To remedy this situation the mind produces signs that mediate between oppositions. These mediators, in essence, act as in-between categories, ones that have characteristics of both of the original binary categories.

To understand Lévi-Strauss' model of how the mind works, think of a traffic light. It works on the basis of opposing colors. The human mind breaks the light spectrum, which is continuous, into discrete categories that are then identified as particular colors. In the traffic signal, colors are used to set up a binary opposition between two signs that are then mediated by a third sign. Red is a sign carrying the meaning "stop," while green is a sign carrying the meaning "go." But there is no natural association of red with stopping and green with going. Nor is there only one way to divide the light spectrum into discrete and particular categories of color.

This arbitrariness requires the binary opposition set up between stop and go to be mediated by a third term, the yellow light. The meaning of yellow in this system of signs is neither go nor stop but something in between the two. It means "slow down" and "be cautious" (this, at least, is the legal meaning of the yellow light; we all know that some drivers interpret this sign as "speed up"). The yellow light, in structuralist terms, mediates between stop and go.

What does this have to do with gender and sexual asymmetry? As you will see, according to Lévi-Strauss, it has to do with the origin of marriage in which women become signs in a system of meaning. As signs, women are exchanged between groups of men in order to create alliances between them. Creating such bonds arises out of the need of humans to transcend nature and to come together into groups that are orderly and structured.

Nature/Culture and the Incest Taboo

According to Lévi-Strauss, the categories "nature" and "culture" are a pair of binary oppositions that the human mind develops to organize the world. We know something is natural because it does not belong to the category "culture," and we know something is cultural because it does not belong to the category "nature." What about humans who are at once natural and cultural? This logical paradox, according to Lévi- Strauss, is solved by the development of an **incest taboo,** which is a supposedly universal law that prohibits mating with close kin.

The incest taboo works to overcome the randomness of mating found in nature by establishing orderly kinship relations required for cultures to function (Murphy 1971:199). It is a mediator between the categories "nature" and "culture," because it allows the natural act of mating to continue, but in a way that is regulated by culture. The incest taboo functions to define the categories into which one can and cannot mate, thereby forming the basis for marriage rules in all societies. These rules of exogamy extend the incest taboo by requiring individuals to find marriage partners from outside their social group. For Lévi-Strauss, the development of the incest taboo marks the critical

Global News

8.1: Geneticists Say There's No Reason for Cousins Not to Have Children

Contrary to popular beliefs and long-standing taboos, cousins who have children together do not face extremely high risks of birth defects or genetic disease, according to a new study. In the general population, the risk that a child will be born with a serious problem such as spina bifida or cystic fibrosis is 3 to 4 percent. The study said first and second cousins face an additional risk of 1.7 to 2.8 percentage points. Although the increase represents a near doubling of the risk, the result is still not considered large enough to discourage related people from having children, said Dr. Arno Motulsky, an emeritus professor of medicine and genome sciences at the University of Washington, the senior author of the report. [*Star Tribune* 4/4/02:A1]

transition of humans from nature to culture and is at the foundation of all social organization.

Marriage and the Exchange of Women

Lévi-Strauss (1971) asserted that what is essential about marriage is that it is governed by rules that call for the reciprocal exchange of women by men. This exchange creates alliances among biologically unrelated groups of individuals so that society can be formed (p. 355). As with language, which enables communication through an exchange of signs, marriage enables relationships among social groups through an exchange of signs, that is, through the exchange of women. The universal incest taboo ensures that

> the risk of seeing a biological family become established as a closed system is definitely eliminated; the biological group can no longer stand apart and the bond of alliance with another family ensures that dominance of the social over the biological, and the cultural over the natural. [Lévi-Strauss 1971:355]

Lévi-Strauss viewed **women as objects of exchange** who cement the relationship between two groups. Because the male sex drive, unlike other "instincts," can be delayed, a network of relationships based on the anticipation of eventual gratification can arise. A system of generalized reciprocity thus devel-

ops in which a man from one family gives a daughter in marriage to a man in another family with the expectation that yet another family, sometime in the future, will provide a daughter for one of his sons to marry. Women are thus the gifts exchanged among men to cement relationships and ensure group cohesion, much as in many societies gifts are exchanged at Christmas between different families to facilitate the continuation of a social relationship into the future.

Since it is men who exchange women, at least according to Lévi-Strauss, it is men who are the beneficiaries of the exchange. Since women are for men to exchange, they are in no position to give themselves away (Rubin 1975:175). Women are objects in this system—things to be exchanged. Men are subjects—people who are able to act on their own volition.

Marriage and the Sexual Division of Labor

According to Lévi-Strauss, in order for marriage and kinship systems to operate there must be interdependence between the sexes so that the union of man and woman will take place. This interdependence arises from the sexual division of labor, which is found in all societies. This division classifies tasks into those that can be performed by men and those by women. Men and women must, therefore, depend on one another since each is incapable of doing all the tasks necessary for survival. Since the particular tasks allotted to each sex vary across cultures,

> it is the mere fact of [the sexual division of labor's] existence which is mysteriously required, the form under which it comes to exist being utterly irrelevant, at least from the point of view of any natural necessity... the sexual division of labor is nothing else than a device to institute a reciprocal state of dependency between the sexes. [Lévi-Strauss 1971:347–48]

The oppression of women, according to Lévi-Strauss' structuralist model, arises from the nature of all social systems that must use women as objects to cement social relationships. Since humans became cultural by instituting an incest taboo that initiates this exchange, women's subordination is synonymous with the very emergence of human beings. In summary, to be human, women are required to be subordinate while men are social initiators, even though there is interdependence between the sexes in the division of labor.

Critique of Lévi-Strauss

Lévi-Strauss explained the universal subordination of women not through invoking biological factors per se but through focusing on the cultural interpretations of biological attributes. He assumed that the explanation for women's secondary status in all societies is due to universal cognitive processes. According to him, stereotypes about males and females are not based on the needs of specific social systems but on the common need of all humans to mediate the transition from nature to culture. As Ortner states, for Lévi-Strauss and for herself: "Local variables of economy, ecology, history, political and social structure, values and worldview... could explain variation within the universal, but they could not explain the universal itself" (1974:83).

For Lévi-Strauss, women's universal subordination is grounded in the role women play as signs in a system of exchange. Men are more highly valued than women, not because of some innate superiority that is genetically grounded or based on some physical characteristic such as speed or strength, but because of the very way the human mind organizes the world into opposing categories.

Several problematic assumptions lie at the base of this structuralist argument, many of which have not been substantiated by data. For example, there is no evidence that people at all times and in all places think through the construction of binary oppositions. Since

Western thinking has been based on such oppositions, some have accused Lévi-Strauss of ethnocentrism: projecting Western ideas on to all other human beings.

Lévi-Strauss' ethnocentrism, according to one of his critics, Carol MacCormack, is also apparent in his assumption that there is a universal human need to transcend nature. She argues that the idea that humans have developed out of a state of nature is not some truth about what happened, but is instead the origin myth of Western capitalism. The opposed categories of nature and culture, according to her, are historically specific, not universal. Their opposition can be traced to a specific time and place: eighteenth-century Europe (MacCormack 1980:7).

While the nature/culture dichotomy may not be universal, Michael Peletz (1996) has suggested that this concept may not be confined to Western thinking. Peletz argues that the association of women with animality (nature) and men with reason (culture) in Islamic societies may date back to a period before the eighteenth century, which suggests that there is still work to be done to clarify the roots of such gender constructs.

Lévi-Strauss' analysis has also been criticized for its assumption that kinship systems are dependent on women being circulated as objects in a network of exchange. The assertion that it is men who must necessarily be in control of an exchange of women neglects evidence to the contrary. According to Gayle Rubin, "Kinship systems do not merely exchange women, they exchange sexual access, genealogical standing, lineage names, and ancestors, rights and people—men, women, and children—in concrete systems of social relations" (1975:177). Only if the active role of women in kinship structures is denied can Lévi-Strauss' formulation be given credence.

Ortner's Structuralist Model of Women's Oppression

Lévi-Strauss' ideas had an important impact on feminist anthropologists writing in the 1970s, especially on Sherry Ortner (1974), whose article "Is Female to Male as Nature Is to Culture?" is now considered a classic in feminist studies. In it, Ortner drew heavily on Lévi-Strauss' work to explain what she assumed were women's devaluation and subordination in all societies. Ortner integrated structuralist assumptions with the ideas of another French writer, philosopher Simone de Beauvoir, whose work we discussed earlier. Beauvoir, if you remember, is best known for her claim in *The Second Sex* that "woman is not born, but made" (1953). This phrase summarizes Beauvoir's understanding of gender as a cultural construct—as the meaning given to the physical or biological traits that differentiate males and females. Beauvoir's influence on Ortner, as well as on many other feminist writers, resides in her focus on the role that Western categories like male and female, and self and other, play in women's subordination and on how ideas about the body are related to notions about who a person is or can be.

As we have seen, many theorists argue that women's bodily functions predispose them to particular gender roles and behaviors, which, in turn, give rise to a sexual division of labor and women's position in society. As we've also discussed, these investigators focus on the "naturalness" of such outcomes, claiming that they have resulted from evolutionary processes having to do with the survival of our species. Beauvoir, by contrast, argued that if women's bodies have constrained them, it is because women have been interpreted through the lens of culture, thought of as "natural" by men who have created the very category of "nature" to serve their own aims.

To explain why women are considered inferior to men in all societies, Sherry Ortner (1974) expanded Lévi-Strauss' conceptualization of women's oppression and drew on Beauvoir's conclusions that men's creative abilities contribute to their superiority over women. Women's inferiority, according to Ortner, cannot be due to what women contribute to society, because what women do in all societies is significant to the overall maintenance and perpetuation of the social group. Why, then, she asks, are women always thought of as inferior? Why are they so often associated with what is defiling? Why are they always excluded from the highest forms of power?

Women as Closer to Nature

Ortner (1974) argues that it is women's association with nature in all societies that gives rise to the universal evaluation of women as inferior to men. According to her, this categorization occurs because a woman's body and its functions are involved more of the time than men's with "species life," with giving birth to, and caring for, children. Women are placed closer to the physical world and thus closer to nature.

According to Ortner, men, lacking the natural procreative abilities of women, exhibit their creativity externally through the manipulation of symbols. In this view, culture itself is seen a system of symbols. Like a sign, a symbol stands for something else. But in contrast to a sign, a symbol has complex meaning and may have multiple meanings. The act of creating symbols is the act of creating meaning, and the act of creating meaning is the act of creating culture. Thus, men's activities "make culture" and men are regarded as cultural by members of the group, just as mating and marriage outside the family group in Lévi-Strauss' scheme are associated with the cultural. Men are also seen as closer to culture because of their involvement in public affairs beyond the family. Thus, men transcend nature, while women lack this ability.

Ortner's debt to Beauvoir is evident in the following statement from *The Second Sex* that Ortner quotes in her article:

> Here we have the key to the whole mystery. On the biological level the species is maintained only by creating itself anew; but this creation results only in repeating the same Life in more individuals. But man assures the repetition of life while transcending Life through Existence [i.e. goal-oriented, meaningful action]; by this transcendence he creates values that deprive pure repetition of all value. In the animal, the freedom and variety of male activities are vain because no project is involved. Except for his services to the species, what he does is immaterial. Whereas in serving the species, the human male also remodels the face of the earth, he creates new instruments, he invents, he shapes the future. [Beauvoir quoted in Ortner 1974:75]

According to Ortner, because human society arose when humans made the transition from nature to culture, natural processes are devalued in relationship to cultural ones in all societies. Women's social roles, associated as they are with nature, are considered to be of a lower order than those of men. This circumstance is not one that just occurs in some societies. Indeed, Ortner asserts her arguments are "intended to apply to generalized humanity; they grow out of the human condition, as humanity has experienced and confronted it up to the present day" (1974:74).

Women as Mediators of Nature and Culture

Ortner asserts that a complicating factor arises in classifying women as natural because, at some level, it must also be recognized that women are cultural beings. They are not, after all, living in the same state of nature as other animals. Another complication arises when women's role as the socializer of children is considered. This role involves the conversion of "animal-like" infants into socialized or cultural beings (Ortner 1974:84). Because of this activity, women mediate between nature and culture. Ortner argues that this intermediate position accounts for the ambiguous way in which women are represented in cultural ideology. On the one hand, for example, they are often symbolized negatively in myth, religion, and art as witches or castrating mothers. On the other hand, they can be depicted positively as transcendent figures, such as in the United States where a statue of a blindfolded woman is used to represent the ideal of justice as fair.

While women are subordinate to men in all societies, according to Ortner, this status is due not to some natural debility or limitation but to women everywhere being *thought* of as natural. Since the realm of nature is conceptualized as inferior to the realm of culture, which is the domain of men, women are thought of as inferior to men.

The Self/Other Dichotomy

The nature/nurture dichotomy is tied, according to Ortner, to another set of categories: the **self/other dichotomy,** in which men are associated with the first term and women with the second. According to Beauvoir, a man knows what he is by knowing what he is not. And man is not woman. Thus for men, selfhood is created through a comparison with individuals who occupy the category other, that is, women. And women are other because they are defined by their bodies while men are defined by a self that floats free of bodily functions. Beauvoir argued that men profit from the otherness of women. Men have created this concept of woman's nature as other, as trapped in the body, while they have imagined themselves as transcendent, associated with mind, which is an entity free from the constraints of the body (Conboy et al. 1997a:2). As Conboy and her associates put it, this entrapment of women in their bodies means that "women have been made the other and the other is inferior—'the second sex,' always defined by a lack of masculine qualities that men assume results from natural defectiveness" (1997a:7).

Beauvoir demonstrated that the self/other, subject/object, man/woman, masculine/feminine, mind/body divisions so pervasive in Western thought are part of a system of oppositions that deprives women of autonomous selfhood and defines men as the central actors in culture. Since woman has been defined by her body, and this definition has rendered her as object not as subject, as passive not as active, feminists have searched to uncover the ways in which women continue to internalize the values associated with being a body/object. As we will see in chapter 9, recent studies have focused on how women are continuously reminded of the central role their bodies play in their self-perception.

Critique of Ortner

While Ortner's early work has been important in furthering thinking about how cultural categorizations and ideas affect women, it can also be questioned. For example, not all anthropologists accept her assertion that women in all societies are devalued. She based this conclusion on the information received by anthropologists from informants during fieldwork. But as Karen Sacks has suggested, there were few anthropologists prior to the 1970s who asked members of other societies "who is worth more, men or women?" Instead, anthropologists tended to translate symbolic statements and forms of behavior into answers to this question, offering interpretations that may have been based on their own Western assumptions.

It has also been argued that it is men's valuation of women that is given preeminence in Ortner's formulation, not the value women place on themselves. For example, Carol MacCormack (1980) reports conversations with women informants who are chiefs and heads of descent groups, secret societies, and households. MacCormack points out that they would not agree with the statement that women are inferior to men (p. 16). Neither would the Batek of Malaysia who have a gender egalitarian society. There, neither women nor men, "as groups, controlled the actions of the opposite sex or the terms by which their actions and characteristics were judged" (Endicott and Endicott 2008:6).

Ortner can also be criticized for invoking evidence of female subordination selectively. While she uses instances in which women are viewed as defiling as an indicator of female devaluation and subordination, she would not interpret the symbol of justice in the United States, for example, as indicating a high status for women. Instead she explains constructions such as this by proposing an intermediate position of women between nature and culture.

The Value of Structuralism

Regardless of the specific drawbacks of a structuralist interpretation of gender roles and sexual asymmetry, its insights have been valuable. So have criticisms of it. As Caroline Brettell and Carolyn Sargent point out, "the critique of the concepts of universal subordination and the nature-culture dichotomy" resulting from the work of such theorists as Lévi-Strauss and Ortner "has stimulated significant research on how gender identity and gender roles are constructed in particular cultural contexts" (2005:186).

In particular, the ideas of Beauvoir continue to have an important impact on anthropology and how contemporary anthropologists think and go about their own work. Beauvoir's notion of the other as a category devised by men to construct themselves as agents capable of acting in the world has been expanded to include non-Western people. As we saw in chapter 3, anthropologists now scrutinize how Western researchers and writers have constructed non-Western societies as objects in need of study and analysis. This construction of the other, they argue, acts as a backdrop against which the West can define itself and legitimize its activities. The West comes to know what it is by knowing what it is not, and it is not the other. In this construction, some of the characteristics of the other include these: primitive, exotic, erotic, and underdeveloped, as we saw in our discussion of Orientalism and the harem.

But, structuralism's most enduring legacy is the contribution it has made to practice theory, which provides feminist and other twenty-first-century anthropologists with a powerful model for understanding culture, power, and difference. Many contemporary feminist writers have followed Beauvoir's lead and have analyzed how cultural constructions of womanhood continue to affect women's lives. Some of these analyses show how such constructions can have devastating effects on women, while others focus on how women work within the constraints of these ideas and representations to construct identities that manipulate and refute cultural norms.

Practice Theory

In 1984, Ortner moved away from her primary focus on structures of power and oppression and provided a fundamental agenda for a "practice" approach to anthropology. Practice anthropology should not only analyze how a society constrains people's actions but also how society is made through human action (Ortner 1984:159). In, "Is Female to Male as Nature Is to Culture?" (1974), Ortner explained how men have come to exert control over women. How, she asked, did the idea that women are closer to nature come to have meaning in society?

With a shift in emphasis to practices, Ortner's question became, to what extent are women able to negate men's capacity to subordinate them through their own actions? To answer this question, Ortner argued that feminist anthropologists need to consider both how power is maintained and how meaning is made. Understanding the production of meaning requires feminist and other twenty-first-century anthropologists to identify the specific context within which ideas about what it means to be a woman or a man, as well as a white or black woman or man, are shaped, negotiated, and resisted.

Early Focus on Women as Actors in Feminist Anthropology

Although a practice approach did not become a dominant focus in feminist anthropology until the 1980s, some feminist researchers in the 1970s were already arguing that understanding women's position in society requires paying attention not only to oppressive structures—such as women's association with nature, their role in the domestic sphere, or their role as objects of exchange that cement alliances among men—but also to how women **negotiate** their position. How, in other words, do women and other oppressed groups work within the confines of society to create options that grant them social power or the ability to cope with economic circumstances?

The situation of women in Taiwan identified by Margery Wolf (1972) provides one type of example. In Taiwan, a young wife is subjugated to her husband and his mother. When she has sons of her own and becomes a mother-in-law herself, she is able to wield considerable power and attain a high status within the household. Thus, women use the powerful bond that exists between them and their sons to gain access to power and prestige.

Among the Nandi of Kenya, a patrilineal people who practice a mixed economy of herding and farming, a woman can raise her status by marrying another woman. According to Nandi ideology, men must manage the most important property: livestock and land (Oboler 1993:136). When a woman marries, she acquires rights to some of her husband's property, which she will pass on to her sons. For a woman with no sons, this situation presents a problem. She will be unable to pass down her property unless she opts either to adopt a male child, to stay in her natal household, to have her husband control her property, or to become a female husband. In this latter case, the woman takes another woman in marriage who will bear her sons (through impregnation by a man, of course). The female husband, who also may have a male husband (Oboler 1993:139), has all the nonsexual prerogatives of a male husband in regard to his wife, and she also acquires other rights associated with being a man, such as the right to manage family property and to exercise legitimate authority over children. This increases the woman's status significantly in this male-dominated society (Oboler 1993:138–139). Women who do this are said to be "negotiating" their position.

Using an early practice approach (known as an interactionist approach), Carol Stack (1974) found that among African Americans living in poverty in the U.S. Midwest, women create women-centered families that are bound together by female kinship and friendships. These networks provide women with economic and emotional support. Such kinship connections create a network of relationships within which women exchange goods and services and cope in the face of harsh conditions. Women-centered households are common. For example, they can be found in the Dominican Republic (Brown 1975), among sectors of the British working class (Morpeth and Langton 1973), and among Japanese Americans (Yanagisako 1977).

Micaela di Leonardo (1997a) has also found similar kinship networks among Italian American women in northern California. Her analysis reveals the extent to which women are involved in initiating, maintaining, and celebrating cross-household kinship ties through such devices as visiting, telephoning, sending cards and presents, and organizing holiday events (p. 341). She found that while such "kin work" is unpaid labor and is sometimes viewed as a burden, it is also a source of satisfaction for women and a route for attaining power not available to them in the labor market (p. 347).

Meaning and Practice

Feminist and other twenty-first-century anthropologists have built on these insights to develop a feminist practice approach. They have also drawn on the ideas of Clifford Geertz and Pierre Bourdieu, two theorists who have had a wide impact on anthropology; Geertz is interested in how people give meaning to their lives, Bourdieu in how people's everyday practices aid in the reproduction of society's oppressive structures. Thus, a central concern of feminist practice theory, and other twenty-first- century anthropological thought, is how women and other oppressed groups actively produce meaning within such structural constraints as class, race, ethnicity, and gender.

Clifford Geertz and Interpretive Anthropology

Just as Lévi-Strauss focused on how meaning is created in a system of signs such as language, so Geertz (1973) focused on how meaning is created in a system of symbols. While a symbol stands for something else, a **symbolic system** is the set of relationships among symbols, or among groups of symbols, and the meanings attached to them. For Lévi-Strauss humans are shaped by mental structures. For Geertz, humans actively create meanings and interpret their worlds.

This system of symbols is what Geertz calls culture. In his approach, **culture** is a system of meaning that individuals share by being members of a group. It is what imposes meaning on the world for a person living in a particular society (1973). These meanings are passed down from one generation to the next and provide people with a way to communicate.

For example, culture is what allows a person of U.S. society to understand that when a man twitches his eye in a particular way in the presence of a young woman, that it is not because he has something in it, but because he is flirting with her, using a wink to send a sexual message. She can understand this message because both she and the young man know what a wink means; they share this understanding by virtue of their shared membership in a particular society. The wink is a symbol. And the goal of the anthropologist, according to Geertz, is to interpret symbols in order to understand how people use them to give meaning to their world (1973). This means that understanding culture requires understanding the meanings of its creators and users. This approach to understanding culture is called **interpretive anthropology.**

One of the important implications of focusing on people's interpretations is that meaning is understood as something that is produced in a particular cultural context. This view calls into question theories like Lévi-Strauss' that make broad generalizations and claim the existence of universal ways of thinking. For

Geertz and other interpretive anthropologists, there is no one thing we can call culture. But there are many groups of people who create meanings for themselves as a group and therefore there are many cultures.

Pierre Bourdieu and Practice Theory

Pierre Bourdieu's (1977, 1984) practice approach synthesizes the ideas of a number of theorists we have discussed. Like Lévi-Strauss, Bourdieu (1977:78–87) focuses on the limitations structure places on people and on how structures get reproduced. But, he also shares with Geertz (1973) the idea put forward by the sociologist Max Weber, whom we discussed in chapter 6, that people's actions can change cultural structures. Thus, although Bourdieu (1977, 1984) thinks that society shapes humans, he also argues that human action shapes society. This is the fundamental premise of practice theory, which Sherry Ortner describes this way: "culture constructs people as particular kinds of social actors, but social actors, through their living, on-the-ground, variable practices, reproduce or transform . . . the culture that made them" (Ortner 2006:129).

Another way of saying this is that Bourdieu (1984) believes that structure and agency exist in a dialectical relationship, that is, in tension with one another. As we have seen, Marx and Engels also focused on structural tensions. Bourdieu's focus, however, is not on people's position within classes, but within "fields."

Fields. Bourdieu's (1984:226–229) basic argument is that people are social agents who interact with one another in **fields,** which are spaces of conflict where they compete to achieve their objectives, of which the main one is to gain capital. Capital refers to the resources one has to invest in pursuit of profit. Different fields have different forms of capital; for example, in the economic field, people compete for money, while in the cultural field, they compete for recognition and prestige.

People's options within fields are constrained by the nature of the resources they hold in that field. While fields are also spaces of opportunity where people might change their position, there is no such thing as a "level playing field." All fields are structured by power differentials so that different people hold different positions within them. People's perception of where they fit in a field will affect their behavior in that field. People estimate, although unconsciously, what actions will enable them to achieve their desired outcome, an estimate based on their previous experiences and, thus, on their sense of their place within a field. People's choices are structured by their position within a field.

Forms of Capital. Like Marx, Bourdieu (1984) also recognizes the relationship between the material conditions of life and social inequality. Marx (1992) argued that people's positions in the world are determined by their economic capital: their control over the relations of production, and over material assets such as property. Bourdieu (1986) suggests that there is another form of capital, which he calls **symbolic capital:** the amount of prestige and honor a person has within a social field that affects his or her behavior, choices, and opportunities.

Thus, for Bourdieu, humans not only seek material resources but also social recognition. Bourdieu suggests that an individual's position in a society is made up of the amounts of each kind of capital a person possesses, both symbolic and material. Specifically, there are two types of symbolic capital: **social capital** refers to the advantages people have because of their membership in a network of social relations; they are key to a person's achievement (Bourdieu 1986).

For example, if one or both of the parents of a student who is applying to an elite university attended that school, the applicant likely will be accepted, even if his or her grades are not as good as those of other applicants. Although some U.S. colleges and universities have begun to question this policy, the fact that the applicant is the child of a previous graduate (i.e., the child is a legacy) still, in most cases, advantages him or her over others A person's social capital is widened or restricted to what he or she can get hold of through his or her connections.

Cultural capital refers to advantages that grant individuals higher status based on the forms of knowledge they have, the skills they possess, and the qualifications they hold (Bourdieu 1984, 1986). Cultural capital is usually acquired through socialization and education and is often achieved through the display of what other members in a society think of as superior aesthetic taste. For example, if your taste in music includes classical music and opera, this could be taken in the United States to indicate that you are educated, refined, and have superior taste. If, however, your predilection is for country music, you could be seen as lacking refinement and taste.

People are often judged on the basis of the distinctions they make, between, let's say, what they think is beautiful and what they think is ugly or what

Left, cultural capital, certain forms of knowledge or skills, can confer class advantages. *Below,* social capital, a person's network of social relations, can also confer class advantages.

they consider polite or what they consider crude and offensive. The music you listen to, and the other cultural products you consume such as the clothes you wear, the books you read, and the travel you are able to do reproduce class difference and inequalities. Cultural capital makes and maintains distinctions among people.

Habitus and Symbolic Violence.   Class position is not only signified by such obvious markers as taste in music and clothes, choice of food, or overall lifestyle. It is also displayed through bodily habits such as the way one walks or "carries" oneself. Bourdieu (1984) calls this **habitus.** These body habits are learned through socialization and become part of a person's deeply buried "self." They shape a person's character, or what Bourdieu calls a person's disposition. In other words, a person's habitus is what *disposes* a person— makes a person willing—to act in certain ways, in particular how to act in ways that reproduce a person's class position and therefore his or her subordination (Ortner 2006). It is the practices or habits people have that reproduce structures of power.

Practice theory enables us to understand how what is socially constructed comes to be seen as something that is natural or inevitable or real (Morris 1995). People are largely unaware or unconscious of their habitus. Habitus is a part of a person, and therefore it structures and affects the way people experience their bodies. Every move you make, in other words, signifies your position within a class struture: you have internalized your class position. And these class markers are observable in the daily practices of the body. According to Bourdieu:

> The body is the most indisputable materialization of class taste, which it manifests in several ways. It does this first in the seemingly most natural features of the body, the dimension (volume, weight, height) and shapes (round or square, stiff or supple, straight or curved) of its visible forms, which express in countless ways a whole relation to the body, i.e., a way of treating it, caring for it, feeding it, maintaining it, which reveals the deepest dispositions of the habitus. [1984:190]

Class distinctions can be maintained through the idealization of certain body types that must be developed, but which are often available only to those who can afford the products and services required to produce the ideal. In contemporary U.S. society, for example, an ideal of slimness may require a kind of diet often found impossible to maintain by hardworking individuals who must work long hours and also tend to a home and family, leaving little time for thinking about or finding time to cook "healthy" meals. It might also demand hours of working out in a gym, requiring both time and money that many working-class people do not have.

When habitus is identified with a person who has limited social capital, and both of these factors are incorporated into that person's life, there exists an opportunity for what Bourdieu calls "symbolic violence." **Symbolic violence** is a form of domination that is exercised on social actors with their own involvement and complicity. When a holder of symbolic capital uses the power this confers against someone who holds less capital, thereby altering the person's actions, he or she exercises symbolic violence.

One of Bourdieu's key examples of symbolic violence is the effect of the educational system on children from different class backgrounds, which differentially privileges middle-class students over working-class or poor students in a school setting (1984). Successful students, Bourdieu argues, inculcate not only behaviors directly related to learning but also others that are not strictly academic but are valued by their teachers. This prepares them with the proper disposition for success.

For example, privileged children learn passive behaviors: how to sit still and remain quiet, use "proper" English, and pay attention. These behaviors fit their teachers' expectations. In contrast, children from less privileged backgrounds who have not internalized these behaviors are seen as misbehaving and difficult. Middle-class parents who invest a great deal of social labor in teaching their children "proper" behavior reap the benefits when their children do well in school, attend good colleges, and get decent jobs. Because of it, their children are likely to reproduce their class position and share in the privileges it bestows.

What is significant about proper behavior or "good taste," whether it is displayed in one's choice of clothes, school behavior, or by one's body, is that it is seen as an inner quality of people. It is not seen as something that is unconsciously learned to maintain class distinction, distinguishing a "higher" and "lower" class of people. For example, the ease with which mid-

dle-class children act in school is attributed to a natural ability that distinguishes them from their unprivileged classmates. Thus, people are thought to have good or bad taste, proper or improper behavior, because of who they are naturally. Bourdieu thus suggests that cultural capital is "misrecognized," or seen as inborn rather than created.

Here Bourdieu's ideas are similar to Antonio Gramsci's, who was discussed in chapter 6. Just as Gramsci argues that power relations are naturalized through notions of common sense, so Bourdieu argues that they are naturalized through misrecognition.

How then are the structures of society that privilege some people over others able to change, especially when they appear natural and inherent to people? Several answers have been given to this question: some theorists argue that control can never work perfectly because dominated people always know that they are dominated and therefore can **resist** oppression (Ortner 2006:5). As we saw in chapter 6, Gramsci argued that hegemony can never be a complete or total system of domination because of the discrepancy between ideology and people's actual material and social experience. For example, people who are denied access to education, such as most U.S. women in the nineteenth century, may have trouble with the statement in the U.S. Declaration of Independence that all are created equal and use this contradiction to fight for equal rights.

Anthropologist Marshall Sahlins points out that even if people respond to such contradictions, especially those arising from new circumstances, their actions may produce change but not necessarily in intended ways. Although Bourdieu similarly suggests that contradictions between habitus and field can result in structural changes, he has been criticized for focusing more on how structures are reproduced than on how they are transformed. His emphasis has been more on stability and continuity than instability and change (Ortner 2006:17).

Practice Theory and Feminism: Ortner's Serious Games

To balance a focus on stability with one on change, Ortner (1996) has developed what she calls a feminist, minority, subaltern, theory of practice. This theory makes practice theory more cultural (more focused on the production of meaning), more historical (more focused on how conditions are created over time and in particularly historical moments) and more

Close-Up

8.1: Unintended Consequences

Some practice anthropologists focus on how large historical transformations have taken place, raising questions about the role played by the motivations and intentions of actors in cultural change. Anthropologist Marshall Sahlins (1996), for example, argues that although humans are agents who can transform society through their actions, those social changes are not necessarily, or even often, the result of intended consequences. He uses the major transformations that occurred in Hawaiian society after its encounter with Captain Cook as an example. He suggests that changes resulted not directly from the actions of the Hawaiians, but from unintended consequences of their behavior. Ortner summarizes insights about the conquest of Hawaii this way:

> Setting out to conceive children with superior mana [supernatural power] by sleeping with British sailors, Hawaiian women became agents of the spirit of capitalism in their society. Setting out to preserve structure and reduce anomaly by killing a "god" who was really Captain Cook, the Hawaiians put in motion a train of events that ultimately brought down their gods, their chiefs, and their world as they knew it. To say that society and history are products of human action is true, but only in a certain ironic sense. They are rarely the products the actors themselves set out to make. [Ortner 1984:157]

Reference

Ortner, Sherry B. 1984. Theory in Anthropology since the Sixties. *Comparative Studies in Society and History* 26 (1):126–166.

Sahlins, Marshall. 1996. *How "Natives" Think about Captain Cook, for Example.* Chicago: University of Chicago Press.

political (more focused on contests over power). She integrates practice theory with feminism to uncover the relationship between gender and power in everyday life.

All people, Ortner argues, are enmeshed within relations of power, inequality, and competition. How, then, she asks, are power and meaning used and negotiated as people confront one another with differing agendas? Although these agendas may not necessarily be about having power and control, Ortner points out that preexisting power differentials between people shape even the most well-meaning encounters, producing friction.

One way to understand how this works is to focus on what Ortner (1996) calls **serious games,** the inter-

actions of individuals trying to control change. People enter into these games—fields of predefined social positions—with some degree of agency. Thus, a serious game is actively played by social actors and is oriented toward shared cultural goals. Actors can act intentionally in serious games, using skill, knowledge, and intelligence to manipulate and modify the social field of the game. Ortner demonstrates how serious games work in her ethnographic study of Sherpas in Nepal.

Some feminist writers have argued that understanding gender as a form of capital helps explain why, even after structural changes occur, gender identities do not necessarily change. As we have seen, women and men have deep-seated and unconscious investments in their gender identities, based on cul-

Ethnography in Focus

Life and Death on Mt. Everest: Sherpas and Himalayan Mountaineering by Sherry B. Ortner

Sherpas are members of an ethnic group who live in the environs of Mount Everest and some of the other highest Himalayan peaks, and who have provided climbing support for Himalayan mountaineering expeditions since the first decade of the twentieth century. . . . The Sherpas have made major contributions to Himalayan mountaineering, have made money, become famous, and often died in the course of it. But Himalayan mountaineering was originally, and is still, for the most part, defined by the international mountaineers. It is their sport, their game, the enactment of their desires. . . . [But] despite the mountaineers' control of the sport, the Sherpas managed to make extraordinary gains in their position over the course of the twentieth century. The story of Himalayan mountaineering "from the Sherpa point of view" is the story of . . . complex and changing relations. [pp. 3–4]

***

I introduced the idea of "serious games" as a way of thinking about the cultural framing of intentions within which people operate at any given time. The idea of the game includes the purposes of the activities, the discursive categories through which it is viewed, the organization and relative power of the players, and so forth. Mountaineering as an activity has been situated within a number of overlapping and intertwining games—the countermodernity game; the romantic, testing-the-existential-limits, game; the masculinity game—and to know this is to begin to understand the kind of language mountaineers speak; the kinds of risks they are willing to take, and the kinds of control they exert over themselves and others. Games are social, indeed intensely social; people play against each other, with each other, for each other. Games thrive on difference; there is no game without difference. Within mountaineering . . . is the Sherpa/sahib [Western mountaineer] difference, and its multiple permutations. [p. 150]

***

Competition is probably the most consistent strand of sahib masculine discourse in Himalayan mountaineering. . . . At issue above all in postwar sahib competitiveness was individual physical superiority in relation to all others on the mountain, including the Sherpas. [But] the Sherpas have their own tradition of competition. . . . From the Sherpa point of view, reaching back into their earliest folklore, everyone . . . competes for status and recognition, for being recognized as superior in some way or other to one's rivals. . . . At one level, the sahibs have always appreciated the Sherpas' strength and endurance, from the earliest years of Himalayan mountaineering to the present. . . . [But,] given the sahibs' extraordinary competitiveness, the fact that the Sherpas were often stronger than they were, and had a greater endurance, was occasionally a source of anxiety. . . . Both the sahibs' competitiveness and their real dependence on the Sherpas thus constituted a weak point that the Sherpas would mischievously exploit from time to time . . . [and this is one way they] established themselves as operating at least in part on equal footing with the Sahibs. [pp. 162–169]

(continued)

***

Intercultural relations are never gender neutral. . . . In the context of all-male expeditions, Sherpa masculinity was played upon by both Sherpas and (male) sahibs as a way of "making equality" between them. At the same time, contradictorily, the Sherpas may well have been coded metaphorically as female . . . [a practice that] is probably true of many forms of Western "othering". . . . The Sherpas' job could be seen as basically mothering the sahibs—cooking, cleaning, carrying their loads, and occasionally even carrying them. Indeed it may in part be because Sherpas were coded female, as well as because of their smaller size, that their frequently superior physical strength, speed, and stamina were so disturbing to the sahibs. [pp. 227–228]

From: Sherry B. Ortner, *Life and Death on Mount Everest.* © 1999 Princeton University Press. Reprinted by permission of Princeton University Press.

tural beliefs about what it means to be feminine or masculine. But because femininity and masculinity are embedded in a person's habitus, they cannot be easily reshaped.

For example, the entry of more women into the workplace in the United States in the 1970s gave women access to new forms of economic capital, but it did not free them from the responsibility for doing certain feminine "emotional work." Although the workplace emphasizes the value of individuals being able "to live their own life," constructions of femininity expected women to "be there for others." This conflict complicated and slowed the process by which women formed new identities. In other words, a gendered habitus continued to work even after the conditions that gave rise to it started to change.

The idea of the gendered habitus also explains how women participate in their own subordination. For example, the belief in women's intellectual inferiority in the United States and Europe well into the twentieth century constrained women's options in the cultural field. Women were seen as lacking in the required abilities for success, and inequality was made to seem normal. Girls' lack of achievement was attributed to natural inabilities, not structured power relations. Moreover, girls were taught that showing their intelligence would limit their choices in the social field, making them seem less feminine, and consequently narrowing their pool of desirable marriage partners, potentially lowering their access to economic capital as well.

Because of these conventional views of femininity, women, in turn, reared their own young daughters within a constrained cultural field, teaching them to

be desirable though their femininity, even though this denied them equity in the field of economic accumulation. It would be incorrect, however, to assume that women are entirely conscious of what they risk by looking, acting, walking, and talking in an unfeminine way. Their habitus itself is gendered and it is within that habitus that women come to experience who they are (Bourdieu and Passeron 1977).

Thus, the "class of women" is socially reproduced by mothers who "teach femininity." It is not difficult to imagine how race would compound a woman's lack of access to cultural, social, and economic capital, reproducing social inequalities and economic distinctions: As Paula Black and Ursula Sharma put it, the ability of women to transfer their gender capital into economic capital is structured by their class position. In looking specifically at the beauty industry, it is important

to note that one woman's leisure is another woman's work. The beauty industry itself, whilst providing the site for carefully packaged and segmented parcels of free time, is also the site of work involving physical labour, emotional work, long hours, low pay, and often poor work conditions for those employed within it. [Black and Sharma 2001:104]

In *Flexible Citizenship*, Aihwa Ong (1999) uses a practice model to understand a situation that emerged in Hong Kong with its repatriation to the People's Republic of China in 1997. She describes how, in response to fears about what such incorporation might mean, Hong Kong's business elite negotiated their new milieu by adopting a strategy of "flexible citizenship": choosing to work in China but to hold citizenship elsewhere by obtaining foreign passports. They also developed economic and cultural strategies to negotiate the structural inequalities they would confront in their newly adopted countries. For example, although they keep their businesses in Southeast Asia, they also buy homes in the United States and send their children to the best U.S. colleges. Nonetheless, it is difficult for them to transform economic capital into social capital because of racial prejudice in the United States. Some have turned to philanthropy as a means to increase their social status and prestige. At the same time, men and women are differently constrained within these structures: flexibility and mobility are seen as masculine traits and flexible citizenship is not an option for the large working classes in China. Ong describes flexible citizenship as "basically a structure of limits and inequality for the many and of flexibility and mobility for the few" (p. 117).

Researchers have also used a practice approach to understand racial oppression. Using "white identity" as a category of analysis, scholars of Critical Race Studies argue that racism in the United States is maintained because white people consent to it or, more precisely, because they do not contest the privilege granted them on the basis of skin color. In return for the social status that "whiteness" gives them, white people demonstrate loyalty to various forms of racism, opposing attempts by people of color to level the "playing field." In other words, they uphold "ideological whiteness," which acts as a structure of domination. Critical Race scholars argue that if white people in the United States do not withhold their consent of the current system of racial oppression, there is little hope for social justice.

Cultural Studies

Many of the ideas discussed in this chapter came together in the 1960s within an academic discipline known as Cultural Studies, in which scholars draw on Marxist theories to understand the relationship of political economy to cultural forms. Drawing on Gramsci they analyze hegemonic forces of domination, especially hegemonic representations and ideologies of class, gender, race, ethnicity, and nationality. What effects, they ask, do newspapers, radio, television, film, and other popular cultural forms have on their audiences, the people who watch and consume them?

Cultural Studies scholars are not just interested in how people are dominated through hegemonic ideas and cultural forms. In line with practice theorists, they are also concerned with how people act as agents in the production of cultural meanings. They argue that no matter how much people are dominated or marginalized, they still seek to make meaningful lives for themselves. They do this through the different ways that they consume cultural products and interpret cultural texts, whether that text is a film, photograph, fashion, or hairstyle. Meaning is created through a range of everyday cultural practices including how people watch TV, shop, and wear their clothes. These cultural practices affect the meaning of the product being consumed. Through the production of new meanings, people are able to reject or challenge the hegemonic meaning of a product and therefore resist it.

Cultural Studies researchers are particularly interested in how oppositional subcultures, such as the working-class culture and youth subcultures, resist dominant forms of culture and identity by creating their own style and identities. For example, young people from British working-class culture look and act differently from those in the mainstream. They adopt different fashion codes, behaviors, and ideologies, which produce their own group identity by differentiating them from mainstream groups, such as middle-class British men and women.

Feminist Cultural Studies

Feminist Cultural Studies scholars share these interests and concerns, focusing on how women and other dominated groups consume products to produce oppositional identities. They have shown that women's consumption of mass culture, whether through shopping at the mall, reading mass-market romance novels, or watching soap operas, does not simply indicate women's subordination to dominant cultural forces; it can also help them imagine and create oppositional identities (Lennox 2007).

For example, in *Adorned in Dreams: Fashion and Modernity*, Elizabeth Wilson (1985) argued against those who see women's fashion—such as high heels—as merely oppressive to women. As we discuss in chapter 9, fashion can be used as a form of self-expression, self-enhancement, and to signal one's affiliation with a subcultural group, often with a strong political orientation. The punk fashion of the 1970s with its torn and slashed clothing; vinyl; bondage gear; and outrageously dyed, spiked, and sculptured hair, for example, presented a mockery of traditional style. Punk style and other "anti-fashion aesthetics," such as the slacker styles of the 1980s and the cyberpunk styles of the 1990s, were attempts to resist standard encodings of beauty, femininity, female sexuality, and class. As we have seen, this argument has been made for the chador or burqa as well.

Janice Radway (1984) has written one of the most influential examples of a Feminist Cultural Studies approach. She focuses on women who read romance novels. Do these readers, she asks, identify with the women in these stories whose are portrayed as passive? If so, do women readers just reproduce their own subordination? Radway found that readers of romance novels do not just passively identify with the stereotypical women characters in the texts. Instead, she shows that women read romance novels actively, using them to work through the disappointments and tensions arising from their attempts to negotiate the competing feminine roles of mother, wife, and worker. Radway suggests that by understanding how women interpret romance novels and put their own interpretations to work, we can see how women produce complex identities. They stitch together the various aspects of who they are.

Global News

8.2: Sounds of Assimilation

Last weekend, Britons of various races and religions flocked to a public park near West London's South Asian heartlands of Hounslow and Southall. . . .

. . . They reveled to records being spun by . . . BBC Radio disc jockeys who have led the public broadcaster's championing of British South Asian urban music (a fusion of hip-hop, bhangra, R&B and Bollywood better known as "desi beats").

The performance was part of the London Mela, an annual festival of South Asian culture and food. . . .

Since the London bombings of July 7, 2005, conventional wisdom has held that when it comes to racial integration, Britain has botched it, and that our long-standing policy of promoting multiculturalism has kept us from sustaining a common, over-arching culture and national identity toward which different races and religions can feel loyal. . . .

. . . [Nevertheless] at the level of popular culture, the great British melting pot works incredibly well, allowing British South Asian youth to coexist and integrate with mainstream Britain instead of living in a state of victimhood or voluntary segregation. . . .

The boys and girls I interviewed would describe assimilated "coconuts" (brown on the outside, white on the inside) not in terms of ethnic characteristics but of street-savviness and gender: they were either "saps" (uncool), "ponces" (effeminate) or "batty" (homosexual). The interviewees implied that South Asian boys who asserted their ethnic identities instead of assimilating were just bolstering their machismo and virility. Selling out involved sacrifices that bordered on emasculation—the universal teenage angst of trying to be a man. [Malkani Gautum, *New York Times* 8/19/06; http://www.nytimes.com/2006/08/19/opinion/19malkani.html?n=Top/Reference/Times%20Topics/Subjects/I/Immigration%20and%20Refugees&pagewanted=print (accessed 9/21/07)]

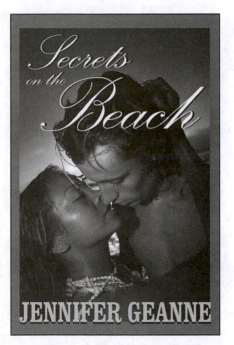

Women who read romance novels often do so as a way to deal with the tensions in their daily lives.

Feminist and other twenty-first-century anthropologists have also turned their attention to investigating the increasingly global circulation of mass media images. They focus on the impact on individual and group identities of cultural practices involving the production, distribution, and consumption of media such as films, television, radio, and video. What role do these cultural practices play in the production of

meaning? Do mass mediated images and technologies reproduce hegemonic ideologies or do they enable people to resist power? Do they maintain inequality or undermine it? Do they dampen people's ability to create oppositional meaning or do they provide the raw materials for new imaginings of identity? (Ginsburg et al. 2002:3).

To study these issues, feminist and other twenty-first-century anthropologists have investigated the media practices of indigenous people and people from the Global South. Feminist anthropologist, Lila Abu-Lughod (2002b), for example, investigates how TV melodramas (soap operas) in Egypt use heightened emotional drama to elicit strong response by viewers, leading them to see their own daily lives as dramas. She suggests that this creates new ideas about what it means to be a person, ideas that are consistent with the government's interest in producing modern citizens and consumers. Specifically, she argues that this heightened emotionality encourages individuality, which, she argues, is essential to neoliberal capitalism (p. 113).

Feminist anthropologist Louisa Schein (2002) focuses on the media practices of Hmong to understand how their production and use of videos and popular music creates transnational relationships and a sense of identity for a diasporic people. She argues that images of an idealized, but lost, homeland provide them with a sense of order in an otherwise disordered world in which they have been displaced from home and yanked out of history (p. 231). Video production becomes a way for them to make a space for themselves

Close-Up

8.2: The Politics of Indigenous Media by Emily McDonald

When we think of "media" what may come to mind are the many ways in which we are used to being entertained and informed: big-budget films from Hollywood, popular television series, nightly news programs, radio, magazines, newspapers, and, increasingly, online media such as blogs and podcasts. Anthropologists, however, are interested in looking at media from a differ-

(continued)

ent perspective. Forms of media that are imagined, produced, and controlled by indigenous and historically marginalized groups provide a window into understanding more about how a group of people see themselves, the issues that are important to their lives, and how they want the rest of the world to understand who they are. Feminist and other twenty-first-century anthropologists are actively debunking the myth that media are only created in "the West." Instead, they are looking at how and why marginalized peoples create and distribute media and how media are connected to issues as diverse as the preservation of history, the mobilization of political and social change, the creation of collective identity, and the reproduction of gender ideologies.

One important focus has been on how marginalized peoples and communities use media to advance their own social and political strategies. Anthropologist Faye Ginsburg (1991) introduced the term "indigenous media" to label all those media-related activities that minority indigenous groups use as a strategy to represent themselves to each other and the world beyond. She looks at several Aboriginal media groups in Central Australia and how these groups use media as both a strategy of self-determination and a way to resist outside forces of cultural domination. Ginsburg shows that Aboriginal filmmakers are taking on the project of recovering and re-creating collective histories that have been erased or refused by the dominant culture and, by doing so, are ensuring that the memory of these traumatic histories remains alive within their communities (Ginsburg 2002:40). This use of media by marginalized groups is connected to the increasing availability and affordability of the equipment and technology needed to create media—as things such as hand-held video cameras, DVD players, Internet connections, and satellite links become increasingly commonplace aspects of people's everyday lives.

Terence Turner (1992) also examines indigenous uses of media, focusing on how the Kayapo people of Brazil use media to represent themselves to an external "Western" audience (including environmental activists and the World Bank) as part of building international opposition to the use of their land for logging and mining. As part of these media practices, the Kayapo often highlight, or represent, those parts of their identity that would seem most "authentic" or "exotic" to an outside audience, thus strengthening their argument for the protection of their lands as an ecological and cultural resource. While Turner points to a number of ambiguities and contradictions in the Kayapo's media representations, he points to the power of indigenous media in enabling marginalized groups to challenge local power hierarchies and build international alliances as part of social movements.

Both Ginsburg and Turner reveal the variety of ways that indigenous groups can access, produce, and strategically use media as part of representing themselves to an outside audience and pursuing their own social and political goals.

References:

Ginsburg, Faye. 1991. Indigenous Media: Faustian Contract or Global Village? *Cultural Anthropology* 6(1): 92–112.

———. 2002. Screen Memories: Resignifying the Traditional in Indigenous Media. In *Media Worlds: Anthropology on New Terrain*. Ruth Ginsburg, Lila Abu-Lughod, and Brian Larkin, eds. Berkeley and Los Angeles: University of California Press.

Turner, Terence. 1992. Defiant Images: The Kayapo Appropriation of Video. *Anthropology Today* 8(5): 5–16.

and their stories and a means by which they can process their past.

Much work in Feminist Cultural Studies has focused on how women consume products focused on their bodies to resist oppressive structures and ideologies. We therefore turn our attention to these kinds of examples in the next chapter focused on the body.

Conclusions

Crafting meaning is a fundamental human activity. How different groups of people are constrained or enabled in this activity depends on structures of power. But as the global circulation of materials, ideas, images, and objects enter people's lives, new raw materials are used, changed, and modified. This involves people everywhere in the production of culture.

WORD PORTFOLIO

agency: an individual's capacity to act independently of oppressive structures.

binary thinking: way of thinking that divides the world into sets of oppositional categories.

culture: a system of meaning that individuals share by being members of a group.

cultural capital: the advantages that grant individuals higher status based on the forms of knowledge they have, the skills they possess, and the qualifications they hold.

fields: spaces of conflict where people compete to gain capital.

habitus: what *disposes* a person—makes a person willing—to act in ways that reproduce his or her class position.

interpretive anthropology: an approach to understanding culture by interpreting symbols in order to understand how people give meaning to their world.

incest taboo: a supposedly universal law that prohibits mating with close kin.

negotiate: one process by which oppressed people work within the confines of society to create options that grant them some social power.

practice theory: an approach that focuses on how social structures influence human activities and how, in turn, human actions influence social structures.

resist: the act of exerting an oppositional force to domination.

self/other dichotomy: the process by which selfhood is created through a comparison with individuals who are seen not as active creators of their lives but merely as objects.

serious games: the interactions of individuals trying to control change.

sign: something that stands for something else.

social capital: the advantages people have because of their membership in a network of social relations, which are key to a person's achievement.

structuralism: theoretical approach in anthropology that understands culture as the product of the universal structures of the human mind.

structure: the societal context that differentially constrains and enables people's actions based on their position in society due to such factors as gender, race, class, and ethnicity.

structure/agency debate: debate over whether people are completely determined by a society's ideas, institutions, and structures or whether they are free to make independent decisions.

symbolic capital: the amount of prestige and honor a person has within a social field that affects his or her behavior, choices, and opportunities.

symbolic system: a set of relationships among symbols, or among groups of symbols, and the meanings attached to them.

symbolic violence: a form of domination that is exercised upon a social agent with his or her complicity.

women as objects of exchange: the idea that women cement alliances between groups of men by being offered as gifts in marriage.

RECOMMENDED READING

Screening Culture, Viewing Politics: An Ethnography of Television, Womanhood, and Nation in Postcolonial India, by Purnima Mankekar. 1999. Durham, NC: Duke University Press. Examining mass media, gender, consumption, and nationalism, Purnima Mankekar helps us understand how media powerfully shape meanings, practices, and experiences both in local places and global contexts. Her ethnography of Doordharsan, the state-run television network in India, provides a lens though which to understand changing notions of national identity. Additionally, Mankekar demonstrates how media cre-

ate postcolonial subject positions for viewers and, in the process, transform understandings of gender, class, and caste.

Off White: Readings on Power, Privilege, and Resistance, edited by Michelle Fine. 2004. London: Routledge. This interdisciplinary collection of essays brings together authors from the fields of psychology and education to argue that we must focus on whiteness as a racial category in order to better understand racism, hierarchy, and exclusion. They argue that critically theorizing whiteness will allow us to see unmarked structures of power, contributing to collective efforts toward antiracist education and activism.

Media Worlds: Anthropology on New Terrain, edited by Faye D. Ginsburg, Lila Abu-Lughod, and Brian Larkin. Berkeley and Los Angeles: University of California Press.

If you are interested in learning more about the burgeoning new focus in anthropology on the ethnography of the media, you'll appreciate this pioneering collection of essays. They address how film, television, and video are used in a range of societies around the world, covering such topics as the effects of transnational media on local societies, state-controlled and indigenous media, social sites of media production, and cultural activism and minority claims through media use.

Re-Orienting Fashion: The Globalization of Asian Dress, edited by Sandra Niessen, Ann Marie Leshkowich, and Carla Jones. 2003. Oxford, UK: Berg Publishers.

This collection of essays will be of interest to you if you want to learn more about the globalization of Asian fashion from its origin in the colonial era and continuing today with the opening of the Shanghai Tang boutique on New York's Madison Avenue, the appeal of sarongs to the London elites, and the many clothes with "made in Asia" labels in U.S. closets. This collection of case studies explores the cultural politics of fashion, focusing on how Asian fashion is part of an ongoing Orientalism that understands Asia as a feminine "other" to the Western masculine self.

The Personal as Political

Once we begin to feel deeply all the aspects of our lives, we begin to demand from ourselves and from our life-pursuits that they feel in accordance with that joy which we know ourselves to be capable of. Our erotic knowledge empowers us, becomes a lens through which we scrutinize all aspects of our existence, forcing us to evaluate those aspects honestly in terms of their relative meaning within our lives.

—*Audre Lorde*

9

Embodying Politics

In this chapter you will . . .

gain an understanding of the importance of the body in today's globalizing world both inside and outside the academy • examine the body as a social construct • learn about body politics • look at how differently gendered and "raced" bodies have been, and continue to be, directly and symbolically controlled, normalized, and disciplined • analyze Western discourses of the body and their implications for notions of masculinity and femininity worldwide • assess the different consequences of the medicalization of the body for white men and women and men and women of color • analyze the increasing commodification of the body and its implications for ideal notions of beauty and constructions of gender and race • discover the body as a site to protest restrictive constructions of gender

Attention to the body has exploded in recent years. This has occurred throughout the globalizing world and is reflected in the intense interest in the body by scholars in many academic disciplines. Today, both in the United States and around the world, identity has become linked to what we wear and do to our bodies. The body is an object of seduction by advertising and a canvas for self-expression.

The body is also an important site of struggle, as anthropologist Terence Turner makes clear: it is the object of torture by a broad spectrum of political regimes, a site of bitter conflicts over reproductive rights and health care, an entity threatened by new epidemic diseases, and a place where struggles for alternative sexual identities are waged. It is also the object of new technologies that alter physical attributes, which were once thought of as naturally determined. This includes cosmetic surgery, asexual and extrabodily fertilization, the modification of genetic traits, and the artificial extending or shortening of the life span (1994:27).

Globalization has even given rise to a new market based on the buying and selling of human organs, as anthropologist Nancy Scheper-Hughes documents in Close-Up 9.1.

Bodies all over the world are vulnerable to seduction, control, and manipulation through direct and indirect means, whether physical or symbolic. The human body is thus a place where power relationships are worked out. Although historically the body has been understood primarily as flesh and bones, there are cultural and political forces at work on the body: bodies are modified, mutilated, contorted, distorted, and controlled in the name of everything from religion to beauty to self-expression. But bodies can also be

A Chinese woman with bound feet (c. 1905).

204

Close-Up

9.1: The Global Traffic in Human Organs
by Nancy Scheper-Hughes

Amidst the neoliberal readjustments of the new global economy, there has been a rapid growth of "medical tourism" for transplant surgery and other advanced biomedical and surgical procedures. A grotesque niche market for sold organs, tissues, and other body parts has exacerbated older divisions between North and South, haves and have-nots, organ donors and organ recipients. Indeed, a kind of medical apartheid has also emerged that has separated the world into two populations—organ givers and organ receivers. Over the past 30 years, organ transplantation—especially kidney transplantation—has become a common procedure in hospitals and clinics throughout the world. The spread of transplant technologies has created a global scarcity of viable organs. At the same time the spirit of a triumphant global and "democratic" capitalism has released a voracious appetite for "fresh" bodies from which organs can be procured. The confluence in the flows of immigrant workers and itinerant kidney sellers who fall prey to sophisticated but unscrupulous transnational organ brokers is a subtext in the recent history of globalization. [From: Nancy Scheper-Hughes, 2002. The Ends of the Body—Commodity Fetishism and the Global Traffic in Organs, p. 61. *SAIS Review* 22 (1):61–80]

used by individuals and groups to protest standard cultural definitions, as we discussed in the last chapter. The ideal image of beauty can be resisted through the antiaesthetic of "punk style," restrictive identities can be transformed through plastic surgery, ideas about masculinity and femininity can be reworked and contested through androgynous fashion, and a belief in the natural body can be rejected through embracing images of the cyborg, a part human, part robot creature (see Haraway 1991).

These examples illustrate that the body is a cultural construct whose meaning and significance vary around the world. In this chapter, we discuss how the concept of the body as a cultural construct allows researchers to analyze the relationship of the body to power, control, and domination. After investigating forms of physical bodily domination, we turn to how bodies can be controlled and constituted symbolically. We focus specifically on how discourses differentially construct and discipline bodies marked by gender and race.

Changing Ideas about the Body

From Natural Entity to Social Construct

The conceptualization of the body as a social construct underlies almost all recent scholarship on the body in the social sciences. Viewing the body as a cultural construct is a relatively new development in Western thought. Until recently, the body was conceptualized primarily as a natural, physical entity. The study of the body was thus found in the physical, not the social, sciences. Within the last few decades, however, this has changed significantly: now research on the body has come to focus on the cultural meanings and experiences of the body.

Understanding Power and the Body: The Influence of Feminism

The shift from understanding the body as a natural object to conceptualizing it as a cultural construction is due, in large part, to the centrality of the body in feminist political struggles, particularly in the United States. Since the 1970s, feminists have been concerned with understanding how the body is constituted and affected by social and cultural forces and how the body has been used for purposes of political domination. They have focused on direct forms of bodily control, such as forced sterilization, abuse, and rape, as well as on less direct forms, such as codes of fashion and ideal notions of femininity and beauty.

As we saw in chapter 4, feminists have also been concerned with how inequalities become naturalized and seen as normal, proper, and inevitable. One important way this naturalizing has occurred is through linking the social inequalities of gender and race to visible, bodily markers such as anatomical sex differences or skin color. This linkage has made understanding the body a significant topic for feminist research. Feminist anthropologists have made particularly im-

Close-Up

9.2: Foot Fetish?

Historically, and across cultures, women's bodies have been stretched, scarred, corseted, crippled, pierced, and deformed in the name of everything from religion to fashion in many societies around the world. In China, for example, the feet of high-status females were once painfully broken and tightly wrapped to produce tiny, erotically charged "lotus-feet" so small that many of these women were unable to walk.

Today's high-heeled shoes are similarly considered fashionable and erotic by many—as their ubiquity in pornography suggests—and they too can deform women's feet, sometimes severely enough to require surgery. New forms of cosmetic surgery are now performed on women's feet in the United States to make them more desirable: toes can be shortened through bone removal or lengthened by the insertion of plastic implants.

Bunions are a common problem experienced mostly by women. The deformity can develop from an abnormality in foot function, or arthritis, but is more commonly caused by wearing improper fitting footwear. Tight, narrow dress shoes with a constrictive toe box (toe area) can cause the foot to begin to take the shape of the shoe, leading to the formation of a bunion. Bunions can worsen to the point where surgery is necessary.

Corns develop from an accumulation of dead skin cells on the foot, forming thick, hardened areas. They contain a cone-shaped core whose point can press on a nerve below, causing pain. Some of the common causes of corn development are tight fitting footwear and high heeled shoes. Complications that can arise from corns include bursitis and the development of an ulcer.

There is controversy over whether the fashion for bound feet should be compared to the fashion for high heels. What do you think?

portant contributions to our understanding of how meanings and experiences of the body are shaped by differing cultural ideas and practices. They have found the work of Michel Foucault, as we discussed in chapter 6, to be particularly useful for understanding how bodies are constructed through power.

In this chapter, we follow the line of research set out by contemporary scholars, investigating **body politics:** how notions and experiences of the body have been embedded in historic, political, economic, and social inequalities and how the body is constituted as a site of power in today's globalizing world.

Controlling the Body through Force

The most obvious relationship between the body and power occurs when bodies are subject to direct forces of social control. Historically, and cross-culturally, both male and female bodies have been controlled through direct physical constraints and punishments, often violent ones. The treatment of bodies within a society, however, differs according to how power is distributed. Because in many societies around the world, both in the past and in the present, women have less power than men, female bodies have tended to be significantly more vulnerable to extremes of cultural manipulation and control than male bodies (Bordo 1993:143).

Rape as a Form of Social Control

In countless societies around the world, assaults on women's bodies serve to constrain their movements, acting as a powerful form of social control. Among the Mundurucú of Brazil, for example, any woman found walking alone is seen to be stepping beyond male control, a circumstance demanding punishment that often comes in the form of gang-rape (Murphy and Murphy 2004). The systematic rape of women has also been commonplace in European warfare since at least the time of the Greeks, and continues today, such as in conflicts in Rwanda and Somalia.

Studies indicate that one-quarter to over one-half of women in many countries of the world today report being physically abused and that between one in five and one in seven women in the United States, Canada, New Zealand, and the United Kingdom report being raped (Heise 1997:414). Gendered-based physical violence in today's world is staggering and has far-reaching and multiple implications for women: it not only constrains physical movements, but it also affects their sexuality, sense of self, and psychological and reproductive health, among other things (see Heise 1997).

Racial Politics and Rape

Differential power relations associated with ethnicity, race, class, and sexual diversities are also expressed in forms of bodily violence. The rape of black female slaves by white men was an institutionalized and commonplace form of social control in the U.S., one that continued long after legal freeing of slaves.

Darlene Hines (1997) has shown the far-ranging effects of this circumstance on black women's choices and sense of self. Rampant sexual assaults terrorized black women and were an important reason for black women's migration out of the South in the first part of the twentieth century. Assault also gave rise to what Hines calls a "cult of secrecy" in which black women protect their inner lives by refusing to reveal their feelings, even as they appear to be doing so. The rape of black women by white men has also served to exert white male supremacy over black men who were emasculated through their inability to protect their mothers, wives, sisters, and daughters.

Ironically, it is the black male who has long been associated with the rapist in the white imagination. For example, throughout the British colonial empire, the fear of sexual assault on white colonial women by colonized African men was referred to as the "Black Peril" and was widely used as a rationale for the development of repressive controls of local populations. Yet, as anthropologist Ann Stoler has shown, "the rhetoric of sexual assault and the measures used to prevent it had virtually no correlation with actual incidences of rape of European women by men of color" (1997:20). Similarly, the image of the "rapist as black male" has been a predominate one in U.S. society, despite "the tiny percentage (perhaps one in nine) of all sexual assaults that fit the heavily symbolic strange-black-on-white-woman model" of rape (di Leonardo 1997b:54).

The use of rape to control relationships between men and women, and between men of differing social positions, occurs in many societies today. In 2002, the rape of a young Pakistani woman was ordered by a local village jury composed of all men as punishment for what the jury said was an inappropriate sexual relationship between the woman's brother and a higher-status woman. Although the rape was reported and the rapists punished, this is far from usual. It has been estimated that in Pakistan a woman is raped every two hours, but most sexual assaults are unreported. It is not difficult to understand why; often a woman who is raped is punished herself as a result of Islamic laws known as the Hudood ordinances: to convict a rapist, four adult Muslim males must have witnessed the rape or the rapist must confess. When this is not the case, the woman risks being accused of consenting to an improper sexual relationship.

A woman can be condemned to death for being raped as part of a practice known as "honor killings," in which a family, dishonored by the sexual activity of one of its female members, kills her to restore family honor. Condemning a woman to death for rape, as though she chose to have an "illicit" sexual relationship, involves the practice of "blaming the victim." Blaming a woman for her own victimization is a widespread tendency in many societies, including the United States. "Honor killings" have been reported in Jordan, Egypt, Syria, Lebanon, Yemen, Iraq, and the Palestinian territories, and among Israeli Arabs (LaFont 2003:330). As we discussed in chapter 3, such practices are often understood as "human rights" abuses but are frequently guarded by members of these societies as "cultural rights." Attempts to abolish them are seen as a form of Western cultural imperialism.

Violence and Masculinity

Violence against women also has implications for men, including for their sexuality. As Lori Heise puts it:

> To the extent that masculine ideals are associated with violence, virility, and power, it is easy to see how male sexual behavior might emerge as predatory and aggressive.... When masculinity is associated with aggression and sexual conquest, domineering sexual behavior and violence become not only a means of structuring power relations between men and women but also a way of establishing power relations among men.... When the behavior of men or boys does not live up to the masculine ideal, they are frequently rebuked by invoking another gendered symbol: the male homosexual, however culturally defined. [1997:426]

In the United States today, ideas about manhood continue to be entangled with violence: boys learn from a young age that violence is not only an acceptable form of behavior but also an admirable one. This association of Western manhood with power and aggression has a long history, although the specific asso-

ciations that are highlighted at any particular moment in time may vary, as we saw when discussing hegemonic masculinity in chapter 6. Michael Kimmel (2001) has traced the change in U.S. thinking about manhood from the late eighteenth and early nineteenth centuries to the present. During this earlier period, the ideal man was equated with the aristocrat and was seen as someone who derived power from land ownership. By the mid-1900s, a new ideal began to emerge, based on the capitalist notion of "Marketplace Man," who had to "prove" manhood through competition with others, both women and other men.

This new model of masculinity derived much of its effectiveness from playing on a male's anxiety that other men might out-compete, and even emasculate, him. Such an "oppositional manhood" required men to repudiate anything that was feminine and go to great lengths not to be seen as a "sissy," a "role" long associated in the U.S. popular imagination with male homosexuality. This fear of emasculation produces, according to Kimmel, not only a man's willingness, but also his desire, to fight in order to feel and be seen as "manly" (Kimmel 2001:37–38). Kimmel suggests that this anxiety also helps explain rampant male homophobia in U.S. society: hating homosexuality stems from fear of one's own potential "unmanliness," which gives rise to all manner of exaggerated masculine behaviors and attitudes on the part of many heterosexual men.

The equation of manhood with aggressiveness and violence is a widespread one found in many societies, but it is not the only conceptualization of manhood. Among the Semai of Malaya, for example, men neither routinely engage in physical violence nor see themselves as violent. Instead, as Robert Dentan has detailed in his ethnography of these people, men who are engaged in a quarrel try to avoid each other and seek out a mediator to help them resolve their conflict (1986:56–57).

Controlling the Body Symbolically

Direct physical assault and violence are not the only ways bodies are subjected to social control. Symbolic meanings of the body also act as powerful constraints on people's conceptions of who they are and how they can act.

Maintaining Social Order through Symbolic Constructs of the Body

Anthropologist Mary Douglas was one of the first anthropologists to show how core cultural values are etched onto human bodies. Her work has focused specifically on how the body is used symbolically to express and maintain social order and on how regulating the body even in subtle ways can also regulate society. In her book, *Purity and Danger* (1966), for example, she argues that a society or social group that is deeply concerned with maintaining strict boundaries is likely to symbolize those concerns in beliefs about the margins of the body. In such societies, body parts and substances that are seen as ambiguous, as existing both on the inside and the outside of the body—such as hair, blood, milk, tears, fingernails, saliva, urine, and feces, for example—are seen as "unclean" and surrounded by prohibitions and taboos, referred to as **pollution beliefs.** Societies that are vulnerable to attack from the outside may similarly conceptualize the body as having rigid boundaries and may institute rituals that strictly police the boundaries of the body. Such beliefs can have differential consequences for men and women. For example, in many societies, it is contact with women's bodies that is thought to be polluting and capable of weakening male strength.

Maintaining Power through Using the Body as a Metaphor

In a later book, *Natural Symbols* (1970), Douglas elaborated these ideas, demonstrating further how the body acts as a metaphor for culture, and how, in the process, abstract cultural ideals are given concrete form. Elaine Scarry's work (1985) on torture vividly illustrates this idea. According to Scarry, because the body has a material reality, it is often used both to concretize abstract ideas as well as to ground notions of "truth." In her book, *The Body in Pain* (1985), Scarry argues that using the body this way occurs particularly at times of societal crises and high uncertainty. Under such circumstances, the sheer material factualness of the human body is borrowed to lend an aura of "realness" or "certainty" to intangible ideas and social constructs (Scarry 1985:14). For example, Scarry argues that torturing the body is a way of concretizing and making visible the power of an oppressive political regime:

> The physical pain [of torture] is so incontestably real that it seems to confer its quality of "incontestable reality" on that power that has brought it into being. It is, of course, precisely because the reality of that power is so highly contestable, the regime so unstable, that torture is being used. [Scarry 1985:27]

Torture, Scarry shows, also operates to "unmake" the world of the victim: intense pain obliterates consciousness, reducing victims to the excruciating experience of their bodies. Scarry argues that this condition makes speech virtually impossible and prevents victims from extending themselves into the world through language, resulting in the destruction of a victim's "self" and world.

Normalizing Discourses of Gender, Race, and the Body

As we have seen, Foucault (1979) argues that biopower operates to make the body docile both through disciplinary practices and disciplinary discourses. A **discourse,** if you remember, is a system of knowledge that creates a picture for people of what is true and what is not. Men and women's gender identities in Western societies are intimately connected to discourses of the body that construct ideas about ideal femininity and masculinity. Historically, in Western societies, various discourses—religious, philosophical, and medical, for example—have produced knowledge about women as frail, helpless, dependent, passive, submissive, childlike, and emotional creatures, defining these traits as inevitable, natural, and normal. These discourses have pronounced these as "truths" about women. The ideal man, by contrast, has been constructed in these same discourses as the opposite of a woman, as a strong, autonomous, active, and rational being.

In the following sections, we focus on three particular constructs of the body embedded in Western thinking that have had far-reaching implications not only for women and men in Western societies but also for people in many other places throughout the world: mind/body dualism, the natural body, and the body as canvas. These conceptions are not contained within any one particular discourse but are found in the often-overlapping discourses of philosophy, religion, and medicine. Although Western philosophical and religious ideas about women and men continue to play a significant role in the lives of many people, science and medicine have become particularly privileged realms of knowledge in the twenty-first century throughout the world. Therefore, after a discussion of these particular discourses of masculinity, femininity, and the body, we turn our attention to the body as a medicalized object of knowledge.

Discourses of Mind/Body Dualism

In the tradition of Western thought, at least since Plato, the body has been juxtaposed with the mind and seen as inferior to it. This distinction between mind and body is an aspect of what is often referred to as Cartesian dualism, named for the French philosopher, René Descartes. Descartes' famous dictum, "I think, therefore, I am," vividly encapsulates the widespread association in Western thinking of the mind, and its reasoning processes, with the self. The body places limitations on the self, according to this view, and must therefore be transcended. Everyday language encodes this understanding of the body as an entity distinct from the self: a person is likely to say "I have a body" not "I am a body" (Mairs 1997:298).

Mind/body dualism is part of the Christian tradition that has also influenced Western thinking: the body is seen in opposition not only to the mind and the self, but also to the "soul" and the "spirit." The body, in this view, represents the animal side of human existence, possessing unruly appetites and desires that must be willfully controlled and suppressed to attain salvation.

What is most significant about this conceptualization for understanding constructions of gender in Western thinking is that "woman" has been associated with the body, while "man" is linked with the mind. "Woman" equated with the body is, therefore, not mind and not self. She is not subject but object, not spirit but flesh. She is aligned against reason (a woman is more emotional, intuitive, and irrational than a man, we still hear today) and against spiritual salvation (woman, it is still widely believed, is naturally a temptress and seductress). She is in need of control. In contrast, "man" is associated with rationality, selfhood, and the soul, attributes that allegedly predispose him to controlling "woman."

This set of associations has had profound significance for how men and women have been differentially valued, treated, and constrained in their opportunities and choices. As we have seen, Simone de Beauvoir argued in 1953 in *The Second Sex*, the entrapment of women in their bodies means that women have been made "the second sex," defined by a lack of masculine qualities and traits, which men assume stem from a natural defect (see Conboy et al. 1997b). More recently, Susan Bordo has remarked:

The cost for such projections to women is obvious. For if, whatever the historical content of the duality, the body is the negative term, and if woman is the body, then women are that negativity, whatever it may be: distraction from knowledge, seduction away from God, capitulation to sexual desire . . . failure of will, even death. [1993:5]

Discourses of the Natural Body

The Female Body as Natural. Women's association with the body also allies them with the negative term in another set of associations in European and North American societies: nature/culture. In Western thinking, the body has been seen as natural and the mind as the source of human cultural control over nature's destructive forces. Traditionally in Western thought the predominant view has been that nature acts against human interests and, therefore, needs to be tamed and subdued.

The association of women with nature may have arisen from the function of woman's body in giving birth and nurturing children. But Simone de Beauvoir's (1953) insights are again instructive; she argues that if women's bodies have constrained them, it is not because this is natural or inevitable but because women have been interpreted through the lens of culture, thought of as "natural" by men who have created the very category of "nature" to serve their own aims.

Evidence from around the world supports Beauvoir's claim: women have combined motherhood with almost every task imaginable. This evidence suggests the cultural, rather than the natural, character of such limitations in Western culture in which "woman" has been defined by her body and seen as trapped in nature because of it. As Beauvoir suggests, this alignment has served as a rationalization for women's domination and subordination.

The Other as Natural. The Western construction of the female as natural has had particular consequences for non-Western women and women of color who have been seen as doubly natural and other due to both gender and race. In Western racial discourse, the naturalness of black and brown bodies has been equated with animality, in particular with an animal-like sexuality. This belief was perhaps nowhere clearer than in Victorian England where, under the guise of scientific interest, the African woman Saartjie Baartman, known as the "Hottentot Venus," was displayed nude in a public pornographic exhibition disguised as science (see Collins 2000). She was probed and poked

Global News

9.1: Exploited in Life and Death, South African to Go Home

The young Khoi-khoi woman . . . boarded a ship for England from South Africa in 1810 apparently convinced that she would make a fortune there.

Instead, she was put on display around Europe as a sexual freak, paraded naked on runways by a keeper who obliged her to walk, sit or stand so that audiences could better see her protruding buttocks and large genital organs.

Even when she died, destitute and diseased, the "Hottentot Venus," as she was called, did not get a decent burial. Napoleon Bonaparte's surgeon general made a plaster cast of her body and put it, along with jars of her pickled body parts, on display at the national Musée de L'homme.

But Saartjie Baartman may finally be going home, closing a particularly sordid chapter in Europe's colonial history. . . .

With the end of apartheid [in South Africa], the image of Ms. Baartman's body rotting on shelves of a Paris museum has become a rallying point for a new movement to reclaim the country's history. . . .

Her proper burial was seen as a necessary part of rebuilding self-respect. . . .

. . . "The return of South Africa to the international community marked the beginning of the process of healing and restoring our national dignity and humanity," Mr. Nzo [South Africa's foreign minister] said. . . . "The process will not be complete while Saartjie Baartman's remains are still kept in a museum." [Suzanne Daley, *New York Times* 1/31/02:A4]

by anatomists and stared at by a repulsed, but fascinated public audience.

Her distinctive bodily traits—enlarged vaginal lips and protruding buttocks—were taken as signs of a wild and animalistic sexuality (Gilman 1985). This conclusion acted to reinforce the notion at the time that African women were savages, devoid of the sexual modesty necessary for achieving "true" femininity. More recently this equation of the black female body with nature and a "primitive" sexuality can be found in advertisements to entice consumers to buy everything from vacations in the Caribbean (see Cohen and Mascia-Lees 1993) and perfumes (see Bordo 1993) to unwanted hair remover (see Williamson 1986).

During the late nineteenth and early twentieth centuries, not only were racial bodies displayed for public consumption, so, too, were those of "disabled" people. Thought of as "freaks," extraordinary bodies were viewed as exotic spectacles in U.S. and European circuses, fairs, and zoos (see Thomson 1996). For example, the boys known as "Ancient Aztecs," who had a genetic condition characterized by a small and pointed head known as microcephaly, were promoted as descendants of a "lost primitive society" (Bogdan 1988). This assertion made sense to many European viewers who were steeped in the cultural discourse of progress that viewed non-Western people as mentally inferior and associated this inferiority with small brain

The Hottentot Venus.

Not all "non-Western others," however, were constructed as naturally animalistic. As we saw in chapter 3, other discourses operated alongside this one: for example, the discourse of "Orientalism," identified by Edward Said in 1978 as a deeply political construction of the East by the West, viewed Asian and Middle Eastern women through a lens of sexual exoticism based on fantasies of the harem. Although their bodies have been represented as erotic and exotic, unlike the bodies of black women, they have not been associated with savagery and animalistic desire. Women of the Far East in particular have been desired by men in Western societies for their smallness, timidity, and subservience. This perception has even led to the development of a highly profitable mail-order business in which Asian women are sold to Western male consumers as brides, as will be discussed further in chapter 11.

Although Asian women were eroticized through Orientalist discourse, Asian men were feminized. As Evelyn Nakano Glenn (2002) has pointed out, this was reflected in employment practices in California and Hawaii in the late nineteenth and early twentieth centuries. In these places, Asian men were hired in large numbers as domestic servants, whether Chinese houseboys and cooks in San Francisco or Japanese male retainers in Honolulu.

As we saw in chapter 4, the discourse of the natural continues to affect how the bodies of men and women are conceptualized and treated, perpetuating the mistaken view that gender differences are innate and normal. For example, the idea of nature is continually used for political purposes in discussions of medical and reproductive technologies. For those who wish to control women's bodies, especially their reproductive functions, medical technologies are often considered unnatural and therefore in need of societal intervention and regulation (see Horn 1994). Technologies viewed by some as contrary to nature include birth control pills and in vitro fertilization, which allows a woman who is having difficulty becoming pregnant to have her egg fertilized with sperm outside of her body.

Discourses of Creativity

The Female Body as Canvas.   The ideal female body in Western thinking has also been conceptualized as a "blank page." This conceptualization of woman's body has meant that women have traditionally been consigned to the role of object of male artistic representation, and not as a subject capable of acting creatively in

size. Just as women's intelligence was assumed inferior to men's based on skull size, as discussed in earlier chapters, so was the intelligence of nonwhite peoples.

The connection is not surprising. On the one hand, Western women were equated with primitives and were viewed as irrational and inferior in intelligence to white Western men of the upper classes. On the other hand, non-Western people were feminized and were viewed like Western women as in need of protection and assistance. The West, it was claimed, was obligated to civilize "primitives," a mission termed by Rudyard Kipling "The White Man's Burden" (1899). This ideology was used to justify colonialism. Contemporary studies show that men who have a disability continue to be feminized, while women who have a disability are desexualized. Such constructions place wide-ranging constraints on how individuals with disabilities can construct notions of identity and selfhood.

the world. Their bodies have been seen as the instigator of male desire, spurring male creativity: woman is a muse, but cannot be an active creator of art herself in this discourse.

Susan Gubar (1982) has shown how at least since the nineteenth century, the Western literary tradition in particular repeatedly excluded woman from literary creation through such ideas. Woman, she argues, has been conceptualized not as writer; instead her body has been understood as a "blank page" in need of inscription by the male pen, which itself has been conceptualized as a metaphorical penis. She provides a number of illustrations that encapsulates this idea. For example, the poet Ezra Pound has written about the female poet H. D., "You are a poem, though your poem's naught."

The African American novelist Ishmael Reed has written this description of sex that conceptualizes the female body as a text: "He got good into her Book tongued her every passage thumbing her leaf and rubbing his hands all over her binding" (Gubar 1982:75–76). Gubar asserts that in this tradition, where the female body and women's sexuality are identified with textuality, "many women experience their own bodies as the only available medium for their art" (Gubar 1982:78). Gubar hypothesizes that this conceptualization of the female body as blank canvas may help account for women's historical preference for media like dance and acting that directly use the body.

"Writing the Body"

Although many women have protested the construction of woman as blank page, incapable of artistic creation, and have reclaimed her as mind, others have appropriated the equation of the female body with text and turned it to their politically desired ends. In her performances, contemporary feminist artist, Carolee Schneemann, for example, has read from a long scroll she removes from her vagina, thereby symbolically equating women's body with text, but also suggesting it as a creative wellspring, not just of babies, but also of words.

French feminists, such as Hèléne Cixous and Luce Irigaray, have theorized that because women's difference from men is located in the body, it is the female body and female sexuality to which women must turn for a source of female creativity that is authentic and disruptive. Cixous has referred to this as *l'écriture féminine*, "writing in the feminine." In her article, "The Laugh of the Medusa," she exhorts women to "write

yourself. Your body must be heard. Only then will the immense resources of unconscious spring forth" (Cixous 1981:250). Cixous turns to a mythical maternal body for the source of this creative inscription.

Marking the Body: Women and Tattoos.   In both the contemporary United States and other places throughout the world, many women have begun to take this idea literally: through tattooing, piercing, and henna painting, they inscribe their own bodies and use them to "write their own stories."

Woman with tattoos: writing the body.

U.S., Canadian, and European women often explain their body modifications in terms of exerting control over meaning, as a means of replacing cultural meanings of the body with their own marks of signification. As anthropologist Margo DeMello writes, for women, the tattoo is often "an important step in reclaiming their bodies, and the narrative in which they describe this process is equally important" (2000:173).

In their research, Fran Mascia-Lees and Pat Sharpe (1994) have found that young U.S. women "write their bodies" for a range of reasons. Some women in their sample reported using piercing and tattooing to control pain as they could not in situations in which they felt victimized. Others saw tattooing and piercing as a way to dictate their own sexualization and eroticization of their bodies and as a means of accepting the body as desirable. Many women saw these practices as a way to resist being defined from without; they used their body as a canvas for their own self-expression. As one woman puts it:

> Whatever reason you have to choose tattooing and a particular tattoo image, keep in mind that each tattoo image is not a word, not a sentence, but an entire *pamphlet* on who you are, what you think of yourself and of others, what group you do and do not belong to, the beliefs you hold, the memories you wish to broadcast. [Vander Straeten 2007]

Contemporary U.S. women are part of a larger group of Westerners to use tattooing the body in the service of their own identity. Because tattoos have long been associated with the non-Western savage or primitive, they have historically been a resource for many individuals wishing to protest aspects of Western culture. The word "tattoo" comes from the Polynesian word "ta-tu," which found its way into English during the eighteenth century when the European explorer, Captain James Cook, returned home after traveling to Pacific islands. Just as Saartjie Baartman was displayed in public as a spectacle because of her anatomical differences from Europeans', which supposedly signified her savagery, so tattooed Polynesians were exhibited at European world fairs as examples of the primitive.

Marking the Body: Tattoos and the Other. In *Bodies of Inscription* (2000), DeMello traces shifts in the Western meaning of tattoos since their introduction into Western societies by Cook and other sailors. Although first viewed as marks of savagery, tattoos soon became signs of adventure, travel, freedom, and the exotic. After a brief period of signaling the wealth and leisure of the British aristocracy, tattoos emerged as a predominantly U.S. art form connected with patriotism and later with such societal outcasts as bikers and prisoners. DeMello argues that tattoos went mainstream in the United States in the last decades of the twentieth century because they partially indicated working-class status and because they were also somewhat severed from their association with social misfits.

This partial disassociation was initiated, she argues, by the convergence of several developments: disaffected middle-class youth sought external symbols of their rebellion against what they saw as a politically corrupt and spiritually bankrupt capitalist social order and looked to the non-West for alternatives. At the same time influential tattooists turned to Eastern societies for new design ideas. This transformation of meaning was accomplished primarily through media discourse and was given cultural weight by the "new class of social movements" of the 1970s and 1980s, which were focused on personal transformation, self-actualization, and spiritual growth: the New Age, self-help, feminist spirituality, ecology, and men's movements (DeMello 2000:137).

Paradoxically, then, although many North American and European women use tattoos to express individuality, reclaim power, make their bodies their own, and "write their own stories," these meanings are made possible because of the long and complex social history of colonial and class relations in which tattooing is embedded.

It is not only in North America and European societies that women use body marking for self-expression. Deborah Kapchan (1993) has shown, for example, that in Morocco, drawing on the body with henna has become a way for women to use their bodies as a canvas for displaying female artistry and celebrating an all-female community. Traditionally, elaborate designs were painted on women's hands and feet during Moroccan marriage ceremonies to symbolize a woman's initiation into womanhood and wifely duties. Today, henna decorations are also applied in secular ceremonies that give women "a time and space for self-expression rather than inhibition" (Kapchan 1993:16). In a society that has traditionally kept women covered and out of public view, and used henna markings to primarily signify women's status as wives, women-initiated secular henna ceremonies give women some control over their bodies. This appropriation and transformation of the marriage ritual, Kapchan argues, "effectively reestablishes women's claims to their own bodies," and under such circumstances, henna designs come to signify "sexual self-possession rather than initiation" into marriage (1993:16–19).

Marking the Body: Initiation Ceremonies. In many societies around the world, body markings are used to indicate a man or woman's social status. Bodies are often marked during an **initiation ceremony,** a type of rite of passage in which a young girl or boy is transformed into an adult through symbolic and ritual actions. Among the Tiv of West Africa, for example, a pubertal girl's abdomen is cut, or scarified, marked with incisions that heal as raised bumps on the skin.

According to Bruce Lincoln (1991), the design produced through this procedure acts as a visual representation of her position within a long history of ancestors and potential descendants. Through a series of raised lines and circles, the girl who is about to be a woman is shown to be an heir of her ancestors and a bearer of descendants (Lincoln 1991:48).

In many societies, marking the body has also been a part of ceremonies initiating boys into manhood. This initiation may involve scarifying a boy's body, usually his chest or forehead. More commonly, a boy's body is "marked" through genital modification. These modification practices range from small incisions made on the penis to draw blood—found among peoples of the East African coast, inland Asia, and Oceania, and a few populations in the New World—to subincision, the cutting open of the urethra on the underside of the penis down to the scrotum, a practice undertaken among the native people of Australia and some Pacific Islands groups (see DeMeo 2003).

Circumcision, the removal of the foreskin of the penis, is the most widely practiced form of male genital modification performed during puberty rituals, found throughout the Middle East and among peoples of sub-Saharan Africa, Central Asia, and some Pacific Island groups. Only during the last century has circumcision become a widespread medical practice in the United States where it is performed on infants in the name of "health," although infant circumcision has long been practiced among Jews. Genital surgeries performed during rites of passage frequently use pain as a means of indoctrinating boys into manhood. Psychologically oriented anthropologists have suggested they also act to induce "castration anxiety," which strengthens cultural prohibitions against incest.

Recently, some scholars have come to understand genital surgery as a form of mutilation of, and abuse against, children, both boys and girls. As we saw in chapter 3, the debate over the clitoridectomies and infibulations performed on girls is a complicated and heated one. There has been much less said about genital surgeries performed on boys, especially in non-Western societies, although some groups now protest the circumcision of male babies in the U.S.

James DeMeo is a notable exception; he has focused on male genital surgery cross-culturally. His analysis suggests that "male genital mutilations are found present in a cultural complex where children, females, and weaker social ethnic groups are subordinated to elder, dominant males in rigid social hierar-

chies of one form or another" (2003:125). His analysis focuses on unequal power relations among groups of individuals and assesses genital surgery as a form of psychological and social domination. This understanding diverges from, and adds an important layer of understanding to, the more traditional anthropological view, still widely accepted today, that has interpreted bodily mutilations during initiation ceremonies primarily as external indicators of a young girl's or boy's changing social status (see Van Gennep 1908).

Experiences of the Body: Embodiment

A number of anthropologists have criticized the "body as text" understanding of the body because it reinforces the idea of the body as an object that can be "written upon." Ultimately this objectification, these anthropologists claim, maintain the Western notion that the mind and body are separate. They have also been concerned not only with how *meanings* of the body differ according to how power is distributed but how *experiences* of the body do as well.

The focus on the body as "experienced" or "lived" has traditionally been the domain of the philosophical tradition known as **phenomenology.** The experience of the body is referred to as **embodiment.** Anthropologists have combined a phenomenological focus on embodiment with their concern with cultural difference and have shown how differing cultural conceptualizations of the body affect how individuals in different times and places experience their own bodies. You may remember the example in chapter 3 of Muslim women in Egypt who, wearing the veil, experience their bodies as pure and holy.

Anthropologists focused on embodiment have often concentrated on illness, suffering, and pain because during these experiences the division of self and body is collapsed and the body is experienced as the self. In such circumstances, the body does not disappear from a person's awareness. Instead it is ever-present, highlighting the experience of being in the world.

Poet and essayist Nancy Mairs has written eloquently about how, as a woman with multiple sclerosis, she experienced her body as doubly shameful: first, because she had a body at all and, second, because her body had become "weakened and misshapen by disease" (1997:301). She echoes the experi-

Close-Up

9.3: Hooked on a Feeling: Anthropology of the Senses and Emotions by Nell Quest

What makes people sad? What does a peach taste like? Many people think that answers to these questions are universal, or that variations in how people feel or sense the world around them are due to individual rather than cultural differences. Some people would even argue that "feelings," in both the emotional and sensory meanings of the word, are determined by neurological, hormonal, or biological causes. In this view, for example, a peach tastes the way it does because it has a particular chemical makeup that interacts with our taste buds and, ultimately, is communicated to our brains. And, similarly, they feel that happiness or sadness might be understood as brought on by changes in levels of hormones and neurochemicals, such as serotonin, or by common experiences of tragedy.

One of the most important roles of feminist and other twenty-first century anthropologists has been to closely examine the assumptions contained in commonsense notions of how the world works, and to reveal how such commonsense notions are culturally specific and privilege particular people's ideas of "normal" over others. Since the late 1980s, feminist anthropologists and others interested in embodiment have devoted increasing attention to studying sensory and emotional experiences, both of their research subjects and of anthropologists themselves. This work shows how senses and feelings are not "common" at all, but are in fact culturally mediated, contingent, and affected by relations of power.

For example, Catherine Lutz (1988) has demonstrated that words used to talk about emotion often do not translate well across cultures or languages, and that each culture's conceptions of particular emotions are dependent on their local circumstances. In her research in the Caroline Islands in the Western Pacific, for example, she found that the meanings of the local word for what in English is called "love" simply did not correspond to the notion of love most Americans have. The native word also applied to what in English is labeled "compassion" and even "sadness." Her study therefore led her to challenge notions of emotion as largely physiological, and to argue that the idea that the typical Western opposition between emotion and rationality—often associated explicitly with the opposition between body and mind, women and men—is not a fact about the world.

How a particular food tastes is also affected by cultural meanings, as Elinor Ochs and her colleagues have demonstrated. They examined the dinner-table interactions of Italian and U.S. middle-class white families and discovered that our sense of taste is "socialized" (1996). In other words, they found that children in the two cultures are taught to think about food differently based on the way their parents discuss it. Italian families emphasize how food builds family ties and that it is pleasurable, while U.S. parents emphasize foods' nutritional content and health benefits, and bargain with their children over food ("If you eat your vegetables, you can have dessert"). This process of socialization through talk makes a difference in what children claim to like, and what it even means to like the way something tastes.

Like other theorists of embodiment, for anthropologist Paul Stoller (1989) the body is not just an object that exists in the world; it is also the very medium through which people experience the world and come to know it. Thus, he argues that anthropologists' sensory experiences are central to how they understand and interpret the situations they encounter in fieldwork, and are important data in themselves. He makes a point of including descriptions of his own sensory experiences in his ethnographies, and shows that sometimes these experiences can indicate important divisions within a community.

Along similar lines, anthropologist Judith Farquhar (1994) has demonstrated that her informants' ideas about and descriptions of their sensory experiences of medicine, food, and pleasure in China are intimately linked to particular historical circumstances, repressive state practices, and citizens' attempts to resist them. These anthropologists have shown that sensory experiences are therefore not dictated by "nature," but are important sites of socialization, conflict, difference, and struggles for power over how the world is defined.

References

Farquhar, Judith. 1994. Eating Chinese Medicine. *Cultural Anthropology* 9 (4):471–497.

Lutz, Catherine. 1988. *Unnatural Emotions: Everyday Sentiments on a Micronesian Atoll and their Challenge to Western Theory.* Chicago: University of Chicago Press.

Ochs, Elinor, Clotilde Pontecorvo, and Alessandra Fasulo. 1996. Socializing Taste. *Ethnos* 61 (1–2):7–46.

Stoller, Paul. 1989. *The Taste of Ethnographic Things: The Senses in Anthropology.* Philadelphia: University of Pennsylvania Press.

ence of many people with disabilities when she recounts how those around her rendered her invisible and erased her sexuality because her body did not conform to standard notions of beauty and health. Other anthropologists interested in embodiment have focused on the senses and emotions.

Like meanings of the body, experiences of the body differ not only across cultures but also within a society by such factors as race, ability, and age. Anthropologist Carolyn Martin Shaw describes how racist ideas affected her experience of her own body and sexuality as a young African American woman growing up in the United States in the 1950s. She was caught between contradictory messages from a popular culture littered with images of sexy women on the one hand, and religion and racial discourse on the other: "While I wanted to be sexy and alluring," Shaw writes, "I was constrained by my need for social approval in the black community and by my fear and mistreatment at the hands of whites who would see me as a workhorse or a whore" (2001:110).

Medicalizing the Body

Constructing the Female Body through Medical Discourse

Scientific discourse has been central in defining men's and women's bodies in both Western and non-Western societies. This definition and control has occurred primarily through the **medicalization of the body:** constructing the body as an object of knowledge of medicine, thereby placing it under the gaze and control of the medical establishment. In Europe and the United States in the nineteenth century, the body became a site of medical knowledge and practice as the field of medicine became professionally organized.

This had particular consequences for women because prior to that time, women had been healers, midwives, and even physicians and surgeons. But as medicine became an increasingly commercial activity—rather than a part of caretaking centered in the home—women were excluded from the business of medicine, and often forcefully so. Medicine became a male-dominated profession charged with gaining "knowledge" of the body. As we have already seen, the male was taken as the norm and women were found deficient by comparison. In medical discourse, such bodily functions as menstruation and menopause were understood as pathologies. Women's bodies were thus viewed as inherently diseased.

In her analysis of contemporary medical discourse, *The Woman in the Body* (1987), anthropologist Emily Martin reveals that these views are still widespread today. She shows how the language used to describe physiological processes in medical textbooks is far from objective and neutral. Frequently, the metaphors that have been used to explain female bodily processes like menstruation and menopause have not been drawn from science, but from aspects of Western economic systems. Menstruation, for example, has been likened to the failure of a factory system: the female body fails to create a useful embryo, instead producing a worthless product, menstrual blood. Menstruation, in this conceptual framework, is therefore seen as a productive system gone awry (Martin 1987:46).

Production metaphors drawn from the world of the factory are also used to describe childbirth. Women are seen as passive laborers in a process in which doctors produce a desirable "product" in the form of a healthy child. Women's "productive capacities" are also described in such negative language. A young woman recently reported being told by her physician that her difficulty in becoming pregnant is due to her "incompetent cervix."

Menopause is described in medical texts through a language derived from the communication industry with its focus on "information-transmitting systems with a hierarchical structure" (Martin 1987:41). Martin describes the depiction of menopause in one of these texts:

> In menopause, according to a college text, the ovaries become "unresponsive" to stimulation from the gonadotropins, to which they used to respond. As a result, the ovaries "regress." On the other end of the cycle, the hypothalamus has gotten estrogen "addiction" from all those years of menstruating. As a result of the withdrawal of estrogen at menopause, the hypothalamus begins to give "inappropriate orders." . . . What is being described is the breakdown of the system of authority. . . . At every point in the system, functions "fail" and falter. [1987:42]

This portrayal of menopause as a failure of the authority structure of the body contributes to our society's negative view of it. As one textbook says, with the onset of menopause "a woman must readjust her life from one that has been physiologically stimulated by estrogen and progesterone production to one devoid of these hormones" (Guyton quoted in Martin, 1987:51). This statement implies that women cannot continue a vigorous life after menopause (they are no longer "stimulated") and must think of themselves as lacking something that invigorated them previously (they are now "devoid" of hormones).

U.S. society is not the only one that has constructed negative notions of female bodily processes. As mentioned above, in many societies menstruating women are viewed as polluting and dangerous, as capable of defiling anyone or anything that comes in contact with them. In some societies, this belief has given rise to taboos that require women's seclusion during their menstrual period. Such taboos may not always have negative implications. Among some Native Americans, for instance, menstrual blood is seen as a source of power.

Women in the United States are not affected equally by the language and practices of medical discourses of the body. Martin found, for example, that white middle-class women are more likely to hold a worldview consistent with a scientific one and thus are more apt to accept the views of their bodies offered by contemporary medical discourse. In contrast, women from working-class backgrounds and women of color are more likely to resist such views. Martin proposes that these different responses arise because the people most oppressed by a system are more likely to be critical of it and to call for fundamental changes in it (1987:190–191).

Rayna Rapp's (2000) study of **amniocentesis**—the extraction of genetic material from the amniotic fluid surrounding a fetus to reveal fetal anomalies such as Down syndrome—has produced similar results regarding a variety of responses from women in the United States to the claims of medical discourse. Rapp has shown how a woman's race, class, and ethnicity can affect her decision to abort a child who, in medical discourse, is seen as "defective." White middle-class women in Rapp's sample tended to be more ambivalent about the idea of raising a child with a disability than were Latinas, for example. According to Rapp, Latinas recall friends and family members with children who were born with a disability and see the care given to these children by their mothers as consistent with a self-sacrificing view of motherhood that is valued by them. They were therefore less likely to end their pregnancies through abortion. A number of other studies have substantiated Martin's and Rapp's conclusions that responses to the medicalization of women's bodies vary by ethnicity and class.

Martin has extended her focus on the medicalization of the body to consider the link between larger cultural ideas and medical understandings of the body's immune system in U.S. society. Unlike a mechanical system that breaks down, the immune system is seen as one that can readily adapt to new circumstances. It is flexible bodies that are praised in this discourse, which should not be surprising given the views highlighted in the discussion of neoliberalism.

In *Flexible Bodies* (1994), Martin demonstrates how, in popular culture in particular, disease is depicted as a foreign enemy that attacks the body, whose immune system comes to its defense. Headlines on magazine covers such as *Time* and *U.S. News and World Report* illustrate her point: they proclaim, "The Battle Inside Your Body: New Discoveries Show How the Immune System Fights Off Disease" and "The Body at War: New Breakthroughs in How We Fight Disease." But "war" is a gendered endeavor, and thus we should not be surprised that "the body at war" contains images loaded with gendered associations: for example, "higher order" T cells, like men at war, are depicted as killing invaders; they are described as "virile heroes of the immune system," and "highly trained commandos." In contrast, macrophages, a "lower form of cell" that surrounds and digests foreign organisms to rid the body of them, are feminized, seen as "the 'housekeepers' of the body," who "clean up the dirt and debris" (Martin 1994:55–57).

Constructing the Male Body through Medical Discourse

Although Martin focuses on how medical and popular depictions of the body draw on conceptualizations of both masculinity and femininity, the focus of most research on the medicalization of bodies has been on white women and people of color, not white men. The neglect of men's bodies in such research is centrally tied to the long-standing idea discussed above that "man" is mind, not body. Men's bodies have rarely been made into an object of study in the same way as female bodies (Sheets-Johnstone quoted in Bordo 1999:18).

This situation, however, has begun to change. Recently scholars have started to investigate how discourses and practices constitute male bodies as well as female bodies. This change in focus is partially tied to changing theoretical conceptualizations, like the ones discussed throughout this chapter, which understand the body as a site of power. In particular, as many scholars have pointed out, in Western thinking the white male body has been the "unmarked" body, taken as the norm against which all other bodies have been assessed. It therefore could go "unnoticed," not brought under scrutiny as an object of knowledge by medical discourses.

This may seem paradoxical since so much medical knowledge has been based on studies involving men, not women. But, in such studies, the male body has traditionally been taken as the generalized body, not a *male* body, and thus could stand in for all bodies. The increasing identification of a specifically male body is not only the result of changes in theorizing, it is also the product of the increased commodification of the body in general. As we will see later in the chapter, the shift in the U.S. economy from marketing to a broadly defined consumer to marketing to increasingly narrow consumer niches associated with particular identities has brought the male body directly into view as never before, and with it, men's body "fitness" has become a central concern.

Leonore Tiefer (2002) provides an example of the new research on the medicalization of the male body, focusing specifically on the medicalization of male sexuality and its relationship to cultural conceptualizations of masculinity. During most of the twentieth century, Western concerns with white masculinity were intimately tied to ideas of virility and men's ability to perform sexually. This link is evident in the very medical term used to describe a man who has difficulty getting an erection: this inability has been thought of as a disease and labeled "impotence," a word that implies not merely a physical difficulty but also a loss of vigor, strength, and power (Tiefer 2002:150).

Although early in the twentieth century it was typical to view impotence as a psychological problem, throughout the century, it increasingly came to be understood as a physical problem in need of medical intervention. In pre-Viagra days, the cure for impotence was usually the surgical implantation of a device into the penis. Despite the costs and risks of this procedure, many U.S. men opted for this solution, Tiefer argues, because it offered an explanation and solution to "impotence" that removed responsibility for "sexual failure" from men themselves.

With the shift in focus away from psychologically based "impotence" to medically based "erectile dysfunction," the inability to get an erection was conceptualized as a "failure of hydraulics," inscribing the male body as a machine. An important consequence of this medicalization, as Tiefer points out, is that it "denies, obscures, and ignores the social causes" of "impotence," removing sexuality from the realm of relationships (2002:160).

Constructing the African Body through Medical Discourse

As we saw earlier in this chapter, Saartjie Baartman's body was probed and studied in the name of gaining scientific medical knowledge. Yet her display was only one instance of the medicalization of the non-Western body by the West. Alexander Butchart (1998) has chronicled how Western medical discourses created an "African" body. As we have seen, one important aspect of Foucault's (1990) argument about discourses is that they actively create new objects of knowledge, making them visible and allowing them to be controlled. According to Butchart, this is precisely what happened to the African body under conditions of colonial control. This construction of the African body began during the seventeenth century, the "Classificatory Age" in Europe, when the predominant mode of knowledge construction involved the careful examination of things in terms of their visible physical structures. These things were then classified and ordered into hierarchical systems. As Butchart puts it:

> It was therefore at this point that the African body first emerged into Western knowledge in something approximating to the distinctly human form we now take for granted, as along with the plants and animals of Africa it was made an object of natural history and installed in the botanical classification system of [Carolus] Linnaeus as "Afer Niger" under the category "homo sapiens." [1998:xii]

This classification effort, according to Butchart, focused on the external appearance of the African body. Facial and bodily surfaces were measured, compared, and grouped in a hierarchical chain of being from ape to man, with the African body filling the space in between.

With the advent of missionary medicine, which constituted the first set of properly "scientific-medical" discourse and practices in Africa, attention moved from the surface of the body to its interior, from a focus on external appearance to one on internal disease. In Christian missionary thinking, diseases of the body were associated with problems with the soul, and thus healing was equated with the "casting out of devils" (Butchart 1998:79). Healing thus came to involve freeing the "African soul" from "the grip of superstition," unburdening Africans, in other words, from their traditional beliefs and practices, which, in medical missionary discourse, were seen as backward and harmful.

A Medical Hierarchy of Black and White Bodies

The differential medical construction of black and white bodies has had significant implications not only for blacks in Africa but for blacks in the United States as well. Well into the twentieth century, the placement of black and white bodies in a medical hierarchy left open the possibility of medical abuse of African Americans long after such treatment of whites was seen as immoral or made illegal.

The most infamous case of such abuse is chronicled by James Jones in *Bad Blood: The Tuskegee Syphilis Experiment* (1993). This abuse occurred between 1932 and 1972 when 399 African American men were used as human subjects by the U.S. Public Health Service in medical studies known as the "Tuskegee Syphilis Experiment," which focused on this venereal disease. The rationale for the experimentation was the theory that white and black bodies were affected differently by the disease: whites, it was thought, experienced more neurological complications from syphilis, blacks more cardiovascular damage.

The men in the study, mostly illiterate sharecroppers from one of the poorest counties in Alabama, were in the late stages of syphilis and were informed merely that they had a condition known as "bad blood." Although these men were led to believe they were being treated for this condition, they were left untreated so that when they died, data could be collected from their autopsied bodies to reveal the damage of late-stage syphilis. The Public Health Service prohibited the men from receiving treatment for any venereal disease. Their untreated syphilitic symptoms included tumors, heart disease, paralysis, blindness, insanity, and ultimately death.

Jones has pointed out that the experiment continued despite passage of the Henderson Act (1943), a public health law requiring testing and treatment for venereal disease, and despite the World Health Organization's Declaration of Helsinki (1964), which required that "informed consent" be obtained from subjects for experiments involving human beings. In 1997, President Bill Clinton issued an apology to eight survivors of the experiments: "The United States government," he declared, "did something that was wrong—deeply, profoundly, morally wrong. It was an outrage to our commitment to integrity and equality for all our citizens . . . clearly racist" (Clinton 1997).

Questionable medical experiments continue to be carried out in many countries around the world today, especially by pharmaceutical companies seeking big profits. As Cheryl Mwaria (2001) points out, studies can be ethically questionable even when they appear to meet the criteria that experiments involving human subjects benefit their participants. To illustrate her point, she cites clinical trials using Third World women to test AIDS medications:

> African women who tested HIV positive were not told that the virus could be passed through breast milk and that therefore they should refrain from breastfeeding. Apologists for the studies have argued that the complex regimen necessary to reduce mother-to-child transmission rates in the United States is simply not feasible in the Third World, primarily because it is expensive. Such arguments serve to reinforce the status quo of hierarchical privilege of Western countries. [Mwaria 2001:196]

Today, medicine, and its discourses and practices, penetrates into bodies and minds in more far-reaching ways than ever before. Human organs can now be transplanted, DNA removed and tested, and every inch of the body—from head to toe, from inside to outside—imaged and surveyed, at least for those who can afford such "benefits." Health and fitness have become dominant values in many countries today as such concerns have increasingly become big business opportunities.

Commodification and the Body Beautiful

Today, both in the United States and throughout the globalizing world, the marketplace has become increasingly central to the construction of women's and men's bodily needs and desires, and to their very sense of who they are. Although, as we have mentioned, the male body has become commodified in the last few decades, the consumption of products and services has become particularly fundamental to many women's lives, with their diverse bodily wants mediated by mass-produced images in commercial advertisements found in magazines, on television, and on the Web. Furthermore, in the commodified world of Hollywood film, the female body is constructed as an object to be consumed.

Through such images, women are offered more than simply products; they are promised a more beautiful body, a more gratifying life, and a happier self (Rosenblatt 1999:8). Everyday life, these images suggest, can be transformed through the style on view or on sale. Yearning for these better ways of looking, living, and being drives consumption. As we will see, commodification is fueled not only by images of "the body beautiful" but by the everyday normalizing and disciplinary practices that Foucault has described. Individuals engage in these practices to produce the ideal body.

Women and the Development of Consumer Society

Since the late nineteenth century, with the rise of industrial and consumer society in Europe and North America, women have been seen as the ideal consumer. The department store was a product of the European Industrial Revolution—a revolution that allowed for the manufacture of large quantities of relatively cheap goods, enabled by the cheap labor of working classes and colonial subjects. With the development of such stores as the Bon Marché in Paris, elite women were titillated by commodities that offered fantasies of a more desirable self.

With the increasing "democratization of consumption" throughout the twentieth century, Western women from the working classes could buy more and more products that, they were led to believe, would offer them compensation and relief from the bodily drudgery of their daily lives. Such "democratization" did not, however, do away with class distinctions. To the contrary, class fashion continued to be expressed in strict rules about how certain items of dress were to be used. For every occasion there might be only one "proper" fashion ensemble, complete with different gloves or shoes. Those without the means to purchase the "correct" attire wore their "inferior" class position on their bodies for all to see (see Crane 2000:134).

Throughout most of the twentieth century women from all classes were enticed to buy newer and better commodities to improve the home, which was seen as their proper domain. For our purposes here it is important to know that, especially in the United States, but increasingly also in other parts of the world, the act of consumption is seen as elite and middle-class women's primary responsibility—buying products and services to turn their bodies and themselves into an object of desire.

In the last decades of the twentieth century, as we have seen, a new form of economic strategy arose, called flexible accumulation. Producing more and more different kinds of products required a corresponding diversification of consumers. This was accomplished through advertisements that increasingly targeted a person's individuality and identity as a means of stimulating consumption. Donald Lowe has outlined the significance of these changes:

> [A] commodity in late capitalism has . . . become a package of changing "product characteristics." Moreover by means of a relay of juxtaposed images and signs, advertising connects product characteristics with prevailing social and cultural values. As a result, we no longer consume commodities to satisfy relatively stable and specific needs, but to reconstruct ourselves in terms of the lifestyle associated with the consumption of certain commodities. [1995:47]

Selling Identity through the Body: Consumer Society

As we discussed in chapter 7, the introduction of assembly-line technology in the early twentieth century allowed mass production and manufactured items to become increasingly standardized in North America and Europe. This standardization became a selling point for products themselves, especially in the United States: advertisers praised the virtues of consumer items that were dependable and consistently of the same quality. Standardized products were marketed to a mass audience, who, in the process were homogenized: notions of the ideal consumer as an assimilated middle-class "smart buyer," were widely disseminated.

People were encouraged to buy more and more products to "keep up with the Joneses"; the goal was not to own distinctly different items from one's neighbors but to attain the same outdoor grill, style of car, or dependable refrigerator. Even today there are satirical depictions of this aspect of mid-twentieth century U.S. middle class, criticizing it for the blind confor-

mity it demanded: In the film, *The Stepford Wives,* for example, white women are characterized as unthinking, robotlike entities, lacking individuality. In *American Beauty,* white men are depicted as unfulfilled and in need of resisting the values of middle-class society, as Kevin Spacey portrayed.

Today, more than ever, and in more and more places, individuals purchase lifestyles and identities largely by acquiring products aimed at their bodies. Women and men distinguish themselves by the products they buy, items that are supposed to reflect "who they really are." Although these commodities might include one's car or living room furniture, they also importantly include products aimed at the body, whether tangible ones like makeup, shampoo, and clothing, or intangible ones like gym memberships and subscriptions to health and fitness magazines. What one wears or imprints on the body, how toned one's muscles are, or how fit one's diet is, are indicators of lifestyle and identity, accomplished through acts of bodily self-creation. Not only do advertising slogans encourage buyers to purchase products that will allow them to "be one's self" or to "create an expression of self" (see Mascia-Lees et al. 1990), so, too, do some progressive political discourses: self-creation is often equated with freedom from oppression by some feminists, for example.

As we saw above, the related idea of "writing one's body" to "tell one's own story" has been adopted by many women as a way of resisting power. We will return to this point later and will assess whether women's attempts at self-creation are liberating or oppressive in capitalist society. As we have already seen, according to Foucualt, such ideas are a technique of power: being an autonomous, self-creating individual with high self-esteem, for example, serves the needs of capitalism.

The role of consumer, which was traditionally ascribed to women of privileged classes in capitalist society, had its counterpart in the one ascribed to men: producer and provider. Well into the 1970s in U.S. society, this division was celebrated and mythologized throughout the culture. But as more and more women moved into the workplace during this period—fueled partly by an economic crisis that made it increasingly difficult to maintain a family's standard of living on one paycheck alone—the strict division began to give way, although slowly and not entirely.

At the same time, "niche" marketing targeted at a more narrowly defined group of consumers created a new site for consumption: the male body. The male body had only been infrequently pursued as a target for products and services before the 1970s. After this time, advertising and discourses of health and fitness increasingly addressed men. Not surprisingly, studies began to demonstrate a rising dissatisfaction among men with their bodies. Susan Bordo has tied this dissatisfaction to the demands of the new consumer capitalism:

> Calvin [Klein] gave us those muscled men in underwear. Then the cosmetics, diet, exercise, and surgery industries elbowed in, providing the means for everyone to develop that great Soloflex body. After all, why should [consumer capitalists] restrict themselves to female markets if they can convince men that their looks need constant improvement too? The management and enhancement of the body is [sic] a gold mine for consumerism, and one whose treasures are inexhaustible, as women know. Dieting and staving off aging are never-ending processes. Ideals of beauty can be endlessly tinkered with by fashion designers and cosmetic manufacturers, remaining continually elusive, requiring constantly new purchases, new kinds of work on the body. [1999:220]

Such changes are implicated in new incidences of eating disorders among men and in increasingly high rates of cosmetic surgery. According to the American Society of Plastic Surgeons, since 1992, there has been a nearly 50 percent increase in cosmetic surgery procedures among men, with liposuction now the number-one male procedure performed (http://www.plasticsurgery.org/mediactr/webmen.htm, accessed October 21, 2002). When asked, U.S. men rarely cite increased targeting by marketers as their reason for such surgery. Instead they suggest that they find it more and more necessary to appear young to stay competitive in a shrinking job market.

Ideal Images of Beauty: Race and Ethnicity

Yet, it is women's consumption that remains critical to the success of a capitalist economy. In the United States, for example, women account for 85 percent of all purchases (Maine 2000:7). Much of this expenditure is directed at the body and, in particular, at the pursuit of beauty. U.S. women spend over $20 billion each year on beauty products, and yet, U.S. women feel more negatively about their bodies than women in most other societies (Faludi 1991).

Standards of beauty and notions of the ideal body vary across societies, and also within them due to differences based on such factors as alternative sexuality, age, and ethnicity. But media images of ideal beauty are so ubiquitous in the world today that they exert a powerful normalizing and homogenizing effect. As Laura Spielvogel describes in the Ethnography in Focus: *Working Out in Japan* (on the following page), young women today often seek the beautiful body rep-

Desirable body practices and adornment vary considerably across societies, as this Dayak woman from Borneo demonstrates.

resented by the white, Western supermodel. The ultraslim, toned body of the tall white woman continues to be the dominant image in advertising, although increasingly women of color can be found in advertisements and on the "high fashion" runways, often sought out for their particularly "exotic" look.

Nonetheless, the relationship of skin color to ideas of beauty and self-worth continue to be important ones for many people. Toni Morrison's provocative novel, *The Bluest Eye* (1970), portrays the devastat-

Ethnography in Focus

**Working Out in Japan: Shaping the Female Body
in Tokyo Fitness Clubs** by Laura Spielvogel

How is beauty defined in contemporary Japan? Coherent yet complicated, current standards of beauty revolve around an unobtainable combination of wholesomeness, youth, sex appeal, cuteness, and thinness. . . . Although men must also conform to a certain body type, it is the women who have been consistently subjected to rigorous standards of perfection that focus on size, symmetry, and appearance (e.g., Bordo 1993; Wolf 1991; Chernin 1981). . . . It is no coincidence that the contemporary feminine ideal in Japan plays up bone-thin skinniness, wide-eyed innocence, cuteness, and youth. The frail, prepubescent ideal poses little emotional, intellectual, or sexual threat to the patriarchal status quo, and this ideal can only be achieved with strict self-control of appetite, wild emotions, and independent thoughts. Most women are all too aware of the paths to success in Japan. The discrimination against women deemed unattractive is evident in this revealing, albeit dated, memorandum recovered from a major Japanese corporation's personnel department: "Be wary of young women who wear glasses, are very short, speak in loud voices, have been divorced, or are the daughters of college professors (quoted in R. Smith 1987:17). [pp. 6–8]

***

To begin to pin down the shifting yet coherent standards of female beauty in contemporary Japan, I asked well over one hundred men and women, young and old, [fitness] club members and nonmembers, and [fitness club] instructors and managers to define female beauty and the ideal woman's body in their own words. Answers ranged from the specific names of supermodels Kate Moss and Cindy Crawford to detailed prescriptions for perfection that break the body apart feature by feature and limb by limb, but most answers converged on four defining characteristics of female beauty: youth, good proportions, attractive legs, and thinness. [p. 150]

***

Downtown Fitness, located within walking distance of well-known bars, restaurants, and clubs that line the cosmopolitan streets of Roppongi, is the club of choice for many of the foreign dancers, models, and bar hostesses employed in the area. . . . The foreigners hail from the United States, Australia, New Zealand, Canada, Israel, Europe, and Mexico. . . . The foreign community obviously has had a profound effect on the way fitness and the ideal body are constructed in Japan, and the interactions between Japanese members and staff and foreign members proved to be quite insightful. . . . Downtown Fitness understands the appeal of the idealized American model and ran a very provocative and controversial campaign, featuring a series of black-and-white photographs of nude Caucasian models. . . . It is significant to note that . . . the majority of . . . female models who are photographed half-dressed or nude in Japanese advertisements are Caucasian (this discussion does not include pornography). Certainly, North American women and, in most cases, Caucasian women are constructed as the body ideal in contemporary Japan. [pp. 155–156]

***

The sexy, attractive body seen in the advertisements resonates with the overall fitness goals of Downtown Fitness. A handout, tellingly printed in English, describes the variety of activities offered at the club, in which the same image of sexiness and beauty is reproduced: "Discover the [Downtown Fitness] that suits you best. With the refreshing feeling you get after having exercises [*sic*], and a strong, healthy and supple figure, you'll look gorgeous just as you are. The best brand-name clothing couldn't make you look better. For you to wear the look of a physically fit, healthy person, we have prepared a variety of programs under the brand name [Downtown Fitness]." In this excerpt, the club has defined fitness in a very specific way: strong, striking, physically fit, and foreign. The emphasis is on appearance, with good health, well-being, and exercise serving as the means to achieve good looks. The message is clear: exercising at Downtown Fitness will produce a beautiful body, idealized by the American model. [pp. 157]

From: Laura Spielvogel, "Young, Proportionate, Leggy, and Thin: The Ideal Female Body (excerpt)," in *Working Out in Japan*, pp. 142–173. Copyright 2003, Duke University Press. All rights reserved. Used by permission of the publisher.

ing consequences for black women of this idealized notion of the beautiful, desirable woman as white. It tells the story of 11-year-old Pecola, who yearns to be white, to have the blondest hair and the bluest eyes so that she will be thought beautiful and be loved, like the white children around her.

Hair is almost as significant as skin color to the lives of many African American women struggling with dominant images of beauty. As Ingrid Banks documents in her ethnography, *Hair Matters: Beauty, Power and Black Women's Consciousness* (2000), hair is one of the most significant topics of discussion among African Americans, especially women. From an early age, black women come to recognize hair as a significant marker of identity particularly given media representations of what constitutes beauty (Banks 2000:23). Their tightly curled hair defines them as inferior in appearance to their straight-haired white counterparts, calling into question notions of their attractiveness and self-worth. However, Banks' interviews also show that while many women of color straighten their hair, many others retain their "natural" look as a means of contesting ideal images of beauty in the United States.

In *The Color Complex: The Politics of Skin Color among African Americans* (1993), Kathy Russell, Midge Wilson, and Ronald Hall trace the historical development in the United States of the "color politics" that provide the larger political context in which notions of beauty and self-worth continue to be embedded. Their analysis shows how a color hierarchy existed not only

between blacks and whites but also within the black community itself as a result of racist assumptions and policies that favored lighter skinned individuals over darker skinned ones. Even while on the trading block, slaves were differentially valued based on skin tone:

In some parts of the South mulattos [a person of both black and white ancestry] were actually bred and sold for huge profit on the female slave market. Pretty quadroons (one-quarter Black) and exotic octoroons (one-eighth Black) were in particularly high demand. Light skinned beauties, called "fancy girls," were auctioned at "quadroon balls" held regularly in New Orleans and Charleston. [Russell et al. 1993:18]

This preference for lighter-skinned individuals laid the basis for a pattern of skin "classism" in the black community itself, resulting in the development of segregated elite social clubs, vacation resorts, neighborhoods, and even churches (Russell et al. 1993:23–27). Today, "light skin" has become a standard of beauty in many places in Africa, where it is often not only associated with beauty but also with wealth and higher levels of education.

Although the tall white model continues to be the dominant image in advertising, we must be careful not to assume that there is no resistance to it or that there are not local and nuanced interpretations that can transform it. Susan Ossman, who has studied "beauty salons" in Casablanca, Paris, and Cairo argues in *Three Faces of Beauty* (2002) that even in the way people talk about their looks or the season of fashion, distinctions that draw on national, ethnic, or social difference persist. Fashion might promote a specific kind of modern body, but its progressions through time thrive not on sameness but on claims to seasons marked by different looks. [Ossman 2002:5]

Distinctiveness is featured in a neofolk fashion show.

Noliwe Rooks (1996) has shown that dominant Western definitions of beauty are often rejected by African American women. Studies in the United States and Britain indicate that black and, to a lesser extent, Asian women tend to be more positive about their bodies and less prone to eating disorders than white women. But, studies also suggest that the more these women integrate into middle-class society the more critical they become of their appearance; caught in a double bind, they may ultimately become more likely to develop problems with food than white women (*The Guardian*,

10/15/01; http://education.guardian.co.uk). This situation may help explain the rise in incidences of plastic surgery among nonwhite women in the last decade.

Ideal Images of Beauty: The Slender, Youthful Body

Whether 14 years old or 60, women across the United States are bombarded with images of the ideal body as slender, leading to extremely high rates of dieting, especially among middle-class girls and women. The impact of the ideal of a slim body is also reflected in studies of the increased incidence of anorexia nervosa and bulimia among recent immigrants to the United States, which has been reported for Korean, Latina, African, Middle Eastern, and Asian women. A number of studies have found significant differences in the body images and dieting behavior of white American and African American teenagers. These studies document that African American women have lower levels of body image disturbance and eating disorder behavior and are more satisfied with their body size, weight, and overall appearance than white women (see Lovejoy 2001).

Mimi Nichter and Nancy Vuckovic's (2002) ethnographic study, however, confirms the prevalence of the ideal slender body among one sample of white, Hispanic, African American, and Asian girls from lower- to upper-middle-class backgrounds in junior high and high school. Many of the girls in their study believe that a perfect body, one that is five feet seven inches tall and weighs no more than 110 pounds, leads to a perfect life.

This study also reveals that for these girls, the desire to remain thin is not only a matter of aesthetics—of what they think looks good—but also one of hope for acceptance from their peers. Girls seek this acceptance through what these researchers call "fat talk." Throughout a typical day, the girls in this study repeatedly declared that they were fat as a means to illicit a sympathetic reaction from those around them. According to these researchers:

"I'm so fat" is not just an observation about one's weight. It is a call for support from one's peers, for affirmation that one is in fact not fat. It can also act as an apology or excuse for behavior, or as an invitation to listeners to reaffirm group solidarity. [Nichter and Vuckovic 2002:137]

Given the importance of working on one's body in the United States today, perhaps it is not surprising

Close-Up

9.4: Cosmetic Surgery and Ethnicity

The impact of the Western ideal of beauty as white can be seen in the rise in incidences of plastic surgery among women of color in the United States, who seek cosmetic surgery procedures that are racially specific (Kaw 1993). The American Academy of Facial Plastic and Reconstructive Surgery recently surveyed their members and found that in 2001 procedures on Hispanics had increased by 200 percent; African Americans by 323 percent; and Asians by 340 percent (see AAFPRS 2001 Statistics on Trends in Facial Plastic Surgery, http://www.facial-plastic-surgery.org/media/stats_polls/m_stats.html). Overall, however, white women still constitute the bulk of cosmetic surgery patients: according to the American Society for Aesthetic Plastic Surgery, in 2001, Hispanics represented only 7 percent of cosmetic surgery procedures, African Americans 5 percent, and Asians 4 percent.

In Asian countries today the most prevalent form of cosmetic surgery is one that alters the shape of the eyelid to mimic the appearance of the "double-lidded Western eye." Latinas often seek lip augmentation while black women increasingly undergo liposuction to slenderize their shapes. Nose surgery (rhinoplasty) is popular with almost all nonwhite groups, and the most popular procedure among African Americans; south Asian women have their noses reduced and tilted at the tip, Afro-Caribbean women have theirs narrowed, and east Asian women have implants inserted to give more defined bridges (*The Guardian*, 10/15/01; http://education.guardian.co.uk).

Although some commentators argue that women of color undergo cosmetic procedures such as these to look whiter, others suggest that it is so they can look more beautiful. The two, however, may not be distinct. Sander Gilman (1991) has shown that undergoing surgery to bring one's appearance in line with a dominant cultural ideal is not a new practice. Plastic, or aesthetic, surgery has been used since the late nineteenth century to erase signs of racial difference, as Sander Gilman has shown (1991). According to Gilman, Jacques Joseph, an orthopedic surgeon performed the first modern "nose job" in Berlin in 1898. His clientele consisted primarily of Jewish patients wishing to remove a visible external sign of their "race," the "Jewish nose." What motivated individuals to undergo such surgery at the time may have had less to do with ideals of beauty than with "racial passing" for economic reasons. Gilman points out that, "The visibility of the Jew made it impossible for him to compete equally with the non-Jew in the economic world. Only vanishing into the visual norm and passing as non-Jewish in terms of his appearance enabled the young Jewish male to become part of the general society." It should not be surprising then that the number of such operations rose as increasing anti-Semitism propelled more and more men and women to alter their bodies to become racially invisible (Gilman 1991:187).

Reference

Gilman, Sander. 1991. *The Jew's Body*. New York: Routledge.
Kaw, Eugenia. 1993. Medicalization of Racial Features: Asian American Women and Cosmetic Surgery. *Medical Anthropology Quarterly* 7 (1):74–89.

TOP 5 SURGICAL COSMETIC PROCEDURES IN 2007			
SURGICAL PROCEDURES	1. Breast augmentation 347,500	**MINIMALLY INVASIVE PROCEDURES**	1. Botox™ 4,600,000
	2. Liposuction 302,000		2. Hyaluronic acid 1,051,000
	3. Nose reshaping 285,000		3. Chemical peel 1,025,000
	4. Eyelid surgery 241,000		4. Laser hair removal 906,000
	5. Tummy tuck 148,000		5. Microdermabrasion 897,000

Source: American Society of Plastic Surgeons, 2008. http://www.plasticsurgery.org/d.xml?comp=x3309

that "fat talk" also has a moral valence: a woman able to control her weight is seen as morally superior to those who "let themselves go." A young woman who is concerned about her weight reveals that she is a good person, responsible for herself and her looks.

In a number of other societies, a thin body is not considered ideal. In Kenya, the South Pacific, and Western Polynesia, for example, where a large-sized body is associated with abundance and wealth, studies reveal positive valuations of "fat" individuals. According to Ann Becker, in Fiji there is consensus on the ideal body type, but unlike in the United States, few individuals there are interested in attaining or cultivating their ideal body as a personal goal (1995:38). This is because the body is seen as part of the larger community and is experienced as a manifestation of that community. Since the body is used neither to distinguish an individual's position nor to define the self, individuals do not discipline their bodies to conform to ideal notions. Instead, weight loss and thinness are associated with social neglect or deprivation.

The ideal body in U.S. society is not only thin but also young. Because it deviates from the idealized body of youth, the aging body is largely viewed as unattractive in U.S. society. Older women are bombarded with advertisement for products to remove their wrinkles and erase their gray hair, convincing them that their physical appearance is undesirable and the aging process objectionable. Whereas age in some societies is valued for the wisdom it brings, older women in many places today increasingly undergo expensive and often dangerous cosmetic surgery, including face lifts, liposuction, and the injection of materials, such as the botulism toxin, into the face to erase

wrinkles and to retain the youthful sense of beauty prescribed by the larger culture. However, the economic basis of cosmetic surgery is becoming ever clearer. Reports indicate that with the recent economic downturn, more and more people are cutting back on elective surgeries (Shute 2008).

Ideal Images of Beauty: Disciplinary Practices

Pursuit of the "body beautiful" requires not only a large amount of money but also an inordinate amount of time. U.S. women today, for example, spend both more money and more time on their appearance than ever before. The requirements for obtaining a beautiful body and appearance have become more stringent as fashion magazines promote new ideas, new images, and new products (Maine 2000:65). New discourses of health overlay these images of beauty: the ideal female body today is also a healthy one that is toned and firmed by hours in the gym. Some women spend nearly as much time trying to look good as they do working. As Naomi Wolf puts it, "Women today work three shifts: one at their job, one taking care of their home and family, and the third trying to meet the beauty demands of our culture" (quoted in Maine 2000:65).

Women's bodies are constructed as much through bodily practices of posture, manner of bearing, and demeanor—as well as the automatic and habitual activities of their daily regimens—as they are through internalized images and cultural values. The time-consuming regimen many women undertake daily in the pursuit of a feminine ideal of beauty acts to discipline women's bodies, as cultural critic Susan Bordo points out:

> Through the pursuit of an ever-changing, homogenizing elusive ideal of femininity—female bodies become

Global News

9.2: Mao's Nightmare: Revolutionaries in Bare Midriff

. . . Ms. Kan, 51, has taken her one-woman cultural revolution to China's children with a Barbie-like doll that she wants to represent the Chinese ideal of beauty. Like her American cousin, the Yue-Sai doll comes freighted with the politics of consumerism, body image, and gender stereotypes. . . .

The doll idea was born, Ms. Kan told the children and assembled guests, when an American friend in New York asked her to bring back a Chinese doll for the friend's 6-year-old daughter. To her dismay, she could not find any Chinese dolls in China other than a series representing the country's 56 minority groups. The brochure she handed out at the fashion show said: "Yes, I did find some ugly Chinese 'minority' dolls but nothing really modern and beautiful, nothing representing us!" (There is no strong tradition of playing with dolls in Chinese culture.)

"All of a sudden," Ms. Kan said, "I realized this is one of the reasons why so many Asians don't find themselves beautiful!" So she set out to create her own doll, working with the best doll makers in Hong Kong, who had previously just made Western dolls. And after 12 head molds and a lot of tinkering with eyebrows, she finally had "a doll that we can be proud of as Chinese." . . . [Craig S. Smith, Shanghai Journal. *New York Times* 12/18/2000]

docile bodies—bodies whose forces and energies are disciplined and habituated to external regulation, subjection, transformation, "improvement." Through the exacting and normalizing disciplines of diet, makeup and dress—central organizing principles of time and space in the day of many women—women are rendered less socially oriented and more internally focused on self-modification. [1993:166]

The Cult of Beauty and Resistance

But must the demands of the cult of beauty be understood as nothing more than expressions of women's oppression in capitalist society? Cultural critic Mary Russo (1986) suggests not, theorizing an "anti-aesthetic of the body," noting that in Western culture, the ideal body has been the classical body of the male that is monumental, static, and closed, "corresponding to the aspirations of bourgeois individualism" (p. 325). By contrast, the woman's body, with its oozing bodily fluids of menstruation and lactation, disrupts the boundaries of the enclosed body and challenges respectability and social order; it is the open, protruding, extended, secreting body of the "grotesque." It is a body conceptualized by society as impure, threatening, and dangerous, as anthropologist Mary Douglas has theorized. Russo suggests that the grotesque body need not be despised and contained as has traditionally been the case; instead, she argues that women can co-opt this unruly body, and its "aesthetic of the ugly," recognizing that the grotesque presents us with a body "of becoming, of process." It provides an image of transgression and change that can be used toward political ends.

Processes of self-creation, resistance, and transgression through fashion and other bodily expression do not exist outside of capitalist formations and gendered power relations, and thus will necessarily be influenced, mediated, and constrained by them. But women are active creators and, as such, can use the resources offered by these formations, if not to escape or transcend them, at least to negotiate, protest, and resist them. To understand shopping and fashion only as frivolous, empty-headed feminine activities reproduces the denigration of the body with which women have so long been associated. It devalues a traditional sphere of women's activities and concerns, and it does not allow for the diverse ways in which women can use these activities to improve their lives.

Some women might starve themselves to death in the pursuit of impossible images of beauty and perfection, but others will playfully adorn themselves and seek pleasure in their own bodies (see Mascia-Lees et al. 1990). Some will subject themselves to potentially dangerous cosmetic surgery, but others will find empowerment in the strong and sculptured body they build at Club Fit. In addition, a strong body is an important element of self-defense, which can serve as a valuable tool in providing women with a sense of comfort and security.

Nevertheless, it is also important to remember that practices of fashioning the body are deeply embedded in worldwide relations of economic, political, and social inequality: it depends on the hard physical labor of the bodies of women in poor countries, their tired backs, exhausted limbs, and failing eyesight, as we saw in chapter 7.

Conclusions

The body is a complex construction: it is a material entity whose movements can be both forcefully and subtly controlled and manipulated, and a symbolic construct to which notions of selfhood, identity, and self-worth are intimately tied (see Conboy et al. 1997a:7–8). It also continues to be seen by many as a natural entity. Seeing the body as natural, however, is itself a cultural construct, which has served to make social and cultural differences appear real, inevitable, and right. But naturalizing the body and tying it to "difference" is problematic: there is little, if any, direct evidence of a simple link between the physical form and the physiological and genetic makeup of the body on the one hand, and what are considered gender or racial behaviors on the other, as we saw in chapter 4. The link between the body and supposed gender and racial differences is a highly tenuous one.

Because the body is socially constructed, the meaning of the body differs across cultures and can vary within societies according to how power is distributed. Because the body is not a stable ground of difference, the meaning of the body can change over time. It can also be used to contest and resist constraining definitions of identity, whether based on gender, race, or other social factors.

WORD PORTFOLIO

amniocentesis: probing a fetus for genetic testing, usually to reveal fetal anomalies, such as Down's syndrome. This technique can also reveal the sex of an unborn child.

body politics: the use of the body as a site of power through which political, economic, and social inequalities are inscribed.

discourse: a system of knowledge, supported by institutions and practices, which creates a picture for people of what is true and what is not.

embodiment: the lived experience of the body.

initiation ceremony: a rite of passage in which a young girl or boy is transformed into an adult through symbolic and ritual actions.

medicalization of the body: constructing the body as an object of knowledge of medicine, thereby placing it under the gaze and control of the medical establishment.

phenomenology: a branch of Western philosophy focused on understanding how the body is "experienced" or "lived."

pollution beliefs: prohibitions and taboos based on the belief that body parts and substances are "unclean."

RECOMMENDED READING

Unbearable Weight: Feminism, Western Culture, and the Body, by Susan Bordo. 1993. Berkeley: University of California Press.

Susan Bordo offers a poststructuralist feminist analysis of various experiences of embodiment and the reproduction of femininity. Through an examination of the enduring legacy of mind/body dualism, Bordo discusses

reproductive rights, eating disorders, and the relationship between postmodern subjects, bodies, and resistance.

Life and Words: Violence and the Descent into the Ordinary, by Veena Das, 2006. Berkeley: University of California Press.

Drawing on powerful fieldwork exploring the role of violence and mourning as part of women's everyday lives in India, Veena Das examines how violence links the individual to the community and nation-state. Focusing on the role of agency within the realm of ordinary life, Das concentrates on the mundane work that women must undertake to integrate the experiences of extreme violence into daily life.

Freakery: Cultural Spectacles of the Extraordinary Body, edited by Rosmarie Garland Thomson. 1996. New York: New York University Press.

This anthology brings together a diverse range of essays examining the notion of "the freak," and the role extraordinary bodies play in the construction of "normal" selfhood. Ranging from the exploration of circus and carnival sideshows, evolutionary oddities in 19th-century science, to postmodern examples of bodybuilders and celebrities, *Freakery* draws our attention to how historically and culturally particular notions of gender, sexual, racial, and bodily "otherness" serve as the ever-changing limits of what is understood to be human.

Embodied Lives: Figuring Ancient Maya and Egyptian Experience, by Rosemary A. Joyce and Lynn M. Meskell. 2003. New York: Routledge.

Using the concept of embodiment as a lens through which to understand the role of self in a society, Rosemary A. Joyce and Lynn M. Meskell compare the high status of the body in ancient Maya and Egyptian civilizations. While many similarities connect the status of the body across these two societies, Joyce and Meskell reveal the critical differences that existed in how the body was treated, understood, and experienced.

Unnatural Emotions: Everyday Sentiments on a Micronesian Atoll and their Challenge to Western Theory, by Catherine Lutz. 1988. Chicago: University of Chicago Press.

In her unique ethnography of emotion, Catherine Lutz draws on fieldwork done in Ifaluk, a Micronesian atoll, in 1977–1978. Drawing comparisons between Ifaluk and the United States, Lutz critiques the understanding of emotions as both natural and universal, arguing instead that they are constructed within a particular cultural context. Drawing on Foucault, she argues that emotions are "ideological practices" at the complex intersection of actors, actions, interpersonal relationships, and social events.

Three Faces of Beauty: Casablanca, Paris, Cairo, by Susan Ossman. 2002. Durham, NC: Duke University Press.

Looking at beauty salons as a window into the relationship between society and self, Susan Ossman offers a "linked comparison" between salons in Casablanca, Cairo, and Paris. These beauty parlors, she argues, are places where the body is deconstructed and put back together again, often in relationship to stereotypical notions of "oriental beauty." Ossman weaves together ethnographic observations with analyses of film, beauty magazines, and poetry, showing how salons both produce and resist normalized notions of the body.

10

Minding Gender and Difference

In this chapter you will . . .

find out how language produces and maintains inequalities • explore the meaning of such terms as "personality," "identity," "self," and "subjectivity" • learn about societies that have more than two gender categories • examine "identity politics" • focus on the relationship of gender identity to national and ethnic identity • see how an individual's sense of "self" is related to cultural discourses • investigate how scholars have explained the differences between male and female personality types

Globalization has had far-reaching effects on how people conceptualize who they are and how they think about where they belong. Images from movies, satellite TV, and the Internet flow across the world, circulating novel ideas about personhood, gender, and sexuality. Dislocation, war, and migration affect ideas about gender and cultural identity, while increasing rates of hunger, poverty, disease, environmental devastation, and social unrest worsen social suffering (Härting 2005). What impact do the power relations inherent in a global economy have on a person's sense of self?

In this chapter we explore the contributions feminist and other twenty-first-century anthropologists have made to our understanding of the relationship of power to the development of "personalities," "identities," and "subjectivities." As we will see, which of these three terms becomes the focus of a researcher's study is an indicator of a different theoretical orientation, each of which draws on different understandings of the human psyche.

Some feminist anthropologists have focused on female and male personality differences, drawing on the psychoanalytic theories of Sigmund Freud. Others have raised questions about identity and have made important contributions to our understanding of the variation in gender identities across societies and of how globalization is changing notions of gender, national, and ethnic identity. Still others have shown how power works to shape who we think we are and how we situate ourselves in the world. These later researchers prefer the term "subject," and focus on how "subjectivity" or selfhood is created, especially through language. In what follows, we trace the history of these approaches from the late nineteenth to the early twenty-first centuries.

Gender and Personality

A major focus of the psychologically oriented anthropological literature concerned with gender has been on explanations of the differences that exist between the male and female **personality,** the consistent behavior patterns and intrapersonal processes that are thought to originate in the individual. The interest in defining and specifying the exact nature of personality differences between the sexes has its roots in Freudian psychology, but it has also involved a critical examination of Freud's ideas.

Freud and Social Evolutionism

Social evolutionism had many adherents outside of anthropology. The most well-known and influential was Sigmund Freud, the founder of psychoanalysis. Anthropology was a consuming interest of Freud and played a significant part in the formulation of some of his major concepts (Wallace 1983). Freud linked the process by which "primitive" societies developed into "civilized" ones with notions of how girls and boys develop from children into adults. Like other nineteenth-century thinkers, Freud believed in the assumption of the natural inferiority of women, and equated the female with the "primitive" and the child.

Like social evolutionists, Freud was searching for the foundations of Western civilization, especially for the basis of the Western mind. He turned to social evolutionary ideas about primitive societies to find them. For Freud, the civilized mind differed from the primitive mind in terms of what was conscious and unconscious in it. He argued that the mind of civilized Western Europeans was at one time like that of primitives. In the course of human prehistory, however, civilized people repressed certain behaviors and ideas, those that are still observable in primitive societies. Freud thus turned to "primitive" societies to uncover the past of "civilized man" and to reveal what was lurking unknown in his unconscious.

The social institution of totemism, found among some non-Western people, was also of particular interest to Freud. The social evolutionist John McLennan had described totemism as a religion in which primitive people worshipped a plant or animal as a god (Kuper 1988:82). An important aspect of totemism was that the group that venerated an animal or plant totem could not eat it during the year. It could be consumed, however, at special times in a ceremony that produced a communion between a people and their god.

Noting this practice, Freud set out to explain its occurrence in his book *Totem and Taboo* (1918). According to him, the first human group was a **primal horde** composed of an all-powerful, patriarchal father and a group of women to which he had exclusive sexual access. This arrangement meant that his sons could not have sexual relations with anyone. Tiring of this situation, the sons committed patricide and incest; that is, they killed their father and had sexual intercourse with the women of the group, their mothers. Afterwards, in their shame for having had incestuous relations, the sons instituted the incest taboo; if you remember, it is a rule requiring that sexual relations occur outside of the biological family. According to Freud's reconstruction, the sons were also overcome with great guilt for killing their father. To show their remorse and love for him, they ate his body and communed with him.

It is debatable whether Freud believed that such an event took place in some remote past. Nonetheless, he did propose that the practice of totemism recorded by some nineteenth-century evolutionary anthropologists could be understood as a repeat performance of the (real or imagined) original act of patricide he described in the primal horde story.

Freud suggested that the Western mind has repressed this event, which now lies only in the unconscious. The memory of this event, and the guilt associated with it, plagues the "civilized mind" today. It is a memory that each individual replays as he or she undergoes the process of psychological development. Since males and females played different roles in the primal horde event, Freud concluded that males and females also undergo different processes of personality development.

Freud's Psychoanalytic Approach to Personality Development

Freud proposed two psychological developmental processes, the Oedipus complex and the Electra complex. According to him, in order for boys to develop proper masculine behaviors, they must learn to renounce their attachment to their mothers and to identify with their fathers. Freud termed this process the **Oedipal conflict,** naming it after the mythical Greek character, Oedipus, whose life was tragic because he unknowingly killed his father and had sex with his mother. Girls, Freud argued, must undergo a different process, one that allows them to forgive their mothers for their inadequacy—the lack of a penis—and to reestablish an attachment with them. Freud called this process the **Electra complex,** naming it after the figure in Greek mythology who incites her brother Orestes to murder their mother.

According to Freud, every boy must resolve the Oedipal conflict in order to develop the appropriate masculine personality. A young boy who has an attachment to his mother as his first love object grows to desire sexual intercourse with her. Having the knowledge that women lack a penis, however, the boy dreads the same fate. He fears that his all-powerful father will castrate him if he acts on his sexual desires. This **castration anxiety** leads the boy to repress his sexual feelings for his mother, to reject her, and to disdain all women because they lack a penis. The boy also begins to identify with his father, leading him to model his father's behaviors and to develop a bond with him.

A girl undergoes a different version of this process of psychological development. She comes to recognize that she lacks a penis and develops **penis envy.** Since her mother also does not have a penis, the young girl blames her mother for this shortcoming. The girl not only regards boys and men with envy because they have this organ but also rejects and disdains her mother and all other women for their lack of one (Freud [1933] 1965:589). Girls come to hate their own mothers and see them as rivals for their father's attention.

Spurred on by penis envy, the girl remains in the Electra complex until she learns to identify with her mother as a symbolic means of possessing her father and, through this identification, obtaining the penis she desires. But since the girl does not identify directly with the father as a boy comes to do, she never develops the traits Freud associated with men: a clear sense of justice and the ability to work actively in the larger world.

Women are confined to the domestic sphere by this natural developmental process, which is based on their anatomical "lack." Later, however, their penis envy can be lessened by "gaining" a penis through marrying a man and having male children. Women, according to Freud, are naturally dependent and passive. They are also masochistic and vain, hating themselves for what they lack and trying to compensate for it by making themselves beautiful and desirable in other ways. Thus, according to the Freudian model, women are naturally inferior to men and will remain that way. For Freud, **anatomy is destiny.**

Margaret Mead and the Culture and Personality School

Early studies, such as those of famed anthropologist Margaret Mead, focused on personality as well. Like Freud, Mead was interested in understanding the differences that characterize male and female personality types, but while Freud presented a universal model of personality development, Mead's work revealed that female and male personality types vary across cultures. Applying a Freudian model to understanding personality development in non-Western cultures, Mead asked, are men always aggressive? Are women inevitably nurturing?

Mead compared personality differences in three different societies in New Guinea, reporting her findings in her book, *Sex and Temperament in Three Primitive Societies* (1935). She noted that anatomical differences provide a first point of identification for boys and girls. However, she argued that early in childhood, boys and girls compare themselves to others. They learn what traits, in their culture, are privileged

or denigrated. Through this, they develop a sense of sexual selfhood. In each of the three societies she studied, Mead found recognizable personality traits, but they existed in different configurations than in the United States. Among the Arapesh, for example, both men and women were "womanly" and "unmasculine" (p. 165), while among the Mundugumor, both men and women were "masculine," "virile," and "aggressive" (pp. 165, 279). The Tchambuli had yet another gender configuration: women were dominant and impersonal while men were less responsible than women and more emotionally dependent, spending much of their time working on their appearance, decorating themselves and primping (p. 279). Given this variation, Mead determined that gendered personality types are culturally constructed, not biologically determined. As she put it:

> We may say that many, if not all, of the personality traits which we [in the United States] call masculine and feminine are as lightly linked to sex as are the clothing, the manners, and the form of the head that a society at a given period assigns to either sex. [Mead 1935:280]

Chodorow's Psychoanalytic Model

While Mead's work called into question some of Freud's underlying assumptions, other feminists have taken his focus on the "family drama," which he saw as underlying personality formation, as a starting point for their own explanations of gender identity. These feminists, however, do not depend on Freud's androcentric assumption of male superiority and do not suggest that universal personality traits doom women to a position of inferiority to men. Neither do they take males as the norm and see anyone who deviates from this norm as pathological or inferior. If you remember, Freud characterized men by what they possess—the penis—and held them in high regard because of it, while he defined women by what they lack.

Freud's influence is especially evident in Nancy Chodorow's article, "Family Structure and Feminine Personality," which appeared in the founding text of feminist anthropology, *Woman, Culture, & Society* (1974) and which has itself become a classic in feminist anthropology. While Freud sought explanations for differences in personality in the biological differences between the sexes, Chodorow focused on how cultural forces are at work in the psychological formation of individuals.

Chodorow was interested in explaining, as Freud was, what she presumed were "nearly universal differences that characterize masculine and feminine personality and roles" (p. 43). But unlike Freud, she argued that the consequences of male and female personality traits depended on a society's particular interpretation of them. Indeed, Chodorow's work has been an important impetus for research in feminist anthropology on the *cultural* and *social* factors influencing psychological development and gender identity.

According to Chodorow (1974), personality development is a result of relational experiences developed in infancy, which become generalized as one grows older. Chodorow claimed that the critical factor giving rise to the different experiences males and females have as infants is that women are responsible for child care. While both male and female infants have an early identification with their mothers, a mother will tend to identify more closely with her daughter.

By contrast, a mother will push her son away, emphasizing a boy's masculinity in opposition to her own femininity. A boy therefore becomes more differentiated from his mother than does a girl. Moreover, Chodorow claimed, a boy has to learn to identify with a more distant father. A boy thus identifies with diffuse and generalized male traits rather than with an actual individual. All these factors contribute to the establishment of strong and rigid boundaries between self and other in boys, making them more independent and self-reliant than girls.

In contrast, a girl's gender identification is of a more personal nature. It is based on close identification with her mother, the person with whom she has had a genuine and continual relationship since infancy. This intimacy results in a girl never completely rejecting her mother in favor of men. The feminine personality, then, is founded on relation and connections, producing a secure sense of gender identity and more flexible boundaries between self and other than males have.

These traits can cause problems for women in societies that do not value women, according to Chodorow. For example, in societies in which women have low status, the process of gender formation will require girls to identify with a devalued figure. In this case, a girl's rejection of her mother also involves the "rejection and devaluation of herself, because of her pre-oedipal identification and boundary confusion with her mother" (Chodorow 1974:65). By contrast, in societies in which women have important kinship roles

or influential authority, women will not be devalued. Therefore, a girl's close identification with her mother will not be problematic. While Chodorow agrees with Freud that male and female personality types are universal and determined by gender, she disagrees with Freud's idea that gender development will always result in women being considered inferior to men.

A Maasai woman, her head shaved and her arms, neck, and ears bedecked with bangles and beads, stands with her baby in front of the house she constructed from mud, sticks, grass, and cow dung, while her husband tends his cattle in distant fields.

Other Explanations of Personality Differences

Unfortunately, neither Chodorow nor Freud provides clear evidence that male and female personality types are universal across all cultures. Clinical studies suggest that there is no evidence to support such a generalization (Maccoby and Jacklin 1974), and some researchers have suggested that there may be more personality differences among individuals than be-tween males and females (see, for example, Freize et al. 1978:2).

Some early anthropological studies suggested that cultural characteristics could explain many of the differences. Traits traditionally associated in Western culture with women, such as nurturance and a sense of responsibility for others, and with men, such as independence and dominance, seem to vary not by sex but by women's labor responsibilities. In a study of six cultures, Whiting and Whiting (1975) found that where women perform many necessary subsistence tasks that are hard and time-consuming, children, regardless of gender, will be organized to help, and responsibility for others will be stressed. Nurturance training is also emphasized for children regardless of the sex of the caregiver if children are caregivers themselves.

Although a mother's workload may have an impact on gender personality and behavior, psychologist Eleanor Maccoby has argued that a focus on parents' efforts in making girls feminine and boys masculine is too limited (1999:8). She has investigated the importance of same-sex peer groups on personality development, finding that they exert a strong influence on boys' and girls' behaviors. She identifies significant differences in the way children interact within all-male or all-female playgroups as opposed to when they are on their own.

Children act far more alike when not with peers. Within all-male groups, boys take risks, play rough, strive for dominance, confront others, and resist revealing their weaknesses to one another. In all-female groups, girls disclose more about themselves to others in the group, participate in more reciprocal and sustained discussions, avoid conflict, and pay more attention to maintaining positive social relations (p. 289). These contexts give rise to distinct interactive styles. Such "interactive repertoires," which are learned in same-sex groups, Maccoby asserts, will be used for same-sex interaction throughout an individual's lifetime. Maccoby concludes that the behaviors we associate with gender are not due to individual personality but to the relationships and interactions we have with others.

Finally, as we'll see in chapter 11, Freud and Chodorow's construction of motherhood as universal is problematic given variation in ideals of motherhood and mothering practices across cultures.

Identity

During the 1950s and 1960s, some psychologists began to focus more exclusively on identity, rather than on models of how the self and personality are created. **Identity** refers to how an individual views him- or herself in relationship to others. **Gender identity** refers to how an individual views him- or herself in relation to being male or female. The traditional view of gender identity is that there is a natural con-

This Dominican Carnival participant does not conform to simplistic notions of gender identity.

nection between it and biological sex, defined in terms of bodily characteristics such as chromosomes and sex organs. Individuals whose biological sex and gender identity do not match have been viewed as abnormal or unnatural. Anthropology, however, has been at the forefront of studies recording a range of gender identities in societies around the world, which have helped to inform and expand simplistic notions about the relationship of gender to anatomy.

Third Gender Categories

As we saw in our discussion of the Hijra in chapter 2, anthropologists have documented how, in some societies, men and women are not forced to conform to two strictly defined gender identities but are allowed to act as what some have called a **third gender** category. In Thailand, for example, a man can take on the personality, dress, and behavior more often associated with women and can take either a man or a woman as his sexual partner (Morris 1994). Third gender categories also existed in many native societies of the United States and Canada before the nineteenth and twentieth centuries. Among the Mohave, for example, "transvestitism" was permitted. A man could become a woman, and a woman could become a man through a special ceremony, although a choice needed to be made. It was not possible for the person to act as both a man and a woman. Whether such individuals are honored or abhorred by other members of their society depends on the particular cultural context in which they exist. Such studies call into question standard Western assumptions about the relationship of sex to gender, as we'll discuss further in chapter 11.

Global News

10.1: Legislative Bargain Frays Some in LGBT Community

While a Nov. 6 [2008] poll by Human Rights Campaign found that 70 percent of lesbian-gay-bisexual-transgender, or LGBT, people expressed support for the Employment Non-Discrimination Act of 2007, a significant faction say transgender people were singled out and left behind when the initial version of the bill was derailed in Congress.

In addition to banning discrimination against people based on homosexuality, bisexuality or heterosexuality—as the bill passed by the House of Representatives states—the initial version also protected "gender identity."

A less familiar idea than sexual orientation, gender identity is crucial for transgender people because it recognizes that while much of the population may be "cisgender"—possessing a sense of gender identity in sync with their sex organs at birth—not everyone is.

Providing gender identity protection would mean such things as not being fired for making a gender transition while employed or not having to worry about being denied employment when birth certificates or drivers' licenses don't reflect a person's gender presentation. It would also help people who live androgynously and are not easily identified as male or female.

The original version of the bill—introduced in late April by Reps. Barney Frank, D-Mass.; Deborah Pryce, R-Ohio; Tammy Baldwin, D-Wis.; and Christopher Shays, R-Conn.—would have prevented discrimination based on "appearance, or mannerisms or other gender-related characteristics of an individual, with or without regard to the individual's designated sex at birth."

(continued)

The original bill was expected to pass out of the House and the Senate relatively easily. Supporters believed that even if President Bush vetoed the bill, the next administration might be more favorably disposed.

But in late September, Frank, who is openly gay and the bill's lead sponsor, told advocates that ENDA—the Employment Non-Discrimination Act—did not have the votes to pass the House if it included gender identity. Frank said that, particularly for Democrats in vulnerable districts, having to vote on a bill with protections for transgender people so soon before the election would be damaging.

When Frank replaced the bill with one that only discussed protection based on sexual orientation, advocates of gender identity inclusion organized a coalition—United ENDA—to lobby to restore the reference to gender identity. Spearheaded by the National Gay and Lesbian Task Force, the ultimately unsuccessful effort drew 400 allied organizations into a national grassroots outreach and lobbying effort focused on Congress, media and citizens.

Eighty-five percent of the Democrats voted in favor of the compromise, sexual orientation-only bill; 80 percent of Republicans voted against the bill. [The Senate has yet to vote.]

Matt Foreman, executive director of the National Gay and Lesbian Task Force, based in Washington and New York, expressed dismay at the loss of the gender identity provision. "We are deeply disappointed," Forman said the day after the vote. "The past six weeks have been among the most difficult and challenging our community has ever faced."

The inclusion of transgender people in the lobbying activities of the Washington-based Human Rights Campaign has been a source of controversy for the civil rights organization dating back to the mid-1990s; it was not until 2004 when the group agreed to add gender identity to their lobbying efforts for the bill. [Julie R. Enszer, *WOMENSENEWS* 11/16/07; http://www.womensenews.org/article.cfm?aid=3387 (accessed 5/29/08)]

Identity Politics

In the last decades of the twentieth century, strong ethnic, nationalist, and minority movements based on the notion of a shared identity developed all over the world. For example, we witnessed the rise of Scottish separatism, the anti-immigration Front National in France, the Taliban in Afghanistan, Hindu nationalism in India, political Islam in North Africa, and indigenous and other minority movements across the globe (Eriksen 1999). Each of these movements is a powerful expression of collective identity (Castells 1997:2) whose aim is to strengthen the collective sense of uniqueness of a particular group and to demand recognition and equal rights based on that identity (Eriksen 1999).

Using group identity to forward such political causes is known as **identity politics.** Within the framework of identity politics, differences among groups rather than the similarities are emphasized. This forms group identity through the process of excluding some individuals and establishing and policing group boundaries.

Many indigenous or minority peoples today see the borders of the nation-states within which they live as arbitrarily created by Western colonial powers. Indeed, more than 80 percent of the conflicts in the world today are those that arise between nation-states and minority peoples living within them (Nettle and Romaine 2000:21–22). Lacking a voice in politics and controlled by people who do not represent their interests, such groups turn to group identity to claim rights and resources. Such movements protesting this situation today can be found, for example, among the Welsh, the Hawaiians, the Basques, and the Kurds in Iraq and Turkey.

Identity politics can be understood as a means for disenfranchised groups to resist or challenge the spread of global capitalism, Western values of individualism, and increasing inequalities, all of which threaten local distinctiveness and self-determination (Eriksen 1999).

In some cases, the group that forms this challenge is an **ethnic group,** a collection of people who identify with one another based on common cultural, linguistic, or religious traits or their belief that they share ancestry. Often the stated aim of these identity groups is to reestablish their shared traditions. Although these groups claim that they are "returning to tradition," identity politics is not just about going back to some actual shared past; it is also a modern response to the loss of traditions and political power that are experienced in situations of rapid change. The appeal to shared, but lost, traditions can mobilize people who feel under siege (Tomlinson 1999). The belief that an ethnic group has the right to be an independent or autonomous political unit and its appeal to tradition to establish this claim is referred to as **ethnic nationalism.**

Gender and National Identity

It is not infrequent in identity movements for women's goals to be subsumed within the collective identity or for women to bear the brunt of the creation of group identities. This has been particularly well documented in nationalist movements. Grace Mitchell, for example, describes how both pro–U.S. and anti–U.S. battles over nationalist identity in Korea were waged on the body of a particular kind of woman. There, the image of the *yanggongju*—a woman who "sexually serviced" U.S. soldiers during the Korean War—was stigmatized, bearing the mark of foreign "contamination." She was a reminder to Koreans of their subordinated status to the U.S., a position that has been at the core of Korean national identity since the American military occupation in 1945. She was also a racialized figure, and her biracial children, the product of unions between the yanggongju and U.S. servicemen, were highly stigmatized (Mitchell n.d.).

Ideas about women have similarly interacted with constructions of national identity in post–Maoist China. Louisa Schein documents how part of the development of that identity involves China seeing itself as a multiethnic nation (2000:73). This has required the official recognition of 56 minority groups, including the Miao, its fifth largest, who were persecuted for their traditions in the past. Today, Chinese nationalists have become newly fascinated with the Miao woman: she has become not only an object of desire but also a nostalgic reminder of an idealized "untarnished" past. This serves to exclude Miao women from the "new prosperities" available in a postsocialist China, as they come to signify tradition at the same moment that China, with its growing market economy, seeks to establish itself as a *modern* nation-state.

Gender and Diasporic Identity

Among **diasporic peoples**—groups of people or ethnic populations forced or induced to leave their native countries—women may also shoulder the heavy responsibility of maintaining tradition. Such women often experience emotional stress stemming from this expectation as well as from their unstable position within the socioeconomic structures of the society. Parin Dossa has documented the impact of this on Iranian women living in Canada. There, stress manifests itself in women feeling that they are unable to improve their lives or to cope "meaningfully with life situations in their adopted country" (2004:42). Feeling isolated, they describe feeling "tired of life" and having "nothing to live for" (pp. 35–36). Although social service providers blame their depression on the unrest in the women's home country, the women themselves acknowledge the social and economic causes of their situation—especially being away from their homelands. Diasporic women's social and economic concerns are seen as individual problems and are medicalized through the concept of "refugee mental health." This intensifies their stress and makes acceptable the impact of disruption on these women's daily lives (pp. 2–4).

Subjectivity

Critics claim that the idea of gender identity is problematic because it rests on a particular notion of "self," which is seen as a self-knowing, unified, free, and stable being. This is the classic Cartesian self of Western thinking who is seen first and foremost as an individual. In relationship to gender, this notion of the self assumes that an individual can at some point conceive of herself as being "just a woman," free from the kind of social, historical, and economic constructions we have been describing (Härting 2005, Butler 1990:3). Yet, this understanding of the autonomous self, as we have seen, came into being with the rise of capitalism to create the very concept of a person who is an individual, free to sell his or her labor and consume products.

Close-Up

10.1: Diasporic Identity and Food by Nell Quest

As we have discussed throughout this text, cultures have probably never been bounded, separable, or predictably located, but this is especially true in a globalizing world. We have seen that senses of cultural belonging are becoming increasingly complex, especially for migrants, those who have moved from their home countries. The cultural sentiments and senses of belonging for diasporic peoples—those who are forced or induced to leave their homelands—are especially complex. They must struggle continually to create senses of belonging in local contexts, while also simultaneously working through experiences of trauma and addressing questions of how to maintain their cultures or assure that their political experiences are remembered.

Women's and girl's roles can be especially complex for migrants and refugees. They are expected to do much of the work of maintaining cultural identity in a new location through their work in the home. Women are the ones who are expected to educate children about cultural and family history, maintain traditional housekeeping practices, find ways to shop for, or otherwise obtain, familiar cultural products for their households, and prepare meals that are similar to those their families used to enjoy in their homelands. But they are expected to do this in conditions vastly different from those in their homelands.

Anthropologists have shown that food is a particularly important element in diasporic populations' attempts to maintain their cultural traditions. They have also, however, shown how diasporic populations can use food practices to integrate into a local culture, to distance themselves from the troubles they faced in their homelands, and to highlight how much better their situation is than it would have been had they not left. Cubans living in Australia and Miami, for example, go to great lengths to prepare items that they think of as part of pre-Castro Cuban cuisine, and value their perceptions of themselves as able to enjoy foods that may not be accessible to Cubans still on the island (Cardona 2004). Although they may sometimes view food nostalgically as a connection to their homelands, members of the Vietnamese diaspora in Australia also attempt to integrate culturally through altering their food practices, whether by youth consumption of fast food or older generations' founding of Asian-fusion restaurants designed to appeal to Australian consumers (Thomas 2004). Starting a restaurant is one way diasporic and migrant populations sometimes make a living in their new homelands.

References

Cardona, Euridice T. Charon. 2004. Re-Encountering Cuban Tastes in Australia. *Australian Journal of Anthropology* 15 (1):40–53.

Thomas, Mandy. 2004. Transitions in Taste in Vietnam and the Diaspora. *Australian Journal of Anthropology* 15 (1):54–67.

Given these connotations, many feminist theorists have preferred the word "subjectivity." Chris Weedon provides the following understanding of **subjectivity** in feminist theory: it "refers to the conscious thoughts and feelings," of a person, "her sense of herself." (1987:112). Subjectivity is a person's ways of understanding her relation to the world. Subjectivity, unlike selfhood, is not seen as a singular entity, but as a combination of the many positions and identifications a person has. This idea of the subject takes into account the many axes of identification through which a person comes to know herself: as, for example, a woman, a black woman, a black woman from the middle class, a black women from the middle class from a Third World country, and so on. These multiple identifications may be contradictory and may change. In the conceptualization of the subject, the self is not an unchanging and essential part of a person; it is multiple, unstable, and shifting. This suggests that our sense of who we are is, as Foucault would say, an effect of power.

Subjectivity and Subjection

Thinking about meanings of the word "subject" helps in understanding subjectivity and subjection—the subject of a sentence; an entity that is subjected to ideas, and therefore acted upon; and someone who is under the rule of another, such as a subject of the King or of the state. The word "subjective" is also used to stress personal feelings and experience in contrast to "objective."

For a sentence to be complete, it must have a subject associated with a verb. Thus, a subject is something that acts. A human subject, then, is capable of action or agency. A human subject is also an entity that is dominated by, and subjected to, the forces of power embedded in discourses. The subject thus becomes a subject of that rule. Thus, subject means two things: an entity that can act and be responsible for its actions and a subjected (or oppressed) being, one who submits to a higher authority.

Through identifying with the subject of language people come to recognize that they belong to a particular identity. This process is referred to as **interpellation.** Marxist philosopher Louis Althusser introduced this term, using it to describe how we come to recognize ourselves through the way we are "addressed" in language. If, for example, you are in a situation in which the police yell, "Hey you!" and you then turn back as if guilty, you come to think of yourself as a "guilty subject." This sense of self does not exist before this act of interpellation; it is a product of it.

As you may remember, discourses produce people's very sense of who they are. They create a picture for people of what is true and what is not. They are **regimes of truth,** according to Foucault (1994). What is particularly important about discourses as regimes of truth, Foucault asserts, is that people cannot construct subjectivity outside of them. Indeed, just the opposite is true. People recognize themselves in a discourse and find meaning in it.

As we discussed in chapter 6, although feminists and other twenty-first-century anthropologists have found Foucault's ideas about subjectivity, discourse, and power exciting and useful, they have also pointed to Foucault's lack of interest in discourses that construct masculinity and femininity in particular. They fault him for his failure to distinguish between discourses that may construct male and female bodies and sexuality differently. Indeed, feminists have suggested that, in some ways, Foucault is like some of the traditional theorists he criticized for developing the idea of universal "man." By using privileged white males as the standard, Foucault does something similar: he develops the notion of a universal "body." In other words, he invokes the white male body as the norm (see Mascia-Lees and Sharpe 1992).

Judith Butler's Performative Subjectivity

For feminist theorist Judith Butler, gender is not something people have, it is something people do. In her book, *Gender Trouble* (1990), she expands our understanding of the relationship of discourse to the production of subjectivity, especially gendered subjectivity. While Foucault and Althusser understand the subject as an entity interpellated—called up—through language, Butler argues that the subject is created through repeated performances of acceptable and conventional ideas about, in the case of gender, what it means to be a man or a woman. For Butler, this means gender is not an essential identity; it is created through **performativity.** It is re-created as individuals take on their society's ideas about femininity and masculinity and enact them. This repeated performance makes it seem as though gender is natural and coherent. It allows us to think that it springs from some underlying biological reality of the body. But Butler argues that in actuality, it is the product of gendered discourses. The sexed body is similarly constructed by discourses. That we come to believe that gender and sex are natural biological facts is testament to how deeply our ideas about gender and sex are embedded in discourses of truth.

Language and Power in a Globalizing World

Not all theorists interested in the relationship of language to power concentrate on discourses. Linguistic anthropologists, for example, are more interested in how language is used. Language is one of the most fundamental and multifaceted activities in which people engage. In today's world, there are almost 6,000 languages. Since there are only approximately 200 countries in the world, it is easy to see that there is a great deal of language variation within national borders (Nettle and Romaine 2000:21). There are also large numbers of people who are **bilingual,** who understand and speak two languages, and **multilingual,** who understand and speak more than two languages.

Yet, many governments recognize only one or two national languages. It is estimated that by the year 2050, 50 percent of the world's languages may be extinct (*Time,* 6/10/02:22).

Linguistic anthropologist Deborah Cameron (2002) makes it clear that language is caught up in one or more significant ways in the developments that we have discussed under the heading of globalization. For example, she notes that the large and complex migration of people that characterizes the world today means people are increasingly living in complex linguistic circumstances. Globalization also affects how people think about language. And today, some of the most important discussions among anthropological linguists revolve around many of the debates we discussed in chapter 1: Will globalization result in linguistic homogeneity? In other words, is it leading to the "Americanization" or "Englification" of language? Or will it increase multilingualism? What are the effects of globalization on currently "endangered" languages? How do ideas about, and access to, certain

Global News

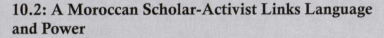

10.2: A Moroccan Scholar-Activist Links Language and Power

Until 2007, Moroccan women who married foreigners could not pass citizenship to their children—who had to apply, year after year, for residence permits to live in their own country. Finally, after decades of feminist protest, parliament has guaranteed paternal and maternal equality in determining nationality.

The new citizenship law follows the 2004 Moudawana (Family Law), which entitles women to a range of civil rights. The minimum marriage age was raised from 15 to 18; women may now wed without the consent of a male wali (marital tutor); polygamy is restricted to cases in which wives, including the new bride, consent by written contracts approved by a judge; and men may no longer unilaterally "repudiate"—divorce—their wives without compensation.

One feminist responsible for such rights is Fatima Sadiqi, a Moroccan-Berber professor at the University of Fes and a linguist specializing in how women and men use language in Morocco. She found that Berber-speaking persons lack access to information and resources because they speak a "female language" associated with the home and hearth. In this country, where Arabic, French and English predominate, many more women and girls than men speak only Berber, don't attend school and are illiterate—approaching 90 percent in some rural areas.

Sadiqi has shown powerful connections between language and women's rights. "I see the official recognition of Berber as a recognition of Berber women," says Sadiqi, author of the first grammar textbook for this ancient language still spoken by millions. She has also struggled for the inclusion of women's voices in Moroccan education. "I wanted to help democratize our higher education by introducing gender studies," says Sadiqi, who also founded the first gender-studies program in North Africa when she realized the absence of women's texts in university syllabi.

"The Family Law has greatly democratized debate on women's issues and introduced the idea of equality between spouses. Of course, not everyone believes in this equality, but at least people discuss it," says Sadiqi. Networking with other Moroccan feminists and keenly aware of the power of words, she agitated for the Family Law by speaking on television and in the printed press, and organizing major international conferences on women, language and development. "The present king [Mohammed VI] made clear in his very first speech that he wanted to improve the lot of women," she says. "Symbolically, this was huge for the feminist movement, which had to constantly negotiate power with both the monarchy and the radical Islamists."

Even before the Family Law struggle, Sadiqi used her work on language and power to strengthen Moroccan feminism. Her studies have led to teaching invitations abroad (including this past year at Harvard), and to her establishment of the ISIS Center for Women and Development in Fes. She is also editor of the forthcoming *Women Writing Africa: The Northern Region* (Feminist Press, 2007), which includes oral and written works of numerous languages and cultures. But she says it all began in her Berber village, where few women read or wrote: "I owe this to my father, who took me to school and believed in me."

Aimee Dowl. Reprinted by permission of *Ms.* magazine. © 2007

languages exclude certain groups of people and increase inequalities?

Linguistic Anthropology

Linguistic anthropologists focus on how language is used in the context of communication. They are interested in what speakers can and cannot do with language in their everyday lives. Their studies are based on the close and careful observation of language use in social interactions between women and men or people from different racial, ethnic, or class backgrounds and the role language plays in the construction of identities, including gender, ethnic, and national identity.

Feminist and other twenty-first-century linguistic anthropologists have focused on a range of topics concerned with language and difference. Some have shown how children acquire knowledge about the society within which they live through language socialization. Through this process, children learn, and come to internalize, the hidden assumptions about gender and other forms of difference in their society.

For example, through the erasure of women referents in language in the United States—that traditionally "man" is meant to refer to both men and women or "he" is used to refer to a male or a female—children learn about the different levels of importance given to males and females. This erasure is accomplished by the hidden assumption that men and the masculine are the norm. Although this practice has changed over the last few decades, it is often still seen as the "proper" way to speak. Other researchers have shown that language trivializes and degrades women through the use of such derogatory metaphors as "baby" and "chick," affecting women's sense of self and self-worth (Diamond and Quinby 1988:xv).

Robert Moore (1988) shows that Standard American English is also permeated with racist stereotypes at multiple levels. It includes not only obvious words of bigotry but also meanings that encode things that are white as good and pure and things that are black as evil and sinister. Moore asks us to think about the following phrases and their connotations: you blacken one's name,

Global News

10.3: Bible's Gender Terms Become Person-ified

America's best-selling modern Bible is about to be updated. Don't expect an entirely peaceful response. "Blessed are the peacemakers, for they shall be called sons of God," Jesus says in the New International Version. In the newest edition, that "sons of God" in Matthew 5:9 will be changed to "children of God." The update will use other gender-neutral wording, too. For example, the Roman 3:28 verse saying "a man is justified by faith" will be rephrased as "a person is justified by faith." The issue is "incredibly serious to evangelicals, how the Bible is translated," said Randy Stinson, executive director of the Council on Biblical Manhood and Womanhood. [Peg Meier and Rosalind Bentley, *Star Tribune* 1/29/02: A1, A9]

blackball an enemy, and blacklist an undesirable person. But frivolous lies are white, and the good guys in the old cowboy movies wore white hats and rode white horses.

Moore extends his analysis of terms that encode inferior status to labels that position certain experiences as secondary. The phrases used in chapter 6 by dependency theorists are an example: underdeveloped countries are judged in relationship to developed ones and Third World nations take last place when compared to First World nations. People of these nations often come to see themselves and their lifestyles in terms associated with the idea of underdevelopment: as backward, inferior, and primitive. Both of these phrases use the dominant white cultures of the Global North as the norm and standard for judging what is best.

Studies show that nondominant groups are not only often invisible in language but are also frequently defined in terms of their sexuality. For example, Julia Stanley's research reports that there are more than 200 terms for sexually active women compared to approximately 20 such terms for men (Stanley cited in Nielsen 1990:20). Anthropologist Shirley Ardener (1975) has described how language can suppress women in other ways. She claims that women are a **muted group** whose voices are often silenced because their experiences are not easily expressed through the dominant communication system of their culture, one that has been developed to serve male interests.

Difference in Communication Styles

Feminist linguistic anthropologists also focus on the differences in men's and women's speech patterns or styles of communication. Linguistic anthropologist Deborah Tannen provides an explanation for how different communication styles come into being:

> Women and men have different past experiences. . . . Boys and girls grow up in different worlds. . . . And as adults they travel in different worlds, reinforcing patterns established in childhood. These cultural differences include different expectations about the role of talk in relationships and how it fulfills that role. [1987:125]

Some conversational styles may disadvantage women in conversations between men and women. In an early study focused on this issue, Dale Spender (1980) noted that there is a long history in Western culture of women being stereotyped as the talkative sex. This is the case despite the many studies that document the tendency of men to talk more than women do in conversations between women and men. She suggests that this discrepancy exists because women are not being compared to men but are being compared to silence. Any talk by women is seen as too much. Other studies have shown that English-speaking men control conversations with women by talking more and by interrupting them frequently.

Researchers Henley and Kramarae (1994) have called attention to how "problematic talk," such as cross-gender communication, is different for white women than for women of color. Women of color from households headed by women, such as those described in chapter 11, for example, may not experience the same difficulties in conversations with men as white women because they have not grown up in families dominated by fathers. They may, however, experience difficulty in communication with white women.

Language Ideologies

Membership in speech communities shapes a person's sense of identity and belonging. By assessing how competent other speakers are in everyday language practices, speakers can determine who is part of a group and who is not. In all societies, ideas about gender are encoded in language ideologies. A **language ideology** consists of "shared bodies of commonsense notions about the nature of language in the world" (Rumsey 1990:346). It includes unquestioned beliefs about the world and the way the world should be with respect to language (Wolfram and Schilling-Estes 2006).

Language ideologies operate to create, maintain, and perpetuate inequality among groups of people. Janet Chernela (2003) provides a fascinating example of the interconnection of language ideology with gender ideology in her study of language in the Northwest Amazon. There she discovered distinct descent groups, which are highly valued and whose distinctness is maintained by perpetuating linguistic difference. In this society, rules require that only women and men from different descent groups may marry one another and that women must live with their husband's group after marriage, a practice referred to as patrilocal residence. This situation produces villages in which the men and their children share a language, while the women speak languages different from that of their husbands and children and often also different from other women who have married into the group. A woman's speech always marks her as an outsider, reinforcing her political subordination. Because of the value placed on distinct groups, children, who are exposed to the speech of their mothers, are prohibited from speaking it in public, underscoring their mother's exclusion.

Language ideologies also shape notions of belonging in nationalist movements where language acts as an important symbol for helping to create a separate identity for a group: for example, in Quebec, a nationalist movement seeking independence from England claims the superiority of French over English and regulates what language can be used, even on signs. The belief in the United States that the country is better off using English as the only language of instruction in schools is another example of a language ideology. It is based on the assumption that a single language creates national unity and is vital to establishing a resident's identity as an American. This ignores the fact that, many people in the United States identify themselves as American even though they speak a language other than, or in addition to, English (Gibson 2004).

The debate over whether English alone should serve as the language of the United States or if Spanish should be included affects the way Spanish speakers see themselves, and therefore it has an effect on ethnic identity. Those who argue against making Spanish an official language do so based on assumptions about what the United States is supposed to be and the role of English in that national image. Because of this widespread ideology, in school, Latina/o children may be considered less intelligent than their English-speaking classmates, making it more difficult for them to succeed within the U.S. educational system.

Language and Identity

The link between language and identity is complex: all speakers are part of at least one speech community. Members of a speech community use language in a unique and mutually accepted way among themselves. Members share understandings, values, and attitudes about language varieties in their community. People use language to indicate which groups they are members of and which groups they are not. Speakers who accept the identity of a particular community will engage in positive identity practices, that is, they will engage actively in order to construct a chosen identity (Bucholtz 1999:211) Those who reject the identity will use negative identity practices to distance themselves from it.

For example, in her analysis of students at a U.S. high school, Mary Bucholtz found that "nerds" actively take up this identity through language practices that are specific to their group, such as using formal words and adhering to hypercorrect spelling and pronunciations. They also differentiate themselves from others through negative identity practices such as avoiding the use of another group's slang phrases (Bucholtz 1999:211–212).

A person usually belongs to more than one speech community, interacting differently within each particular one. Individuals thus may have multiple perceptions of themselves, allowing them to have multiple identities (Gibson 2004). However, as Mary Gibson points out:

> Language is not only a means for individuals to present their own notion of "who we are," but it is also a way for others to project onto them their own suppositions of the way "we must be." Conflict arises when the hearer has a different understanding of the speaker's identity than the one the speaker desires.

The tension is further compounded when the hearer is in a position of power and cannot only misinterpret the desires of the speaker, but can actively thwart this expression, forcing the speaker into an entirely different, perhaps unwanted, identity. [2004:1]

Thus, language expresses the way individuals position themselves in relationship to others, the way they group themselves, and the power they claim for themselves and allocate to others (Gibson 2004). This is evident in Don Kulick's ethnography of a group of transgendered individuals living in Brazil.

Ethnography in Focus

Travesti: Sex, Gender, and Culture among Brazilian Transgendered Prostitutes by Don Kulick

What is most characteristic about travestis in . . . Brazil, is that they adopt female names, clothing styles, hairstyles, cosmetic practices, and linguistic pronouns, and they ingest large amounts of female hormones and pay other travestis to inject up to twenty liters of industrial silicone directly into their bodies in order to acquire feminine bodily features such as breasts, wide hips, large thighs, and most importantly, expansive buttocks. . . . [Most travestis] live in extremely humble conditions, in tiny three-by-four-meter rooms, and they support themselves primarily by prostituting themselves on the streets of the city. . . . [But] despite the fact that they live their lives in female clothing, call one another by female names, and endure tremendous pain in order to acquire female bodily forms, travestis . . . do not consider themselves to *be* women. They are not transsexuals. They are instead, they say, homosexuals—males who ardently desire men, and who fashion and perfect themselves as an object of desire for those men. [pp. 5–7]

* * *

Travesti ideas about women and travestis exist in a problematic, tense, and antagonistic relationship. . . . The antagonistic logic of this relationship makes it impossible for travestis to grant that any travesti might legitimately lay claim to female subjectivity, because were she allowed to do so, she would immediately think of herself—as women are believed to do—as superior to travestis. To prevent any individual from ever being able to make such a claim, travestis have developed a number of practices . . . designed to remind any travesti who may pretend otherwise that she is a male, not, ever, a woman. . . . One subtle way [for doing this] . . . is through the forms and address and reference they use in their talk. Travestis regularly address one another with the feminine vocatives *menina* (girl), *mulher* (woman), and *minha filha* (my daughter). . . . But even though these feminine terms are common, much more frequent in travesti talk are the address forms *viado*, *bicha*, and *mona*—words that can all be translated as "effeminate homosexual." And when referring to other travestis, words like *menina* or *mulher* are *never* used; the preferred term is *bicha*. . . .

Address and reference terms meaning "effeminate homosexual" . . . often occur as responses to intimations by a travesti that somebody might think she is a woman. Hence, the pragmatic force of such words is to remind the addressee that she is most definitely not a woman. A typical occurrence of this kind happened one afternoon when Banana, Tina, and I were sitting on the doorstep on São Francisco Street. . . . At one point, the ash from the joint she was smoking fell into Banana's lap. As she brushed it off her skirt, she discovered that one of her testicles had slipped away from its usual position against her perineum and was dangling outside of her panties. "Yuck," she laughed as she stuffed it back in, "a bit of my cunt was slipping out and I wasn't even noticing." . . . Tina, who was sitting with her back to Banana, looked archly over her shoulder and shot at her, "What bit of cunt, viado? It's a bit of your ball for sure that's slipping out. I never saw a piece of cunt with hanging wrinkled skin like that." . . . This kind of humor occurs regularly in travestis' conversations with each other, but it is risky humor, because no travesti will accept being called a man by somebody who she thinks says it to hurt her feelings. [pp. 204–207, Portuguese-language version of dialogue omitted]

From: Don Kulick, *Travesti: Sex, Gender, and Culture among Brazilian Transgendered Prostitutes.* Copyright © 1998. Permission granted by The University of Chicago Press.

Conclusions

Studies of the development of people's sense of themselves—who they are and where they fit in—make it clear that personality, identity, and subjectivity are complex aspects of human existence. Upbringing, relations with others, family forms, cultural discourses, language practices, and the inculcation of a society's beliefs about sex and gender form dense and complex environment within which humans are created and create themselves.

WORD PORTFOLIO

anatomy is destiny: the belief, associated with Freud, that the anatomical difference between the sexes is responsible for women's and men's different personality traits.

bilingual: being able to understand and speak two languages.

castration anxiety: a boy's fear that his all-powerful father will castrate him if he acts on his sexual desire for his mother. It motivates the Oedipal conflict.

diasporic peoples: groups of people forced or induced to leave their native countries.

Electra complex: the process that a girl must undergo, according to Freud, in order to develop proper feminine behaviors. It requires her to forgive her mother for her lack of a penis and to reestablish the mother-daughter bond. See also *penis envy.*

ethnic nationalism: a belief that an ethnic group has the right to be an independent or autonomous political unit.

ethnic group: a group of people, whose members identify with each other, based on belief in a shared ancestry and/or shared cultural, linguistic, or religious traits.

gender as performative: the idea that the subject is created through repeated performances of acceptable and conventional ideas about what it means to be a man or a woman.

gender identity: how an individual views him- or herself in relation to being male or female.

identity: how an individual views him- or herself in relationship to others.

identity politics: the use of group identity to forward a political cause.

interpellation: the process through which people come to recognize that they belong to a particular identity by identifying with the subject of language.

language ideology: ingrained and unquestioned beliefs about the way the world is and should be with respect to language.

multilingual: being able to understand and speak more than two languages.

muted group: idea applied to a group whose voices are silenced because their experiences are not easily expressed through the dominant communication system of their culture.

Oedipal conflict: the process that boys must undergo, according to Freud, in order to develop proper masculine behaviors. It requires the boy to renounce his attachment to his mother and to identify with his father. See also *castration anxiety.*

penis envy: a girl's jealousy of males because they have a penis and she does not. It motivates the Electra complex.

performativity: See *gender as performative*.

personality: the consistent behavior patterns and intrapersonal processes that are thought to originate in the individual.

primal horde: according to Freud, the first human group composed of an all-powerful, patriarchal father and a group of women to which he had exclusive sexual access.

regimes of truth: discourses that create a picture for people of what is true and what is not.

subjectivity: who we think we are and how we situate ourselves in the world.

third gender: a man or woman who is not forced to conform to one or two strictly defined gender identities.

RECOMMENDED READING

Women without Class: Girls, Race, and Identity, by Julie Bettie, 2002. Berkeley: University of California Press.
Julie Bettie looks at the lives of young white and Mexican-American women attending high school in central California. Exploring how these women use race and ethnicity to understand the differences between them, Bettie discovers that understandings of class difference are largely absent from their conceptions of self. Bettie suggests that class has not been developed as a category of identity in the same way as gender and race and proposes that researchers work to theorize class subjects in ways that also take into account other aspects of identity.

Language and Sexuality, by Deborah Cameron and Don Kulick. 2003. Cambridge: Cambridge University Press.
Looking at the complex relationship between language and sexuality, Deborah Cameron and Don Kulick present a range of research that demonstrates how our ideas about sex are deeply connected to how we talk about them. Defining sexuality broadly, Cameron and Kulick move beyond the emphasis on sexual identity present in much current literature and instead examine a variety of constructions and expressions of erotic desire.

Educated in Romance: Women, Achievement, and College Culture, by Dorothy Holland and Margaret Eisenhart. 1992. Chicago: University of Chicago Press.
Dorothy Holland and Margaret Eisenhart follow the lives of twenty-three black and white women as they attend college and enter the workforce during 1979–1987. Tracing the way in which these women's early academic and career expectations gave way to their involvement in heterosexual romantic relationships, the authors focus on the seemingly insignificant, everyday decisions that reproduce gender hierarchies and ask how culturally constructed ideas of romance affect women's academic and career success.

You Just Don't Understand: Women and Men in Conversation, by Deborah Tannen. 2001. New York: Harper Paperbacks.
Concentrating on gender-based linguistic differences between U.S. men and women, Deborah Tannen analyzes dialogues as part of understanding differences in conversational strategy and styles. She finds that women tend to engage in "rapport-talk," a style of private communication, whereas men are more likely to engage in public forms of speaking, which she terms "report-talk." Tannen's insights into gender differences in communication contributes to our understanding of the everyday social practices that create and maintain inequality.

11

Reproducing Gender and Difference

In this chapter you will . . .

investigate how sex practices vary across cultures • explore the idea that homosexuality is created through discourse • learn about queer theory • find out if there is such a thing as a family • look at differing ideas about motherhood • focus on how marriage practices in other cultures differ from those in the United States • examine how women's reproduction is controlled for state interests erhaps no phenomenon is as iconic of globalization as HIV/AIDS. As Dennis Altman has written:

AIDS fits the common understanding of "globalization" in a number of ways, including its epidemiology [how it spreads], the mobilization against its spread, and the dominance of certain discourses in the understandings of the epidemic. [2001:69]

As Altman chronicles, HIV/AIDS has been enabled by global population movements. Its dispersion follows the same pattern as other global flows, specifically the trade in illegal drugs. Its treatment has been hindered by neoliberal policies that have reduced public expenditures for public health care. Its transmission has been facilitated by social dislocation and poverty.

Attempts at its prevention have led to the increasing imposition of a Western biomedical model of health, disease, and healing on people and cultures around the world (Altman 2001). In this model, disease is thought of as emanating from the invasion of the body by outside organisms, and treatment is seen as something that attacks the invader. Also in this model, diseases are categorized and treated with standardized procedures that have been objectively validated using principles of the natural sciences, such as biology. Although the biomedical model excels at treating infectious diseases and injuries, it has been shown to be less successful treating chronic, multifac-

eted, and terminal illnesses, such as HIV/AIDS or cancer, diseases that are amenable "to multiple therapeutic interventions through a variety of systems of care, including biochemical, environmental, social, psychological, behavioral, and spiritual systems" (Cohen 1998:4).

Anthropologist Jean Comaroff (2007) also points to how HIV/AIDS is implicated in the global processes that shaped the twentieth century, adding an important dimension by showing the role Africa has come to play in Western nightmares about the emerging new world order of which HIV/AIDS was a part.

HIV/AIDS has had profound effects on people's sexuality and sexual practices, on sexual mores, on marriage practices, on women's reproduction functions and rates, on who raises children, and on how families are organized. And as is so often the case, women are differentially affected by these effects: as the majority of the world's poor, they are prone to higher rates of infection and greater disparagement for the shame the disease brings to their communities.

Much research in feminist and other twenty-first-century anthropology today focuses on the impact of global processes on sexuality, reproduction, and the family. This continues a commitment to analyzing these domains as important sites of power, which has characterized feminist anthropology since its inception.

In this chapter, we focus on sexuality, reproduction, marriage, and the family in traditional societies

Close-Up

11.1: HIV/AIDS as African Nightmare

Anthropologist Jean Comaroff (2007) argues that ideas about the disease reflect the world order that was emerging in the last quarter of the twentieth century: "the disease served as both a sign and a vector of a global order-in-formation," resulting from the restructuring of the geopolitical landscape after the cold war, of liberal-democratic nation-states and of capitalism itself (p. 198). In the United States, HIV/AIDS was conceptualized in a way similar to the other post-cold war enemies: a changeable, hard to pin down "deterritorialized invader," which could hijack our existence and terrorize the nation. Although Muslim terrorism emerged as a dominant intruder in this scenario, it is Africa, she argues, who came to stand for the other against which the West constructed itself in the new world order; in the process, colonial images of Africa as primitive were reasserted (p. 201). As Comaroff puts it: Africa once more

> becomes a site for European philanthropy [and paternalism] and adventurism. Once more it is depicted as a horrific exemplar of all that threatens the natural reproduction of life: mothers whose wombs incubate death, genocidal leaders who court dissident science, men who rape virgins—even babies—to rid themselves of infection, children bereft of innocence who are driven to preternatural sex and violence for profit. [2007:201]

HIV/AIDS reveals the human costs of economic and political marginalization, the limited impact of humanitarian intervention, the toll on an ever more monopolistic control over the means of life itself (pp. 201–202).

Reference

Comaroff, Jean. 2007. Beyond Bare Life: AIDS, (Bio)Politics, and the Neoliberal Order. *Public Culture* 19 (1):197–219.

as well as in today's globalizing world. We document a range of variation in people's conceptions of sex, sexuality, marriage, and the family and explore how they are embedded within the social and political context of a society. The goals in this chapter are twofold: to disrupt and complicate the idea that these aspects of human life are natural and that there are simple connections between sex, gender, and sexuality, and to expose the ideological basis of some widespread ideas about sex, sexuality, reproduction, motherhood, marriage, and the family that create and sustain difference. In other words, we will explore the politics of sexuality, reproduction, motherhood, marriage, and the family.

Traditional Anthropological Approaches

Since the nineteenth century, understanding the role of sex, reproduction, marriage, and the family in the development and perpetuation of societies has been a central concern to the entire discipline of anthropology. As you may remember, for social evolutionists such as Lewis Henry Morgan, new forms of family and social institutions—such as monogamy—lay at the base of Western society's progress and superiority. Although Marx and Engels did not extol the virtues of Western industrial capitalism, they too understood its development in terms of changing family forms: "mother right" societies evolved into capitalist societies through male control of private property, instituted through rules of marriage and inheritance that privileged men. Contemporary evolutionary theories posit that the very evolution of humans and human society rests on women's "loss of estrus" and its subsequent impact on female sexuality and women's role in childbearing and rearing. In each of these scenarios, ideologies of marriage and the family come together with assumptions about sexuality and gender to explain and maintain contemporary structures of power and difference.

Twenty-First-Century Anthropological Approaches

It is not surprising, then, that feminist and other twenty-first-century anthropologists have made ideologies of sex and reproduction, and of such social institutions as marriage and the family, central sites of analysis and critique. Many feminist anthropologists in the 1970s, as we have seen, argued that women's inferior status resulted from their association with nature because of their procreative role and their subsequent relegation to the private world of domesticity. Unlike social and contemporary evolutionary thinkers who made a similar case, they focus on how *ideologies* of sex, gender, motherhood, marriage, and the family have operated to exclude women from access to material and symbolic resources.

Just as feminist and other twenty-first-century anthropologists have revealed gender as a cultural construct, so, too, have they shown that sex and sexuality are ideological constructions. To do so, they have had to disentangle sex from gender, and sexuality from both sex and gender. They have contributed to this endeavor by exposing numerous instances in which sex, gender, and sexuality are not aligned according to the Western binary opposition—female and male.

A major part of this effort has involved revealing the way such ideologies naturalize women's roles. As we discussed in several chapters, arguments that assert a biological basis for the differential roles, behaviors, motivations, and aptitudes among groups of people naturalize these differences, making an unequal distribution of power, privileges, and resources appear nor-

mal and inevitable. Since marriage and the family are widely seen as based on the natural facts of reproduction and maternal instinct, analyzing these institutions has been of particular significance. Contrary to the claim that many anthropologists make, that the family is universal, feminist anthropologists have shown that what constitutes a family varies both within and across societies, as does how people think about motherhood and how they practice marriage.

Sex and Sexuality

In scientific discourses and everyday beliefs, Western thinking has understood gender as the natural outcome of sexual anatomy. The work of early sexologists and anthropologists, however, documented variation in how people think about, organize, and practice sex. This began to erode any simple ideas about the naturalness of Western conceptions. This early work was often discounted, and alternative sexualities were pronounced unnatural and deviant. Recent work by feminist and queer theorists has been particularly influential in rethinking ideas about normal and abnormal sexuality.

As we will see in the next sections, by the mid-twentieth century, studies of sexuality were already providing ample evidence of variation in sexuality in the United States, while anthropological studies revealed variation in sexual practices across cultures. Both sets of examples chipped away at the "anatomy is destiny" assumption.

Documenting Variation in Sexual Practice within the United States

In the 1940s and 1950s, American researcher Alfred Kinsey conducted an extensive survey of the sexual behavior of women and men in the United States. His findings, based on interviews, astonished his contemporaries. He found many people engaging in a range of sexual behaviors considered to be atypical by standards of the time. Masturbation and oral genital sex were found to be practiced by a significant proportion of the population. Kinsey and his associates also documented a vast number of both men and women who demonstrated at least some "homosexual response" over their lifetimes (Kinsey cited in Johnson n.d.).

Beginning in the 1960s, the work of sex researchers, William Masters and Virginia Johnson continued to produce unexpected results. Their research was an influential corrective to long-held heterosexist and androcentric beliefs about female sexuality. For example, their finding that orgasms result from clitoral stimulation, and that the phases of female sexual response are the same regardless of the source of stimulation, rejects the notion that a woman's full sexual satisfaction requires sexual intercourse with a man. Their studies indicated that women generally reach orgasm more quickly and with greater intensity from manual stimulation of the clitoris (Masters and Johnson 1966).

Although laboratory studies of sexuality and physiological sexual responses have discredited many old assumptions about sexuality and raised new possibilities, they are limited in addressing the varied and changing experience and meaning of sexuality for diverse individuals. With their focus on physical responses, Masters and Johnson privileged biology, and therefore did not go far to disentangle sexuality from sex. By the 1970s, feminists argued that sexuality cannot be reduced to objective measures about orgasms or divorced from its social and personal context. African American feminist poet Audre Lorde made the significance of understanding sexuality as more than a biological process abundantly clear. She identified "the erotic"—women's deepest sexual feelings—as a creative resource and basis of power (1984).

Documenting Variation in Sexual Practice Cross-Culturally

By focusing on a wide range of sexual behaviors found around the world, anthropologists also helped to call into question the naturalness of any one construction of sexuality. They revealed that there is great variation in the way people view sex in different societies. For example, there are differences in how people in different societies think about the importance of sexual foreplay to sexual satisfaction, the physical traits considered erotic, and their preference for sexual positions; whether same-sex sexual behavior is encouraged, tolerated, or completely prohibited; and the relationship of sexuality to ideas about violence. We focus on a few of these traits, especially those catalogued by Suzanne Frayser in *Varieties of Sexual Experience* (1985) and Patrick Gray and Linda Wolfe (1999) in their work on anthropological approaches to human sexuality.

Societies differ in terms of whether sexuality is seen as pleasurable or not. For example, in the Hawaiian Islands prior to the arrival of missionaries in 1820, a wide range of erotic pastimes were deemed desirable for members of the hereditary elite. Such activities as engaging in freely formed heterosexual and homosexual relations or having sexual relations with a sibling were permitted. Among Yap islanders (Micronesia),

Global News

11.1: China Survey on Teenage Sex Surprises Educators

A survey of 2,300 high school students in the Xuanwu district of Beijing found that half said there was nothing wrong with one-night stands and that an overwhelming majority of the girls would not reject a boyfriend's request for sex, *The China Daily* reported. The survey also found that six percent of the students had already had a sexual experience and that the average age of students losing their virginity was 15. The results surprised educators, the newspaper said. "The new generation is open-minded about sex," Zhang Meimei, a professor at Capital Normal University who was involved in the survey, was quoted as saying. "We can only conclude that it is a result of a fast-changing society." [by Ginger Thompson, Reuters 1/12/07, Late Edition-Final, Section A, p. 8] by contrast, sexual relations are seen as unhealthy, while for the Manus of Papua New Guinea even sexual intercourse between a husband and wife is considered degrading.

Some societies link sexual arousal with hostility and aggression. Among the Guisii of Kenya, for example, it is thought that a husband has to overcome, through force, pain, and humiliation, what is seen as women's natural resistance to sexual intercourse. In an early feminist study, Peggy Sanday (1981) found that sexual violence against women is related to constructions of masculinity and femininity in a number of societies. She found no incidence of rape, for example, in the ancient Ashanti kingdom of West Africa where women were highly respected and influential members of the community. By contrast, in societies like the United States, where men and boys are encouraged to be tough and aggressive and violence is tolerated, rape is prevalent. Violent sexual relations also can be found in societies in which the construction of masculinity calls for competition among men. Roger Lancaster has found in Nigeria, for example, that violence against women is "performed with two audiences in mind: first other men, to whom one must constantly prove one's masculinity and virility; and second, one's self, to whom one must also show all the signs of masculinity" (1995:140).

What is considered erotic also varies from society to society. Some societies, for example, view full nudity as repugnant while others find it highly stimulating. Some cultures prohibit any kind of same-sex sexual behavior while others do not. Bisexuality is socially acknowledged in some Melanesian societies, for example, while in some Arab societies, lesbian relations are acceptable as long as they occur between widows. These early studies of sexual variation helped to displace the idea that there is one natural form of sexuality. Since then, feminist and other twenty-first-century anthropologists have focused on how sexuality is related to power, domination, and oppression.

Discourses of Sexuality

Just as discourses have produced "truths" about the body, so, too, have they created sexual identities. Michel Foucault's ideas have been instrumental to how we understand sexuality and its relationship to power today. Discourses of science and medicine in the nineteenth century worked not only to construct ideal notions of the body but also to gain hold over sexuality. This process has had significant consequences

for how women and men experience their bodies and their selves. Susan Bordo describes how, during this time period, the incessant probing of the body and the mind of the patient for knowledge about sexual practices paradoxically forced sexuality inward, interiorizing it. What may have been just sexual acts prior to being subjected to science's scrutinizing eye became "perversions," as sexual behaviors were pathologized:

> The medicalization of sexuality in the nineteenth century . . . recast sex as a family matter into a private, dark, bodily secret that was appropriately investigated by such specialists as doctors, psychiatrists, and school educators. The constant probing and interrogation . . . ferreted out, eroticized and solidified all sorts of sexual types and perversions, which people then experienced (although they had not done so originally) as defining their bodily possibilities and pleasures. The practice of the medical confessional, in other words, in its constant foraging for sexual secrets and hidden stories, actually created new sexual secrets. [Bordo 1993:142–143]

Medical and psychiatric researchers produced knowledge of women's and men's sexual behaviors and declared certain of those behaviors natural, and others abnormal, based on standard assumptions of ideal femininity and masculinity. For example, women who displayed little or no sexual desire, but who, nonetheless, complied to satisfy their husbands' sexual needs and to have children, were deemed "good" women. In contrast, the sexual woman was viewed as sick, dangerous, and whorelike.

Freud believed that women's sexual fulfillment could only come about in the form of vaginal orgasm (as distinct from clitoral orgasms, which Freud considered "masculine" and childish) and the subsequent bearing and nurturing of children. Lesbian sexuality, according to Freud, was a neurosis based on lesbian women's inability to give over their early masculine identification with the clitoris, the "inferior penis," to the vagina, thereby rejecting their true feminine role as passive receptacles in heterosexual vaginal intercourse. Such "normalizing discourses" created women's and men's sexual appetites and behaviors as well as new identities.

Constructing Homosexuality

Nowhere has the effect of discourses on identity, especially "homosexual" identity, been more vividly illustrated than in Foucault's *History of Sexuality* (1980). Foucault argued that as people's sexuality became an important object of knowledge, medical and psychiatric researchers and practitioners sought and gained information about same-sex sexual behaviors, organizing them into a "discourse of homosexuality," deeming heterosexuality normal, and homosexuality abnormal. This created the very idea of "the homosexual." Before this time homosexual acts occurred, but same-sex sexual relations were identified by the name of the practice. For example, for men, these practices were referred to as "sodomy." The social *identity* "homosexual" did not exist (Foucault 1980). Medicine and psychiatry created this category of identity through organizing information about same-sex sexual relations under the heading homosexuality. In other words, Foucault revealed that homosexuality is an invention.

John D'Emilio (1997) has also shown that homosexuality has a history, coming into existence only under conditions of capitalism, but his analysis focuses more on a changing economic system. During the nineteenth century, the rise of capitalism led to the decline of household production in the United States, changing the meaning of the nuclear family, family life, and same-sex relations (p. 170). The family came to be seen not as the site of production but of emotional satisfaction and happiness. The decline in household production also loosened the link between sex and procreation as children were decreasingly needed for their labor power. As a result, D'Emilio argues, marriage became a site for intimacy and the center of one's personal life, providing the conditions for some women and men to organize their personal life around erotics rather than procreation. In other words, capitalism began to undermine the idea of families as natural, leading to autonomous individuals created through consumer and sexual desire. Eventually this led to new constructions of gay men's and lesbians' identity and the formation of gay and lesbian communities (p. 171).

The constructed nature of homosexuality is also evident when same-sex relationships are examined cross-culturally. For example, although the Sambia in New Guinea engage in same-sex erotic behavior, they have no word for homosexuality. For them, same-sex relations are part of a normal life cycle that begins with such relations but ends in heterosexual marriage. The Sambia believe that boys must be cleansed from the "pollution" of their mothers in order to grow and become men (Herdt 1997:xii). This is accomplished through a ritual system in which younger boys per-

form oral sex on older boys; the swallowing of semen is seen as providing them with the substance needed for masculinity. Later these young men take the role of inseminating even younger boys. Only then do they go on to marry and have sexual relationships with women, living the rest of their lives in a heterosexual relationship (Herdt 1997:7).

Race and Sexual Discourse

Siobhan Somerville has studied the connection between sexuality discourses in the late nineteenth and early twentieth centuries and the development of discourse of racial difference in the United States (1997:39). She shows how racial discourse provided a model for researchers trying to understand homosexuality. Just as discourses of race sought to locate difference in the body, so too did discourses of homosexuality. And just as the genitalia of the Hottentot Venus were taken as signs of a rampant and animalistic sexuality, the supposedly larger clitoris of lesbians was seen as an indicator of homosexuality. Like race discourse, sexual science used an evolutionary model to link anatomy to race, homosexuality, and primitiveness. The large clitoris associated with both homosexuality and black women positioned both lesbians and African American women as evolutionary throwbacks or primitives (p. 43). Models of homosexual desire were also likened to interracial desire: each was evidence of an abnormal choice of sexual object and therefore seen as perverse (p. 45).

Queer Theory

As we saw in chapter 2, the field of gay and lesbian studies that emerged out of the gay liberation movement in the United States in the late 1960s took "gay identity" as one of its central topics of investigation. By the 1980s, **queer theory** emerged as an outgrowth of lesbian, gay, bisexual, and transgender (LGBT) studies and critiqued LGBT identity-based scholarship on sexuality, seeing it as limiting and essentialist.

Queer theory questions all identity categories, such as heterosexual, homosexual, male, and female as fixed and instead places sexuality along a continuum. Queer theorists have argued that to understand the "homosexual" or "homosexuality," scholars must move beyond an exclusive focus on identity to an approach that emphasizes same-sex practices. Like Foucault, queer theorists argue that homosexuality is not a natural category; that identities draw on multiple axes of difference and are not fixed; and that sexual de-

Global News

11.2: Gays in Latin America: Is the Closet Half Empty?

Most analysts haven't noticed, but a major social revolution is taking place in Latin America. The region is becoming gayer. It's not that there are more gays and lesbians living in Latin America (we would never know). Rather, the region is becoming more gay-friendly. A generation ago, Latin America was the land of the closet and the home of the macho. Today, movements fighting for lesbian, gay, bisexual, and transgender (LGBT) rights are taking advantage of the region's more globalized, open regimes. They are promoting their cause through smart, mainstream political and economic alliances. So, though closets and machos are still ubiquitous, Latin America is now the site of some of the most pro-gay legislation in the developing world. . . .

. . . Change hasn't simply come on paper. Latin American cities are also becoming increasingly gay-friendly. The number of gay-owned or gay-friendly establishments (e.g., bars, support groups, services) per capita in Latin American cities is on the rise, with some cities outperforming even the most liberal Western capitals. . . . Nobody really ever thought the region was a gay desert, but there is plenty of evidence now that Latin America—at least legally and in urban centers—is coming out. [Javier Corales, *FP/Foreign Policy* 2/09; http://www.foreignpolicy.com/story/cms.php?story_id=4713 (accessed 3/31/09)]

sires, identities, and sexual practices do not always align (Corber and Valocchi 2003:1).

One of queer theory's most powerful concepts is that of **heteronormativity,** which refers to the set of norms that make heterosexuality seem natural and normal while homosexuality is constructed as its binary opposite. Heteronormativity constructs homosexuality as a deviation from heterosexuality, which is taken for granted (p. 4). The idea of heterosexuality, thus, depends on the idea of homosexuality for its very existence.

Some anthropologists, however, have cautioned against the use of the term "queer" because it does not acknowledge that women and men who engage in same-sex relationships are differently located. Lumping the two together, they warn, obscures gender hierarchies and women's oppression (Wieringa and Blackwood 1999).

The Sex/Gender System

Gayle Rubin's article, "The Traffic in Women," first printed in the important volume *Toward an An-*

thropology of Women (1975), strongly influenced the development of Queer Studies, providing a starting point for thinking about heteronormativity. Rubin argued that gender is not the inevitable outcome of biological sex differences; instead, sex differences are created by suppressing similarities between the sexes.

She argued that one way this is accomplished is through the development of a sexual division of labor that sees some tasks as women's work and others as men's work. This division requires men and women to join their work efforts, which, according to Rubin, ensures heterosexuality. But what is important about Rubin's argument for understanding heteronormativity is that she claims that the prohibition against incest, which regulates heterosexual unions, presupposes "a taboo against *non*-heterosexual unions." As she explains:

Gender *is* not only an identification with one sex; it also entails that sexual desire be directed toward the other sex. The sexual division of labor is implicated in both aspects of gender—male and female it creates them, and it creates them heterosexual. The suppression of the homosexual component of human sexuality, and by corollary, the oppression of homosexuals, is therefore a product of the same system whose rules and relations oppress women. [Rubin 2006:95]

Regulations about sexuality are part of what Rubin calls the **sex/gender system:** the set of arrangements by which a society transforms biological sexuality into products of human activity, and in which these transformed sexual needs are satisfied (1975:159).

In a later article, "Thinking Sex" (1993), Rubin elaborated on her idea of the sex/gender system, calling into question the idea of sexual essentialism. She argues that sexuality is not a consequence of gender, as Western thinking has supposed, but is constructed through a system of sexual stratification in which forms of sexuality are differently valued. This creates a hierarchy that legitimates some expressions of sexuality while persecuting others. Such ideas have been highly influenced by religious conceptions of what is and is not appropriate sexual activity (p. 35). As Rubin puts it, "Modern Western societies appraise sex acts according to a hierarchical system of sexual value" (1993:11). This system is as follows: marital, reproductive heterosexuality is valued the most highly. It is followed by unmarried monogamous heterosexuality, which, in turn, trumps the following: solitary sex; stable long-term homosexual couples; "bar dykes" and promiscuous gay men; transsexuals, transvestites, fetishists, sadomasochists, and sex workers; and, finally pedophiles. This valuation system is encoded in law, enforced by the state, and policed by medical professionals and popular ideas about appropriate and inappropriate sexual behavior.

Reproductive Politics

As we have seen throughout this book, because of their role in procreation, in Western thinking women's bodies have been associated with the natural. This construction has been used to deny them full participation in society and equal access to prestige, status, and resources. Because of procreation's centrality to the reproduction of social life, it has been a significant site of power and control in many societies past and present. Women have had their procreative functions regulated through political and religious ideologies in a number of ways: for example, in China state policies have restricted women to giving birth to one child in the name

of curbing overpopulation; in Germany and the United States, mentally impaired women have been forcefully sterilized, an action motivated by an ideology of eugenics; and in a number of countries, including the United States, women have been denied abortion rights based on religious ideologies and political stakes. Women have had their fertility controlled to meet the needs of states for centuries, making analysis of the "politics of reproduction" a central feminist concern.

State Control of Women's Reproduction

Population regulation has occurred throughout human history through the control of women's fertility. In foraging, horticultural, and small-scale agricultural societies, population numbers are regulated through women's own practices, such as long periods of breast-feeding, infanticide, or abortion. With the rise of the state, however, women's reproductive functions came under state control, to fit its needs of social and biological reproduction. In such cases, natal policies, laws, punishments, and incentives in accord with the state's own interests are instituted and enforced. At times, states institute policies to restrict the number of children women can bear, as in the case of China's "one child rule." In other cases, state policies and laws restrict women's access to birth control and abortion, at the same time offering them positive incentives to increase their number of children.

For example, David Horn chronicles how in Italy in the first half of the twentieth century population control became central to state goals, and reproduction became a "taken-for-granted object of scientific knowledge and medical intervention" (1994:5). During that time, Italy was understood as a national "body politic" plagued by the "disease" of infertility. This construction led to procreation being understood as a social, not an individual, problem, one that needed to be studied and managed by the government in the name of the good of society. The government instituted two types of interventions: directly oppressive "negative" ones that punished women who had abortions or used contraception, and "positive" ones, which encouraged marriage, childbirth, and large families.

Such state intervention into reproduction has recurred repeatedly throughout history. In Nazi Germany, for example, women were removed from the workplace into the home through a series of legislative efforts while at the same time they were provided increased maternity benefits and family allowances as the size of their families grew.

A billboard in China promoting "one family, one child."

Gail Kligman (1995) has focused specifically on documenting state intervention in population control in socialist Romania under the rule of Nicolae Ceausescu. Her example vividly illustrates the disastrous consequences of state control not only for women, but also for their children. Due to falling birthrates, policies encouraging women to have children were enacted in the 1960s: "contraceptives were banned, abortions were restricted, incentives were installed to encourage larger family size, and the virtues of motherhood were extolled" (pp. 234–240).

To ensure control, Ceausescu initiated a campaign requiring the health of women of childbearing age to be closely policed. Some women were given gynecological exams three times a year, while pregnant women who had had a previous abortion were confined to hospitals (Kligman 1995:243). As living conditions worsened under strict state control of the economy, it became difficult for families to feed the children they had, and consequently illegal abortion rates rose and with them women's death rate. Un-

wanted children were abandoned to the "care" of the state, which Kligman describes as, at best, systematic neglect, resulting in the "institutionalization of the innocent, the rise of infant AIDS, and international trafficking in babies and children through adoption" (pp. 244–245).

The consequences of reproductive policies without regard for the material conditions of life were severe; as Kligman puts it, "Many women were unable to fulfill their 'patriotic duties' and 'noble mission' in life, [giving] up their lives—and, frequently, those of their children in the service of the state" (Kligman 1995:246). Susan Gal and Gail Kligman have documented the significant role of reproductive politics in postsocialist societies after the fall of communism in 1989.

Stratified Reproduction

Racial, ethnic, and class differences are often used within a nation to empower some women to reproduce and nurture children, while disempowering others (Ginsburg and Rapp 1995:3). This is referred to as

Close-Up

11.2: Reproductive Politics after Socialism by Susan Gal and Gail Kligman

It is a striking fact about the collapse of communism in 1989 that abortion was among the first issues raised by virtually all the newly constituted governments of East Central Europe. In Romania, liberalization of abortion was the second decree issued by the provisional government upon the fall of the Ceausescu regime. Abortions' legality in East Germany and its restriction in West Germany almost derailed German unification. In Poland the question has become virtually a permanent feature of the parliamentary agenda. But abortion was only one of the issues associated with sexuality and human reproduction that have taken center stage since 1989. In the former Yugoslavia, rape was a weapon of war. Because women who had been raped and had children that resulted from rape were ostracized and rejected by their own ethnic groups, rape was also and intentionally a tool of "ethnic cleansing," through its tragic reproductive consequences. Unwanted babies became a political issue in Romania and Germany, but in different ways. A private adoption market in babies, not all of whom were unwanted by their birth mothers, emerged in Romania. The rate of voluntary sterilization increased dramatically among eastern German women, which produced a political scandal when it was noticed and labeled a "birth strike" by mass media. [From: Susan Gal and Gail Kligman, eds. 2000. *Reproducing Gender: Politics, Publics, and Everyday Life after Socialism*. Princeton, NJ: Princeton University Press, p. 215]

stratified reproduction. In the United States, for example, representations of minority women's fertility have been used historically and recently in the service of conservative political interests. Black women, Latinas, and poor women, in particular, have been viewed and portrayed as threats to the nation and its commitments.

For example, black "unwed mothers" were relentlessly demonized in the 1980s, represented as "welfare mothers" who undermined the nation's values by living "off the backs of taxpayers" through receipt of social assistance. This idea was successfully used as the rationale for withdrawing government support for the poor, who are primarily women and children. In 1996, the U.S.'s major support program, Aid to Families with Dependent Children, was dismantled.

Latinas have been negatively depicted as having "dangerous" and "abnormal" reproductive behaviors. In 1994, California adopted Proposition 187, called the "Save Our State" initiative, to deny undocumented immigrants social services, particularly prenatal care and education for their children (Chavez 2004). Although this legislation was eventually repealed, such policies have had severe political and economic consequences for Latinas and their children, despite a lack of evidence to support alarmist rhetoric about Latinas' reproduction:

> Latinas do not begin sexual activities at a relatively early age nor do they have relatively more sexual partners than Anglo women. . . . Most Latinas have used birth control pills at some point in their lives. . . . All Latinas have fewer than 2.0 children per woman. Mexicans who immigrated to the U.S. as adults and second- and third-generation Mexican Americans (U.S.-born) had fewer children . . . than their counterparts nationally. All U.S.-born Latinas had almost the same number of children as Anglo women nationally.

Age, education, and marital status . . . predict whether women have more or less children. . . . Ethnicity was an important, but not a statistically significant, variable for understanding fertility differentials in the 18–44 age group. [Chavez 2004:185]

In the U.S., depictions of poor white and minority women's dangerous reproduction have also been used to privilege other—mostly middle-class white—women's reproductive possibilities. For example, beginning in the 1980s, young, especially poor women who give birth on their own—outside of the American medical system—were portrayed as "monster mothers," who "stuff their children in garbage bags and take them out to the trash" (Tsing 1990:282).

Global News

11.3: After a Devastating Birth Injury, Hope

. . . [T]he bed was in a crowded hospital ward [2], and between the moments of laughter, Sarah Jonas, 18, and Mwanaidi Swalehe, 17, had an inescapable air of sadness. Pregnant at 16, both had given birth in 2007 after labor that lasted for days. Their babies had died, and the prolonged labor had inflicted a dreadful injury on the mothers: an internal wound called a fistula, which left them incontinent and soaked in urine.

Last month at the regional hospital in Dodoma, they awaited expert surgeons who would try to repair the damage. For each, two previous, painful operations by other doctors had failed.

"It will be great if the doctors succeed," Ms. Jonas said softly in Swahili, through an interpreter.

Along with about 20 other girls and women ranging in age from teens to 50s, Ms. Jonas and Ms. Swalehe had taken long bus rides from their villages to this hot, dusty city for operations paid for by a charitable group, Amref, the African Medical and Research Foundation. . . .

. . . Obstructed labor can kill the mother, too, or crush her bladder, uterus and vagina between her pelvic bones and the baby's skull. The injured tissue dies, leaving a fistula: a hole that lets urine stream out constantly through the vagina. In some cases, the rectum is damaged and stool leaks out. Some women also have nerve damage in the legs.

One of the most striking things about the women in Ward 2 was how small they were. Many stood barely five feet tall, with slight frames and narrow hips, which may have contributed to their problems. Girls not fully grown, or women stunted by malnutrition, often have small pelvises that make them prone to obstructed labor. . . .

. . .[W]omen with fistulas frequently became outcasts because of the odor. . . .

. . . Fistulas are a scourge of the poor, affecting two million women and girls, mostly in sub-Saharan Africa and Asia—those who cannot get a Caesarean section or other medical help in time. Long neglected, fistulas have gained increasing attention in recent years, and nonprofit groups, hospitals and governments have created programs, like the one in Dodoma, to provide the surgery. . . . [Denise Grady, *New York Times* 2/23/09; http://www.nytimes.com/2009/02; http://www.nytimes.com/2009/02/24/health/24hospital.html (accessed 3/31/09)]

Feminist anthropologist Anna Tsing reviewed several cases of such unassisted births and points out that even those in which the circumstances surrounding the child's death was unclear, women were charged with child endangerment and treated as criminals. Tsing connects these over-the-top depictions to the political climate in the United States at the time, including a growing antiabortion movement and an increasing number of women entering the labor force. Just as antiabortionists depicted fetuses as in need of protection from their own mothers, so, too, did they portray the babies of these "monstrous women" as needing to be rescued. This representation, as Tsing puts it, was "asserted in reaction to what was seen as female 'selfishness,' evidenced by women's increased participation in wage labor, career development, and political activity" (Tsing 1990:297).

State control of reproduction continues to be a hotly debated topic in the United States today. Although conservative political ideologies champion individual rights in relationship to the state, and seek to protect individuals from intrusive policies that might deny them the right to own a gun or fly the Confederate flag, such attitudes fall by the wayside when women's right to control their reproductive functions is in question. Proponents of "family values" have, since the 1980s, made their desire to make abortion illegal a cornerstone of their ideology and political efforts. Their larger agenda includes a belief in the superiority of families made up of married, heterosexual couples and their biological offspring, an ideal that continues to affect many women's reproductive decisions in the United States today (Stacey 1997).

These ideas affected women around the world in the Bush administration, a situation that has recently changed. Within his first week in office, U.S. President Barack Obama upturned two Bush administration policies: one had blocked $34 million that Congress had approved in 2002 for the United States to contribute to the United Nations Population Fund (UNPF); the other had banned U.S. government aid for family-planning organizations that promoted or conducted abortions. Obama pledged to reinstate the allocation to the UNPF and he signed an order reversing the Bush administration ban (Revkin 2009).

The Politics of Reproductive Technologies

From conception to birth, technology plays a role like never before in a women's procreative life. A woman's fertility can be enhanced with drugs, her eggs removed from her body and implanted in another's, the DNA of her fetus removed and tested for "birth defects," and, increasingly throughout the world, her child's birth monitored and assisted in a hospital. New technologies have so changed the face of procreation that a reproductive politics has emerged that reflects global inequalities. Reproductive practices and policies today unfold on a transnational landscape of inequalities where poor women's bodies are the testing ground for new birth control options for women in the Global North and the devaluation of currencies in the global marketplace make fertility drugs too expensive for importation to poor countries (Ginsburg and Rapp, 1995:1–7).

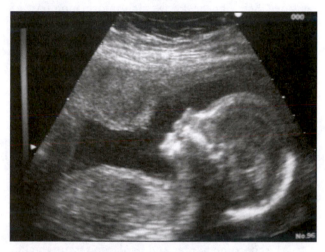

Health care professionals routinely use ultrasound scans for diagnostic purposes during pregnancy.

Biomedical practices and technologies affecting women's reproduction have both been welcomed and opposed by women around the world. Some have appreciated the chance to give birth in a hospital under sterile conditions while others, such as Inuit women of Canada, have resisted attempts to take birth out the hands of local women (see O'Neil and Kaufert, 1995). Feminists have organized locally, as well as on an international scale, to voice their concerns about new reproductive technologies and to exert pressure on policy makers. Women in India, fearing the differential abortion of female fetuses, for example, successfully waged a campaign against the use of amniocentesis—the extraction of genetic material from the amniotic fluid surrounding a fetus for genetic testing that we discussed in chapter 9—to determine the sex of an unborn child. Despite the 1994 ban on such tests, however, their use has become commonplace and female fetuses are routinely aborted. This practice of sex selection through selective abortion continues a trend that became marked in India in the 1980s: in 1981, the number of girls per 1,000 boys was 962; in 2001 that number dropped to 927 (Dugger 2001:12).

Debates over new reproductive policies can pit groups of women against each other, just as in the fight over abortion in the United States. U.S. women are also divided in their stance on the testing of fetuses for genetic diseases. Amniocentesis is now routinely used to test a fetus for a range of genetic abnormalities and diseases, and women are counseled to seek abortions if tests indicate their presence. Many women consider their right to know such information part of their reproductive freedom. Other women, particularly disability rights activists, argue that aborting a fetus is a new form of **eugenics,** selective breeding against undesirable traits. They argue that such practices narrowly define what is normal and desirable and perpetuate discrimination against those living with disabilities (see Rapp 2000). Many women wonder what will happen when genetic technologies are used not only to screen for potential diseases and disabilities but also to create "designer" children with "desirable" traits. The popularity of prenatal genetic testing has risen as both men and women have come to see a wide range of traits as biologically based and therefore inheritable (Browner and Press 1995).

It has become harder and harder to sustain the fiction of reproduction as a natural process in our world of highly technologized reproduction. Indeed, the body has now crossed into the realm of the **cyborg** (cybernetic organism), a part human/part machine organism, as such technological prostheses as pacemakers, artificial hearts, and ceramic hip joints become increasingly prevalent.

The feminist social scientist Donna Haraway has written a manifesto in which she argues that although the cyborg body created through today's technologization of the body and reproduction might be taken as just the latest imposition of the scientific domination of women, it should not simply be seen as oppressive. Instead, she suggests that we embrace it as an image of transgression:

> A cyborg world might be about lived social and bodily realities in which people are not afraid of their joint kinship with animals and machines, not afraid of permanently partial identities and contradictory standpoints.

The political struggle is to see from both perspectives at once because each reveals both dominations and possibilities unimaginable from the other vantage point. Single vision produces worse illusions than double vision or many-headed monsters. Cyborg unities are monstrous and illegitimate; in our present political circumstances, we could hardly hope for more potent myths for resistance. [Haraway 1991:154]

Haraway offers the image of the cyborg as a strategy for developing a new politics of human liberation. Yet, it is too early for celebration, making continued analyses of how women's reproduction is controlled and constrained in the name of power essential.

Views of Motherhood

Ideas about motherhood vary in different historical and cultural contexts and along dimensions of race, class, and ethnicity, affecting the meanings of mothering and mothering practices. Like gender, motherhood is deeply embedded in cultural ideas about femininity and masculinity. For example, motherhood is not seen everywhere as a necessary, exclusive, and primarily natural bond between a woman and her child, as it is largely conceptualized in contemporary North America and Europe. Some feminists have argued that this conceptualization instills guilt in women who participate in the public world of paid labor, maintaining the subordination of women (Sharon Hays cited in Barlow 2004).

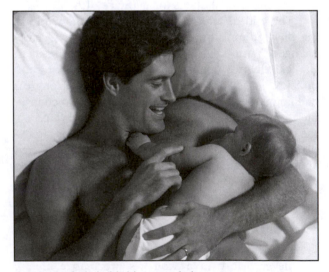

A man tenderly holds his young baby.

Others argue that the incompatibility seen to exist between motherhood and paid labor in the United States can act as a hegemonic discourse, affecting women's choices and their sense of self. Just as social evolutionists used women's role as mothers to justify development of the patriarchal family, so widespread beliefs about mothering today also condition the way we think about alternative forms of child rearing, such as dual or same-sex parenting and paid child care (Barlow 204:515, 518).

Women's role as mothers as we have seen, has led social evolutionists, Marxists, and many feminists to conclude that women's procreative functions can explain their lower status in society. Yet, the development of new reproductive technologies—including surrogate motherhood and in vitro fertilization—has made many people think differently about motherhood. More and more, today in the United States, a genetic mother and a legal mother have to be distinguished in the life of a child. In contrast, fatherhood, once considered "uncertain" compared with motherhood, can now readily be discerned through DNA testing. The way in which different forms of motherhood are understood and valued—whether genetic motherhood, surrogate motherhood, single motherhood, lesbian motherhood, or adoptive motherhood—reveals a good deal about underlying ideological notions about personhood and kinship. So, too, do discourses about fathers' rights

Feminist anthropologist Kathleen Barlow (2004) has shown that ideas about motherhood as a natural part of women's lives, as Freud proposed, are not universal. She documents alternative ideas and practices among the Murik of Papua New Guinea. In Murik society, mothers, fathers, and siblings are distinguished generationally, so that a woman's sister is also a mother to her child. Since women rarely devote sole attention to mothering, Murik cultural beliefs value shared child care. Children are reared in a group of related houslolds or in households with multiple adults and siblings, including men, all of whom participate in taking care of them. Although the Murik conceptualize mothering in ways consistent with U.S. ideals—a mother is a nurturer, a protector, and teacher of her children—this role is neither confined to women nor devalued. Instead, these maternal traits are seen as the model for the ideal person, existing in everyone, male and female.

For a child to become an adult, she or he must learn how and when to exhibit these attributes and how to use them to create and secure relationshiops based on exchange and obligation. These traits are seen as a road to power and prestige; as Barlow describes it: "she or he who provides food, gives resources, teaches, and protects is powerful whereas she or he who takes food, accumulates goods, lacks knowledge, or is unskilled is childlike, indebted, and weak" (p. 525). This set of beliefs contrasts sharply with those in the United States where the mother–child bond is seen as a natural one-on-one relationship, arising from a maternal instinct.

Feminist anthropologist Nancy Scheper-Hughes also calls into question the instinctual basis of maternal love in her powerful book, *Death Without Weeping: The Violence of Everyday Life in Brazil* (1993). The very poor and powerless women in the shantytown Alto do Cruzeiro, whom she studies, live in desperate conditions, plagued by severe hunger, chronic illness, and violence. Under these circumstances women prefer infants who struggle to survive and consequently fail to bond with their weak, listless babies during their first year of life, neglecting and expressing indifference toward them. Claiming that these infants have an aversion to life and are doomed to death, mothers do not feel grief upon the deaths of these "angel babies" and, instead, view their dying as a "blessing." Is this behavior unnatural? Inhumane? Scheper-Hughes suggests not: she sees these mothers' reactions toward frail children as a reasonable response to desperate circumstances in which there is a very high rate of starvation. Women nurture more vital infants who are more likely to withstand these deprivations, concentrating their economic and psychological child resources on them. This example demonstrates how cultural circumstances shape and condition not only maternal behavior but also emotions.

Reproductive technologies have gone a long way in calling into question the naturalness of motherhood. Surrogate motherhood and test tube babies are loosening the link between biological reproduction and motherhood. This connection is also increasingly challenged by the decision made by more and more people today to form families through adoption, to nurture and rear children who are not their biological offspring. In the United States in 2005, Americans adopted more than 20,000 foreign children.

Underlying ideologies about the biological basis of motherhood are tenacious in the United States. For example, Christine Gailey (2000) shows how the idea of motherhood as natural persists in assumptions about adoptive motherhood: that attachment through caregiving cannot substitute for connection through giving birth and that, therefore, adoptive motherhood is inferior to, and less real than, genetic motherhood (p. 18). Discourses about lesbian motherhood and single motherhood as inferior forms of motherhood reinforce heteronormativity and the underlying assumption of the nuclear family as superior.

A U.S. mother enjoys a special moment with her adopted Asian daughter.

Ellen Lewin (1993) has shown that when lesbian women make similar claims about motherhood as those of mothers in heterosexual marriages—that, for example, motherhood is at the core of their identity—they are able to claim a specific location in the sex/gender system (that of mother) in the United States otherwise denied them based on their homosexuality. This can also reinforce the hegemonic ideal that motherhood is essential to definitions of womanhood (Lewin 1993).

Global forces have had a tremendous impact on the structure of families and mothering all over the world. Transnational migration, for example, has greatly increased the number of children in poorer countries who are not raised by their biological mother or father. Unlike transnational migrant households in the past, transnational households today are the result of the migration of women and the feminization of the transnational labor force, which we discussed in chapter 7 (Parreñas 2006). In the Philippines

an estimated nine million children grow up in households where a migrant mother, a migrant father, or both do not live with them (Parreñas 2006). Filipino women who are forced to leave their children for employment are disparaged in their society and their children are portrayed as deviant and prone to drinking and drug use, despite the lack of statistics to substantiate this claim (Parreñas 2006).

Women who must leave their own children behind to find work elsewhere may feel the separation as deeply painful (Hondagneu-Stelo and Avila 1997). In their ethnographic study of Latina immigrant workers in California, Pierrette Hondagneu-Stelo and Ernestine Avila found that these mothers often fear that their own children are being harmed, neglected, and even abused by the caretaker back home or that they will lose their children's allegiance and affection to the "other mother" (1997:560–561).

Can Marriage Be Defined?

Anthropologists have long struggled to find a definition of marriage that has cross-cultural validity. Anthropologist Linda Stone suggests that it is impossible to define "marriage" cross-culturally:

> Anthropologists have learned . . . from a global, cross-cultural perspective, "marriage" is . . . extremely difficult, some would say impossible, to define. . . . It is true that virtually every society in the world has an institution that is very tempting to label as "marriage," but these institutions simply do not share common characteristics. [Stone 2004]

Exceptions can be found to almost all of the characteristics that people in the United States, Canada, and Europe tend to think of as defining marriage, even though these characteristics may seem fundamental to them. For example, doesn't marriage always involve a sexual relationship between spouses? Usually this is the case, but not always. In Europe cases of "celibate marriages" could be found among early Christians (Stone 2005). In addition, spouses often do not even live together. A separate residence of husbands in "men's houses," away from their wives and children, has been common in many places. Among the Nayar of India, wives and husbands remain in their own natal groups with husbands periodically "visiting" their wives; children are raised by their mothers and mothers' brothers. Indeed as Linda Stone (2005) puts it, the only feature of marriage that is apparently universal is that it creates intimate and highly charged interactions and a set of relationship with one's **affines,** those who are related to a person through marriage. But even so, affinal relationships are themselves varied.

Only recently has the question of marriage as a *heterosexual* union been raised in the United States. Although marriage in most places of the world involves heterosexual unions, there are important exceptions. Among the Nuer, and some other African groups, woman–woman marriages are sanctioned. In this instance, a woman unable to bear children could divorce her husband, taking another woman as her wife. The **female-husband** would then arrange for a surrogate to impregnate this woman, but the children would refer to her as "father" and become members of the female-husband's natal group. Among some Native American groups, males who preferred to live as women adopted the names and clothing of women and often became wives of other men.

A very young Sumatran girl, in her wedding dress, prior to the ceremony.

Daughter-in-law marriage is yet another form of women-marriage. It allows a woman unable to bear a son to marry the woman "who was always meant for her son." Children born to the daughter-in-law (impregnated by a lover) would be recognized as the heirs of the son (Wieringa and Blackwood 1999:5).

Debates about gay marriage have become particularly pronounced in the United States since 1996 when Hawaii agreed to allow them, even though ultimately this decision was blocked. Soon after, President Clinton signed the Defense of Marriage Act, refusing recognition of such marriages in other states, although Vermont has officially recognized the legitimacy of same-sex partnership since then, and several other states followed.

In 1989, Denmark became the first country to recognize same-sex relationships, and in 2005, Canada became the fourth country in the world to legalize same-sex marriage nationwide. As in the United States, many other European nations are still debating the issue (Altman 2001). In 2001, Colombia became the first Latin American country to legally recognize gay marriage.

Marriage differs along a number of other dimensions as well, each one of which creates significantly different experiences of marriage for women and men across cultures. Who is an acceptable marriage partner, how marriages are formed, and how many spouses one may have all vary considerably.

Whom to Marry

All societies have rules about with whom a women or man may have sexual relationships and whom they may marry. At a minimum, the incest taboo requires individuals to have sexual relations outside of the immediate family, leading to **exogamous marriage.** In most, but not all, societies, there are also rules about **endogamy,** which regulate into which group a person must marry. Sometimes these rules are explicit, as among Hindus, where marrying outside of one's caste is forbidden. Although only implicit, there is great pressure in many European societies to marry within one's own class, a circumstance agonized over by parents of all those young women in nineteenth century "domestic dramas," like *Pride and Prejudice.* Interracial marriage has been heavily regulated in a number of societies. In the United States laws have prohibited **miscegenation,** the marriage or cohabitation between people of different races. In 1958 one law against interracial marriage within the United States read this way:

If any white person intermarry with a colored person, or any colored person intermarry with a white person, he shall be guilty of a felony and shall be punished by confinement in the penitentiary for not less than one nor more than five years.

In many societies cousin marriages are preferred, frequently as a means of consolidating resources. The Bible, for example, describes the ideal marriage for Hebrews as one between a young man and his father's brother's daughter.

How to Marry

How one obtains a legitimate spouse has multiple variations too: in some societies, a prospective husband, with the help of his family, must provide his future wife's family with **bridewealth** or "bride price." Among the Zulu and the Swazi of South Africa, for example, bride payments in the form of cattle are required (Kuper 1988). Since in some societies, this "payment" gives the husband and his family rights to any children of the union, this practice is also sometimes called **progeny price.**

Bridewealth societies also offer some women opportunities. Among the Dahomey of Africa, for example, if a woman has enough to pay the bride price, she can take a wife and become a female husband with all the privileges granted to males in that society. Among the Azande of Africa a young man unable to obtain a woman for a marriage partner may make a bridewealth payment and take a boy as his wife until the opportunity arises for him to marry a woman (Evans-Pritchard quoted in Rubin 1975).

Among the Cheyenne, a group of Native Americans, marriages were contracted through an equivalent exchange of gifts between the two families, while in Japan a man could obtain a wife by having her adopted into his family and reared by his parents until she was old enough to marry. In some societies, as in the United States, couples might elope, although in some Native American societies this might be so shameful that the brother of the young woman might commit suicide. Many marriages continue to be arranged by the parents or families of the bride and groom, although this is happening in fewer and fewer places as the contemporary Western ideal of marriage as a union based on companionship and love spreads to all corners of the globe.

Today, it is even possible to order a bride. Mail-order brides have existed for some time. They are famous in depictions of the American "Wild West." The market in brides reveals inequalities between poor countries and wealthier ones, with women moving from their homes in the former to live with their husband's elsewhere.

Ethnography in Focus

Romance on a Global Stage: Pen Pals, Virtual Ethnography, and "Mail-Order" Marriage
by Nicole Constable

There are over 350 web sites whose stated aim is to introduce marriage-minded western men to foreign women. . . . The United States represents to some [Filipina and Chinese women] a place with modern amenities, modern government freer of corruption, and modern values and attitudes toward marriage and gender relations in contrast to the imagined shortcomings of the homeland. Although women are often attracted to the United States in part for its promise of modernity, U.S. men are often drawn to women from the Philippines and other parts of Asia for the promise of so-called traditional family values and gender roles. [p. 93]

* * *

Although meeting marriage partners from abroad is not new, the Internet has fueled a global imagination and created a time-space compression that has greatly increased the scope and efficiency of introductions and communication between men and women from different parts of the world. . . . This study focuses primarily on the views and experiences of Chinese and Filipino women and U.S. men who are contemplating [such] correspondence, in the process of correspondence, recently married, or about to be reunited. [p. 4]

* * *

Filipinas and Chinese women rarely objected to the idea that their relationships with U.S. men were related in part to political relations and the global flow of capital. U.S. men, by contrast, often objected strongly. Most men considered it distasteful to connect politics and market forces with personal lives and intimate relationships, or to propose that love might not be the single or most essential ingredient of a marriage. Women from China and the Philippines often articulated the importance of love, but were not so resistant to the idea that marriage involves personal and political considerations. [p. 116]

* * *

Simon's description of meeting Xaoli illustrates the blending of emotional and practical considerations into a relationship that is thinkable and attainable. . . . "My own choice to find a foreign woman started with practical considerations of the cultural type. In other words, I knew if I fell I love with someone who tended to view a husband as 'competition' or 'an obstacle to success,' we'd have big problems. . . . The Chinese idea of marriage is much like the America of 50 years ago, and I like it." [pp. 126–127]

* * *

For the women, meeting a foreign man was desirable for a number of practical reasons, but this did not necessarily preclude feelings of love. . . . Although Chinese women are often pragmatic about the appeal of foreign men and the desire to live abroad . . . they seemed unwilling to sacrifice themselves for "just any" foreign man, nor were they willing to forego the possibility of love, caring, and affective ties to their prospective partners. . . . Filipinas most often referred to foreign men as handsome and kind men who knew how to "take care of" their wives. [p. 134]

* * *

I argue that correspondence relationships are often based on ideals of romantic love or, at the very least, reflect attempts to define them in such terms. They are thus sorely misrepresented if boiled down to crude materialist motives. But it is also important to consider how and why love, romance, and marriage are linked—despite a strong American cultural reluctance to burst the fairy tale bubble and see it this way—to money, class and power, as represented by and embodied in nationality, race, gender, and place at a particular time. [p. 118]

From: Nicole Constable, *Romance on a Global Stage: Pen Pals, Virtual Ethnography, and "Mail Order" Marriages.* Copyright © 2003. Permission granted by University of California Press.

How Many to Marry

It might strike you as interesting that monogamy, or the marriage of only two people at a time, is not the most preferred type of marriage union in the world. In many places, **polygamy,** a practice in which a person may have more than one spouse at a time, is preferred, although this preference takes the specific form of **polygyny,** which allows a man to have multiple wives. Polygynous marriages exist throughout Africa and can be found among Muslims: Islam allows a man to have four wives. Polygyny is often a way for a man to acquire wealth and status. Bringing more women into the household increases the productive labor available to it as well as the number of children a man has, which is often a source of great prestige. In some societies, as among the Inuit, co-wives are often sisters.

Polyandry, which allows a woman to take multiple husbands, however, is extremely rare. In Himalayan regions, polyandry is related, at least in part, to scarce resources, which cannot support a large population. Even among some of the fiercest defenders of "family values" in the United States, strict monogamy is not enforced: a man may have several wives and a woman several husbands as long as they only have one at a time. This type of marriage practice is called **serial monogamy.**

What such marriages mean for the men and women of different societies also varies considerably, making it difficult to argue that women fare worse, for example, in polygynous societies than in monogamous ones. Monogamy can isolate a woman from her family and other women while polygyny offers women companionship and other women's help. Sometimes jealousy is rampant in polygynous households, and sometimes it is not.

Is the Family Universal?

Some anthropologists claim that the family is a universal institution, found in all places to fulfill the universal need for nurturing and rearing children. Yet, on close inspection, the notion of the family on which this claim is based seems to have a history; that is, this conceptualization can be shown to have come into being with the rise of capitalism and, therefore, cannot be some natural human formation based on some needs that all humans share.

Feminist anthropologists Jane Collier, Michele Rosaldo, and Sylvia Yanagisako make this case in their provocatively titled article "Is There a Family?" (1997). They argue that anthropologists who have made the case for the family's universality assume that all families share a basic set of characteristics: they are bounded units localized in a particular place that function to nurture children, and are based on emotional and affectionate bonds between a mother and child (p. 72). However, as the authors show, there is a basic flaw in this conceptualization: just "because a social institution is observed to perform a necessary function

does not mean either that the function would not be performed if the institution did not exist or that the function is responsible for the existence of the institution" (p. 73).

In addition, they argue that it is not at all clear that people in all societies make a distinction between, on the one hand, a mother and her children and, on the other, outsiders to this "basic unit." Many languages have no word for the unit of parents and children that we call "a family." The authors similarly find that "just as some languages lack words for identifying units of parent and children, so some 'families' lack places" (Collier et al. 1997:73). In some cultures, for example, men and boys live separately from their wives and mothers. What about the idea that love and affection cement familial relations? The authors find that this is an ideological construction that fits with the Western conception of a mother as loving and self-sacrificing. However, this characteristic of motherhood is not, as we've seen and as Scheper-Hughes has shown, universal (1993:74).

Instead, Collier and her colleagues (1997) show how each of these defining characteristics is based on a symbolic opposite, a set of binaries that helped conceptualize gender and sexual relations under capitalism. As we discussed, capitalism required a split between the public world of work and the private sphere of the home. As we have also seen, this split was buttressed by a wide array of ideological claims about who women were and what they could and could not do and who men were and what they could and could not do. In other words, both the market and the home were constructed in relationship to the other. If the world of work is based on competition, temporary relations, and underwritten by law, then the private realm of the family must be based on cooperative and enduring natural bonds of love and affection, and regulated by moral concerns.

Ideal forms of marriage and the family not only vary from society to society but also over time. For example, in the United States the nature of marriage, husband–wife relationships, parent–child relationships, family structure, and household structure have all undergone considerable transformation since the 1700s, and rapidly so since the 1960s (Coontz 1988). The 1960s saw rising rates of divorce, resulting in greater numbers of single-parent households. A rise in remarriage following divorce additionally brought about the growth of "blended families," or "brave new families" (Stacey 1998). Many children in the United

States today live in households with various combinations of step-parents and step-siblings. Others are raised in two separate households, where one or both may consist of a previous parent and a newer set of step-relations.

The 2000 census suggests the extent of these new family practices. According to Archer and Lloyd, by 2000 one-third of all households in the United States were composed of nonfamily members, that is people living on their own or with people unrelated to them (Archer and Lloyd 2002:162). Only 23.5 percent of all households in 2000 were composed of married couples with children under 18 years of age compared to 45 percent in 1960. The number of single-woman–child households increased by 25 percent during 1990–2000 (Archer and Lloyd 2002:162).

Lesbian and gay practices have had an important impact on how we think about family and family composition. As Kath Weston has described, the underlying notion of the family unit as natural and based on biological connections was called into question by lesbians and gay men. Encountering rejection from members of their biological family such as parents and siblings, they formed a range of new types of voluntary, nonprocreative families (1991:35). This reinvention of the family has linked gay men, lesbians, and straight men and women into new family configurations. Gay families have also broken the link between the idea of family and heterosexuality, giving way to a new conception of kinship as a relation based on personal choice and commitment (Stone 2004).

Conclusions

Whether to have children, how to have them, and with whom; whom to marry, how, and why; how to form families; and how to think about and practice one's sexuality are all aspects of life that vary around the world. These questions are fundamental to how people experience their lives and present the context within which they struggle, negotiate, and cope on a daily basis. As we have seen in this chapter, global forces are transforming reproductive and marriage choices and options for parenthood and family forms; as always, different groups of people have varying opportunities and constraints. Structures of power are deeply intertwined with cultural options. They dictate people's intimate lives, making continued analysis by feminist and other twenty-first-century anthropologists crucial for our understanding of power, domination, and change.

WORD PORTFOLIO

affines: those people to whom one is related through marriage; one's in-laws.

bridewealth: the goods or money that a man is required to give to a woman's family to gain the right to marry; also called bride price.

cyborg: a part human/part machine organism.

eugenics: selective breeding against undesirable traits.

endogamy: rule requiring a person to marry within a particular group.

exogamous marriage: type of marriage produced by a rule requiring a person to marry outside of a particular group.

female-husband: a woman, unable to bear children, who takes a woman as her wife.

heteronormativity: the set of norms that make heterosexuality seem natural and normal while homosexuality is constructed as its binary opposite, marked as different, and seen as a deviation from heterosexuality.

miscegenation: the marriage or cohabitation between people of different races.

polyandry: a marriage form allowing a woman to have multiple husbands.

polygamy: a marriage form allowing a person to have multiple spouses at the same time.

polygyny: a marriage form allowing a man to have multiple wives.

progeny price: the goods or money that a man is required to give to a woman's family to gain the right to marry her, granting the husband and his family rights to any children of the union.

queer theory: an approach to understanding sexuality that assumes that homosexuality is not a natural or fixed category, and that sexual desires, sexual identities, and sexual practices do not always align with the Western binary, male/female.

serial monogamy: a marriage practices allowing a man to have several wives or a woman to have several husbands as long as they only have one at a time.

sex/gender system: the set of arrangements by which a society transforms biological sexuality into products of human activity, and in which these transformed sexual needs are satisfied.

stratified reproduction: policies and practices that empower some women to reproduce and nurture children, while disempowering others.

RECOMMENDED READING

The Gay Archipelago: Sexuality and Nation in Indonesia, by Tom Boellstorff. 2005. Princeton, NJ: Princeton University Press.

Tom Boellstorff explores the connection between sexual subjectivity, global interconnection, and national identity in Indonesia. He argues that Western terms such as "homosexuality," "sexuality," and "gender" cannot adequately explain non-Western experiences of same-gender sexuality and identity. Instead, he develops the concept of *dubbing culture* as the practice of shaping identity and local meanings by drawing on cross-cultural media. The practice of *dubbing culture* challenges the idea of an "authentic" Indonesian identity, even as it is used to remake Western terms and ideas as uniquely Indonesian.

Margaret Mead Made Me Gay: Personal Essays, Public Ideas, by Esther Newton. 2000. Durham, NC: Duke University Press.

This collection of essays from one of the early scholars of lesbian and gay studies brings together more than thirty years of writing on a range of topics including drag culture, the performance of gender, the role of theater in gay communities, and Newton's personal reflections on her own butch identity. Her essays make critical contributions to the field of anthropology, including the role of the erotic in fieldwork, the social construction of homosexual identities, and the importance of gay and lesbian issues to the field.

Cross-Border Marriages: Gender and Mobility in Transnational Asia, edited by Nicole Constable. 2005. Philadelphia: University of Pennsylvania Press.

This collection looks to new and expanding forms of globalization and asks how they are connected to the increasingly common practice of cross-border marriages in Asia. Transnational marriage practices, the authors argue, are shaped by class, nationality, ethnicity, and gender, and embedded within existing cultural, historical, and political-economic landscapes. This analysis of cross-border marriage is critical to understanding new patterns of gendered migration and offers insight into how global hierarchies are affecting women's lives.

Ideologies and Technologies of Motherhood, edited by Heléna Ragoné and France Winddance Twine. 2002. New York: Routledge Press.

Bringing together a diverse set of themes as part of this edited volume, Heléna Ragoné and France Winddance Twine examine how the practices of motherhood are experienced differently, particularly in terms of race, class, religion, and nationality. The contributors cover a variety of topics central to our understanding of motherhood, including kinship, adoption, disability, personhood, choice, genetics, and identity. These essays examine how identity is transformed through motherhood and how particular forms of motherhood are reproduced.

Birthing the Nation: Strategies of Palestinian Women in Israel, by Rhoda Kanaaneh. 2002. Berkeley: University of California Press.

Providing a nuanced alternative to the often-dehumanizing representations of Palestinians living in Israel, Rhoda Ann Kanaaneh examines the everyday experiences of marginalization through the lenses of sexuality, reproduction, and family. Looking at family planning as a social process affecting ideas about economy, politics, body, and gender, Kanaaneh discusses women's imagination of community, the negotiation of modernity, and the relationship between identity and nationalism.

Epilogue

In September 2008, it became clear that the global economy was in crisis. Although the mass media identified "corporate greed" as the culprit, the unraveling of the global financial system that we are witnessing at the time of this writing calls into question the very legitimacy of the neoliberal paradigm. The neoliberal belief in a "free market," unencumbered by governmental regulations, has not resulted in the predicted prosperity for all; to the contrary, it has exacerbated inequities along traditional lines of difference, widening the gap between the haves and have-nots, both within and among nations.

There is little doubt that there will be greater suffering for women and children, people of color, workers, low-income families, the rural and urban poor, and indigenous peoples as the crisis grows. In many countries, the financial recession has already begun to spread beyond traditionally disadvantaged groups to affect higher income families as unemployment rises. And as more and more people are thrown into a deep sense of hardship and insecurity, there is increasing danger that political movements—especially reactionary ones that exploit people's xenophobia or fear that "foreigners" will take their jobs—will rise, increasing intolerance and violence.

The circumstance is bleak, but the election of Barack Obama as president of the United States is a testament to the transformative possibilities of political movements for equality. It suggests that if people, despite their differences, come together to fight for social justice, there is hope. An essential aspect of these struggles is to dig deep below the surface of political rhetoric and ideology, of accepted ideas and assumptions, to understand the forces that create and maintain inequities in all their complexity. Twenty-first-century anthropology offers a powerful tool for doing so.

References

Abu-Lughod, Lila. 1990. Writing Against Culture. In *Recapturing Anthropology: Working in the Present*. Richard Fox, ed. Pp. 137–162. Santa Fe, NM: School of American Research.

Abu-Lughod, Lila. 1990/91. Can There Be a Feminist Ethnography? *Women's Performance* 5:7–27.

Abu-Lughod, Lila, ed. 1998. *Remaking Women: Feminism and Modernity in the Middle East*. Princeton, NJ: Princeton University Press.

Abu-Lughod, Lila. 2002a. Do Muslim Women Need Saving? *American Anthropologist* 104 (3):783–790.

Abu-Lughod, Lila. 2002b. Egyptian Melodrama: Technology of the Modern Subject? In *Media Worlds: Anthropology on New Terrain*. Faye Ginsburg, Lila Abu-Lughod and Brian Larkin, eds. Pp. 115–133 Berkeley: University of California Press.

Altman, Dennis. 2001. *Global Sex*. Chicago: University of Chicago Press.

Anderson, Terry H. 1995. *The Movement and the Sixties: Protest in America from Greensboro to Wounded Knee*. New York: Oxford University Press.

Andriolo, Karin. 1998. Gender and the Cultural Construction of Good and Bad Suicides. *Suicide and Life-Threatening Behavior* 28 (1):37–49.

Anzaldúa, Gloria. 1987. *Borderlands/La Frontera: The New Mestiza*. San Francisco: Aunt Lute Books.

Archer, John and Barbara Lloyd. 2002. *Sex and Gender*. 2nd ed. Cambridge: Cambridge University Press.

Ardener, Shirley, ed. 1975. *Perceiving Women*. London: Malaby.

Aristotle. 1943. *The Generation of Animals*. Vols.1 and 4. A. L. Peck, trans. Cambridge, MA: Harvard University Press.

Atwood, Margaret. 1985. *The Handmaid's Tale*. Boston: Houghton Mifflin.

Babcock, Barbara. 1995. "Not in the Absolute Singular": Rereading Ruth Benedict. In *Women Writing Culture*. Ruth Behar and Deborah Gordon, eds. Pp. 104–130. Berkeley: University of California Press.

Bachofen, J. J. 1861 [1992]. *Myth, Religion, and Mother Right: Selected Writings of J. J. Bachofen*. Ralph Manhein, trans. Princeton, NJ: Princeton University Press.

Bamberger, Joan. 1974. The Myth of Matriarchy: Why Men Rule in Primitive Society. In *Woman, Culture, & Society*. Michelle Zimbalist Rosaldo and Louise Lamphere, eds. Pp. 263–280. Stanford, CA: Stanford University Press.

Banks, Ingrid. 2000. *Hair Matters: Beauty, Power and Black Women's Consciousness*. New York: NYU Press.

Barlow, Kathleen. 2004. Critiquing the "Good Enough" Mother: A Perspective Based on the Murik of Papua New Guinea. *Ethos* 32 (4):514–537.

Basow, Susan. 1992. *Gender: Stereotypes and Roles*. Pacific Grove, CA: Brooks/Cole.

Baumgardner, Jennifer and Amy Richards. 2000. *Manifesta: Young Women, Feminism, and the Future*. New York: Farrar Straus & Giroux.

Baxandall, Rosalyn and Linda Gordon. 2000. *Dear Sisters: Dispatches from the Women's Liberation Movement*. New York: Basic Books.

Beauvoir, Simone de. 1953 [1949]. *The Second Sex*. H. M. Parshley, ed. and trans. New York: Knopf.

Beck, Ulrich. 2000. *The Brave New World of Work*. Cambridge: Polity Press.

Becker, Anne E. 1995. *Body, Self, and Society: The View from Fiji*. Philadelphia: University of Pennsylvania Press.

Behar, Ruth. 1994. *Translated Woman: Crossing the Border with Esperanza's Story*. Boston: Beacon Press.

Behar, Ruth. 1997. *The Vulnerable Observer: Anthropology That Breaks Your Heart*. Boston: Beacon Press.

Berend, Ivan T. 2006. *An Economic History of Twentieth-Century Europe*. Cambridge: Cambridge University Press.

Black, Pamela and Ursula Sharma. 2001. Men are Real, Women are "Made Up": Beauty Therapy and the Construction of Femininity, *Sociological Review* 49:100–116.

Boddy, Janice. 1997. Womb as Oasis: The Symbolic Context of Pharonic Circumcision in Rural Northern Sudan. In

The Gender/Sexuality Reader: Culture, History, Political Economy. Roger N. Lancaster and Micaela di Leonardo, eds. Pp. 310–324. New York: Routledge.

Bogdan, Robert. 1988. *Freak Show: Presenting Human Oddities for Amusement and Profit.* Chicago: University of Chicago Press.

Bolles, Lynn. 1996. *Sister Jamaica: A Study of Women, Work and Households in Kingston.* Lanham, MD: University Press of America.

Bolles, Lynn. 2001. Seeking the Ancestors: Forging a Black Feminist Tradition in Anthropology. In *Black Feminist Anthropology: Theory, Politics, Praxis, and Poetics.* Irma McClaurin, ed. Pp. 24–48. Piscataway, NJ: Rutgers University Press.

Bordo, Susan. 1993. *Unbearable Weight: Feminism, Western Culture, and the Body.* Berkeley: University of California Press.

Bordo, Susan. 1999. *The Male Body.* New York: Farrar, Straus and Giroux.

Boris, Eileen and Elisabeth Prügl, eds. 1996. *Homeworkers in Global Perspective.* New York: Routledge.

Boserup, Esther. 1970. *Women's Role in Economic Development.* London: Allen and Unwin.

Bossen, Laurel. 1984. *The Redivision of Labor: Women and Economic Choice in Four Guatemalan Communities.* Albany: State University of New York Press.

Bourdieu, Pierre. 1977. *Outline of a Theory of Practice.* Cambridge: Cambridge University Press.

Bourdieu, Pierre. 1984. *Distinction: A Social Critique of the Judgement of Taste.* R. Nice, trans. London: Routledge.

Bourdieu, Pierre.1986. The Forms of Capital. In *Handbook of Theory and Research for the Sociology of Education.* John Richardson, ed. Pp. 241–258. New York: Greenwood Press.

Bourdieu, Pierre. 1993. *The Field of Cultural Production.* New York: Columbia University Press.

Bourdieu, Pierre and J.-C. Passeron. 1977. *Reproduction in Education, Society and Culture.* London: Sage.

Brah, Avtar. 2003. Diaspora, Borders, and Transnational Identities. In *Feminist Postcolonial Theory: A Reader.* Reina Lewis and Sara Mills, eds. Pp. 613–634. New York: Routledge.

Breckenridge, C. and A. Appadurai. 1989. On Moving Targets. *Public Culture* 2 (1):i–iv.

Brennan, Denise. 2004. Women Work, Men Sponge, and Everyone Gossips: Macho Men and Stigmatized/ing Women in a Sex Tourist Town. *Anthropological Quarterly* 77 (4):705–733

Brettell, Caroline and Carolyn Sargent, eds. 2005. *Gender in Cross-Cultural Perspective.* 4th ed. Upper Saddle River, NJ: Prentice-Hall.

Brown, Judith. 1970. A Note on the Division of Labor by Sex. *American Anthropologist* 72 (5):1073–1078.

Brown, Susan. 1975. Love Unites Them and Hunger Separates Them: Poor Women in the Dominican Republic. In *Toward an Anthropology of Women.* Rayna R. Reiter, ed. Pp. 322–332. New York: Monthly Review Press.

Browner, Carole and Nancy Ann Press. 1995. The Normalization of Prenatal Diagnostic Testing. In *Conceiving the New World Order.* Faye Ginsburg and Rayna Rapp, eds. Pp. 307–322. Berkeley: University of California Press.

Bucholtz, Mary. 1999. Why be Normal?: Language and Identity Practices in a Community of Nerd Girls. *Language in Society* 28 (2):203–225.

Bunch, Charlotte. 1972. Lesbians in Revolt. *The Furies: Lesbian/Feminist Monthly* 1 (January):8–9.

Burton, F. 1972. Sexual Climax in Female *Macaca mulatta.* Proceedings of the Third World International Congress of Primatology 3:180–191.

Butchart, Alexander. 1998. *The Anatomy of Power: European Constructions of the African Body.* London: Zed Books.

Butler, Judith. 1990. *Gender Trouble: Feminism and the Subversion of Identity.* New York: Routledge. Reprinted 2007, 2008.

Cameron, Deborah. 2001. Current Debates on Language and Globalization. Faculty Seminar Fall. http://www.depauw.edu/univ/facevents/language.html (accessed 8/2/07).

Castells, M. 1997. *The Power of Identity,* Vol. II of *The Information Age: Economy, Society and Culture.* Malden, MA: Blackwell.

Chavez, Leo. 2004. Glass Half Empty: Latina Reproduction and Public Discourse. *Human Organization* 63 (2):173–188.

Chernela, Janet. 2003. Language Ideology and Women's Speech: Talking Community in the Northwest Amazon. *American Anthropologist* 105 (4):794–806.

Chodorow, Nancy. 1974. Family Structure and Feminine Personality. In *Woman, Culture, & Society.* Michelle Zimbalist Rosaldo and Louise Lamphere, eds. Pp. 43–66. Stanford, CA: Stanford University Press.

Christen, Robert Peck, Richard Rosenberg and Veena Jayadeva. 2004. Financial Institutions with a Double-Bottom Line: Implications for the Future of Microfinance. CGAP Occasional Paper, July.

Cixous, Hélène. 1981. Laugh of the Medusa. In *New French Feminisms.* Elaine Marks and Isabelle de Courtivron, eds. Pp. 254–264. New York: Schocken Books.

Clark, Gracia. 2000. Mothering, Work, and Gender in Urban Asante Ideology and Practice. *American Anthropologist* 101 (4):717–729.

Clifford, James. 1997. *Routes: Travel and Translation in the Late Twentieth Century.* Cambridge, MA: Harvard University Press.

Clinton, William. 1997. Remarks by the President in Apology for Study Done in Tuskegee. http://clinton4.nara.gov/textonly/New/Remarks/Fri/19970516-898.html (accessed 5/26/03).

Cohen, Colleen B. and Frances E. Mascia-Lees. 1993. The British Virgin Islands as Nation and Destination: Representing and Siting Identity in a Post-Colonial Caribbean. *Social Analysis* 33:130–151.

Cohen, Michael. 1998. *Complementary and Alternative Medicine: Legal Boundaries and Regulatory Perspectives.* Baltimore, MD: Johns Hopkins University Press.

Cole, Sally. 1995. Ruth Landes and the Early Ethnography of Race and Gender. In *Women Writing Culture*. Ruth Behar and Deborah Gordon, eds. Pp. 166–185. Berkeley: University of California Press.

Collier, Jane. 1974. Women in Politics. In *Woman, Culture, & Society*. Michelle Zimbalist Rosaldo and Louise Lamphere, eds. Pp. 89–96. Stanford, CA: Stanford University Press.

Collier, Jane, Michele Rosaldo and Sylvia Yanagisako. 1997. Is There a Family? New Anthropological Views. In *The Sex/Gender Reader*. Roger Lancaster and Micaela di Leonardo, eds. Pp. 71–81. New York: Routledge.

Collins, Jane. 2002a. Mapping a Global Labor Market: Gender and Skill in the Globalizing Garment Industry. *Gender and Society* 16 (6):921–940.

Collins, Jane. 2002b. Deterritorialization and Workplace Culture. *American Ethnologist* 29 (1):151–71.

Collins, Patricia Hill. 2000. *Black Feminist Thought*. 2nd ed. New York: Routledge.

Comaroff, Jean. 2007. Beyond Bare Life: AIDS, (Bio)Politics, and the Neoliberal Order. *Public Culture* 19 (1):197–219.

Conboy, Katie, Nadia Medina and Sarah Stanbury. 1997a. Introduction. In *Writing on the Body: Female Embodiment and Feminist Theory*. K. Conboy, N. Medina and S. Stanbury, eds. Pp. 1–12. New York: Columbia University Press.

Conboy, Katie, Nadia Median and Sarah Stanbury, eds. 1997b. *Writing on the Body*. New York: Columbia University Press.

Conkey, Margaret. 2005. The Archaeology of Gender Today: New Vistas, New Challenges. In *Gender in Cross-Cultural Perspective*. 4th ed. Caroline Brettell and Carolyn Sargent, eds. Pp. 53–62. Upper Saddle River, NJ: Prentice Hall.

Connell, Robert. 1987. *Gender and Power*. Cambridge: Polity Press.

Coontz, Stephanie. 1988. *The Social Origins of Private Life: A History of American Families, 1600–1900*. New York: Verso.

Corber, Robert and Stephen Valocchi. 2003. *Queer Studies: An Interdisciplinary Reader*. Malden, MA: Blackwell.

Crane, Diana. 2000. *Fashion and its Social Agendas: Class, Gender, and Identity in Clothing*. Chicago: University of Chicago Press.

Crehan, Kate. 2002. *Gramsci, Culture and Anthropology*. Berkeley: University of California Press.

Cummins, H. J. 2002. The Lying Game. *Star Tribune,* February 18:E8.

D'Emilio, John. 1997. Capitalism and Gay Identity. In *The Sex/Gender Reader*. Roger Lancaster and Micaela di Leonardo, eds. Pp.169–178. New York: Routledge.

Dahl, Gudrum. 1987. Women in Pastoral Production: Some Theoretical Notes on Roles and Resources. *Ethnos* 52 (1-2):246–279.

Darwin, Charles. 1871. *The Descent of Man and Selection in Relation to Sex*. London: Murray.

Dawkins, Richard. 1976. *The Selfish Gene*. New York: Oxford University Press.

DeMello, Margo. 2000. *Bodies of Inscription: A Cultural History of the Tattoo*. Durham, NC: Duke University Press.

DeMeo, James. 2003. The Geography of Genital Mutilations. In *Constructing Sexualities: Readings in Sexuality, Gender, and Culture*. Suzanne LaFont, ed. Pp. 120–126. Upper Saddle River, NJ: Prentice-Hall.

Dentan, Robert 1986. *The Semai: A Nonviolent People of Malaya*. New York: Holt, Rinehart, and Winston.

di Leonardo, Micaela. 1991. *Gender at the Crossroads of Knowledge: Feminist Anthropology in the Postmodern Era*. Berkeley: University of California Press.

di Leonardo, Micaela. 1997a. The Female World of Cards and Holidays: Women, Families, and the Work of Kinship. In *Gender in Cross-Cultural Perspective*. 2nd ed. Caroline Brettell and Carolyn Sargent, eds. Pp. 340–350. Upper Saddle River, NJ: Prentice-Hall.

di Leonardo, Micaela. 1997b. White Lies, Black Myths: Rape, Race, and the Black "Underclass." In *The Gender/Sexuality Reader*. Micaela di Leonardo and Roger Lancaster, eds. Pp. 53–68. New York: Routledge.

Diamond, Irene and Lee Quinby. 1988. Introduction. In *Feminism and Foucault: Reflections on Resistance*. Irene Diamond and Lee Quinby, eds. Pp. ix–xx. Boston: Northeastern University Press.

Dossa, Parin. 2004. *Politics and Poetics of Migration: Narratives of Iranian Women from the Diaspora*. Toronto: Canadian Scholars Press.

Douglas, Mary. 1966. *Purity and Danger*. London: Routledge and Kegan Paul.

Douglas, Mary. 1970. *Natural Symbols*. New York: Vintage Books.

Dreyfus, Hubert and Paul Rabinow. 1982. *Michel Foucault, Beyond Structuralism and Hermeneutics*. Chicago: University of Chicago Press.

Dua, Enakshi. 1999. Canadian Anti-Racist Feminist Thought: Scratching the Surface of Racism. In *Scratching the Surface: Canadian Anti-Racist Feminist Thought*. Enakshi Dua and Angela Robertson, eds. Pp. 7–31. Toronto: Women's Press.

Duffy, Kevin. 1996. *Children of the Forest*. Long Grove, IL: Waveland Press.

Dugger, Celia. 2001. Abortion in India Spurred by Sex Test Skew the Ratio Against Girls. *New York Times,* April 22:12.

Edelman, Marc and Angelique Haugerud. 2005. Introduction. In *Anthropology of Development and Globalization*. Marc Edelman and Angelique Haugerud, eds. Pp. 1–74. Malden, MA: Blackwell.

Ember, Carol and Melvin Ember. 1994. War, Socialization, and Interpersonal Violence. *Journal of Conflict Resolution* 38 (4):620–6.

Endicott, Kirk and Karen Endicott. 2008. *The Headman Was a Woman: The Gender Egalitarian Batek of Malaysia*. Long Grove, IL: Waveland Press.

Engels, Friedrich. 1884 [1978]. Excerpt from *The Origin of the Family, Private Property and the State* (1884). In *The Marx-Engels Reader*. 2nd ed. Robert C. Tucker, ed. Pp. 734–758. New York: W.W. Norton.

Enloe, Cynthia. 1989. *Bananas, Beaches and Bases: Making Feminist Sense of International Politics*. London: Pandora.

Enslin, Elizabeth. 1994. Beyond Writing: Feminist Practice and the Limitations of Ethnography. *Cultural Anthropology* 9 (4):537–568.

Eriksen, Thomas Hylland. 1999. Globalization and the Politics of Identity. *UN Chronicle*. http://folk.uio.no/geirthe/UNChron.html (accessed 8/3/07).

Evans, Mary. 1995. *Introducing Contemporary Feminist Thought*. Malden, MA: Blackwell.

Falk, Dean. 1997. Brain Evolution in Females: An Answer to Mr. Lovejoy. In *Women in Human Evolution*. Lori D. Hager, ed. Pp. 114–136. London: Routledge.

Faludi, Susan. 1991. *Backlash: The Undeclared War against American Women*. New York: Crown Books.

Fausto-Sterling, Anne. 2000a. *Sexing the Body: Gender Politics and the Construction of Sexuality*. New York: Basic Books.

Fausto-Sterling. Anne. 2000b. Beyond Difference: Feminism and Evolutionary Psychology. In *Alas, Poor Darwin: Arguments against Evolutionary Psychology*. Hilary Rose and Steven Rose, eds. Pp. 209–227. New York: New York: Harmony Books.

O'Neil, John and Patricia Leyland Kaufert. 1995. Irniktakpunga!: Sex Determination and the Inuit Struggle for Birthing Rights in Northern Canada. In *Conceiving the New World Order*. Faye Ginsburg and Rayna Rapp, eds. Pp. 59–73. Berkeley: University of California Press.

Fedigan, Linda. 1982. *Primate Paradigms: Sex Roles and Social Bonds*. Montreal: Eden Press.

Fedigan, Linda. 1986. The Changing Role of Women in Models of Human Evolution. *Annual Review of Anthropology* 15:25–66.

Fernandez-Kelly, Patricia. 1989. *For We Are Sold, I and My People: Women and Industry in Mexico's Frontier*. New York: State University of New York Press.

Ferree, Myra Marx, Judith Lorber and Beth B. Hess, eds. 1999. *Revisioning Gender*. Thousand Oaks, CA: Sage.

Finn, Janet. 1995. Ella Cara Deloria and Mourning Dove: Writing for Cultures, Writing against the Grain. In *Women Writing Culture*. Ruth Behar and Deborah Gordon, eds. Pp. 131–147. Berkeley: University of California Press.

Foucault, Michel. 1979. *Discipline and Punish: The Birth of the Prison*. Alan Sheridan, trans. New York: Vintage Books.

Foucault, Michel. 1980. *The History of Sexuality: Volume 1: An Introduction*. Robert Hurley, trans. New York: Vintage Books.

Foucault, Michel. 1994. Truth and Power. In *Power*. James Faubion, ed. Pp. 111–133. New York: The New Press.

Frank, Gelya. 1995. The Ethnographic Films of Barbara Myerhoff: Anthropology, Feminism, and the Politics of Jewish Identity. In *Women Writing Culture*. Ruth Behar and Deborah Gordon, eds. Pp. 207–232. Berkeley: University of California Press.

Frayser, Suzanne. 1985. *Varieties of Sexual Experience*. New Haven: Human Relations Area Files Press.

Freeman, Carla. 1993. Designing Women: Corporate Discipline and Barbados's Off-Shore Pink-Collar Sector. *Cultural Anthropology* 8 (2):169–186.

Freeman, Carla. 2001. Is Local: Global as Feminine: Masculine? Rethinking the Gender of Globalization. *Signs: Journal of Women in Culture and Society* 26 (4):1007–1037.

Freeman, Jo. 1971. *The Women's Liberation Movement: Its Origin, Structures and Ideals*. Pittsburgh: Know, Inc.

Freize, I., J. Parsons, P. Johnson, D. Ruble and G. Zellman. 1978. *Women and Sex Roles: A Social Psychological Perspective*. New York: Norton.

Freud, Sigmund. 1918. *Totem and Taboo*. London: Hogarth.

Freud, Sigmund. [1933] 1965. *New Introductory Lectures in Psychoanalysis*. J. Strachey, ed. and trans. New York: Norton.

Friedan, Betty. 1963. *The Feminine Mystique*. New York: Dell.

Friedman, David M. 2001. *A Mind of Its Own: A Cultural History of the Penis*. New York: The Free Press.

Friedman, Jonathan. 2003. Globalizing Languages: Ideologies and Realities of the Contemporary Global System. *American Anthropologist* 105(4):744–752.

Fukuyama, Francis. 2002. *Our Postmodern Future: Consequences of the Biotechnology Revolution*. New York: Farrar, Straus, & Giroux.

Gailey, Christine W. 1998. Feminist Methods. In *Handbook of Methods in Cultural Anthropology*. H. Russell Bernard, ed. Pp. 203–234. Walnut Creek, CA: Altamira.

Gailey, Christine Ward. 2000. Ideologies of Motherhood and Kinship in the United States. In *Ideologies and Technologies of Motherhood: Race, Class, Sexuality, Nationalism*. Heléna Ragoné and Frances Winddance Twine, eds. Pp. 11–55. New York: Routledge.

Gal, Susan and Gail Kligman. 2000: *The Politics of Gender after Socialism*. Princeton, NJ: Princeton University Press.

Garcia, Alma M. and Mario T. Garcia. 1997. *Chicana Feminist Thought: The Basic Historical Writings*. London: Routledge.

Garwood, Shae. 2005. Politics at Work: Transnational Advocacy Networks and the Global Garment Industry. *Gender and Development* 13 (3):21–33.

Geertz, Clifford. 1973. *The Interpretation of Cultures*. New York: Basic Books.

Gero, Joan. 1985. Socio-politics of Archaeology and the Woman-at-Home Ideology. *American Anthropologist* 50:342–350.

Gibson, Kari. 2004. English-Only Court Cases Involving the U.S. Workplace: The Myths of Language Use and the Homogenization of the Bilingual Workers' Identities. *Second Language Studies* 22 (2):1–60.

Giddens, Anthony. 1990. *The Consequences of Modernity*. Cambridge: Polity Press.

Gill, Lesley. 1993. "Proper Women" and City Pleasures: Gender, Class, and Contested Meanings in La Paz. *American Ethnologist* 20 (1):72–88.

Gilligan, Carol. 1982. *In a Different Voice: Psychological Theory and Women's Development*. Cambridge, MA: Harvard University Press.

Gilman, Sander. 1985. *Difference and Pathology: Stereotypes of Sexuality, Race, and Madness*. Ithaca, NY: Cornell University Press.

Ginsburg, Faye and Anna L. Tsing, eds. 1990. *Uncertain Terms: Negotiating Gender in American Culture*. Boston: Beacon Press.

Ginsburg, Faye and Rayna Rapp, eds. 1995. *Conceiving the New World Order*. Berkeley: University of California Press.

Ginsburg, Faye, Lila Abu-Lughod and Brian Larkin. 2002. Introduction. In *Media Worlds: Anthropology on New Terrain*. Faye Ginsburg, Lila Abu-Lughod and Brian Larkin, eds. Pp 115–133. Berkeley: University of California Press.

Glenn, Evelyn Nakano. 2002. *Unequal Freedom: How Race and Gender Shaped American Citizenship and Labor*. Cambridge, MA: Harvard University Press.

Golde, Peggy, ed. 1986. *Women in the Field: Anthropological Experiences*. 2nd ed. Berkeley: University of California Press.

Goodale, Jane. [1971] 1994. *Tiwi Wives: A Study of the Women of Melville Island, North Australia*. Ethnological Society Monograph no. 51. Seattle: University of Washington Press.

Goodale, Jane. 1974. *Tiwi Wives: A Study of Women of Melville Island, North Australia*. Seattle: University of Washington Press.

Goode, Erica. 2000. Human Nature: Born or Made? *New York Times*, March 14:F1, F9.

Gough, Kathleen. 1959. The Nayars and the Definition of Marriage. *The Journal of the Royal Anthropological Institute of Great Britain and Ireland* 89:23–34.

Gough, Kathleen. 1975. The Origin of the Family. In *Toward an Anthropology of Women*. Rayna R. Reiter, ed. Pp. 51–77. New York: Monthly Review.

Gray, Patrick J. and Linda Wolfe. 1999. An Anthropological Look at Human Sexuality. In *Perspectives: Anthropology*. Richard Deutsch, ed. Pp. 117–133. St. Paul, MN: Coursewise.

Gruenbaum. Ellen. 2001. *The Female Circumcision Controversy: An Anthropological Perspective*. Philadelphia: University of Pennsylvania Press.

Gubar, Susan. 1982. "The Blank Page" and the Issue of Female Creativity. In *Writing and Sexual Difference*. Elizabeth Able, ed. Pp 73–94. Chicago: University of Chicago Press.

Guettel, C. 1974. *Marxism and Feminism*. Toronto: Hunter Rose.

Gupta, Akhil and James Ferguson. 1997. Beyond "Culture": Space, Identity, and the Politics of Difference. In *Culture, Power, Place: Explorations in Critical Anthropology*. Akhil Gupta and James Ferguson, eds. Pp. 33–51. Durham, NC: Duke University Press.

Gura, Susanne. 2006. Report prepared for the World Initiative for Sustainable Pastoralism, IUCN EARO. Ober-Ramstadt, Germany: The League for Pastoral Peoples and Endogenous Livestock Development.

Hager, Lori D. 1997. Sex and Gender in Paleoanthropology. In *Women in Human Evolution*. Lori D. Hager, ed. Pp. 1–28. London: Routledge.

Hannerz, Ulf. 1996. *Transnational Connections: Culture, People, Places*. London: Routledge.

Haraway, Donna. 1991. *Simians, Cyborgs and Women: The Reinvention of Nature*. New York: Routledge.

Harding, Sandra. 1987. Introduction: Is There a Feminist Method? In *Feminism and Methodology*. Sandra Harding, ed. Pp. 1–14. Bloomington: Indiana University Press.

Harley, D. 1982. Models of Human Evolution. *Science* 217:296.

Harrison, Faye. 1997. The Gendered Politics of Violence of Structural Adjustment: A View from Jamaica. In *Situated Lives: Gender and Culture in Everyday Life*. Louise Lamphere, Helena Ragoné and Patricia Zavella, eds. Pp. 451–468. London: Routledge.

Harrison, Faye and Ira Harrison. 1999. Anthropology, African Americans, and the Emancipation of a Subjugated Knowledge. In *African American Pioneers in Anthropology*. Ira Harrison and Faye Harrison, eds. Pp. 1–36. Chicago: University of Illinois Press.

Härting, Heike. 2005. Subjectivity. Globalization and Autonomy Glossary. http://anscombe.mcmaster.ca/global1/servlet/Glossary.pdf?id=CO.0036 (accessed 9/9/08).

Harvey, David. 1989. *The Condition of Postmodernity: An Enquiry into the Origins of Cultural. Change*. Malden, MA: Blackwell.

Harvey, David. 2005. *A Brief History of Neoliberalism*. Oxford, UK: Oxford University Press.

Hatch, Elvin. 1997. The Good Side of Relativism. *Journal of Anthropological Research* 53 (3): abstracts.

Hawkes, Terence. 2003. *Structuralism and Semiotics*. 2nd ed. London: Routledge.

Heise, Lori L. 1997. Violence, Sexuality, and Women's Lives. In *The Gender/Sexuality Reader*. Micaela di Leonardo and Roger Lancaster, eds. Pp. 411–433. New York: Routledge.

Held, David, Anthony McGrew, David Goldblatt and Jonathan Perraton. 1999. *Global Transformations: Politics, Economics, and Culture*. Stanford, CA: Stanford University Press.

Henley, Nancy and Cheris Kramarae. 1994. Gender, Power, and Miscommunication. In *The Women and Language Debate: A Sourcebook*. C. Roman, S. Juhasz and C. Miller, eds. Pp. 383–406. Piscataway, NJ: Rutgers University Press.

Herdt, Gilbert. 1997. *Same Sex, Different Cultures: Exploring Gay and Lesbian Lives*. Boulder, CO: Westview Press.

Hernández, Daisy and Bushra Rehman. 2002. *Colonize This!: Young Women of Color on Today's Feminism*. New York: Seal Press.

Hines, Darlene Clark. 1997. Rape and the Inner Lives of Black Women in the Middle West: Preliminary Thoughts on the Culture of Dissemblance. In *The Gender/Sexuality Reader*. Micaela di Leonardo and Roger Lancaster, eds. Pp. 434–439. New York: Routledge.

Hing, Bill Ong. 2004. *Defining America through Immigration Policy*. Philadelphia, PA: Temple University Press.

Hobhouse, G. C. 1924. *Morals in Evolution*. London: Chapman and Hall.

Hochschild, Arlie Russell. 1983. *The Managed Heart: Commercialization of Human Feeling*. Berkeley: University of California Press.

Hondagneu-Stelo, Pierrette and Ernestine Avila. 1997. "I'm Here, but I'm There": The Meanings of Latina Transnational Motherhood. *Gender and Society* 11 (5):548–571.

Hoodfar, Homa. 1997. The Veil in Their Minds and on Our Heads: Veiling Practices and Muslim Women. In *The Politics of Culture in the Shadow of Capital*. Lisa Lowe and David Lloyd, eds. Pp. 248–279. Durham, NC: Duke University Press.

Horn, David G. 1994. *Social Bodies: Science, Reproduction, and Italian Modernity*. Princeton, NJ: Princeton University Press.

Hrdy, Sarah B. 1979. The Evolution of Human Sexuality: The Latest Word and the Last. *The Quarterly Review of Biology* 54:309–314.

Hrdy, Sarah B. 1981. *The Woman That Never Evolved*. Cambridge; MA: Harvard University Press.

Hull, Gloria T., Patricia Bell Scott and Barbara Smith. 1982. *All the Women Are White, All the Blacks Are Men, But Some of Us Are Brave: Black Women's Studies*. New York: Feminist Press.

Hurtado, Aida. 1989. Relating to Privilege: Seduction and Rejection in the Subordination of White Women and Women of Color. *Signs* 14 (4):833–855.

Huxley, Aldous. (1932/1998). *Brave New World*. New York: Harper Perennial.

Inda, Jonathan Xavier and Renato Rosaldo. 2002. Introduction: A World in Motion. In *The Anthropology of Globalization*. Jonathan Xavier Inda and Renato Rosaldo, eds. Pp. 1–36. Malden, MA: Blackwell.

Isaac, G. 1982. Models of Human Evolution. *Science* 217:295.

Jackson, Stevi, Jane Prince and Pauline Young. 1993. Introduction to Science, Medicine, and Reproductive Technology. In *Women's Studies: Essential Readings*. Stevi Jackson, ed. New York: New York University Press.

Johanson, D. C. 1997. In Search of Human Origins. *NOVA* special, air date June 3.

Johanson, Donald and Maitland Edey. 1981a. *Lucy: The Beginnings of Humankind*. New York: Touchstone.

Johanson, Donald and Maitland Edey. 1981b. How Ape Became Man: Is It a Matter of Sex? *Science* (April):45–49.

Johnson, Matthew. n.d. Anthropology. In *GLBTQ: An Encyclopedia of Gay, Lesbian, Bisexual, Transgender and Queer Culture*. http://www.glbtq.com/social-sciences/anthropology.html (accessed 5/30/08).

Johnston, David Cay. 2005. Richest Are Leaving Even the Rich Far Behind. *Class Matters*. New York: New York Times Press, pp. 182–189.

Johnston, David Cay. 2007. US Income Gap Is Widening Significantly, Data Shows. *New York Times*, March 29, 2007, http://www.commondreams.org/archive/2007/03/29/163/.

Jones, James H. 1993. *Bad Blood: The Tuskegee Syphilis Experiment*. New York: Free Press.

Kapchan, Deborah. 1993. Moroccan Women's Body Signs. In *Bodylore*. Katherine Young, ed. Knoxville: University of Tennessee Press.

Kaplan, Caren. 1996. *Questions of Travel: Postmodern Discourses of Displacement*. Durham, NC: Duke University Press.

Kaplan, Caren and Inderpal Grewal. 1999. Transnational Feminist Cultural Studies Beyond the Marxism/Poststructuralism/Feminism Divides. In *Between Woman and Nation: Nationalisms, Transnational Feminisms, and the State*. Caren Kaplan, Norma Alarcón and Minoo Moallem, eds. Pp. 349–364. Durham, NC: Duke University Press.

Kayberry, Phyllis. 1939. *Aboriginal Woman Sacred and Profane*. London: Routledge.

Keough, Leyla J. 2006. Globalizing "Postsocialism": Mobile Mothers and Neoliberalism on the Margins of Europe. *Anthropological Quarterly* 76 (3):431–462.

Kimmel, Michael. 2001. Masculinity as Homophobia: Fear, Shame, and Silence in the Construction of Gender Identity. In *Men and Masculinity: A Text Reader*. Theodore F. Cohen, ed. Pp. 29–41. Belmont, CA: Wadsworth.

Kincaid, Jamaica. 1985. "Girl." http://www.turksheadreview.com/library/texts/kincaid-girl.html (accessed 3/13/09).

Kipling, Rudyard. 1899. The White Man's Burden. *McClure's Magazine*.

Kligman, Gail. 1995 Political Demography: The Banning of Abortion in Ceausescu's Romania. In *Conceiving the New World Order*. Faye Ginsburg and Rayna Rapp, eds. Pp. 234–255. Berkeley: University of California Press.

Kuper, Adam. 1988. *The Invention of Primitive Society: Transformations of an Illusion*. London: Routledge.

LaFont, Susan, ed. 2003. *Constructing Sexualities: Readings in Sexuality, Gender, and Culture*. Upper Saddle River, NJ: Prentice-Hall.

Lamphere, Louise. 1974. Women in Domestic Groups. In *Woman, Culture, & Society*. Michelle Zimbalist Rosaldo and Louise Lamphere, eds. Pp. 97–112. Stanford, CA: Stanford University Press.

Lamphere, Louise. 1986. From Working Daughters to Working Mothers: Production and Reproduction in an Industrial Community. *American Ethnologist* 13 (1):118–130.

Lamphere, Louise. 1995. Feminist Anthropology: The Legacy of Elsie Clews Parsons. In *Women Writing Culture*. Ruth Behar and Deborah Gordon, eds. Pp. 85–103. Berkeley: University of California Press.

Lamphere, Louise. 2005. The Domestic Sphere of Women and the Public World of Men: the Strengths and Limitations of an Anthropological Dichotomy. In *Gender in Cross-Cultural Perspective*. 4th ed. Caroline Brettell and Carolyn Sargent, eds. Pp. 86–95. Upper Saddle River, NJ: Prentice-Hall.

Lancaster, Roger. 1995. *Life Is Hard: Machismo, Danger, and the Intimacy of Power in Nicaragua*. Berkeley: University of California Press.

Lazzarato, Maurizio. 1996. Immaterial Labor. In *Radical Thought in Italy*. Paolo Virno and Michael Hardt, eds. Pp. 133–150. Minneapolis: University of Minnesota Press.

Leacock, Eleanor, ed. 1972. Introduction. In *The Origin of the Family, Private Property and the State*, by F. Engels. New York: International Publishers.

Leacock, Eleanor. 1978. Women's Status in Egalitarian Society. *Current Anthropology* 19:247–276.

Leibowitz, Lila. 1983. Origins of the Sexual Division of Labor. In *Women's Nature*. M. Lowe and R. Hubbard, eds. Pp. 123–147. New York: Pergamon.

Lennox, Sara. 2007. *Feminism and Cultural Studies*. http://daadcenter.wisc.edu/publications/Lennox-cultural&feminism.pdf (accessed 8/24/07).

Lévi-Strauss, Claude. 1971. The Family. In *Man, Culture and Society*. H. Shapiro, ed. London: Oxford University Press.

Lewellen, Ted. 2002. *The Anthropology of Globalization: Cultural Anthropology Enters the 21st Century*. Westport, CT: Bergin & Garvey.

Lewin, Ellen. 1993. *Lesbian Mothers: Accounts of Gender in American Culture*. Ithaca, NY: Cornell University Press.

Lewin, Ellen and William Leap, eds. 1996. *Out in the Field: Reflections of Lesbian and Gay Anthropologists*. Chicago: University of Illinois Press.

Lewin, Ellen and William Leap. 2002. *Out in Theory: The Emergence of Lesbian and Gay Anthropology*. Chicago: University of Illinois Press.

Lewis, Reina and Sara Mills. 2003. Introduction. In *Feminist Colonial Theory*. Reina Lewis and Sara Mills, eds. Pp. 1–21. New York: Routledge.

Lincoln, Bruce. 1991. *Emerging from the Chrysalis: Rituals of Women's Initiation*. New York: Oxford University Press.

Lind, Amy. 2000. Negotiating Boundaries: Women's Organizations and the Politics of Restructuring in Ecuador. In *Gender and Global Restructuring: Sightings, Sites and Resistances*. Marianne H. Marchand and Anne Sisson Runyan, eds. Pp. 161–175. London and New York: Routledge.

Lorde, Audre. 1984. Uses of the Erotic: The Erotic as Power. In *Sister Outsider: Essays and Speeches*, by Audre Lorde. Pp. 53–59. Berkeley, CA: The Crossing Press. (Reprint, 2000, Tucson, AZ: Kore Press.)

Love, Patrick. 2003. Gay and Lesbian Studies—Goals, History, Current Configurations. *Education Encyclopedia*. http://education.stateuniversity.com/pages/2003/Gay-Lesbian-Studies.html.

Lovejoy, C. Owen. 1981. The Origins of Man. *Science* 211:341–350.

Lovejoy, Meg. 2001. Disturbances in the Social Body: Differences in Body Image and Eating Problems among African American and White Women. *Gender and Society* 15 (2):239–261.

Lowe, Donald M. 1995. *The Body in Late-Capitalist USA*. Durham, NC: Duke University Press.

Lugones, Maria and Elizabeth Spelman. 1983. Have We Got a Theory for You! Feminist Theory, Cultural Imperialism, and the Demand for "The Woman's Voice." *Women's Studies International Forum* 6 (6):573–581.

Lutkehaus, Nancy. 1995. Margaret Mead and the "Rustling-of-the-Winds-in-the-Palm-Trees School" of Ethnography. In *Women Writing Culture*. Ruth Behar and Deborah Gordon, eds. Pp. 186–206. Berkeley: University of California Press.

Maccoby, Eleanor. 1998. *The Two Sexes: Growing Up Apart, Coming Together*. Cambridge, MA: Harvard University Press.

Maccoby, Eleanor. 1999. *The Two Sexes: Growing Up Apart, Coming Together*. Cambridge, MA: Harvard University Press [paperback].

Maccoby, Eleanor and Carol Jacklin. 1974. *The Psychology of Sex Differences*. Stanford, CA: Stanford University Press.

MacCormack, Carol. 1980. Nature, Gender, and Culture: A Critique. In *Nature, Culture and Gender*. Carol MacCormack and Marilyn Strathern, eds. Pp. 1–24. Cambridge: Cambridge University Press.

Mahmood, Saba. 2001. Feminist Theory, Embodiment, and the Docile Agent: Some Reflections on the Egyptian Islamic Revival. *Cultural Anthropology* 16:202–236.

Maine, Margo. 2000. *Body Wars*. Carlsbad, CA: Gürze Books.

Mairs, Nancy. 1997. Carnal Acts. In *Writing on the Body*. Katie Conboy, Nadia Median, and Sarah Stanbury, eds. Pp. 296–305. New York: Columbia University Press.

Malik, Kenan. 1996. *The Meaning of Race: Race, History and Culture in Western Society*. New York: New York University Press.

Manning, Marable. 2004. Globalization and Racialization: Building New Sites of Resistance to the New Racial Domain. http://www.manningmarable.net/works/pdf/globalization.pdf.

Manson, W. C. 1986. Sexual Cyclicity and Concealed Ovulation. *Journal of Human Evolution* 15:21–30.

Marchand, Marianne and Anne Sisson Runyan. 2000. *Gender and Global Restructuring: Sightings, Sites and Resistances*. London: Routledge.

Martin, Emily. 1987. *The Woman in the Body: A Cultural Analysis of Reproduction*. Boston: Beacon Press.

Martin, Emily. 1991. The Egg and the Sperm: How Science Has Constructed a Romance Based on Male-Female Stereotypic Roles. *Signs* 16 (3):485–501.

Martin, Emily. 1994. *Flexible Bodies: Tracking Immunity in American Culture from the Days of Polio to the Age of AIDS.* Boston: Beacon Press.

Martin, Kay and Barbara Voorhies. 1975. *Female of the Species.* New York: Columbia University Press.

Martinez, Elizabeth and Arnoldo Garcia. n.d. What Is Neoliberalism? *CorpWatch* (http://www.corpwatch.org/article.php?id=376).

Marx, Karl. 1992. *A Critique of Political Economy.* Ben Fowles, trans. New York: Penguin.

Marx, Karl and Friedrich Engels. [1848] 1967. *The Communist Manifesto.* London: Penguin.

Mascia-Lees, Frances E. and Patricia Sharpe. 1992. The Marked and the Un(re)marked: Tattoo and Gender in Theory and Narrative. In *Tattoo, Torture, Mutilation and Adornment: The Denaturalization of the Body in Culture in Text.* Frances E. Mascia-Lees and Patricia Sharpe, eds. Pp.145–169. New York: State University of New York Press.

Mascia-Lees, Frances E. and Patricia Sharpe. 1994. The Anthropological Unconscious. *American Anthropologist* 96 (3):649–660.

Mascia-Lees, Frances E. and Patricia Sharpe. 1996-1997. Women Writing [and] Their Bodies: Exploring the Conjunction of Writing Difficulties, Eating Disorders, and the Construction of Self and Body among American Female Adolescents. *Berkeley Journal of Sociology* 1996-1997:167–181.

Mascia-Lees, Frances E., Patricia Sharpe and Colleen B. Cohen. 1989. The Post-Modernist Turn in Anthropology: Cautions from a Feminist Perspective. *Signs* 15 (1):7–33.

Mascia-Lees, Frances E., Patricia Sharpe and Colleen B. Cohen. 1990. The Female Body in Postmodern Consumer Culture: A Study of Subjection and Agency. *Phoebe: An Interdisciplinary Journal of Feminist Scholarship, Theory and Aesthetics* 2:29–50.

Mascia-Lees, Frances E., F. Tierson and J. Relethford. 1989. Investigating the Biocultural Dimensions of Human Sexual Behavior. *Medical Anthropology* 11 (4):367–384.

Masters, W. H. and V. E. Johnson. 1966. *Human Sexual Response.* New York: Bantam Books.

Matthiasson, C. 1974. Introduction. In *Sex Roles in Changing Cultures, Occasional Papers in Anthropology.* A. McElroy and C. Matthiasson, eds. Buffalo: State University of New York Press.

McClaurin, Irma. 1996. *Women of Belize: Gender and Change in Central America.* Piscataway, NJ: Rutgers University Press.

McClaurin, Irma, ed. 2001. *Black Feminist Anthropology: Theory, Politics, Praxis, and Poetics.* Piscataway, NJ: Rutgers University Press.

Mead, Margaret. 1935. *Sex and Temperament in Three Primitive Societies.* New York: William Morrow.

Mead, Margaret. 1949 [1928]. *Coming of Age in Samoa.* New York: Mentor Books.

Meadow, Susannah. 2002. Meet the Gamma Girls. *Newsweek* June 3:44–50.

Mernissi, Fatima. 1987. *Beyond the Veil: Male-Female Dynamics in a Modern Moslem Society.* Bloomington: Indiana University Press.

Micklewright, N. 1999. Public and Private for Ottoman Women of the Nineteenth Century. In *Women and Self-Representation in Islamic Societies.* D. Fairchild Riggins, ed. New York: State University of New York Press.

Miller, James. 1993. *The Passion of Michel Foucault.* New York: Simon & Schuster.

Mills, Mary Beth. 2003. Gender and Inequality in the Global Labor Force. *Annual Review of Anthropology* 32:41–62.

Mills, Mary Beth. 2005. From Nimble Fingers to Raised Fists: Women and Labor Activism in Globalizing Thailand. *Signs* 31 (1):117–144.

Mitchell, Grace. n.d. Race, Ethnicity, and National Identity: America, Korea, and Biracial Koreans. Department of Sociology, College of Staten Island, CUNY, course syllabus. http://www.exeas.org/resources/pdf/Korean-race-ethnicity.pdf (accessed 9/9/08).

Moghadam, Valentine M. 1999. Gender and Globalization: Female Labor and Women's Mobilization. *Journal of World-Systems Research* 2:367–388.

Mohamed, Abdi-Noor Haji. 2006. "Globalization." http://authorsden.com/visit/viewPoetry.asp?id=163641&AuthorID=12041 (accessed 3/13/09).

Mohanty, Chandra Talpade. 2002. "Under Western Eyes" Revisited: Feminist Solidarity through Anticapitalist Struggles. *Signs* 28 (2):499–535.

Mohanty, Chandra Talpade, Ann Russo and Lourdes Torres, eds. 1991. *Third World Women and the Politics of Feminism.* Bloomington: Indiana University Press.

Moore, Robert. 1988. Racist Stereotyping in the English Language. In *Racism and Sexism in America: An Integrated Study.* Paula S. Rothenberg, ed. Pp. 269–279. New York: St. Martin's Press.

Moraga, Cherrie and Gloria Anzaldúa, ed. 1983. *This Bridge Called My Back: Writings by Radical Women of Color.* New York: Kitchen Table, Women of Color Press.

Morbeck, Mary, Alison Galloway and Adrienne Zihlman, eds. 1997. *The Evolving Female: A Life-History Perspective.* Princeton, NJ: Princeton University Press.

Morgan, Lewis Henry. 1877 [1985]. *Ancient Society.* Tucson: University of Arizona Press.

Morpeth, R. and P. Langton. 1973. Contemporary Matriarchies, Women Alone: Independent or Complete. *Cambridge Anthropology* 1 (3):20–38.

Morris, Rosalind C. 1994. Three Sexes and Four Sexualities: Redressing the Discourses on Gender and Sexuality in Contemporary Thailand. *Positions* 2:15–43.

Morris, Rosalind C. 1995. All Made Up: Performance Theory and the New Anthropology of Sex and Gender. *Annual Review of Anthropology* 24:567–592.

Morrison, Toni. 1970. *The Bluest Eye.* New York: Simon & Schuster.

Mullings, Leith. 1997. *On Our Own Terms: Race, Class, and Gender in the Lives of African American Women.* New York: Routledge.

Murphy, Robert. 1971. *The Dialectics of Social Life.* New York: Basic Books.

Murphy, Yolanda and Robert Murphy. 1974. *Women of the Forest.* New York: Columbia University Press.

Murphy, Yolanda and Robert Murphy. 2004. *Women of the Forest.* 30th anniversary ed. New York: Columbia University Press.

Mwaria, Cheryl. 2001. Biomedical Ethics, Gender, and Ethnicity: Implications for Black Feminist Anthropology. In *Black Feminist Anthropology: Theory, Politics, Praxis, and Poetics.* Irma McClaurin, ed. Pp. 187–210. Piscataway, NJ: Rutgers University Press.

Nagengast, Carole. 1997. Women, Minorities, and Indigenous Peoples: Universalism and Cultural Relativity. *Journal of Anthropological Research* 53 (3): abstracts.

Nanda, Serena. 1990. *Neither Man nor Woman: The Hijras of India.* Belmont, CA: Wadsworth.

Nanda, Serena. 2000. *Gender Diversity: Cross-cultural Variations.* Long Grove, IL: Waveland Press.

Narayan, Kirin. 1993. How Native Is a "Native" Anthropologist? *American Anthropologist* 95 (3):671–686.

Nash, June and Helen Safa, eds. 1980. *Women and Change in Latin America.* South Hadley, MA: Bergin & Garvey.

Nelkin, Dorothy. 2000. Less Selfish than Sacred?: Genes and the Religious Impulse in Evolutionary Psychology. In *Alas, Poor Darwin: Arguments against Evolutionary Psychology.* Hilary Rose and Steven Rose, eds. Pp. 17–32. New York: Harmony Books.

Nelkin, Dorothy and M. Susan Lindee. 1995. *The DNA Mystique: The Gene as a Cultural Icon.* New York: W. H. Freeman.

Nelson, Sarah. 1997. Diversity of the Upper Paleolithic "Venus" Figurines and Archeological Mythology. In *Gender in Cross-Cultural Perspective.* 2nd ed. Caroline Brettell and Carolyn Sargent, eds. Pp. 67–73. Upper Saddle River, NJ: Prentice-Hall.

Nettle, Daniel and Suzanne Romaine. 2000. *Vanishing Voices: The Extinction of the World's Languages.* New York: Oxford University Press.

Nichter, Mimi and Nancy Vuckovic. 2002. Fat Talk: Body Image among Adolescents Girls. In *Readings in Gender and Culture in America.* Nancy McKee and Linda Stone, eds. Pp. 134–150. Upper Saddle River, NJ: Prentice-Hall.

Nielsen, Joyce M. 1990. *Sex and Gender in Society: Perspectives on Stratification.* 2nd ed. Long Grove, IL: Waveland Press.

O'Hare, William P. 2001. The Child Population: First Data from the 2000 Census. Population Reference Bureau. http://www.prb.org/pdf/KC3_ChildPopulation.pdf.

O'Neil, John and Patricia Leyland Kaufert. 1995. Irniktakpunga!: Sex Determination and the Inuit Struggle for Birthing Rights in Northern Canada. In *Conceiving the New World Order.* Faye Ginsburg and Rayna Rapp, eds. Pp. 59–74. Berkeley: University of California Press.

Oboler, Regina Smith. 1993. Is the Female Husband a Man? Woman/Woman Marriage among the Nandi of Kenya. In *Talking about People.* William Haviland and Robert Gordon, eds. Pp. 136–145. Mountain View, CA: Mayfield.

Ong, Aihwa. 1987. *Spirits of Resistance and Capitalist Discipline: Factory Women in Malaysia.* Albany: State University of New York Press.

Ong, Aihwa. 1999. *Flexible Citizenship: The Cultural Logics of Transnationality.* Durham, NC: Duke University Press.

Ortner, Sherry. 1974. Is Female to Male as Nature Is to Culture? In *Woman, Culture, & Society.* Michelle Zimbalist Rosaldo and Louise Lamphere, eds. Pp. 67–88. Stanford, CA: Stanford University Press.

Ortner, Sherry. 1984. Theory in Anthropology since the Sixties. *Comparative Studies in Society and History,* 26 (1):126–166.

Ortner Sherry B. 1989. Expanding Practice Theory. In *High Religion: A Cultural and Political History of Sherpa Buddhism.* Pp. 11–18. Princeton, NJ: Princeton University Press.

Ortner, Sherry B. 1996. *Making Gender: The Politics and Erotics of Culture.* Boston: Beacon Press.

Ortner, Sherry B. 2006. *Anthropology and Social Theory: Culture, Power and the Acting Subject.* Durham, NC: Duke University Press.

Ossman, Susan. 2002. *Three Faces of Beauty: Casablanca, Paris, Cairo.* Durham, NC: Duke University Press.

Parreñas, Rhacel Salazar. 2001. *Servants of Globalization: Women, Migration, and Domestic Work.* Stanford, CA: Stanford University Press.

Parreñas, Rhacel Salazar. 2006. Understanding the Backlash: Why Transnational Migrant Families Are Considered the "Wrong Kind of Family" in the Philippines. http://64.233.169.104/search?q=cache:CyUNUKG4gW8J:globalchild.rutgers.edu/pdf/Salazar%2520Parrenas%2520Research%2520Note.pdf+transnational+mothering&hl=en&ct=clnk&cd=3&gl=us (accessed 6/27/08).

Peletz, Michael. 1996. *Reason and Passion: Representations of Gender in Malay Society.* Berkeley: University of California Press.

Perez, Gina. 2007. Methodological Gifts in Latina/o Studies and Feminist Anthropology. *Anthropology News* (October):6–7.

Pieterse, Jan N. 1995. Globalization as Hybridization. In *Global Modernities.* Mike Featherstone, Scott Lash and Roland Robertson, eds. Pp. 45–68. London: Sage.

Pratt, Mary Louise. 1986. Fieldwork in Common Places. In *Writing Culture: The Poetics and Politics of Ethnography.* James Clifford and George Marcus, eds. Pp. 27–50. Berkeley: University of California Press.

Preibisch, Kerry and Leigh Binford. 2007. Interrogating Racialized Global Labour Supply: An Exploration of the Racial/National Replacement of Foreign Agricultural Workers in Canada. *Canadian Review of Sociology and Anthropology* 44 (1):5–36. http://goliath.ecnext.com/coms2/gi_0199-6659063/Interrogating-racialized-global-labour-supply.html.

Qadeer, M. A. (1983). *Urban Development in the Third World: Internal Dynamics of Lahore,* Pakistan. Westport, CT: Praeger.

Quinn, Naomi. 1977. Anthropological Studies of Women's Status. *Annual Review of Anthropology* 6:181–225.

Racioppi, Linda and Katherine O'Sullivan See. 2000. Organizing Women before and after the Fall: Women's Politics in the Soviet Union and Post-Soviet Russia. In *Global Feminisms Since 1945: A Survey of Issues and Controversies.* Bonnie G. Smith, ed. Pp. 205–234. New York: Routledge.

Radway, Janice. 1984. *Reading the Romance.* Chapel Hill: University of North Carolina Press.

Radway, Janice. 1986. Identifying Ideological Seams: Mass Culture, Analytical Method, and Political Practice. *Communication* 9:93–124.

Rapp, Rayna. 2000. *Testing Women, Testing the Fetus: The Social Impact of Amniocentesis in America.* New York: Routledge.

Reiter, Rayna R. 1975a. Introduction. In *Toward an Anthropology of Women.* Rayna R. Reiter, ed. Pp. 11–19. New York: Monthly Review.

Reiter, Rayna R. 1975b. Men and Women in the South of France. In *Toward an Anthropology of Women.* Rayna R. Reiter, ed. Pp. 252–282. New York: Monthly Review.

Revkin, Andrew C. 2009. Family Planning and the Path to Progress. *DOT EARTH* (January 24). http://dotearth.blogs.nytimes.com/2009/01/24/family-planning-and-the-path-to-progress/?scp=4&sq=global%20%crisis%20gender%20inequality&st=cse (accessed 3/31/09).

Rodriguez, Cheryl. 2007. "Black Feminist Anthropology for the 21st Century." *Anthropology News* (October):7.

Rooks, Noliwe M. 1996. *Hair Raising: Beauty, Culture, and African American Women.* Piscataway, NJ: Rutgers University Press.

Rosaldo, Michelle. 1974. Woman, Culture, & Society: A Theoretical Overview. In *Woman, Culture, & Society.* Michelle Zimbalist Rosaldo and Louise Lamphere, eds. Pp. 17–42. Stanford, CA: Stanford University Press.

Rosaldo, Michelle Zimbalist and Louise Lamphere, eds. 1974. *Woman, Culture, & Society.* Stanford, CA: Stanford University Press.

Rosaldo, Renato. 1989. *Culture and Truth: The Remaking of Social Analysis.* Boston: Beacon Press.

Roseberry, William. 1996. The Rise of Yuppie Coffees and the Re-imagining of Class in the United States. *American Anthropologist* 98:762–775.

Rosenblatt, Roger, ed. 1999. *Consuming Desires: Consumption, Culture, and the Pursuit of Happiness.* Washington, DC: Shearwater.

Rouse, Roger. 1991. Mexican Migration and the Social Space of Postmodernism. *Diasporas* 1 (1):8–23.

Rowell, T. 1972. Female Reproductive Cycles and Social Behavior in Primates. *Advances in the Study of Behavior* 4:69–105.

Roy, Arundhati. 2001. *Power of Politics.* 2nd ed. Cambridge, MA: South End Press, pp. 32–33.

Rubin, Gayle. 1975. The Traffic in Women: Notes on the "Political Economy" of Sex. In *Toward an Anthropology of Women.* Rayna R. Reiter, ed. Pp. 157–210. New York: Monthly Review Press.

Rubin, Gayle. 1993. Thinking Sex: Notes for a Radical Theory of the Politics of Sexuality. In *Pleasure and Danger.* Carole Vance, ed. Pp. 267–319. New York: HarperCollins.

Rubin, Gayle. 2006. The Traffic in Women: Notes on the "Political Economy" of Sex. In *Feminist Anthropology: A Reader.* Ellen Lewin, ed. Pp. 87–106, Malden, MA: Blackwell.

Rumsey, Alan. 1990. *Word, Meaning, and Linguistic Ideology. American Anthropologist* 92 (2):346–361.

Russell, Kathy, Midge Wilson and Ronald Hall. 1993. *The Color Complex: The Politics of Skin Color among African Americans.* New York: Anchor Books.

Russett, Cynthia. 1989. *Sexual Science: The Victorian Construction of Womanhood.* Cambridge, MA: Harvard University Press.

Russo, Mary. 1986. Female Grotesques: Carnival and Theory. In *Feminist Studies: Critical Studies.* Teresa de Lauretis, ed. Pp. 213–229. Bloomington: Indiana University Press.

Sacks, Karen. 1979. *Sisters and Wives.* Westport, CT: Greenwood.

Sacks, Karen. 1989. Toward a Unified Theory of Class, Race and Gender. *American Ethnologist* 16 (3):534–550.

Said, Edward. 1979. *Orientalism.* New York: Vintage Books.

Salzinger L. 1997. From High Heels to Swathed Bodies: Gendered Meanings under Production in Mexico's Export-Processing Industry. *Feminist Studies* 23:549–573.

Sanday, Peggy. 1981. *Female Power and Male Dominance: On the Origins of Sexual Inequality.* Cambridge: Cambridge University Press.

Scarry, Elaine. 1985. *The Body in Pain: The Making and Unmaking of the World.* London: Oxford University Press.

Schein, Louisa. 2000. *Minority Rules: The Miao and the Feminine in China's Cultural Politics.* Durham, NC: Duke University Press.

Schein, Louisa. 2002. Mapping Hmong Media in Diasporic Space. In *Media Worlds: Anthropology on New Terrain.* Faye Ginsburg, Lila Abu-Lughod and Brian Larkin, eds. Pp. 229–244. Berkeley: University of California Press.

Scheper-Hughes, Nancy. 1993. *Death Without Weeping: The Violence of Everyday Life in Brazil.* Berkeley: University of California Press.

Scheper-Hughes, Nancy. 1995. The Primacy of the Ethical: Propositions for a Militant Anthropology. *Current Anthropology* 36 (3):409–420.

Schlegel, Alice. 1972. *Male Dominance and Female Autonomy: Domestic Authority in Matrilineal Societies.* New Haven, CT: Human Relations Area Files Press.

Schlegel, Alice. 1977. *Sexual Stratification: A Cross-Cultural View.* New York: Columbia University Press.

Schneider, Jane. 2002. World Markets: Anthropological Perspectives. In *Exotic No More.* J. MacClancy, ed. Pp. 64–85. Chicago: University of Chicago Press.

Sen, Amartya. 2001. The Many Faces of Gender Inequality. *The New Republic* (September):35–41.

Shaw, Carolyn Martin. 2001. Disciplining the Black Female Body: Learning Feminism in Africa and the United States. In *Black Feminist Anthropology.* Irma McClaurin, ed. Pp. 102–125. Piscataway, NJ: Rutgers University Press.

Sheehan, Elizabeth. 1997. Victorian Clitoridectomy: Isaac Baker Brown and His Harmless Operative Procedures. In *The Sex/Gender Reader: Culture, History, Political Economy.* Roger Lancaster and Micaela di Leonardo, eds. Pp. 325–334. New York: Routledge.

Shostak, Marjorie. 1983. *Nisa: The Life and Words of a !Kung Woman.* New York: Vintage.

Shute, Nancy. 2008. Amid Economic Pain, Americans Cut Back on Cosmetic Surgery. *U.S. News & World Report,* 12/26. http://health.usnews.com/articles/health/2008/12/26/amid-economic-pain-americans-cut-back-on-cosmetic-surgery.html (accessed 3/2/09).

Simmons, Rachel. 2002. *Odd Girl Out: The Hidden Culture of Aggression in Girls.* New York: Harcourt Brace.

Slocum, Sally. 1975. Woman the Gatherer: Male Bias in Anthropology. In *Toward an Anthropology of Women.* Rayna R. Reiter, ed. Pp. 36–50. New York: Monthly Review.

Smith, Bonnie G., ed. 2000. *Global Feminisms Since 1945: Rewriting Histories.* New York: Routledge.

Smuts, Barbara. 1985. *Sex and Friendship in Baboons.* New York: Aldine.

Somerville, Siobhan. 1997. Scientific Racism and the Construction of the Homosexual Body. In *The Sex/Gender Reader.* Roger Lancaster and Micaela di Leonardo, eds. Pp. 37–52. New York: Routledge.

Spencer, Herbert. 1884. *The Study of Sociology.* New York: D. Appleton.

Spender, Dale. 1980. *Man Made Language.* London: Routledge.

Spivak, Gayatri Chakravorty. 1990. The Intervention Interview. In *The Post-Colonial Critique: Interviews, Strategies, Dialogues.* Sarah Harasym, ed. London: Routledge.

Stacey, Judith. 1988. Can There Be a Feminist Ethnography? *Women's Studies International Forum* 11 (1):21–27.

Stacey, Judith. 1997. The Neo-Family Values Campaign. In *The Sex/Gender Reader.* Roger Lancaster and Micaela di Leonardo, eds. Pp. 453–470. New York: Routledge.

Stacey, Judith. 1998. *Brave New Families: Stories of Domestic Upheaval in Late-Twentieth-Century America.* Berkeley: University of California Press.

Stack, Carol. 1974. Sex Roles and Survival Strategies in an Urban Black Community. In *Woman, Culture, & Society.* Michelle Zimbalist Rosaldo and Louise Lamphere, eds. Pp. 113–128. Stanford, CA: Stanford University Press.

Stephen, Lynn. 1997. *Women and Social Movements in Latin America: Power From Below.* Austin: University of Texas Press.

Stewart, Kathleen C. 1990. Backtalking the Wilderness: "Appalachian" Engenderings. In *Uncertain Terms: Negotiating Gender in American Culture.* Faye Ginsburg and Anna L. Tsing, eds. Pp. 43–56. Boston: Beacon Press.

Stocking, George W. 1987. *Victorian Anthropology.* New York: The Free Press.

Stoler, Ann. 1997. Carnal Knowledge and Imperial Power: Gender, Race, and Morality in Colonial Asia. In *The Gender/Sexuality Reader.* Micaela di Leonardo and Roger Lancaster, eds. Pp. 13–36. New York: Routledge.

Stoller, Paul. 1997. *Sensuous Scholarship.* Philadelphia: University of Pennsylvania Press.

Stone, Linda. 2004. Gay Marriage and Anthropology. *Anthropology News* (May). http://www.aaanet.org/press/an/0405if-comm4.htm (accessed 9/11/08).

Stone, Linda. 2005. *Kinship and Gender: An Introduction.* 3rd ed. Boulder: Westview Press.

Strinati, Dominic.1995. *An Introduction to Theories of Popular Culture.* London: Routledge.

Study Guide: The Rights of Indigenous Peoples. 2003. Minneapolis, University of Minnesota Human Rights Center. http://www1.umn.edu/humanrts/edumat/studyguides/indigenous.html (accessed 7/17/08).

Tannen, Deborah. 1987. *That's Not What I Meant! How Conversational Style Makes or Breaks Relationships.* New York: Ballantine.

Tanner, Nancy. 1981. *On Becoming Human.* Cambridge: Cambridge University Press.

Thompson, E. P. 1993. *Customs in Common: Studies in Traditional Popular Culture.* New York: The New Press.

Tanner, Nancy and Adrienne Zihlman. 1976. Women in Evolution. Part I: Innovation and Selection in Human Origins. *Signs* 3 (1):585–608.

Thomson, Rosemarie Garland, ed. 1996. *Freakery: Cultural Spectacles of the Extraordinary Body.* New York: New York University Press.

Thornhill, Randy and Craig Palmer. 2001. *A Natural History of Rape: Biological Bases of Sexual Coercion.* Cambridge: MIT Press.

Tiefer, Leonore. 2002. In Pursuit of the Perfect Penis: The Medicalization of Male Sexuality. In *Readings in Gender and Culture in America.* Nancy McKee and Linda Stone, eds. Pp. 150–162. Upper Saddle River, NJ: Prentice-Hall.

Tiger, Lionel and Robin Fox. 1997. *The Imperial Animal.* Piscataway, NJ: Transaction.

Tolbert, Kathryn. 2000. Japanese Women Choosing Work Over Children. *Star Tribune* (September 5):D1, D4.

Tomlinson, John. 1999. *Globalization and Culture*. Chicago: University of Chicago Press.

Trinh T. Minh-Ha. 1989. *Woman, Native, Other: Writing Post-coloniality and Feminism*. Bloomington: Indiana University Press.

Tsing, Anna L. 1990: Monster Stories: Women Charged with Perinatal Endangerment. In *Uncertain Terms*. Faye Ginsburg and Anna Tsing, eds. Pp. 282–299. Boston: Beacon Press.

Tsing, Anna L. 1993. *In the Realm of the Diamond Queen*. Princeton, NJ: Princeton University Press.

Tsing, Anna. 2000. The Global Situation. *Cultural Anthropology* 15 (3):327–360.

Turner, Terence. 1994. Bodies and Anti-Bodies: Flesh and Fetish in Contemporary Social Theory. In *Embodiment and Experience: The Existential Ground of Culture and Self*. Thomas J. Csordas, ed. Cambridge: Cambridge University Press.

Tylor, Edward B. 1871. *Primitive Culture: Researches into the Development of Mythology, Philosophy, Religion, Language, Art, and Custom*. 2 vols. London: John Murray.

Van Gennep, Arnold. 1908 [1960]. *The Rites of Passage*. Chicago: University of Chicago Press.

U.S. Bureau of Census. 1998. *Statistical Abstract of the United States*. 118th edition. Washington, DC: Commerce Department.

Vander Sraeten, Katrien. 2007, March 16. Tattoos: Reasons, Responsibilities: The Message on the Body: Personal and Political. http://customsholidays.suite101.com/article.cfm/tattoos_reasons_responsibilities (accessed 9/29/08).

Wallace, Edwin R. 1983. *Freud and Anthropology. A History and Reappraisal. Psychological Issues Monograph* 55:iv. New York: International Universities Press.

Waller, Marguerite R., Jennifer Rycenga and Chandra Talpade Mohanty, eds. 2001. *Frontline Feminisms: Women, War, and Resistance*. London: Routledge.

Washburn, Sherwood and C. Lancaster. 1968. "The Evolution of Hunting." In *Man the Hunter*. R. B. Lee and Irven DeVore, eds. Pp. 293–303. Chicago: Aldine.

Weber, Max. [1905] 1958. *The Protestant Ethic and the Spirit of Capitalism*. New York: Scribner's Press.

Webster, Paula. 1975. Matriarchy: A Vision of Power. In *Toward an Anthropology of Women*. Rayna R. Reiter, ed. Pp. 141–156. New York: Monthly Review.

Weedon, Chris. 1987. Subjects. In *A Concise Companion to Feminist Theory*. Mary Eagleton, ed. Pp. 111–132. Malden, MA: Blackwell.

Weiner, Annette. 1976. *Women of Value, Men of Renown*. Austin: University of Texas Press.

Weston, Kath. 1997. *Families We Choose*. Revised edition. New York: Columbia University Press.

Whiting, Beatrice and John Whiting. 1975. *Children of Six Cultures: A Psycho-Cultural Analysis*. Cambridge, MA: Harvard University Press.

Whyte, Martin K. 1978. *The Status of Women in Preindustrial Societies*. Princeton, NJ: Princeton University Press.

Wieringa, Saskia and Evelyn Blackwood. 1999. Introduction. In *Female Desires: Same-Sex Relations and Transgender Practices across Cultures*. Evelyn Blackwood and Saskia Wieringa, eds. New York: Columbia University Press.

Williamson, Judith. 1986. Woman Is an Island: Femininity and Colonization. In *Studies in Entertainment*. Tania Modleski, ed. Pp 99–118. Bloomington: Indiana University Press.

Wilson, Edward O. 1975. *Sociobiology: The New Synthesis*. Cambridge, MA: Harvard University Press.

Wilson, Elizabeth. 1985. *Adorned in Dreams: Fashion and Modernity*. Berkeley: University of California Press.

Wiseman, Rosalind. 2002. *Queen Bees & Wannabes: Helping Your Daughter Survive Cliques, Gossip, Boyfriends, and Other Realities of Adolescence*. New York: Crown.

Wolf, Eric. R. 1997. *Europe and the People without History*. Berkeley: University of California Press.

Wolf, Margery. 1972. *Women and the Family in Rural Taiwan*. Stanford, CA: Stanford University Press.

Wolfram, Walt and Natalie Schilling-Estes. 2006. *American English: Dialects and Variation*. 2nd ed. Malden, MA: Blackwell.

Wood, J. 1982. Models of Human Evolution. *Science* 217:296–297.

Wright, Robert. 1994. *The Moral Animal: Evolutionary Psychology and Everyday Life*. New York: Vintage.

Wylie, Alison. 1997. Good Science, Bad Science, or Science as Usual? Feminist Critiques of Science. In *Women in Human Evolution*. Lori D. Hager, ed. Pp. 29–55. London: Routledge.

Yanagisako, Sylvia. 1977. Women-Centered Kin Networks in Urban Bilateral Kinship. *American Ethnologist* 2:207–226.

Yanagisako, Sylvia and Carol Delaney. 1995. *Naturalizing Power: Essays in Feminist Cultural Analysis*. New York: Routledge.

Zieger, Robert. 2004. "Uncle Sam Wants You . . . to Go Shopping": A Consumer Society Responds to National Crisis, 1957–2001. *Canadian Review of American Studies* 34 (1):83–103.

Zihlman, Adrienne. 1997. The Paleolithic Glass Ceiling: *Women in Human Evolution*. In *Women in Human Evolution*. Lori D. Hager, ed. Pp. 91–113. London: Routledge.

Zippel, Kathrin S. 2006. *The Politics of Sexual Harassment: A Comparative Study of the United States, European Union, and Germany*. Cambridge: Cambridge University Press.

Zuk, Marlene. 2002. *Sexual Selections: What We Can and Can't Learn about Sex from Animals*. Berkeley: University of California Press.

Index